Berlitz®

English

Doing
Business

Berlitz Languages, Inc.
Princeton, NJ
USA

ISBN 2–8315–2159–9

Illustrations
Jim Woodend

Cover Photo
Images© 1996 PhotoDisc, Inc.

Fourth Edition
Thirteenth printing - November 1999

Printed in Switzerland

For use exclusively in connection with Berlitz classroom instruction

Berlitz Languages, Inc.
400 Alexander Park
Princeton, NJ
U.S.A.

TABLE OF CONTENTS

Chapter 3

Chapter 4

Chapter 5

Chapter 6

Chapter 7

Chapter 8

Chapter 9

Chapter 10

Chapter 14

Chapter 15

Chapter 19

Chapter 20

Chapter 23

Chapter 24

PREFACE

Doing Business in English is an instructional program aimed at the intermediate level student who is studying English for use in the business world. It is designed for use in connection with live instruction in the Berlitz classroom. In addition to the Student Reader, course materials include six one-hour audio cassettes for home review and a Teacher's Manual for the instructor.

The major objective of the *Doing Business in English* program is to build practical communication skills, with emphasis on conversational fluency. While vocabulary and grammar are covered thoroughly, the primary aim of the program is to develop a command of the spoken language.

The 24-chapter program is based on the story of a fictional electronics company and the activities of its managers. In addition to narrative texts and examples of business documents and written communication, the course also includes a rich assortment of written exercises designed to practice key structures and to expand vocabulary and idiomatic usage.

Progress through this program will depend greatly on the degree to which the instructor can motivate the student to begin to take the initiative in the learning process, to break free from the constraints of the classroom and, in the words of M.D. Berlitz, "to get hold of the *spirit* of the language."

LIST OF CHARACTERS

Jack Bell	Account Executive, Creative Talents Advertising Agency
Steve Blake	Director of Marketing, Audio Performance
Jim Burke	President, United Electronics Industries
Charles Campbell	President, Play World
Sue Chandler	Personnel Assistant, Audio Performance
Bob Crandall	Personnel Assistant, Audio Performance
Jane Collins	Executive Assistant, Audio Performance
Peter Crawford	President, Audio Performance
Judy DeWitt	Personnel Office Manager, Audio Performance
Alan Fischer	Director of Export Department, Audio Performance
Philip Hayes	General Counsel, Audio Performance
Bill Jensen	(former) President, Audio Performance
Jeffrey Knowles	Vice-President, Data Masters
Nicholas Kosloff	Director of Research and Development, Audio Performance
Dorothy Lamb	Stockholder, Leisure Time Entertainment
Karen Lawrence	Secretary to the President, Audio Performance
Jeff Martinelli	Vice-President of Planning, Audio Performance
Ben Melnick	Director of Sales, Audio Performance
Carol Nordstrom	Director of Personnel, Audio Performance
Ed Pearson	Production Manager, Audio Performance
Jack Reilly	Assistant Plant Manager (Baltimore plant), Audio Performance
Bob Smith	Plant Manager (Baltimore plant), Audio Performance
Stan Waterman	Controller, Audio Performance
Dave Williams	Director of Purchasing, Shop-Way Stores
Bud Wilson	Director of Public Relations, Audio Performance

1 UNEXPECTED NEWS

Jim Burke has just joined his friend Peter Crawford at a small table in the restaurant on the top floor of the office building where Jim works. Old friends from school, they usually meet for lunch two or three times a year.

"Nice to see you again, Peter! How've you been?"

"Not too bad, Jim. How are things with you?"

"I feel terrific. Waiter! Two menus, please."

Crawford, a 47-year-old business executive, is president of Electronic Specialties, Inc., a medium-sized supplier of electronic components. He has had more than 20 years of management experience, most of it in the electronics field. Since he was named to the position three years ago, Crawford has changed ESI from a small, slow-moving operation into one of the fastest growing and most profitable firms in the industry.

"How are things going at ESI, Peter? I hear you finally solved some of your production problems."

"That's right. In the end, we had to buy all new equipment. It was expensive, but our production is up and our labor costs have even gone down a little."

"That's good to hear, Peter. I knew you could do it."

Jim Burke is more than just a friend to Crawford. He is also president of United Electronic Industries, a conglomerate that includes an electronics firm called Audio Performance, Inc. AP is a well-known producer of stereo equipment and is one of ESI's best customers. The production problems at ESI had cut off AP's supply of one of its most important components, and Crawford's solution to the problem was good news to Burke.

"And how's everything at UEI, Jim?"

"Not too bad. I suppose you've heard that Bill Jensen, the president of Audio Performance, has been ill."

"No, I didn't know. I hope it's nothing serious."

"I'm afraid it is, Peter. It's his heart. The doctors have told him to take it easy and stay away from his desk for at least a few months. But he's sixty-one now, and he's decided to request early retirement. We've approved the request, particularly since Bill hasn't really been up to the job for some time."

"What are you going to do?" asked Crawford.

"We'll have to find a replacement."

"That won't be easy. Running a large operation like Audio Performance is a big job."

"It certainly is. We need someone who can take charge, someone with experience and good business judgment — someone who can give the company leadership."

"Do you have anyone in mind?" Crawford asked.

"Yes, as a matter of fact, I do," answered Burke, looking up from the menu. "And I'm having lunch with him right now!"

Exercise 1   Comprehension Check

Choose the best way to complete the sentences.

1. Jim Burke and Peter Crawford first became friends when they ...
   a) worked in the same building.
   b) worked for the same company.
   c) were students.

2. Crawford's firm, ESI, produces ...
   a) data-processing equipment.
   b) electronic components.
   c) supplies.

3. In the 3 years that Crawford has been president of ESI, the firm has ...
   a) grown quickly.
   b) become more profitable.
   c) both of the above

4. The production problems at ESI ...
   a) cut off AP's supply of an important component.
   b) made AP's operation unprofitable.
   c) made AP's labor costs go up.

5. Bill Jensen, president of AP, is retiring because ...
   a) he's 61.
   b) he's not well.
   c) his doctors ordered him to.

6. Burke wants Crawford to take charge of AP because ...
   a) he has to replace Jensen as soon as possible.
   b) AP is a large corporation.
   c) he thinks Crawford would do a good job.

GREETINGS

"Nice to see you again, Peter! How've you been?"
"Not too bad, Jim. How are things with you?"

more formal

- Hello, Mr. Crawford. It's so nice to see you again. How have you been?

- Mrs. Burke, what a pleasant surprise! How are you? It's been quite a while.

- Yes, it has, hasn't it?

- Good morning, Mr. Stanley. How are you today?

- I'm very well, thank you. And you?

- I'm fine, thank you.

- Good afternoon, Miss Crane. It's good to see you.

- Thank you. It's nice seeing you, too. How are things going?

- Just fine, thanks.

less formal

- Hello, Mary. How are you doing?

- Pretty well, thanks. How's everything with you?

- Not too bad, busy as ever.

- Hi, Ellen! How's it going?

- Great! What's new with you?

- Oh, not too much. You know, the same old thing.

PRESENT PROGRESSIVE *vs.* SIMPLE PRESENT

> "**Do** you **have** anyone in mind?" Crawford asked.
> "Yes ... And I'**m having** lunch with him right now."

Present progressive	Simple present

It's noon. I'**m going** to lunch. →	I usually **go** to lunch at noon.
It's Sunday. Tom **isn't working** today. →	He **doesn't work** on Sundays.
Listen! **Is** the phone **ringing** again? →	**Does** it always **ring** this often?

Exercise 2

Example: (retire)
Mr. Jensen **_is retiring_** for health reasons.
Many executives **_retire_** at age sixty-five.

1. *(read)*
   I always _____ on the train going home from work.
   I _____ an excellent book right now.

2. *(call)*
   May I ask who _____, please?
   How often _____ you _____ clients in the evening?

3. *(take it easy)*
   According to some doctors, people who _____ often live longer.
   Janet _____ today because she has a cold.

4. *(do)*
   What _____ you _____ to solve the labor problem?
   What _____ the firm _____ when labor costs go up?

5. *(grow)*
   We are pleased because our business _____ so fast.
   Businesses often _____ when they are well managed.

6. *(request)*
   Fred usually _____ vacation time a month in advance.
   This year he _____ two weeks off in August.

7. *(include)*
   We _____ a new price list with this shipment.
   As always, the prices _____ postage and handling.

SIMPLE PAST and PAST PROGRESSIVE

Simple past

completed   Peter **started** working for ESI three years ago.
action: He **had** lunch with Mr. Burke yesterday.
   They **discussed** business while they **ate**.

habitual   Charles **lived** in London when he **was** young.
action: He **went** to a small public school.
   We **didn't know** each other in those days.

Past progressive

continuing   **Were** you **working** for AP in June of 1989?
past actions: Karen **was typing** memos all afternoon.
   While you **were talking**, I **was thinking** of something else.

Simple past with past progressive

   We **didn't play** golf because it **was raining**.
   Jim and I **were leaving** when the phone **rang**.
   What **did** you **do** while you **were waiting** to see the doctor?

Exercise 3

Fill in the simple past or past progressive.

Example: *(get off / wait)*
     When Tom _**got off**_ the train, his son _**was waiting**_ for him.

1. *(see / eat)*
   When I _____ Carol and Tom, they _____ lunch in the cafeteria.

2. *(talk / arrive)*
   While Ed and I _____ on the phone, the mail _____.

3. *(go / run into)*
   Jill _____ to the elevator when she _____ her friend Karen.

4. *(take / earn)*
   When Mr. Hill _____ charge, the firm _____ a profit.

5. *(have to / leave)*
   We _____ hurry because our train _____.

ELECTRONIC SPECIALTIES, INC.
PERFORMANCE REPORT
January 1987 - September 1989

Year	Quarter	Sales ($)	Profit ($) (before tax)	Profit Margin (%)
1987	1st	5,125,000	240,900	4.7
	2nd	5,680,000	272,600	4.8
	3rd	7,373,000	464,500	6.3
	4th	10,208,000	765,600	7.5
Total:		28,386,000	1,743,600	6.1
1988	1st	13,776,000	1,171,000	8.5
	2nd	14,924,000	1,417,800	9.5
	3rd	19,642,000	1,801,400	9.2
	4th	11,706,000	772,600	6.6
Total:		60,048,000	5,162,800	8.6
1989	1st	16,109,000	989,600	6.1
	2nd	25,672,000	3,645,400	14.2
	3rd	38,374,000	6,293,300	16.4
(proj.)	4th	48,818,000	7,371,500	15.1
TOTAL: *(proj.)*		128,973,000	18,299,800	14.2

Electronic Specialties, Inc. is a medium-sized
supplier of electronic components.

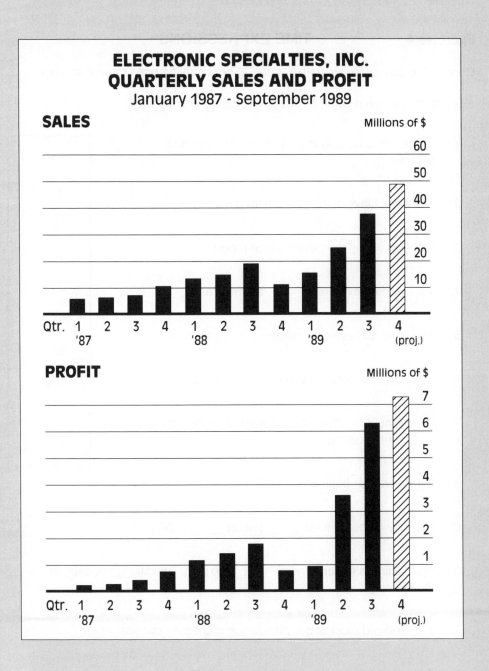

ELECTRONIC SPECIALTIES, INC.
QUARTERLY SALES AND PROFIT
January 1987 - September 1989

SALES   Millions of $

Qtr. 1	2	3	4	1	2	3	4	1	2	3	4
'87				'88				'89			(proj.)

PROFIT   Millions of $

Qtr. 1	2	3	4	1	2	3	4	1	2	3	4
'87				'88				'89			(proj.)

Crawford has changed ESI from a small, slow-moving operation into one of the fastest growing and most profitable firms in the industry.

Exercise 4   TIME EXPRESSIONS

Choose the correct words from the box. Some may be used more than once.

Example: I was out when Mr. Crawford called me **_at_** noon.

1.   Mr. Burke is waiting in your office. He arrived ten minutes _____.

2.   The bank stays open _____ 6:00 p.m. on Fridays.

3.   Is Karen typing the performance report _____?

4.   Tom worked overseas _____ several years.

5.   The train will leave the station _____ 7:52 a.m.

6.   The supplies were delivered _____ Tuesday.

7.   Please hold my calls. I don't want to be disturbed _____ the meeting.

for
during
ago
in
on
to
at
now
until
from

8.   Bill is away on business. He'll be back _____ three or four days.

9.   I usually go out to lunch _____ noon _____ 1:00 p.m.

10.   Ms. Collins is never at home _____ the day. Try calling her early in the evening.

11.   We replaced most of our office equipment over two years _____.

12.   Sally wanted to go into the electronics field _____ a while, but she changed her mind.

8

PUTTING NOUNS TOGETHER

> "[Crawford] has had more than 20 years of **management experience**, most of it in the electronics field."

It's easy to make new words in English by using the ones we already know. If you know the words *phone* and *office*, you'll understand *office phone* (a *phone* in the *office*). Here are a few other examples:

business letter	performance report	shoe factory
coffee break	replacement cost	traffic light
labor costs	steel production	address book

Sometimes words can be put together to make a single new word:

checkbook	housework	teatime
daylight	necktie	weekday
haircut	paperwork	workweek

Exercise 5

Examples: Bill's **office** is in this **building**. It's a very large *office building* .

Here's a **cup** for your **tea**. There are more *teacups* on the shelf.

1. At what **age** will you take **retirement**? The usual _____ is sixty-five.

2. **Production** is up mainly because of improvements the **manager**, Mr. Cramer, has made. He's been the _____ for two years.

3. My favorite **time** of the year is **spring**. It's beautiful in the _____.

4. Everyone used to **work** ten hours a **day**. Now the _____ has been shortened to eight hours.

5. The **report** covers **sales** for May. I turn in a _____ every month.

6. My **card** has my **business** address on it. May I have your _____?

7. Many of the **clubs** here are open late at **night**. Most of the _____ offer live entertainment.

8. There was no **clerk** at the hotel **desk**. Isn't there a _____ on duty?

AUDIO PERFORMANCE
383 MADISON AVE., NEW YORK, NY 10017
TEL (212) 921-8500   FAX (212) 921-9449

William Jensen
President

September 15, 1989

Mr. James Burke, President
United Electronics Industries
100 Rockefeller Center
New York, NY 10020

Dear Jim:

During a recent medical examination I received some rather disturbing news. I was told that my health would be at risk if I continued to hold a full-time position.

The doctor suggested I take a leave of absence for several months. I don't feel that this would be fair to the company, so I am writing to inquire whether some sort of early retirement status might be possible.

I sincerely appreciate the understanding and cooperation I have received from AP over the past few months when my health problems prevented me from giving my full attention and energies to the company.

Very truly yours,

William Jensen

Bill Jensen is sixty-one now, and he's decided to request early retirement.

- How important do you feel the following factors are in reaching the top of the corporate ladder: previous experience, educational background, quality of performance, "connections," and simply being in the right place at the right time?

- Business executives should be allowed to work as long as they are able to perform well, regardless of age. Discuss.

Vocabulary

unexpected – expect	heart
join	take it easy
executive (n, adj)	request (n, v)
supplier supply (n, v)	retirement – retire
component	approve (~ a request) – approval
management – manage	up to (be ~, feel ~)
field (the electronics ~)	replacement – replace
named (to)	run an operation
slow-moving	take charge – in charge of
fast-growing	judgment
profitable – profit	leadership – leader
equipment	have in mind
labor (~ costs)	As a matter of fact ...
conglomerate	
cut off	

2 THE PRESIDENT

It's a cold February afternoon in New York City. Peter Crawford is sitting in his office on the twenty-fourth floor of the Madison Building. He has just finished going over the computer printouts of the last several weeks' sales figures. He has put the papers down and, for the first time in nearly a month, is taking a few minutes to relax and just think.

His lunch with Jim Burke took place only four months ago. Burke made him a very generous offer, including a five-year contract and a large salary increase. At first, Crawford wasn't sure what to do. The offer was hard to turn down. He told Burke he would give him an answer within two weeks.

At that time, Crawford was happy at ESI. The company was growing, and he was growing with it. There was still a lot to do, a lot to finish. He didn't like leaving in the middle of a job. But he knew Audio Performance was a terrific opportunity, one that might not come again. After talking it over with his wife, Peter decided to take the job. He sat down that evening and wrote out a letter of acceptance. He ended the letter to Burke on a personal note: "I've always valued our friendship, and I'm now looking forward to working with you professionally. I appreciate the confidence you've placed in me, and I assure you I'll do my best to live up to it."

Eight weeks after mailing that letter, Crawford was named president of Audio Performance, a major corporation with revenues in excess of $160 million a year, 2,300 employees, and manufacturing plants in Baltimore, Hartford, and Boston. The firm's corporate headquarters are located in New York City.

In addition to Audio Performance, the parent company, United Electronics Industries, includes a number of other subsidiaries, most of them in the electronics field. Each subsidiary has its own management, but they all report to Jim Burke. At the top of the UEI organization is the Board of Directors.

Audio Performance was set up about 35 years ago, at the beginning of the hi-fi boom. Having gotten in on the "ground floor," it led the industry in growth and profits for many years. AP had always produced stereo equipment, but as new developments in technology occurred, they expanded their product line to include audiocassette players and recorders, amplifiers, and speakers, as well as a full line of CD players.

For a long time, most of the competition was domestic. But as foreign producers improved their technology and marketing capabilities, foreign competition increased, particularly from the Far East. Due to these factors, plus generally lower labor costs abroad, foreign manufacturers were selling their products at prices AP could no longer match.

This is just one of the problems that Crawford, as president of AP, is facing. There has been talk of purchasing components from foreign suppliers or even of opening manufacturing plants in other countries in an effort to bring production costs down, but Peter wants to find a way to make a go of it domestically. He knows that there will be a major review of his performance at year-end and that both Jim Burke and the Board are expecting a lot of him. He is determined not to let them down.

Exercise 6   Comprehension Check

Choose the best way to complete the sentences or answer the question.

1. Crawford didn't accept Burke's offer right away because ...
   a) he wanted a five-year contract.
   b) he wanted to take early retirement.
   c) he wanted to think it over.

2. The decision was not an easy one for Crawford because ...
   a) AP had been having problems.
   b) he knew that other opportunities would come along.
   c) he felt there was still a lot left for him to do at ESI.

3. Audio Performance ...
   a) hasn't expanded its product line over the years.
   b) has lower labor costs than its competitors.
   c) no longer leads the industry in growth and profits.

4. Which of the following is a problem Peter Crawford is facing?
   a) foreign competition
   b) expanding the AP product line
   c) neither of the above

5. Peter thinks the company should ...
   a) open manufacturing plants in other countries.
   b) purchase components from domestic suppliers.
   c) open other subsidiaries in the electronics field.

6. United Electronic Industries ...
   a) has several parent companies.
   b) has a number of subsidiaries.
   c) has a number of foreign operations.

EXPRESSING APPRECIATION

"I appreciate the confidence you've placed in me ..."

more formal

— We'd like to express our thanks for your hospitality during our stay, Mr. Walters.

— It was my pleasure. Think nothing of it. I wish I could have done more.

— It's very kind of you to see me on such short notice, Dr. Hill. I really appreciate it.

— That's quite all right, Mrs. Coleman.

— Karen, I'm very grateful for all your help with the report. I can't thank you enough.

— It was nothing, Mr. Crawford. Don't mention it. I was happy to be of help.

— Thank you again for dinner, Jim. It was a lovely evening.

— I'm glad you had a nice time, Jane. I enjoyed it too.

less formal

— I appreciate your driving me to work, Sam. You really saved my life!

— That's O.K. Honestly, it was no trouble at all. It was the least I could do.

— Thanks for sending the copy of the production report, Ed.

— You're welcome, Stan. Anytime.

THE PRESENT PERFECT

"[Peter] **has just finished** going over the computer printouts ..."

Finished time	Unfinished time
I **spoke** to the director yesterday.	I **have spoken** to the director today.
The meeting **took place** last week.	The meeting **hasn't taken place** yet.
I **met** Mr. Edwards two years ago.	I **have met** Mr. Edwards *(in my life)*.
Did you **study** French when you were a child?	**Have** you ever **studied** French?

Exercise 7   **CONTRASTING TENSES**

Fill in the present perfect, simple past, or simple present as needed.

1. *(meet)*
    So far today Tom _____ with six different people.

2. *(sign)*
    Last week we _____ an important contract with UEI.

3. *(check out)*
    The personnel department always _____ each applicant's references.

4. *(hire)*
    Our department_____ just _____ nine new trainees.

5. *(dictate)*
    Mr. Burke usually _____ his letters into a microcassette recorder.

6. *(be)*
    Mr. Hill _____ with the same company for the last ten years.

7. *(keep in touch)*
    I still _____ with a few of my former colleagues.

8. *(take)*
    When I was in school I _____ several computer programming courses.

9. *(have)*
    Ted _____ three different jobs since he started working for the firm.

10. *(be)*
    This year sales are the best they _____ in many years.

Exercise 8   TIME EXPRESSIONS

*Fill in **for**, **since**, **yet**, or **already**.*

1. Eberly's Electronics has been an authorized Tru-Tone dealer
   _____ over 20 years.

2. We haven't gotten our production costs under control _____ .

3. Sales have fallen over 12 percent _____ last year at this time.

4. How many applicants have _____ been interviewed?

5. James hasn't been able to come to work _____ he broke his leg.

6. Sarah and Karen have known each other _____ many years.

7. Haven't Ben and Steve begun working out a long-term strategy
   _____ ?

8. If the price cut has _____ gone into effect, it's almost impossible to
   reverse it.

9. We've been working on the market study _____ February, and we
   haven't finished it _____ .

10. The Baltimore plant has been in operation _____ 1960.

11. As a result of rising labor costs, we've barely broken even _____ two
    months.

12. A number of sites have _____ been evaluated, but we haven't found
    anything suitable _____ .

EXPRESSING PURPOSE AND REASON

> "**Due to** these factors ... foreign manufacturers were selling their products at prices AP could no longer match."

Purpose: Jill is taking a computer course **so** she can get a better job.
She's studying at night **in order to** improve her skills.
She went to a counselor **for** advice about courses.

Reason: Jill wanted a better job. **That's why** she went back to school.
She couldn't take classes during the day **because of** her job.
Since she has experience, she'll be able to get a good job.
Because she works hard, she has a good chance to succeed.
If Jill is successful, it will be **due to** her hard work.

Exercise 9

Example: (because / so)
I went to lunch early __*because*__ I had a 1:00 p.m. meeting.

1. *(for / because of)*
   The invoices were sent out late _____ a computer problem.

2. *(in order to / for)*
   We are working with Mr. Blake _____ solve the problems at the plant.

3. *(due to / since)*
   The phone lines were down for 24 hours _____ the big storm.

4. *(for / in order to)*
   The new machinery was purchased _____ increase efficiency.

5. *(Since / Due to)*
   _____ Mike doesn't have a license, he depends on friends for rides.

6. *(in order to / for)*
   Stan is going to London _____ a business meeting.

7. *(so / since)*
   I wrote myself a note _____ I wouldn't forget to call you.

8. *(Due to / That's why)*
   Bill just bought a new car. _____ he isn't taking a vacation this year.

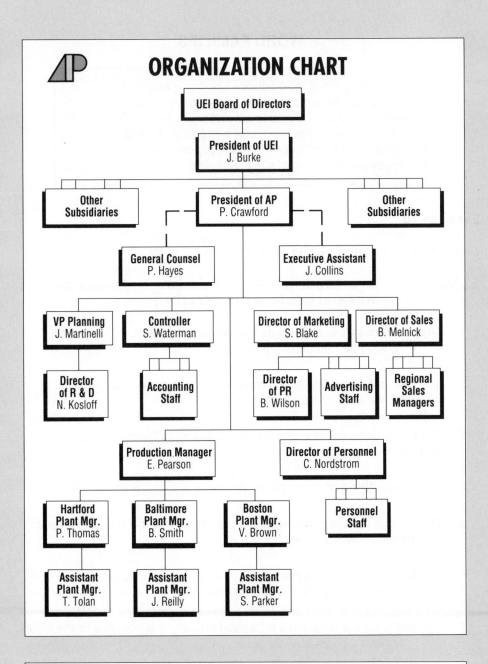

ORGANIZATION CHART

- **UEI Board of Directors**
  - **President of UEI** — J. Burke
    - **Other Subsidiaries**
    - **President of AP** — P. Crawford
      - **General Counsel** — P. Hayes
      - **Executive Assistant** — J. Collins
      - **VP Planning** — J. Martinelli
        - **Director of R & D** — N. Kosloff
      - **Controller** — S. Waterman
        - **Accounting Staff**
      - **Director of Marketing** — S. Blake
        - **Director of PR** — B. Wilson
        - **Advertising Staff**
      - **Director of Sales** — B. Melnick
        - **Regional Sales Managers**
      - **Production Manager** — E. Pearson
        - **Hartford Plant Mgr.** — P. Thomas
          - **Assistant Plant Mgr.** — T. Tolan
        - **Baltimore Plant Mgr.** — B. Smith
          - **Assistant Plant Mgr.** — J. Reilly
        - **Boston Plant Mgr.** — V. Brown
          - **Assistant Plant Mgr.** — S. Parker
      - **Director of Personnel** — C. Nordstrom
        - **Personnel Staff**
    - **Other Subsidiaries**

*As one of the UEI subsidiaries, AP has its own management.
At the top of the UEI organization is the Board of Directors.*

WORD FAMILIES

> Audio Performance **produces** electronic equipment.
> The company is a **producer** of stereos and tapes.
> AP's **products** are sold in several countries.
> Each manufacturing plant has a **production** quota.
> AP wants its employees to be as **productive** as possible.
> **Productivity** has a lot to do with profits.

Exercise 10

Complete these sentences using words from the same family.

Example: The Board has just received Crawford's letter of __*acceptance*__ .
They're pleased he's decided to **accept** the position.

1.   Most countries try to encourage **industrial** development. Many new
_____ have appeared in recent years.

2.   The firm that **supplied** us with many of our components is going out of
business; we have to look for a new _____.

3.   Our major **competitor** is a foreign corporation, but domestic _____ is
beginning to increase as well.

4.   Mr. Hill is **retiring** next month; we're having a _____ party for him.

5.   One reason the company **leads** the industry is that the Board of Directors
has always provided strong _____.

6.   We are considering an **expansion** of our corporate offices. We'd like to
_____ them by about 20,000 square feet.

7.   The company's **profits** have increased steadily; it is now one of the most
_____ firms in the industry.

8.   The project must be submitted to the Board for final _____ once Peter
Crawford has **approved** it.

PUTTING NOUNS TOGETHER WITH NUMBERS

"Burke made him a very generous offer, including a **five-year** contract and a large salary increase."

We can take a noun, put a number before it, and then put another noun after it. So an *apartment* with four *rooms* is called a *four-room apartment.* Here are some other examples:

six-letter word	eight-hour day	40-hour week
two-piece suit	ten-dollar tie	50-page report
four-door car	five-year contract	1000-mile trip

Do you have any plans for the **three-day weekend**?
The Pearsons have just bought a **four-bedroom house**.
The receptionist takes a **ten-minute break** around three o'clock.

Exercise 11

Example: This bottle holds two liters. It's a __*two-liter bottle*__ .

1. Mr. Carlson was on a tour of Europe for three weeks. He really enjoyed his _____ of Europe.

2. There are 50,000 words in that dictionary. How much do you think a _____ costs?

3. We ate a meal consisting of five courses, but _____ aren't unusual in our family.

4. Mary paid $25,000 for her car. How much is the tax on a _____?

5. The firm's corporate plane holds eighteen passengers. The _____ can land at most airports.

6. There are eight people on the committee. An _____ can't make decisions very quickly.

7. The fence around the building is six feet high. The _____ keeps unwanted visitors out.

8. My computer course lasts nine months. I'll finish my _____ in July.

PETER CRAWFORD

155 Valley Road
New Rochelle, NY 10080

October 20, 1989

Mr. James Burke
President
United Electronic Industries
100 Rockefeller Center
New York, NY 10020

Dear Jim:

It was nice meeting with you for lunch. It's always good to catch up on news of you and your family, as well as what's been happening at UEI.

After thinking your offer over carefully, I've decided that the position of president at Audio Performance is an opportunity I simply can't pass up. The terms you've described are quite agreeable, and I'm delighted to accept.

I've always valued our friendship, and I'm now looking forward to working with you professionally. I appreciate the confidence you've placed in me, and I assure you I'll do my best to live up to it.

Best regards,

Peter Crawford

*After talking it over with his wife, Peter decided to take the job.
He sat down that evening and wrote out a letter of acceptance.*

- Discuss the advantages and disadvantages of working for a conglomerate.

- Employees owe loyalty to the firms that first hired them. Discuss.

Vocabulary

go over
printout
figures (sales ~)
take place
offer (make s.o.* an ~)
increase (n, v)
– decrease (n, v)
turn down
talk over
on a personal note
value (v)
look forward to
appreciate
live up to
corporation
corporate
revenue(s)
excess (in ~ of)
– exceed
manufacturing plant
– manufacture
headquarters
parent company
subsidiary

* s.o. = someone

report to
– report (n)
Board of Directors
set up
boom (hi-fi ~)
lead (= be first)
expand
– expansion
product line
competition
– competitor
domestic(ally)
foreign
marketing
market
capability
– capable
abroad
face (v)
– be faced with
effort (in an ~ to)
make a go of (= succeed)
review (n, v)
determined (be ~ to)
let s.o. down

3 PRODUCTION PROBLEMS

Peter and AP's production manager, Ed Pearson, were going over some production reports from the main manufacturing plant in Baltimore. The plant wasn't meeting its quota, and there had been reports of orders not being filled on time. There were several important contracts, and at the current rate of production, the plant wouldn't even come close to meeting the delivery schedule.

"From what I can see, production will have to be increased by at least fifteen percent," said Pearson, looking up from the reports.

"Fifteen percent! That's a lot! It looks like we've really got a problem, Ed. Let's fly down to Baltimore tomorrow and take a closer look at the situation," replied Peter.

The flight to Baltimore was a short one. Peter and Ed were greeted at the gate by the plant manager, Bob Smith, and his assistant, Jack Reilly. When they got to the plant, Pearson suggested starting with a tour of the facility. Crawford agreed, and they began with the assembly line area. During the tour Crawford took a good look at the equipment and asked a lot of technical questions about the operation.

Then Crawford said he would like to spend a few minutes on his own talking to some of the workers. He wanted to find out what their general attitudes were and how they felt about their work. He started in the maintenance department. He was surprised to find that the employees were open, even friendly.

After some small talk, Peter got right to the point. "Look," he said, "I'm here because the plant isn't meeting its production quota. You people are right here where the action is. Why don't you tell me how you honestly feel about the situation? What are the problems as you see them? Your input would be helpful in finding solutions."

After some hesitation, one of the men spoke up. "Mr. Crawford, I'll give you an honest answer. Our biggest problem is that we're working with machines that are constantly breaking down, hard to repair, and dangerous. Sometimes we're faced with a couple of breakdowns at the same time, and we don't have enough people to take care of all the repairs. By the time we get one problem solved, something else goes wrong. We spend so much time on repairs we don't have time for routine maintenance. It's a nightmare!"

"I worry about safety," said another worker. "One man was seriously injured in the loading area just last week. The procedures and safety regulations just don't cover the situations we get into. We're being asked to do the impossible."

"We don't want to complain, Mr. Crawford," said a third worker. "Mr. Smith told us if we complained we could lose our jobs to robots. We're in a difficult situation. We know the plant's productivity has been slipping and we're as unhappy about that as anybody. It's really frustrating!"

Peter was impressed with the group's frank comments. "I appreciate the information. I assure you it will be kept confidential," Crawford said as he shook hands with them one by one. He then rejoined Ed Pearson and Bob Smith, who were in Smith's office.

As Peter walked into the room, Pearson was speaking to Smith. "I'm concerned about the amount of time that's being lost because of breakdowns."

"Most of the equipment is over twenty years old," replied Smith. "I don't think we can do much better with such obsolete equipment."

"I'm not so sure," Peter said. "From what I can see, the maintenance department is overworked, understaffed, and badly trained. There hasn't been enough attention paid to preventive maintenance in the past, and now we're paying for it."

"I assure you, Mr. Crawford, we're doing the best we can," Smith replied.

On the trip back to New York, Peter and Ed discussed the situation. Ed felt the plant wasn't being run as efficiently as it could be. Peter agreed the equipment was old, but felt the problem was more one of management. "If production doesn't increase soon, we may have no alternative but to look for a replacement for Smith. Let's give him two months to begin to turn things around."

Exercise 12   Comprehension Check

Choose the correct words to complete the sentences.

1. The Baltimore plant is having _____ problems.
   a) production   b) delivery   c) labor

2. Crawford wanted to find out how _____ felt about the plant.
   a) Smith   b) the employees   c) Reilly

3. The staff doesn't have time to do _____ maintenance.
   a) repair   b) routine   c) safety

4. One man injured on the job might _____ the company.
   a) quit   b) report   c) sue

5. The plant manager believes the machines are _____.
   a) overworked   b) obsolete   c) efficient

6. The employees are frustrated about the _____ productivity.
   a) rising   b) steady   c) falling

WORRY, CONCERN, AND REASSURANCE

"I worry about safety. One man was seriously injured in the loading area just last week."

more formal

– I'm very concerned about the problems at the plant, Ed. I'm afraid Smith just isn't up to the job anymore.

– I think your concern is justified, Peter. But things may not be as bad as they seem.

– I'm worried, Barbara. Steve Miller was supposed to be here an hour ago. He hasn't called, has he?

– No, but I wouldn't be too concerned if I were you, Bob. He probably just missed his train.

– What will happen if we don't meet our quota, Carl? That's what's bothering me.

– Don't worry, George. Everything will work out somehow.

less formal

– I'm really upset! I can't find the papers I need to do my weekly report. I've looked everywhere!

– Calm down, Alice. You know they must be here somewhere.

– You look worried, Tom. What's bothering you?

– I'm really nervous about my job interview tomorrow.

– Just relax. You don't have a thing to worry about.

RELATIVE CLAUSES

"I'm concerned about the amount of time
that's being lost because of breakdowns."

Things → *"that"*

Berlitz is a company. *It* teaches languages.
→ Berlitz is a company *that* teaches languages.

Berlitz is a company. Everyone knows *it*.
→ Berlitz is a company *that* everyone knows. (1)
Berlitz is a company everyone knows. (2)

Berlitz is a company. The director works for *it*.
→ *Berlitz is a company (that) the director works for.* (2)

We'd like to find a firm **that can supply** electronic components.
The machine **that was repaired** last week is giving us trouble again.
There's no easy solution to the production problems **(that) we have.**
One thing **I'm concerned about** is the age of the equipment.

People → *"who / whom"*

Miss Ames is a secretary. *She* works for Berlitz.
→ Miss Ames is a secretary *who* works for Berlitz.

Miss Ames is a secretary. The director hired *her*.
→ Miss Ames is a secretary *whom* the director hired. (1)
→ *Miss Ames is a secretary (who) the director hired.* (2)

Miss Ames is a secretary. I work with *her*.
→ *Miss Ames is a secretary (who) I work with.* (2)

Customers **who pay by check** must get the manager's approval.
Thomas Hill is the accountant **who was promoted.**
The client I called will be out of town until next Wednesday.
The man I wrote to last week hasn't answered my letter yet.

(1) written form (2) spoken form

Exercise 13

Rewrite the sentences using relative clauses.

Examples: The secretary has some memos. *(They have to be finished.)*
The secretary has some memos that have to be finished.

Mr. Wilson is the supervisor. *(I work for him.)*
Mr. Wilson is the supervisor I work for.

The doctor was very good. *(You recommended her.)*
The doctor you recommended was very good.

1. I've just had dinner with a friend. *(I haven't seen him in years.)*

2. We have twenty new trainees. *(They were hired last month.)*

3. I went over the paperwork. *(You put it on my desk.)*

4. Ted works for a firm. *(It has offices all over the country.)*

5. The Board chose a president. *(He has had many years of experience.)*

6. Mr. Crawford was on the flight. *(It left at one o'clock.)*

7. The client would like you to return her call. *(She called about an order.)*

8. The expansion should increase the company's profits. *(We're planning it.)*

9. There are some problems at the plant. *(The manager is concerned about them.)*

10. The passenger will have to pay another fare. *(She lost her ticket.)*

11. The book is now a best seller. *(It was recommended to me.)*

12. I'm having lunch with some people. *(I met them at the meeting.)*

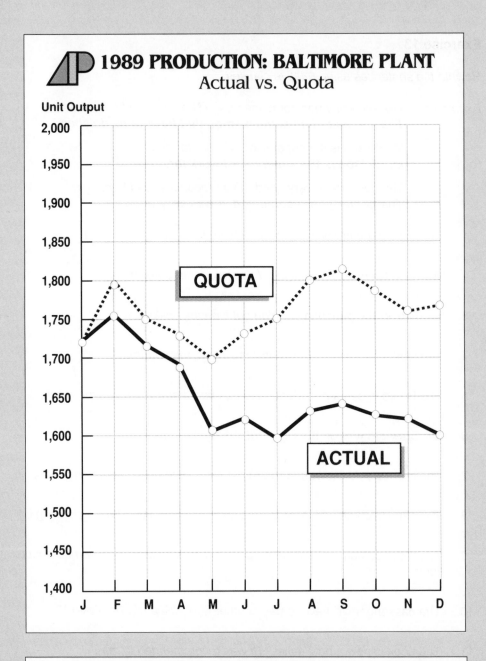

1989 PRODUCTION: BALTIMORE PLANT
Actual vs. Quota

The plant wasn't meeting its quota. At the current rate of production, it wouldn't even come close to meeting the delivery schedule.

PROGRESSIVE FORMS

"I assure you, Mr. Crawford, **we're doing** the best we can," Smith replied.

> Karen **is working** on a report.
> She **was working** on it when I called.
> She **has been working** on it since she arrived.
> How long **will** she **be working** on it?

Exercise 14

Fill in the correct progressive forms.

Example: *(have)*
        At this time tomorrow, I **_will be having_** lunch with the directors.

1. *(go over)*
   Right now John _____ the latest production report.

2. *(leave)*
   I met Jane when she walked into the office; I _____ just _____.

3. *(talk)*
   Mr. Ames is in his office with Mrs. Cohen; they _____ for an hour now.

4. *(have)*
   We _____ dinner when Peter called.

5. *(rain)*
   Do you think it _____ still _____ when we leave?

6. *(meet)*
   The plant _____ its quota ever since it was expanded.

7. *(work)*
   John _____ for a small electronics firm now.

8. *(wait)*
   We can look over the contract while we _____ to see Mrs. Spencer.

9. *(walk)*
   We discussed the production problems while we _____ back from the plant.

10. *(teach)*
    Berlitz _____ languages for more than a hundred years!

Exercise 15

Examples: (opens / is opening)
The secretary __*is opening*__ the mail now.

(arrived / was arriving)
Her boss __*arrived*__ an hour ago.

1. *(keeps / is keeping)*
    The company always _____ close track of travel expenses.

2. *(spoken with / been speaking with)*
    Sara had already _____ her client when his letter arrived.

3. *(be wearing / wear)*
    Will I recognize you at the airport? What will you _____ when you arrive?

4. *(did / was doing)*
    We gave Bob time to turn things around because he _____ his best.

5. *(been coming / come)*
    So far Miss Lyons has _____ in three times asking about employment.

6. *(expected / been expecting)*
    The employees have _____ a salary increase since last January.

7. *(waited / been waiting)*
    When we arrived, Ed had _____ in the reception area for an hour.

8. *(is dictating / dictates)*
    Mr. Crawford usually _____ a few letters in the morning.

9. *(lie / be lying)*
    At this time next week I'll _____ on the beach in Majorca.

10. *(makes / is making)*
    Mr. Barton can't speak with you now; he _____ an urgent phone call.

11. *(was raining / rained)*
    When Peter left his apartment this morning, it _____ quite hard.

12. *(gone over / been going over)*
    I have _____ the most recent printouts for over two hours now.

THE PREFIXES *OVER-* AND *UNDER-*

> "From what I can see, the maintenance department is **overworked**, **understaffed**, and badly trained."

The prefixes *over-* and *under-* change the meaning of a word. If a person eats *too much*, we can say he *over*eats. If he's paid *too little*, we say he's *under*paid. Here are some other examples:

> Jill got to work late because she **overslept**.
> If everyone works **overtime**, we can meet the production quota.
> The company ran into difficulty because they **overexpanded**.
> What a terrible meal! Everything was **undercooked**!
> The purchasing agent **underordered**, and we've run out of parts.

Exercise 16

*Use the prefixes **over-** and **under-** to make new words.*

Example: Terry thinks the assembly line workers are **paid too much**. In his opinion, they're ___*overpaid*___.

1. Our **prices** are **too low**. Everyone agrees our products are _____.

2. Our plant's **production** was **too low** in the fall. Because we _____, there was a shortage of goods during the holidays.

3. Our **supply** of paper is **too large**. Don't order more until we use up the
   _____.

4. The travel agent **charged** me **too much** for the plane ticket. He _____ me $20.

5. Very few people feel that they pay **too little tax**. Do you know anyone who complains about being _____?

6. Tom's **reaction** to the problem was **too strong**. Because he _____, he actually made the problem worse.

7. I thought Maria was **dressed too formally** for the occasion, but no one else felt she was _____.

8. The hotel was given **too low a rating** in the guide book. As a matter of fact, it's one of the most _____ hotels I've stayed in.

RADIOWORLD INC.

225 BUTLER STREET • PARAMUS, NJ 07652 • 201-295-0811

February 8, 1990

Audio Performance, Inc.
383 Madison Avenue
New York, NY 10017

Ref: Order No. 2J725

Attention: Charles Cooper
Order Department

The above-referenced order was submitted to you on January 5, 1990, and delivery promised within four weeks.

Unfortunately, the merchandise has not arrived yet and the delay has caused us considerable inconvenience. I would appreciate it if you would advise me immediately when we can expect delivery.

We have been doing business with Audio Performance for many years, and would like this relationship to continue.

Sincerely,

John S Daley

John S. Daley
Manager

JSD:mm

There had been reports of orders not being filled on time.

- How much responsibility do companies have to long-time employees who start to "slow down" or whose performance is affected by personal problems? Discuss.

- Describe the qualities and skills you feel are most important to supervise employees effectively.

quota (meet a ~)
fill (~ an order)
facility
assembly line
on one's own
maintenance (~ department)
– maintain
small talk
get to the point
input
speak up
break down
breakdown
repair
danger
dangerous
nightmare
safe
safety
injured (be / get ~)

loading area
– load (v)
procedures (safety ~)
cover (~ a situation)
complain
lose (a job, time)
slip (v)
impressed (be ~ with)
frank (adj)
confidential (keep s.t.* ~)
concerned (be ~ about)
do better
do the best you can
obsolete
overworked
– staff (n)
understaffed
preventive
– prevent
alternative (no ~ but to do s.t.)
turn s.t. around

* s.t. = something

4 THE PRESIDENT'S SECRETARY

"Good morning, Mr. Crawford." It was almost ten o'clock when Peter walked into the office. He was usually the first one to arrive, but today he was late because of heavy traffic.

"Good morning, Karen," he answered. Crawford's secretary, Karen Lawrence, was sitting at her desk just outside his office. "Things seem fairly quiet around here this morning. Any messages?"

"Actually, it's been quite hectic. I was trying to finish up these memos before you got here, but I haven't had a chance. Your messages are on your desk. And several faxes have come in too. Oh, one more thing — Jane Collins called just before you walked in."

"I'll get back to her this afternoon," said Peter, "unless it's important."

"No, she said it could wait."

"Fine. Has the mail arrived yet?"

"Yes, but there doesn't seem to be anything very urgent."

"Thanks," Peter said, walking into his office.

Karen had joined the company as a receptionist three years earlier, having answered an ad placed in the classified section of the local newspaper. Although she'd taken all the secretarial and word processing courses offered in school, she hadn't had any practical, on-the-job experience. But it wasn't long before people started noticing her excellent work. She was soon promoted to clerk typist, then to secretary.

Peter had notified the personnel department that he was looking for a secretary when he came to Audio Performance, and Karen was one of the applicants who had been sent in for an interview. Peter liked her immediately and told her the job was hers if she wanted it. Karen accepted enthusiastically. It was a good opportunity. The promotion to executive secretary meant a raise and additional responsibilities. It also meant that, for the first time since she had begun working at AP, she would be working for only one person instead of several at the same time.

In addition to general clerical work and answering the telephone, Karen was now responsible for keeping Crawford's files in order, keeping track of all of his appointments, and making travel arrangements when necessary. From the start, Crawford had been more than satisfied with Karen's performance.

Peter pressed the "talk" button on his intercom. "If you have a minute, Karen, I'd like to get a few memos out."

"I'll be right in," she answered. A few minutes later she was sitting in front of him with a steno pad in her hand.

Peter began dictating. "The first one is to Ed Pearson, copy to Jane Collins ..."

At that moment, the phone rang. Peter picked it up and Karen heard him say, "O.K., Ed. I understand. I didn't think things were quite that bad. I'll see you in a few minutes."

Peter's mood had suddenly turned very serious. "Sorry, Karen. The memos will have to wait. Something has come up at the Baltimore plant that needs my attention. Could you get me the latest production reports from the file, please? And when Ed Pearson gets here, send him right in."

Exercise 17   Comprehension Check

Choose the correct words from the box, then answer the questions.

Example: Was it quiet or fairly **_hectic_** when Peter arrived?
         It was quiet when he arrived.

1.   Where is Karen's desk _____?

2.   Was the call from Jane Collins _____?

3.   How much _____, on-the-job experience had
      Karen had when she went to work for AP?

4.   Had Karen taken any _____ courses in school?

5.   Why was she so _____ about becoming
      Mr. Crawford's secretary?

6.   As Mr. Crawford's secretary, what were some of
      Karen's _____ responsibilities going to be?

7.   How _____ was Peter with Karen's performance?

8.   Who was Peter going to discuss the_____ production reports with?

practical
enthusiastic
satisfied
urgent
hectic
latest
located
additional
secretarial

REQUESTS

"Could you get me the latest production reports from the file, please?"

more formal

less formal

— Karen, would you be good enough to hold my calls for the next twenty minutes or so?
— Certainly, Mr. Crawford. I'd be happy to.

— Would you mind opening the window a little, please?
— Not at all ... Is that better?
— Yes, thank you.

— Ann, could you take these files up to Ed's office for me?
— I'm expecting an important call right now, but I'd be glad to do it after that.
— No, that's all right. I'll take care of it. Thanks anyway.

— If you have a minute, Mary, I'd like to go over these figures.
— I'm afraid I can't, Tom. I have an appointment in ten minutes.
— It'll only take a second.
— All right, I suppose so, if we can make it quick.

— Say, Jim, I have a big favor to ask. Can you give me a ride home tonight?
— I wish I could, but I have to stay late to catch up on some paperwork. Sorry.

— Hey, Jack. Do me a favor, will you? Hand me that stapler.
— No problem. Here you go.

THE PAST PERFECT

"Karen **had joined** the company as a receptionist three years earlier ..."

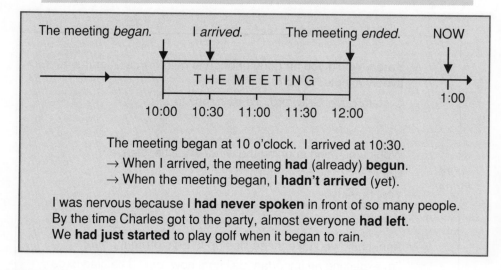

The meeting *began.* I *arrived.* The meeting *ended.* NOW

THE MEETING

10:00 10:30 11:00 11:30 12:00 1:00

The meeting began at 10 o'clock. I arrived at 10:30.
→ When I arrived, the meeting **had** (already) **begun**.
→ When the meeting began, I **hadn't arrived** (yet).

I was nervous because I **had never spoken** in front of so many people.
By the time Charles got to the party, almost everyone **had left**.
We **had just started** to play golf when it began to rain.

Exercise 18

Examples: I read the newspaper at 7:30 a.m. I got to the office at 8:30 a.m.
When I got to the office, _**I had already read the newspaper**_ .

The secretary typed the memos this morning.
When she left last night, _**she hadn't typed the memos yet**_ .

1. I ate at noon. At one o'clock my boss invited me to lunch.
When my boss invited me to lunch, _____.

2. The Parkers got to the airport at 7:45 a.m. The plane left at 8:05 a.m.
When they got to the airport, _____.

3. The Board met on the 7th. On the 1st, Bill requested retirement.
By the time the Board met on the 10th, _____.

4. Miss Ames resigned in September. She found another job a month later.
When Miss Ames resigned, _____.

5. On Tuesday I went to the meeting. I went over the figures on Monday.
By the time I got to the meeting, _____.

Exercise 19   *JUST, STILL* and *ALREADY*

Rewrite the sentences to include the words in parentheses.

Example: I called Karen at 12:15 p.m. She went to lunch. *(just)*
   When I called Karen, she had just gone to lunch.

1. Peter Crawford gave Jim Burke his decision. He talked it over with his wife. *(already)*

2. Janet went to work for AP. It became a subsidiary of UEI. *(just)*

3. I left work at 6:30 p.m. I didn't finish going over the sales figures. *(still)*

4. Your representative contacted us. We signed a contract with another firm. *(just)*

5. Mr. Park left the meeting. We discussed foreign competition. *(already)*

6. The sales manager retired. They didn't find a replacement for her. *(still)*

7. The computer technician arrived after lunch. We solved the problem ourselves. *(already)*

8. We drove through the intersection. The accident took place. *(just)*

9. I spoke to Sally last week. She didn't find an apartment. *(still)*

10. Jim arrived at the garage. They finished repairing his car. *(just)*

11. Stephen invited me to dinner. I made other plans. *(already)*

12. We saw our friends in August. We came back from vacation the week before. *(just)*

Exercise 20   OPPOSITES

Choose the opposites from the words in the box.

Example: There is some **danger** to the job, but ___*safety*___ procedures are strict.

1. A company's _____ must exceed its **expenses** in order to make a profit.

2. If the equipment isn't **repaired** correctly, it will just _____ again.

3. Bill feels his **personal** life is just as important as _____ advancement.

4. Both **foreign** and _____ competition have increased over the past five years.

5. If we can't **lower** our costs, we'll have no alternative but to _____ our prices.

6. You will be **dropped off** at the airport when you leave and _____ when you return.

7. Bob **resigned** from the company within a year after he had _____ it.

8. These files are completely **out of order**. It will take me a while to put them back _____.

9. The personnel manager was surprised when Mary **turned down** the job offer; he had expected her to _____ it.

10. Sales have been going up **gradually** over the past two years. They should rise _____ after we increase our advertising.

11. Although Linda made it seem like a _____ problem, it was really only a **minor** one.

12. The government has recommended an _____ in taxes and a **decrease** in spending to balance the budget.

professional
safety
break down
revenues
domestic
picked up
major
in order
joined
raise
increase
accept
sharply

EASTON
FEB-7'90
PA

U.S.POSTAGE
0.25
P.B.METER
6812849

Peter Crawford
c/o Audio Performance, Inc.
383 Madison Ave.
New York, NY 10017

CONFIDENTIAL

Dwight Office Supply
P.O. Box 1827
Princeton, NJ 08540

PRINCETON
FEB-9'90
NJ

U.S.POSTAGE
0.25
P.B.METER
6812849

Audio Performance
383 Madison Ave.
New York, NY 10017

Attention: Karen Lawrence

LONDON N
9.30PM
2 FEB
1990

OF MEM
USE
POST

Mr Peter Crawford, President
Audio Performance, Inc.
383 Madison Avenue
New York, NY 10017
U.S.A.

By air mail
Par avion

Piccadilly Electronics Ltd.
420 TOTTENHAM COURT RD. LONDON WC2

Peter asked Karen if the mail had arrived yet.

43

Exercise 21   CONTRASTING TENSES

Example: (was / have been / had been)
I __*was*__ on the phone all morning yesterday.

1. *(signed / has signed / had signed)*
Last summer the corporation _____ a contract to supply AP with electronic components.

2. *(met / has met / had met)*
So far this year the Board of Directors _____ three times.

3. *(went out / has gone out / had gone out)*
I called Mr. Ames, but he wasn't there; he _____ for lunch.

4. *(drove / have driven / had driven)*
The trains weren't running, so I _____ to work this morning.

5. *(didn't finish / hasn't finished / hadn't finished)*
When the secretary left the office she _____ typing the memos.

6. *(was / has been / had been)*
Nancy _____ busy going over the figures for two hours now.

7. *(stopped / have stopped / had stopped)*
On my way to work this morning I _____ to buy a newspaper.

8. *(didn't talk / hasn't talked / hadn't talked)*
The president made a decision even though he _____ it over with the Board.

9. *(watched / have watched / had watched)*
Since we hired the new systems analyst, we _____ her performance very carefully.

10. *(didn't leave / hasn't left / hadn't left)*
By 6:30 last night Peter Crawford still _____ the office.

Exercise 22　　　　　　　**IDIOMS**

Choose the correct words to complete the idioms.

Example:　　(making / taking / doing)
　　　　　　Bill has been working too hard. He'd better start **_taking_** it easy.

1.　(get / speak / go)
　　I'm not sure what you're trying to say. Would you _____ to the point?

2.　(told / done / made)
　　The company has _____ me a very good job offer.

3.　(choose / take / have)
　　No one is happy about it, but we _____ no alternative but to close the
　　Birmingham plant.

4.　(took / did / made)
　　Peter was surprised when he _____ a look at the latest sales figures.

5.　(at / in / to)
　　Do you have anyone _____ mind for the position in Hartford?

6.　(make / take / put)
　　We need someone who can _____ charge, someone who isn't afraid
　　of making difficult decisions.

7.　(do / take / meet)
　　If Apex can _____ the price of the other supplier, we will purchase the
　　components from them.

8.　(over / place / charge)
　　At about what time did the accident take _____?

9.　(on / to / of)
　　We've started keeping track _____ all long distance calls made from
　　the offices.

10.　(chance / point / mind)
　　The Millers have been wanting to get away for a weekend, but they haven't
　　had a _____.

**AUDIO PERFORMANCE**
383 MADISON AVE., NEW YORK, NY 10017
TEL (212) 921-8500   FAX (212) 921-9449

# of pages: _(1)_

TO: Mr. R. Smith

FROM: Ed Pearson

DATE: 2/16/90

SUBJECT: Production Levels

This will confirm our telephone conversation yesterday regarding the production levels at the Baltimore plant. The latest figures, for the period February 1 - 14, indicate that production continues to fall significantly below plan levels. At this rate the plant will not even produce 1,600 units this month, as against a quota of 1,850.

At our last meeting we agreed on new production goals and a special maintenance program to ensure that plant output reaches acceptable levels. As plant manager, it will be your job to see that these goals are achieved.

Bob, I want you to realize that this situation is very serious. We expect to see a substantial improvement over the next two months, otherwise we will be forced to re-evaluate your suitability as plant manager.

EP/jp

cc: Peter Crawford
    Jane Collins

*Pearson and Crawford decided to give Smith
two months to start turning things around.*

- What qualities would you look for in an executive secretary?

- Companies are usually better off hiring from the outside because "new blood" brings new ideas. Discuss.

Vocabulary

fairly (~ quiet)	interview *(n, v)*
actually	raise *(n)*
hectic	responsible for (~ doing s.t.)
finish up	in order – out of order
have a chance (~ to do s.t.)	keep track of
get back to s.o.	
join (a company)	arrangements (make ~) – arrange
place (~ an ad)	press (~ a button)
classified section	intercom
notice *(v)*	steno pad
promote – promotion	dictate – take dictation
clerk typist / clerical	mood
personnel (department)	turn (~ serious)
notify	come up *(= happen)*
applicant – apply	

5 BUY, BUILD, OR LEASE

Karen buzzed Peter on the intercom: "Mr. Martinelli is here to see you."

"Oh, good. Tell him to come right in," Peter answered.

In addition to the general inefficiency at the Baltimore plant, Peter was also concerned about rising labor costs. He had asked his executive assistant, Jane Collins, to do a study of labor costs in all of AP's plants. The results indicated that in Baltimore labor costs were rising to the point where the facility would soon do no more than break even.

After a series of discussions, top management had decided to open a new facility located in a more favorable labor climate and to gradually phase out the unprofitable operation. They also recommended taking advantage of the move to expand plant capacity. Peter had asked Jeff Martinelli, the company's vice president of planning, to report on how he felt the expansion should be handled.

"We have just under 100,000 square feet now. As I see it," Jeff began, "we should expand that to at least 175,000 square feet. That should allow us to double our capacity. I've spoken with several real estate brokers already, and new construction seems to be the best way to go. And while we're at it, to minimize our labor costs, we should purchase all new, state-of-the-art equipment, with as many automated and robotized functions as possible."

"New construction? With the price of land in the northeast as high as it is? I was thinking more of leasing or buying an existing facility," said Peter. "Remember, any expansion will require the approval of the Board of Directors. I seriously doubt that they'll go along with such a large capital outlay at this time."

"Why should we limit ourselves to sites in the northeast?" Jeff replied. "There are many areas of the country where unimproved land is still relatively cheap and taxes are reasonable. State governments are eager to attract new business, especially when it's something that's clean and doesn't cause pollution, like the electronics industry."

"I'm aware of that, but I'm also aware that the supply of labor in those areas can be limited, and proximity to transportation is often less than ideal," said Peter.

"You have a point," replied Jeff, "but I think that might be too much of a generalization. Our main objectives on this project are to reduce labor costs and to expand capacity so we can get our unit costs down. I just think we'd better explore all the options before making a decision."

"You're right about that," Peter agreed. "But I still want to focus the search on existing facilities. New construction should be a last resort. Why don't you come up with a list of available facilities in various areas, including the northeast? And evaluate each in terms of the supply and cost of labor, proximity to transportation, taxes, and so on. And if you want to check on properties and construction costs at the same time, I have no objection. Why don't you and Jane work together on this? She did the study on labor costs, and her input will be valuable. I'd like to come up with a plan of action as soon as we can."

Exercise 23   **Vocabulary Check**

Choose the correct words from the box.

Example: AP is looking into __*properties*__ suitable for new construction.

1. It wouldn't be wise to set up a plan of _____ until we have all the facts.	assistant
	transportation
2. AP would rather not build, but they'll have to consider it if there's no other _____.	construction
	outlay
3. The manufacturing _____ to be constructed will have about 175,000 square feet.	proximity
4. Jeff will be out of the office when you arrive, but his _____ will be able to help you.	**properties**
	action
5. The conference room has a seating _____ of 24 people.	results
6. Tom doesn't have a car, so he uses public _____ to get around.	capacity
	objectives
7. The Martins bought their house because of its _____ to good schools, shopping and parks.	option
	project
8. If we construct a new plant, what will the approximate dollar _____ be?	facility

9. The expansion of the plant will be a one-year _____.

10. The major _____ would be to increase capacity and efficiency.

11. I'll call you when the _____ of the marketing study are available.

12. We've bought the property and hope to begin _____ in a month.

AGREEING AND DISAGREEING

"You have a point ... but I think that might be too much of a generalization."

"I feel that relocating to another area would be impractical."

- – I'm in complete agreement with you.

- – Perhaps you're right.

- – That's probably true, but it wouldn't hurt to look into it.

- – With all due respect, I'm afraid I can't agree with you.

- – I'm sorry, but that just doesn't make sense to me.

more formal

"I think we should build a new plant rather than buy an existing one."

- – I couldn't agree with you more.

- – I tend to agree with you. But I want to have all the facts first.

- – I have some reservations about that. It would be a lot more expensive.

- – I'm afraid I can't go along with you on that.

- – I don't really see how you can say that.

less formal

"If you ask me, Tom is the only one who can do the job."

- – You can say that again. That's just what I was thinking, too.

- – I guess you're probably right. He has the background for it.

- – I don't know if I'd go *that* far. There are others who could do it, too.

- – You do? I don't really think he could handle it.

- – You can't be serious! He's overworked as it is.

USING GERUNDS

"I just think we'd better explore all the options **before making** a decision."

It's important to **arrive** on time.	**Arriving** on time is important.
Jeff's secretary **types** well.	Jeff's secretary's **typing** is good.
I **read** good books; I enjoy it.	I enjoy **reading** good books.
First I **made** some calls; then I **read** through the mail.	**After making** some calls, I **read** through the mail.
If we **manufacture** the parts ourselves, we can lower our costs.	**By manufacturing** the parts ourselves, we can lower our costs.
I **smoke** cigars. Do you mind?	Do you mind **my smoking** cigars?

Exercise 24

Example: I work late several days a week.
I don't mind __*working late several days a week*__ .

1. Charles travels all over the world on business.
   He enjoys _____.

2. Tracy Kahn works as a real estate agent.
   She makes good money _____.

3. It's easy to learn to use a word processor.
   _____ isn't difficult.

4. We analyzed the study. We finished on May fifteenth.
   We finished _____.

5. The company will save money if it leases an existing plant.
   _____ will save the company money.

6. Write up the report today. Don't put it off!
   Don't _____ until next week.

7. We discussed the expansion plans with Jane. It was a good idea.
   _____ with her was a good idea.

8. We looked at properties.
   _____ made us realize how expensive real estate is.

Exercise 25

A. *Example:*   Mr. Hazelton called yesterday; I don't remember it.
   I don't remember <u>his calling yesterday</u>.

1. Karen left the office early; Mr. Crawford didn't mind.

2. Don't you remember? The Board members agreed to consider our suggestion.

3. You gave me the information. I appreciate it.

4. Joe found a new job; Susan told me about it.

5. I got up late; that caused a lot of problems at work.

B. *Examples:*   The secretary typed the memos; she didn't stop. *(without)*
   The secretary typed the memos <u>without stopping</u>.

   I saw Jim's new laptop computer. I decided to buy one. *(after)*
   <u>After seeing</u> Jim's new laptop computer, I decided to buy one.

1. The plant can increase production if it buys new equipment. *(by)*

2. Jeff spoke with several brokers. He became aware of the options.
   (as a result of)

3. The sales director read the reports; then he made his decision. *(after)*

4. Kurt is the company's top salesperson; he got a bonus. *(for)*

5. I waited for the elevator and talked to the receptionist. *(while)*

6. Ed talked it over with his wife; then he accepted the offer. *(before)*

7. Steve signed the memo. He didn't read it. *(without)*

8. Paul moved to St. Moritz. He's learned to ski well. *(since)*

9. George is young, but he's had a lot of practical experience. *(in spite of)*

10. We bought an existing facility. We didn't build a new one. *(instead of)*

Jane and Jeff would evaluate a number of sites in terms of the supply and cost of labor, proximity to transportation, taxes, and so on.

Exercise 26   GERUND OR INFINITIVE?

Example: The plant manager suggested __*b*__ the monthly quota.

      a)   to increase   **b)   increasing**

1.   I don't mind _____ your office to discuss the project.
     a)   to stop by   b)   stopping by

2.   The company is planning _____ its present facilities.
     a)   to expand   b)   expanding

3.   I asked the operator _____ the number again.
     a)   to dial   b)   dialing

4.   Janet decided _____ home because the weather was bad.
     a)   to stay   b)   staying

5.   Many people enjoy _____ the paper during breakfast.
     a)   to read   b)   reading

6.   We need _____ this problem before it gets any worse.
     a)   to solve   b)   solving

7.   The firm expects their profits _____ this year.
     a)   to increase   b)   increasing

8.   We hope our costs will stop _____ by next year.
     a)   to rise   b)   rising

9.   Our suppliers are having trouble _____ our specifications.
     a)   to meet   b)   meeting

10.   How can we avoid _____ our prices?
     a)   to raise   b)   raising

11.   Ed hopes _____ his project before he goes on vacation.
     a)   to finish   b)   finishing

12.   We had better buy the land soon. Property keeps _____ more expensive.
     a)   to get   b)   getting

Exercise 27   PREPOSITIONS AFTER ADJECTIVES

Example: *(in / for / to)*
I'm not interested **_in_** buying that car.

1. *(about / for / on)*
I'm so happy _____ your promotion, Nancy!

2. *(of / to / for)*
Are you the person responsible _____ making the arrangements?

3. *(on / for / with)*
Everyone is impressed _____ the sales manager's performance.

4. *(for / to / in)*
I'm eager _____ hear your recommendations on the expansion.

5. *(at / on / with)*
The president is satisfied _____ the performance of the subsidiaries.

6. *(for / of / about)*
When did you become aware _____ the firm's plans for expansion?

7. *(for / with / about)*
Let's see if the Board is as enthusiastic _____ the decision as we are.

8. *(to / with / for)*
We are very grateful _____ all of the help you've given us.

9. *(for / of / about)*
My assistant will be in charge _____ the office while I'm away.

10. *(about / for / of)*
The Board is concerned _____ rising labor costs.

11. *(for / in / about)*
We need someone who is experienced _____ computer programming.

12. *(about / for / of)*
Our company is known _____ its high quality products.

PREFIXES OF NEGATION

"In addition to the general **inefficiency** at the Baltimore plant,
Peter was also concerned about rising labor costs."

Several prefixes give words a negative meaning. If something isn't clear, we say it's *un*clear. If something's not complete, it's *in*complete. There's really no easy rule to know which prefix to use. Here are some examples:

un-:	*un*enthusiastic	*un*known	*un*satisfactory
in-:	*in*complete	*in*dependence	*in*experienced
dis-:	*dis*agreement	*dis*interested	*dis*like
ir-:	*ir*reparable	*ir*replaceable	*ir*responsible
im-:	*im*personal	*im*practical	*im*possible
non-:	*non*existent	*non*taxable	*non*smoker

Exercise 28

Use the prefixes from above to make new words.

Example: Tom and I usually get along, but when it comes to politics, we always
___**disagree**___. *(not agree)*

1. I was _____ with the applicant who was interviewed for the position.
   (not impressed)

2. The manager was _____ of improving things at the plant.
   (not capable)

3. There's no chance we can lower labor costs. It's _____!
   (not possible)

4. Is any portion of your income _____? *(not taxable)*

5. The paintings lost in the fire at the museum were insured, but of course
   they were _____. *(not replaceable)*

6. Bill wants to find a stereo that's fairly _____. *(not expensive)*

7. Is there anything you _____ about where you live? *(not like)*

8. With an _____ supply of capital, our decision would be easier.
   (not limited)

AUDIO PERFORMANCE
383 MADISON AVE., NEW YORK, NY 10017
TEL (212) 921-8500   FAX (212) 921-9449

# of pages: _1_

March 2, 1990

Mr. John Sutherland
Brown & Walker Real Estate
    Associates
535 Lee Avenue
Greenville, SC 29601

Dear Mr. Sutherland:

Confirming our telephone conversation of this morning, I would like to investigate properties suitable for a manufacturing facility in South Carolina. We prefer to buy or lease, but would also consider purchasing land suitable for new construction if we found the right opportunity.

As I mentioned, we require at least 100,000 sq. ft. of manufacturing space, rail access, and parking for about 500 cars. Ideally, the site should be within 5 to 10 miles of a major highway.

Could you please send me a list of sites meeting these specifications, with descriptions of each? Please note that for the time being, all inquiries should remain confidential.

Sincerely,

Jeff Martinelli

Jeff Martinelli
Vice President of Planning

JM/st

Peter asked Jeff to come up with a list of available facilities.

- What are the advantages and disadvantages of buying, leasing, or constructing a property or plant?

- Manufacturing plants should always be located as close as possible to the markets they serve. Discuss.

executive assistant

results

rise *(v)*

break even

climate (labor ~)

phase out

take advantage of

handle *(v)*

square feet

double *(v)*

real estate (~ broker)

automated
– automation

robotized

doubt *(v)*

go along with *(= agree)*

capital *(= money)*

outlay

site

land (unimproved ~,
  improved ~)

cause *(v)*

pollution

proximity

generalization

objective

unit costs

focus on
– focus *(n)*

search *(n, v)*

last resort

come up with

available
– unavailable

in terms of

objection
– object to

6 A BUSY DAY FOR PERSONNEL

When Peter Crawford and Ed Pearson walked into the personnel department, it was filled with activity. In one area job applicants were busy filling out application forms, and in another, people were taking shorthand and typing tests. AP's director of personnel, Carol Nordstrom, was sitting at her desk reading through some letters of application.

It had been over two months since Peter and Ed's visit to the Baltimore plant. Production there had not increased. In fact, there had been a considerable decrease. And in the end Pearson had asked for Smith's resignation. Ed felt strongly that Jack Reilly, the plant's assistant manager, was capable of taking over as manager, but Peter had recommended interviewing a few people from the outside just to be sure. So Ed had arranged to meet with Carol.

On his way to Carol's office Pearson stopped in on the twenty-fourth floor to give Crawford an update on the situation. Peter decided to go along with Ed to personnel. He had some free time before his three o'clock appointment with Jane Collins, and he liked to take such opportunities to visit the various departments.

"To find a replacement we'll probably work through a recruiter," said Carol, turning to Pearson. "What I'll need from you is a job description giving details about the position, including the requirements regarding education and professional experience, as well as the salary you're offering."

"A job description? Of course," Ed answered. "I'll write it up and get it to you first thing tomorrow morning."

"Fine," said Carol. She went on to explain that the applicants would be asked to submit detailed résumés and then would be screened thoroughly. "And, of course, the references of any applicants under serious consideration will be checked out very carefully."

"Naturally, I'd like to interview personally anyone you feel has the necessary qualifications for the position," said Ed.

Before leaving, Peter asked Carol if she would introduce him to some of her staff. Carol started with her assistants. "This is Bob Crandall. Among his other duties, Bob puts together the company newsletter," Carol began.

"It's nice to meet you, Bob. I enjoy reading the newsletter."

"It's a pleasure meeting you, Mr. Crawford."

"And Sue Chandler handles our management training program. She also takes care of all insurance matters."

"Hello, Sue. Nice to meet you."

"I've been looking forward to meeting you, Mr. Crawford."

"And you already know Judy, our office manager. She's in charge of the secretarial pool and finds temporary help when it's needed."

"Hi, Judy. How are you? Nice to see you again." Peter checked his watch and saw that he was late for his appointment with Jane on the twenty-fifth floor. He thanked Carol for her time, said good-bye to Ed, and hurried to the elevator.

Exercise 29   Comprehension Check

Choose the best way to complete the sentences or answer the question.

1. Applicants who had finished filling out forms were ...
   a) taking shorthand tests.
   b) being interviewed by the personnel staff.
   c) waiting for their names to be called.

2. The situation at the Baltimore plant ...
   a) had improved considerably.
   b) had gotten much worse.
   c) hadn't changed at all.

3. The person who recommended interviewing people from the outside was ...
   a) Peter Crawford.
   b) Ed Pearson.
   c) Carol Nordstrom.

4. The job description Ed is going to write up will include everything except ...
   a) educational requirements.
   b) professional experience required.
   c) starting date of the position.

5. According to Carol, the first thing she would do after reviewing the résumés would be to ...
   a) check out the applicants' references thoroughly.
   b) screen all the applicants carefully.
   c) send the applicants to Ed so he could interview them.

6. Which one of the following is not one of Judy's responsibilities?
   a) finding temporary help when needed
   b) being in charge of the secretarial pool
   c) handling insurance matters

INTRODUCTIONS

> "This is Bob Crandall."
> "It's nice to meet you, Bob."

more formal

- Mr. Lee, I'd like to introduce Peter Crawford. He's the president of AP.
- How do you do, Mr. Crawford. It's a pleasure meeting you.
- I'm pleased to meet you too, Mr. Lee.

- I don't believe we've met. Allow me to introduce myself. I'm Kurt Williams.
- Nice to meet you, Mr. Williams. I'm Stephen Becker.

- Tom, I'd like you to meet Kay Brady. Kay is in charge of our Boston office. Kay, this is Tom Clark.
- I've heard a lot about you, Miss Brady. It's nice to finally meet you.
- Nice meeting you, too. Please, call me Kay.

less formal

- Hello. My name is Jim Stanley. I'm the new accountant.
- Welcome to AP, Jim. I'm Chris Thompson. I've been looking forward to meeting you.

- Jim, this is Susan Lewis. If you have any questions, just ask Susan.
- Hi, Susan. How are you?
- Fine, thanks. Let me know if there's anything you need.

THE PASSIVE VOICE

> "And, of course, the references of any applicants under serious consideration **will be checked out** very carefully."

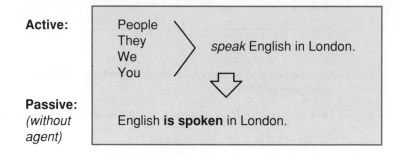

Active:

People
They
We
You

speak English in London.

Passive:
(without agent)

English **is spoken** in London.

The position **was advertised** in the *New York Times*.
Applications for the position **are** no longer **being accepted**.
The matter of salary **has** already **been** thoroughly **discussed**.

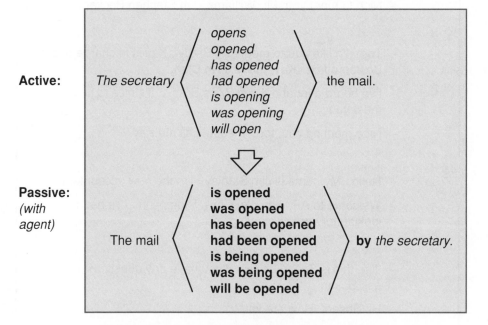

Active:

The secretary

opens
opened
has opened
had opened
is opening
was opening
will open

the mail.

Passive:
(with agent)

The mail

is opened
was opened
has been opened
had been opened
is being opened
was being opened
will be opened

by *the secretary*.

The applicants **will be interviewed** by Mr. Pearson.
The company newsletter **is put together** by Bob Crandall.
All of the résumés **were reviewed** by Carol Nordstrom.

Exercise 30

Examples: We export most of our products.
Most of our products are exported.

Mercedes-Benz manufactures cars and trucks.
Cars and trucks are manufactured by Mercedes-Benz.

1. The secretary schedules all appointments.

2. They pay high salaries to their top managers.

3. We had filled our quota by the end of last month.

4. AP manufactures this stereo component.

5. The Board of Directors makes important decisions.

6. We'll discuss these reports at the next meeting.

7. We finally increased capacity by adding extra shifts.

8. Someone has recommended an increase in the production quota.

9. Modern machines will replace our obsolete equipment.

10. We've trained 25 new employees over the past six months.

11. The director of sales was planning a meeting.

12. They only distribute this product through department stores.

13. All of the applicants have submitted detailed résumés.

14. The interviewer asked many questions.

15. The firm I work for imports many products.

AUDIO PERFORMANCE, INC.
APPLICATION FOR EMPLOYMENT

THIS COMPANY IS AN EQUAL OPPORTUNITY EMPLOYER.   Date _____

PERSONAL DATA

NAME: LAST	FIRST	MIDDLE	TELEPHONE NUMBER

ADDRESS: STREET AND NO.   CITY   STATE   ZIP CODE

If not a U.S. Citizen, do you have a work visa/green card? ☐ Yes ☐ No	NUMBER	SOCIAL SECURITY NUMBER

WORK INTERESTS

Position desired: Referred by: Salary desired:

What type of position are you applying for? ☐ Full-Time ☐ Part-Time	Are you willing to relocate? ☐ Yes ☐ No	Willing to travel? ☐ Yes ☐ No

Have you previously applied to or worked for AP?   ☐ Yes   ☐ No
Location: Dates:

EDUCATION

Year(s)	Name/Location of School	Major Course	Graduated/Degree

EMPLOYMENT RECORD
List below your former employers. Begin with present employer. Continue on reverse.

Employer:	Employed From:	To:
Address:	Salary Starting:	Last:
Position:	Job Description:	
Supervisor:		
Reason for leaving:		
Employer:	Employed From:	To:
Address:	Salary Starting:	Last:
Position:	Job Description:	
Supervisor:		
Reason for leaving:		

Job applicants were busy filling out application forms.

THE PASSIVE WITH MODALS

"[Carol] went on to explain that the applicants **would be asked** to submit detailed résumés ..."

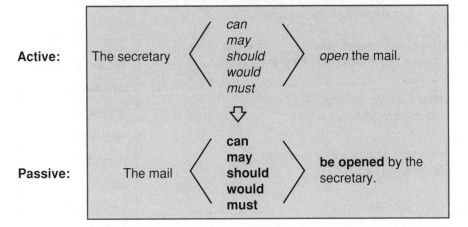

Active: The secretary ⟨ can / may / should / would / must ⟩ *open* the mail.

⇩

Passive: The mail ⟨ **can / may / should / would / must** ⟩ **be opened** by the secretary.

The expansion project **must be approved** by the Board of Directors.
I **can be reached** at my office any time after nine o'clock.
Application forms **should** either **be typed** or **filled out** in ink.

Exercise 31

Examples: Someone must approve these expenditures in advance.
These expenditures must be approved in advance.

Both parties must sign the contract.
The contract must be signed by both parties.

1. We must complete this project by the first of August.

2. Machines can replace some factory workers.

3. We should always type business letters.

4. You can't buy this product in department stores yet.

5. The same company that sold the machines should deliver them.

6. One person alone can't carry that copier.

7. You shouldn't make personal calls from the office.

8. Mr. Burke must review the proposal before we proceed.

Exercise 32   SYNONYMS

Choose words from the box that are closest in meaning to those in italics.

Example: We have the *(choice)* __option__ of hiring Reilly or looking for someone from the outside.

1. The director *(went over)* _____ the report several times before making a decision.

2. Miss Carlson usually *(takes care of)* _____ placing employment ads.

3. Wouldn't it be cheaper to *(buy)* _____ an existing facility?

4. I applied for the *(job)* _____ I saw advertised.

5. The production manager *(suggested)* _____ adding additional shifts.

6. After six months with the company, the salesperson *(asked for)* _____ a raise.

7. The plant manager must *(hand in)* _____ a production report every month.

responsibilities
assembled
reviewed
requested
consider
submit
opportunity
purchase
frank
option
handles
recommended
position

8. After the stereos are *(put together)* _____, they are inspected.

9. Would you ever *(think about)* _____ taking a job in another city?

10. The *(honest)* _____ answers Sheila gave during the interview helped her get the job.

11. An executive secretary has many important *(duties)* _____.

12. I had the *(chance)* _____ to study abroad, but I turned it down.

USES OF *GET*

"I'll write it up and **get it to you** first thing tomorrow morning."

The verb *get* is one of the most widely used words in the English language. You can *get (receive)* a letter or *get (arrive)* home. When we *get (become)* hungry, we can *get (prepare)* ourselves something to eat. Here are more examples:

> Where can I **get** a newspaper around here?
> I met Barbara only last month, but I'm **getting to know** her well.
> It's hard to **get anything done** with the phone ringing constantly.
> How much money **have** you **got** with you?

Exercise 33

Example: Please tell Mr. Hill I called. I'll get __*back*__ to him later.

1. Let's get _____ for lunch sometime soon.

2. I've been dialing Mr. Pearson's number for ten minutes, but I can't get _____.

3. Bill is working full-time and going to night school. He really wants to get _____.

4. Everyone has arrived. Can we get _____ to business now?

5. It's late and I have a train to catch. I really should get _____.

ahead
together
going
point
down
back
through
interesting
across

6. Tell me more; this story is starting to get _____.

7. Since I don't speak German very well, it took me a while to get my point _____ to the Customs officer.

8. The opening speaker at the conference talked on and on without ever really getting to the _____.

```
                                    802 Chambers Street
                                    Westbury, NY  11590

                                    April 10, 1990


Ms. Carol Nordstrom
Director of Personnel
Audio Performance, Inc.
383 Madison Avenue
New York, NY 10017

Dear Ms. Nordstrom:

I am writing in response to your advertisement in
today's New York Times for a clerk-typist.  I am
interested in applying for the position.

I am a recent graduate of the Jefferson Business
Institute in New York City and am currently
working part-time as a clerk for Stettwell Adver-
tising.  My word processing skills are excellent
and I am familiar with all aspects of office
operations.

I am enclosing a copy of my résumé and would very
much appreciate an opportunity to come in for an
interview.  I can be contacted during the day at
(212) 417-9876.

I look forward to hearing from you.

                                    Sincerely yours,

                                    Sarah Jameson

                                    Sarah Jameson


Enclosure
```

AP's director of personnel, Carol Nordstrom, was sitting at her desk reading through some letters of application.

- You are responsible for finding and selecting the best candidate for a position in your firm. Where will you advertise? Who can you eliminate based on the letter of application/résumé? What questions will you ask at the interview?

- Personnel is the most important department in any company. Discuss.

shorthand

considerable

resignation
– resign

strongly (feel ~)

outside *(adj, n)*

take over

update *(n, v)*

work through (~ s.o.)

recruiter (job ~)
– recruit

job description

details

position *(= job)*

regarding

as well as *(= also)*

write up *(v)*

go on to do s.t.

submit

résumé

screen *(v)*

reference

consideration (under ~)
– consider

check out (~ a reference)

put together (~ a report)

newsletter

matters (insurance ~)

secretarial pool

7 A SALES MEETING

Ben Melnick, Audio Performance's director of sales, was already sitting in the conference room on the twenty-third floor when Peter arrived. "I'm sorry, Ben. I hope you haven't been waiting long," Peter apologized. "I've had a very busy morning, and I'm afraid I'm a little behind schedule."

Unit sales of Audio Performance's entire line of stereo equipment, sold under the brand name "Tru-Tone," had been falling an average of 3 percent per quarter for over a year. And the most recent quarter looked even worse. Peter had called the meeting to discuss the problem and see what could be done.

Melnick pointed out that Tru-Tone was distributed largely through a network of authorized dealers. "They account for 71 percent of our business," he said. "We've been trying to increase the amount of merchandise sold through discount and department stores, but we haven't had much success in getting them to carry it."

Melnick went on to explain that Tru-Tone received far less advertising support than the competing products on the market. "As a result, brand awareness is falling off. And, of course, stores don't like to carry products that don't sell. However, they're usually more than happy to stock merchandise that's 'pre-sold' by the manufacturer through advertising and marketing."

Melnick also said he felt that the Tru-Tone line was overpriced. Only one competing brand was priced higher, and it was a well-established product with a premium image, heavy advertising support, and an extensive distribution network. "If we want to sell the line at a premium price, we'll have to spend some money improving the product image. Or we could consider cutting the price. This might help make us more competitive for the time being, but it won't solve all our problems."

"You're right, it won't," said Crawford. "The real challenge is getting our production costs under control. I'm not totally against a price cut, but we'd be taking a risk. Once a cut goes into effect, it's not easy to reverse." Crawford knew that in this case he would have to rely on the people around him, who had a better feel for what was going on. Crawford thanked Melnick and asked him to get together with Steve Blake, AP's director of marketing, to follow up on the discussion. He then phoned Blake and reviewed the situation with him.

Blake's feelings on the matter were quite strong. "In my opinion, there's nothing wrong with our image. The Tru-Tone line has been around for over 30 years. Why, it's practically a household word. If you ask me, the problem isn't with advertising; it's with sales. And that's Ben Melnick's area, not mine."

Peter was aware of the rivalry between Blake and Melnick, but he was determined to get the two of them to work together in spite of it. "There's no point in holding any one department responsible. What we need to decide is where to go from here. And Steve, I'd like you and Ben to put together a complete market study in order to get a better picture of our present position. We need specifics with regard to the overall market and our position in it. We'll have to get data on pricing, advertising, and distribution, as well as technical specifications on the products, both for AP and the industry as a whole. As soon as we have all that, we can begin to develop a long-term strategy."

Blake agreed that this was the best way to proceed. He said he would meet with Ben and get to work immediately on the market study. "We should have the results ready for you within about a month."

Exercise 34　　　　Comprehension Check

Choose the correct words from the box; then answer the questions.

Example: Where did Peter and Ben __*meet*__ ?
They met in the conference room on the twenty-third floor.

1. Did Peter _____ to Ben for having arrived late?

2. Had Tru-Tone sales risen or _____ the past year?

3. What percent of Tru-Tone products was being _____ through authorized dealers?

4. Why was brand awareness of Tru-Tone products _____ off?

5. Did Melnick feel the Tru-Tone line was _____ too high or too low?

6. Was Peter totally against _____ prices?

7. Who did Peter want to _____ the situation with?

8. What department did Blake _____ responsible for the falling sales?

distributed
priced
hold
review
meet
develop
apologize
put together
cutting
falling
fallen

9. Why does Peter want Melnick and Blake to _____ a market study?

10. In addition to technical specifications on the products, what data did they need before they could _____ a long-term strategy?

APOLOGIES

"I'm sorry, Ben. I hope you haven't been waiting long," Peter apologized.

more formal

— I hope you'll forgive me Mr. Hayes, but I'm going to have to cut our meeting short. My plane leaves in an hour.

— I understand, really. We've accomplished a lot today, and we'll be meeting again next week.

— I'm really sorry, Mr. Coe; the report won't be ready on time. The computer is down, and there's nothing I can do about it.

— I'm afraid that's just not good enough, Paul. I asked for those figures a week ago.

— I owe you an apology, Carol. You were right about the problem in personnel, and I was wrong. No hard feelings?

— Not at all. I appreciate your mentioning it to me.

less formal

(after spilling something)
— I'm so sorry. It was an accident. Let me help you clean it up.

— That's all right. Don't worry about it. I've got it.

— Sorry I'm late, Tom. I had a terrible time finding a cab.

— I know how it is. But let's get started, shall we?

PAST PARTICIPLES USED AS ADJECTIVES

"We've been trying to increase the amount of merchandise **sold through discount and department stores ...**"

I received a report that was *written*.
→I received a **written report**. *(participle only)*

The report was *well written*.
→I received a **well-written report**. *(adverb + participle)*

The report was *written by my assistant*.
→I received a report **written by my assistant**. *(participle + phrase)*

The company is proud of its **redesigned** product line.
Has our competition been hurt by the **recently introduced** products?
We've had success using software programs **developed by our staff**.

Exercise 35

Rewrite the sentences using past participles.

Examples: Berlitz is a name that's recognized internationally.
Berlitz is an internationally recognized name.

Everyone enjoyed the meal that was served after the meeting.
Everyone enjoyed the meal served after the meeting.

1. We buy our equipment from a company that's well-known.

2. The applicant who was chosen for the job had ten years of experience.

3. A maintenance person replaced the window that was broken.

4. Increasing competition was one topic that was discussed at the meeting.

5. The purchasing agent ordered some supplies that were badly needed.

6. The personnel director interviewed four applicants who were well-qualified.

7. The ad that was placed in the newspaper got immediate results.

8. Our line is as good as other lines that are similarly priced.

EXPRESSING CONDITION AND CONTRAST

"Peter was aware of the rivalry between Blake and Melnick, but he was determined to get the two of them to work together **in spite of** it."

Condition:

I'll go out for lunch **if** I have time.
I'll go out for lunch (or stay in) **depending on** the weather.
Do you think the weather will be good? **If so**, I'll go out.

You can't do the job **unless** you've been trained.
The job is impossible to do **without** proper training.
Are you trained? **If not**, the job will be difficult for you.

Contrast:

Mr. Dale saw me **even though** I had no appointment.
(Al)though I had no appointment, Mr. Dale met with me.
He saw me **in spite of** his heavy schedule.
Our meeting was short, but we **still** accomplished a lot.

Exercise 36

Use phrases from above to complete the sentences.

Example: Will you be home tonight? __*If not*__, I'll call you tomorrow.

1. We'll be late for work _____ we hurry.

2. Tim is going to buy the car _____ the high price.

3. Prices will rise or fall _____ changes in the cost of labor.

4. I didn't feel well this morning, but I _____ came to work.

5. _____ Mike took over 30 driving lessons, he couldn't pass the test.

6. That restaurant is so busy you can't get a table _____ a reservation.

7. We'll buy the new equipment _____ the expenditure is approved.

8. Will you be in class tomorrow? _____, I'll probably see you.

9. I don't know if I'll be at school. _____, I'll see you on Monday.

10. It started to rain, but we _____ were able to finish our golf game.

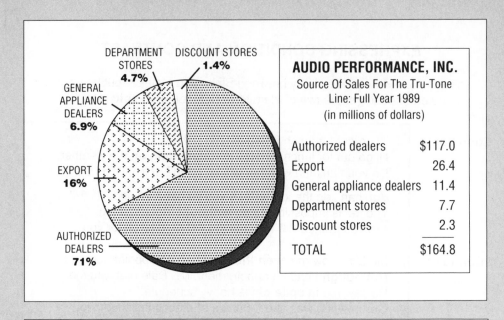

AUDIO PERFORMANCE, INC.
Source Of Sales For The Tru-Tone
Line: Full Year 1989
(in millions of dollars)

Authorized dealers	$117.0
Export	26.4
General appliance dealers	11.4
Department stores	7.7
Discount stores	2.3
TOTAL	$164.8

Tru-Tone was distributed largely through authorized dealers.

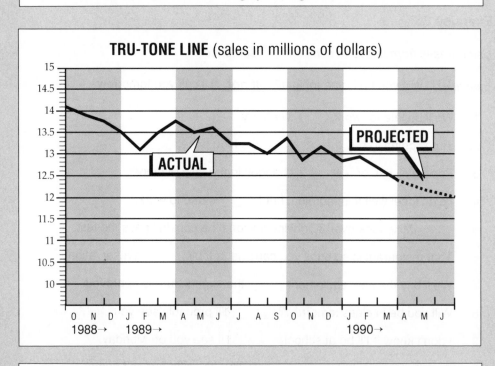

Tru-Tone sales had been falling an average of 3% per quarter.

QUESTION AND ANSWER TAGS

> "[Cutting the price] won't solve all our problems."
> "You're right, **it won't**."

The products *aren't* overpriced, **are they**?
     – Yes, **they are**.   – No, **they aren't**.

You *don't* want to cut prices, **do you**?
     – Yes, **I do**.   – No, **I don't**.

Sales *have* been falling recently, **haven't they?**
     – Yes, **they have**.   – No, **they haven't**.

The report *will* be finished in a few weeks, **won't it**?
     – Yes, **it will**.   – No, **it won't**.

Careful!

I'm not late, **am I**?
I'm at the right address, **aren't I**?

No one called while I was out, **did they**?
Your family lives in London, **don't they**?

Exercise 37

Fill in the correct question tags; then answer the questions.

Example: The rent includes utilities, **_doesn't it_** ? *(yes)*
          Yes, it does.

1. The lease has already been signed, _____? *(no)*

2. We should postpone the planning meeting, _____? *(yes)*

3. The product line doesn't need a premium image, _____? *(no)*

4. Discount stores don't carry that brand, _____? *(yes)*

5. Carol won't be in charge of the market study, _____? *(no)*

6. I'm expected to be there tomorrow, _____? *(no)*

7. Mrs. Harris got a promotion, _____? *(yes)*

8. Someone has followed up on the study, _____? *(yes)*

USING AUXILIARIES

Emphasis:	I don't speak Italian, but I **do** speak Spanish. Tom didn't call me on my birthday, but he **did** send a card.
Comparisons:	Carol's been with the firm longer **than I have**. A manager makes more money **than an assistant does**.
Comments:	I thought the movie was great. – You **did**? The bank isn't open today. – It**'s** not?
Verb substitutes:	I have a car. Because I **do**, I can drive you to the station. Tom is supposed to call. When he **does**, let me know.

Exercise 38

Complete the following sentences using the correct auxiliaries.

1. I've already taken care of the insurance matter. – You _____?

2. Sarah doesn't drive, but she _____ plan to learn.

3. We offer better products than our competitors _____, but their prices are lower than ours.

4. Did you make a plane reservation? If you _____, you might not get on the flight.

5. Can you type? Unless you _____, you shouldn't apply for this job.

6. This fax machine needs servicing. – It _____?

7. Tom didn't have time to visit, but he _____ call while he was in town.

8. Has Mr. Lewis left yet? – I'm not sure whether he _____ or not.

9. Our department will be hiring more employees than yours _____.

10. I can speak English better now than I _____ two years ago.

Exercise 39 **IDIOMS**

Choose the correct words to complete the idioms.

Example: (on / in / under)
If we get our expenditures **under** control, we can make a profit.

1. (on / of / to)
The firm's revenues for 1990 were in excess _____ $92 million.

2. (as / for / in)
The company _____ a whole is doing well, but there are still a few problems.

3. (for / to / on)
Peter wanted Blake to find out everything with regard _____ AP's position in the industry.

4. (until / at / in)
We tried to keep the Houston operation going, but _____ the end we had to close it.

5. (at / for / in)
AP has enough computer workstations _____ the time being, but eventually they'll have to purchase more.

6. (for / by / on)
I offered to help Ed with the project, but he said he could handle it _____ his own.

7. (At / In / By)
_____ first I didn't think the new accountant was up to the job, but her performance has been more than satisfactory so far.

8. (on / at / behind)
The supplier called to tell us their deliveries are running _____ schedule, so the shipment will be a week late.

9. (In / By / With)
_____ addition to high labor costs, the Baltimore plant has problems with efficiency.

10. (for / ahead / on)
Rather than relocating, we've decided to redecorate our offices: painting, getting new furniture, and so _____.

((€ BERLY'S ELECTRONICS, INC.

April 20, 1990

Order Department
Audio Performance, Inc.
383 Madison Avenue
New York, NY 10017

Dear Sirs:

First quarter sales of certain Tru-Tone items have fallen below expectations.
For this reason, we are overstocked and must reduce the quantity we
ordered on April 2. I am attaching a copy of the original order.

The revised quantities to be shipped are as follows:

   50 DCD-84 Stereo Dual Cassette Decks
   50 CDP-6000 High-Performance CD Players
  100 SP-535 Speakers
   60 HD-300 Headsets
   20 RS-2000 Stereo Rack Systems

Sincerely yours,

Arnold Aronson

Arnold Aronson
Purchasing Manager

AA:pt
Att.

Sales of Audio Performance's Tru-Tone line have been falling.

- Channels of distribution include authorized dealers, discount houses, department stores, mail-order catalogs, door-to-door sales, telemarketing, and T.V. "home shopping." Where would you be likely to buy any of the following products: television, computer, camera, washing machine, clothes, telephone?

- Advertising is of little or no value to the average consumer; it only results in higher prices for everyone. Discuss.

Vocabulary

brand (~ name, ~ awareness)

fall *(v) (= decrease)*

average *(n, adj)*

quarter(ly) *(= three months)*

call (~ a meeting)

distribute / distribution

network

authorized dealer

account for *(= make up)*

merchandise

discount store

carry (~ a product)

support *(n, v)*

stock *(n, v)*

established (well-~)

premium *(adj)*

image

cut *(n, v)* (~ prices)

for the time being

challenge *(n)*
– challenging

under control
– out of control

risk (take a ~)
– risky

effect (go into ~)

rely on

feel (have a ~ for s.t.)

follow up (~ on s.t.)

household word

responsible (hold s.o. ~)

specific(s)

specification

long-term
– short-term

strategy

get to work (on) *(= start)*

8 A CASH MANAGEMENT PROBLEM

It was late April. Peter had been with Audio Performance long enough to feel at home in the job. He felt this would be a good time to meet with AP's controller, Stan Waterman, to review the company's financial position at the end of the first quarter. Stan had joined the company only a few months before Peter, after the unexpected resignation of the previous financial controller. He had inherited a fairly chaotic situation, and he had been extremely busy trying to straighten things out.

Peter had been receiving a number of financial documents on a regular basis. Among these were the monthly balance sheets, which provided a good picture of the company's current financial position. When he received the most recent balance sheet, he looked it over and made some notes. Then he went to the computer, called up the file on securities the company was currently investing in, and printed it out. He took copies of both documents with him to the meeting.

The first item Peter discussed with Stan Waterman was the amount of cash being held at various banks the firm did business with. AP was holding about $600,000 on deposit in checking accounts which paid no interest.

"I'd like to make this excess cash work harder for us, Stan. If these funds were invested in short-term securities, they could be earning returns as high as 8 or 9 percent, couldn't they?"

"You're right," said Stan. "The investments would have to be supervised carefully, though. Many times these funds are only available for a few days. I'll certainly keep a closer eye on the situation in the future, and try to keep just enough cash on hand to meet our day-to-day operating expenses."

Next, the two men talked about the accounts receivable figure: $12.4 million. "This figure seems high to me. What is the standard collection policy?" asked Peter.

"Most bills are payable in 30 days, and there's a 1 percent discount on invoices paid within 10 days. Outside collection agencies are used to recover past-due accounts. Even so, it takes an average of 120 days to collect."

"Which means we're making interest-free loans to our customers. I think we should increase the discount to 2 percent. And I'd recommend turning past-due accounts over to outside agencies sooner than at present. Why don't we establish a year-end goal of reducing our collection time to 60 days?"

"That sounds reasonable," said Stan.

They went on to discuss the accounts payable figure which, at $2.4 million, was too low. AP was paying its own bills too promptly. Peter pointed out that the firm's cash position could be improved by delaying payments on certain accounts.

Peter knew that Stan's staff was small and, in the past several months, overworked. He trusted Stan's ability to handle matters on a day-to-day basis, but he wanted to continue meeting with him a least once a month.

Exercise 40　　　　Comprehension Check

*Indicate whether the following statements are **True (T)** or **False (F)**.*

1. ___　　Peter felt at home at AP because he'd been there over a year.

2. ___　　Stan Waterman had been with the company longer than Peter had.

3. ___　　Stan had taken over when the previous controller resigned.

4. ___　　The previous controller had left a lot of problems Stan was trying to straighten out.

5. ___　　The only financial documents Peter had looked at were the monthly balance sheets.

6. . ___　　Peter got information from the computer about current company investments.

7. ___　　The money being held in checking accounts wasn't earning any interest.

8. ___　　Some funds were being invested in short-term securities.

9. ___　　The accounts receivable figure was much lower than it should have been.

10. ___　　The accounts payable figure was low because AP was paying its bills too quickly.

11. ___　　The year-end goal was to reduce collection time to 60 days.

12. ___　　Peter wanted to meet with Stan every month because he didn't have much confidence in his ability.

SUGGESTIONS AND RECOMMENDATIONS

> "Why don't we establish a year-end goal of
> reducing our collection time to 60 days?"

*more
formal*

— You've looked over the records and met the staff, Mr.
Crawford. Do you have any suggestions?

— One thing I'd recommend strongly is hiring at least one
more accountant.

— Tim, we're having a hard time deciding whether to rent a
house or go ahead and buy one. What do you think?

— I'm afraid I couldn't tell you, Steve. You might try asking
Bill. He knows a lot about real estate.

— Sally, I want to buy a home computer. What kind do you
recommend?

— If I were you, I'd get a KMEX. I have one, and I love it.

*less
formal*

— You travel a lot, Ben. My wife and I want to go somewhere
for a week or so, just to relax. Do you have any ideas?

— How about a cruise? We really enjoyed the one we took.

— Where shall we have lunch, Barbara?

— Why don't we try the new place on the corner? I hear they
have great sandwiches.

CAUSATIVES AND PERMISSIVES

"I'd like to **make** this excess cash **work** harder for us, Stan."

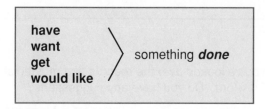

I **had** the memos **typed**.
Peter **wants** the study **finished** by May.
When **did** you finally **get** the fax machine **repaired**?
We'**d like** the new models **tested** as soon as possible.

I **had** my secretary **type** the memos.
The manager **made** everyone **work** late in order to finish.
She **let** me **leave** early because I had a doctor's appointment.
I'**ll have** Mr. Crawford **give** you a call when he comes in.

ask	want	would like	
tell	allow	persuade	someone **to do** something
get	force	encourage	
urge	order	require	

I **want** the secretary **to type** the memos.
The results of the market study **have forced** us **to redirect** our advertising.
We'**ve asked** the company **to send** us a catalog of its products.
How can we **get** discount stores **to carry** our product line?

Exercise 41

Choose the correct causative or permissive forms.

Example: Peter __c__ Karen make his flight reservation.
        a) got   b) wanted   **c) had**

1. The sales manager _____ his assistant to demonstrate the product.
    a) had   b) let   c) asked

2. I'll _____ someone from maintenance to look at the elevator.
    a) have   b) get   c) make

3. We _____ employees to take courses that will improve their skills.
    a) make   b) have   c) encourage

4. Did you _____ your reservations made by the Apollo Travel Agency?
    a) have   b) let   c) order

5. Declining sales _____ the corporation to close two of its retail outlets.
    a) made   b) forced   c) got

6. Please _____ your secretary set up an appointment for me.
    a) get   b) tell   c) have

7. Could you please _____ the accountant to double-check the figures?
    a) ask   b) make   c) have

8. The marketing department _____ the statistics broken down by area.
    a) asked   b) let   c) had

9. Mr. Crawford _____ us to prepare a detailed plan as soon as possible.
    a) will make   b) will have   c) would like

10. The firm _____ you to request vacation time a month in advance.
    a) requires   b) makes   c) has

11. The Halls haven't _____ their phone installed yet.
    a) made   b) gotten   c) asked

12. We _____ our teenage son use the car once in a while.
    a) get   b) allow   c) let

Exercise 42

Choose the correct causative or permissive forms.

Example: The Board asked Peter __***b***__ a replacement.

        a)   recommend   **b)   to recommend**   c)   recommended

1. I couldn't get through so I had the operator_____ the number.

    a)   dial   b)   to dial   c)   dialed

2. The company has all its travel arrangements _____ by the same agency.

    a)   make   b)   to make   c)   made

3. The bad weather forced me _____ my weekend plans.

    a)   change   b)   to change   c)   changed

4. Jim Burke wants me _____ him at the airport on Saturday.

    a)   meet   b)   to meet   c)   met

5. The director wants these letters _____ as soon as possible.

    a)   send out   b)   to send out   c)   sent out

6. Mr. Crawford is out, but I can let you _____ with his assistant.

    a)   speak   b)   to speak   c)   spoken

7. The law requires us _____ our entire income from all sources.

    a)   report   b)   to report   c)   reported

8. We have to get this project _____ before the end of the month.

    a)   finish   b)   to finish   c)   finished.

9. I hope we can persuade our supplier _____ his price.

    a)   lower   b)   to lower   c)   lowered

10. The study results made us _____ that our advertising was misdirected.

    a)   realize   b)   to realize   c)   realized

AUDIO PERFORMANCE, INC.
BALANCE SHEET
AS OF MARCH 31, 1990
(in millions of dollars)

Assets

Current Assets:

Cash	0.6	*too much cash!*
Short-term securities	0.2	
Accounts receivable - net	12.4	*why so high?*
Inventory	7.4	
Total Current Assets:		20.6

Fixed Assets:

Land	1.6	
Plant and equipment (after depreciation)	6.6	
Total Fixed Assets:		8.2
TOTAL ASSETS:		28.8

Liabilities and Stockholders' Equity

Current Liabilities:

Accounts payable	2.4	?
Mortgage and notes payable	1.0	
Interest payable	0.6	
Taxes payable	3.4	
Total Current Liabilities:		7.4

Long-term Liabilities:

Mortgage	10.2	
Note due	3.4	
Total Long-term Liabilities:		13.6

Stockholders' Equity:

Capital stock outstanding	5.2	
Retained earnings	2.6	
Total Stockholders' Equity:		7.8
TOTAL LIABILITIES AND STOCKHOLDERS' EQUITY:		28.8

Peter looked over the most recent monthly
balance sheet and made some notes.

Exercise 43   WORD FAMILIES

Complete these sentences using words from the same family.

Example: Robert has some **managerial** skills, but he's not capable of
     managing a large operation.

1.   We received an **itemized** invoice from the supplier. The price, quantity,
      and stock number of each _____ was listed.

2.   There's more and more **competition**, so we have to keep our prices low to
      remain _____.

3.   I'm sorry to hear you're **resigning**. I understand you submitted your letter
      of _____ yesterday.

4.   A new **supervisor** was hired last week. He'll be responsible for _____
      35 to 40 employees.

5.   Laura was finally **promoted** to sales manager last month. The _____
      was long overdue.

6.   Here are the numbers of the invoices we haven't been able to **collect**.
      They'll be sent to a _____ agency on June 1st.

7.   William has just learned that his grandmother left him an **inheritance**. He
      has _____ nearly $2 million.

8.   There are many things to **consider** in buying a piece of property; price
      shouldn't be the only _____.

9.   The materials needed for production have been carefully **specified**. These
      _____ should be followed closely.

10.   I'm **responsible** for the overall operation of the plant. Training new
      employees is one of my major _____.

11.   If we do decide to _____ prices, I don't think the **reduction** should be
      more than 10 percent.

12.   I'm not _____ to approve expenditures over $500. This will need the
      manager's **authorization**.

VERBS OF PERCEPTION: *SOUND, LOOK, FEEL*

"That **sounds** reasonable," said Stan.

What kind of music is that?	It **sounds**	interesting. *like* Peruvian music.
What kind of fabric is this?	It **feels**	very soft. *like* wool.
Look at that man!	He **looks**	familiar. *like* a friend of mine. *as if* he's lost.

Exercise 44

*Fill in the correct form of **sound, look,** or **feel**.*

Example: What magazine are you reading? It **_looks_** interesting.

1. I _____ too tired to write the report last night. I'll do it this morning.

2. When you spoke to Crawford on the phone did he _____ concerned?

3. It's so cloudy. It _____ as if it's going to rain any minute.

4. We had been gone for a month, so it _____ wonderful to be back home.

5. We enjoyed hearing about your trip to Denmark. It _____ like a beautiful country.

6. Even though we don't speak Danish, we _____ very comfortable.

7. I've spoken to Tom, and he _____ very interested in the position.

8. Bill is taller than his father, but other than that he _____ just like him.

AUDIO PERFORMANCE
383 MADISON AVE., NEW YORK, NY 10017
TEL (212) 921-8500   FAX (212) 921-9449

April 27, 1990

Mr. Frank Gilder
Manager, Accounts Payable
Ames Department Store
13623 Cattleman Boulevard
San Antonio, TX 78200

Dear Mr. Gilder:

This is to advise you that your account is currently in arrears. Your most recent statement, dated March 16, 1990, shows an outstanding balance of $29,824.50. Of that amount, $22,416.91 was carried forward from previous months.

We would appreciate your settling this account promptly. We value your patronage over the years and would like to be able to continue our relationship. We hope you can understand our position in this matter.

Very truly yours,

Mary Crandall

Mary Crandall
Collections

Peter recommended turning over past-due accounts
to outside collection agencies sooner.

- How do the collection procedures described in the text compare with those in your country? What measures can be taken to increase the collection rate on the following types of bills: utility bills such as gas, electric and telephone, consumer loans, and rent or mortgage payments.

- Describe some of the possibilities available, both short- and long-term, for individuals and companies to "keep their money working hard."

Vocabulary

controller (financial ~)
financial / finance(s)
inherit
chaotic
– chaos
straighten s.t. out
provide
basis (on a regular ~)
balance sheet
look over
notes (make ~)
call up (~ a computer file)
securities
invest(ment)
item
amount
deposit (on ~)
account (checking ~, savings ~)
interest (earn ~)
return (~ on investment)

supervise
– supervision
funds
keep an eye on
on hand
operating expenses
day-to-day
accounts receivable
accounts payable
collect (~ money)
collection agency
policy
invoice
past due
recover *(= get back)*
interest-free
loan (make a ~)
– lend
turn s.t. over to s.o.
promptly
trust *(v)*

9 DISCUSSING FRINGE BENEFITS

As part of his overall program to revitalize Audio Performance, Peter knew it was necessary to attract more talented people to the company and to reduce employee turnover. He called Carol Nordstrom into his office to discuss the matter and to find out how the personnel department might help.

He started by asking her to comment on where she thought the company stood in terms of compensation. Carol said she felt the Audio Performance salary package, having been recently upgraded, equaled or exceeded what most other companies were offering.

"And what about fringe benefits?" Crawford inquired.

"I don't think we're doing too badly in that area either," she replied. "As you know, we have a health plan with all costs picked up by the company. We also offer optional life insurance, providing up to $100,000 in coverage, with the premiums shared by the company and the employee. In addition, all employees are eligible for our retirement plan, which provides pension benefits beginning at age 65. And, of course, we provide all the benefits required by law: Social Security, worker's compensation for job-related injuries, and unemployment insurance. It's not a bad package."

"It's costing us enough, that's for sure," Peter said. "According to last month's figures, benefits currently represent more than 30 percent of total payroll costs."

"This is true for most companies," answered Carol. "Many firms offer benefits exceeding 40 percent. I think our present program is about average, both in terms of benefits provided and its cost to the company. As a matter of fact, I was going to recommend that we give some thought to upgrading some of our programs in order to give us a competitive advantage in the job market."

"What exactly did you have in mind?" asked Peter, sensing that the conversation was about to get expensive.

"Well, as you know, many firms offer coverage for dental care, as well as reimbursement for job-related training costs and even costs related to day care for preschool children. And, of course, some firms offer profit-sharing plans, through which they distribute a part of their profits to employees each year. And there are employee stock purchase programs, in which employees are given the opportunity to buy shares of the company's stock at a discounted price."

"And you really feel that adding some of these benefits would help upgrade the quality of the applicants we attract?" Peter asked.

"Definitely. And we wouldn't have to offer everything either. Some companies have implemented a 'cafeteria plan,' allowing employees to select from among a range of benefits offered."

"I'm familiar with that as well. We looked into it when I was with ESI and decided it would be too expensive to administer. I'm not sure AP can afford it either."

"In my opinion, dollar for dollar, benefits are a better investment than salary," said Carol. "They're nontaxable to the employee and deductible for the company. And they could play a major role in attracting the kind of people we need."

"I'll tell you what. Why don't you put together a study of the situation in firms similar to AP. If the results back up what you're saying and the cost of upgrading is reasonable, I'm willing to consider it."

They went on to discuss some ideas Carol had for improving the management recruitment and executive training programs. Having completed their meeting, they decided to break for lunch. "It's noon," said Peter. "Will you join me?"

"I'd love to. Just give me about five minutes to check my office for messages."

Exercise 45   Vocabulary Check

Use words from the preceding text to complete the sentences.

1. AP's salary _____ is above average for the industry, but its benefits program isn't competitive.

2. They could pick up the total cost of life _____ in addition to paying for the health plan.

3. The retirement plan provides _____ benefits beginning at age 65.

4. Unemployment insurance is one benefit that's _____ by law.

5. Some firms provide _____ for job-related training costs.

6. In families where both parents work, _____ benefits are very attractive.

7. Instead of a set program, _____ plans' offer employees a choice of benefits.

8. If the cost of upgrading the benefits program is reasonable, Peter will be _____ to consider changes.

INVITATIONS

"It's noon," said Peter. "Will you join me [for lunch]?"
"I'd love to," [said Carol.]

— I was wondering if you'd care to join me for lunch tomorrow, Mr. Edwards?

— It would be my pleasure. I appreciate the invitation.

more formal

— My wife and I are having a few people for dinner on Saturday. We'd like you to join us if you're free.

— It's very nice of you to invite us. We'd love to come.

— Would you like to play tennis after work tomorrow, Jim?

— Thanks for the invitation, Tom, but I'm afraid I've already made plans. Can I take a raincheck?

— Why don't we continue our discussion over lunch, Tim?

— That's a good idea, Sam. There's a café right next door.

— Anita, are you free for lunch on Thursday?

— Thursday? No, I'll be out of town. Could we make it Friday?

less formal

— Friday is fine with me. How about one o'clock?

— That's perfect.

— Mary! A few of us are going out to a movie tonight. How about joining us?

— I'd love to, Bill, but I have a class. Maybe next time.

PRESENT PARTICIPLES

"Some companies have implemented a 'cafeteria plan,' **allowing employees to select** from among a range of benefits offered."

I *knew* Carol was in her office.
→ **Knowing** she was in her office, I stopped to see her.

I *didn't know* she already had the report.
→ **Not knowing** she already had the report, I gave her a copy.

Exercise 46

Rewrite the sentences using present participles.

Examples: The Blakes thought the bus had left, so they took a cab.
Thinking the bus had left, the Blakes took a cab.

Tom isn't eligible for insurance yet. He has a private policy.
Not being eligible for insurance yet, Tom has a private policy.

1.   Robert works for an advertising agency. He has the opportunity to meet many interesting people.

2.   Because the firm doesn't have a good benefits program, they have trouble attracting top people.

3.   I travel so much, I don't have a lot of time to spend with my family.

4.   Helen isn't familiar with the city, so she may have trouble finding her way around.

5.   Carl won't believe the sales figures. He'll check them over himself.

6.   Because I used the computer, I finished my report in less than an hour.

7.   The Martins may spend two years in Sweden. They would learn a lot about the country.

8.   We didn't remember that Jill and Frank were out of town. We stopped to visit them.

9.   Because Carol is head of personnel, she must make difficult decisions.

10.   I didn't know where you were, so I couldn't return your call.

PERFECT PARTICIPLES

"Having completed their meeting, [Carol and Peter] decided to break for lunch."

We *hadn't decided* on a delivery date, so we didn't sign the contract.
→ **Not having decided** on a delivery date, we didn't sign the contract.

Since then we *'ve agreed* on a date, so we're going to sign the contract.
→ **Having agreed** on a date, we're going to sign the contract.

We *had never dealt with* this firm before. We are happy things went well.
→ **Never having dealt with** this firm before, we are happy things went well.

Exercise 47

Rewrite the sentences using the perfect participles.

Examples: Ed had finished his work, so he left the office.
Having finished his work, Ed left the office.

I hadn't eaten lunch, so I was hungry all afternoon.
Not having eaten lunch, I was hungry all afternoon.

1.   Anita has seen the movie twice, so she's not going to see it again.

2.   I didn't study a language in school, so I'm finding German very difficult.

3.   We had read the newspaper, so we knew about the accident.

4.   Mrs. Perkins had never flown in a plane before, so she was a little nervous.

5.   Carol had done a thorough study on benefits, so she was able to make recommendations.

6.   My wife and I haven't had a vacation for two years, so we're really looking forward to this one.

7.   Tom had worked in accounts payable for many years, so he was a good candidate for department head.

8.   I've never lived in a large city, so I don't know if I would like it.

 **CLAIM FOR MEDICAL BENEFITS**

IT IS A CRIME TO FILL OUT THIS FORM WITH FALSE INFORMATION, OR TO OMIT FACTS YOU KNOW ARE IMPORTANT.

1. EMPLOYEE INFORMATION

NAME: FIRST MIDDLE INITIAL LAST	DATE OF BIRTH MONTH DAY YEAR	SEX ☐ MALE ☐ FEMALE	WORK STATUS ☐ ACTIVE ☐ DISABLED
ADDRESS: STREET AND NO. CITY STATE ZIP		DATE OF DISABILITY MONTH DAY YEAR	

MARITAL STATUS ☐ SINGLE ☐ DIVORCED ☐ MARRIED ☐ WIDOWED	IS CLAIM RESULT OF ACCIDENT OR OCCUPATIONAL ILLNESS? IF YES, COMPLETE SECTION 3. ☐ YES ☐ NO	EMPLOYEE'S ID / SOC. SEC. NO.

2. PATIENT INFORMATION — Complete only if patient is other than employee.

PATIENTS NAME: FIRST MIDDLE INITIAL LAST	RELATIONSHIP TO EMPLOYEE SPOUSE CHILD OTHER - SPECIFY	SEX: M___ F___ DATE OF BIRTH

3. ACCIDENT / OCCUPATIONAL CLAIM INFORMATION

IS THE CLAIM DUE TO AN ACCIDENT? ☐ YES ☐ NO	DATE OF ACCIDENT MONTH DAY YEAR	DESCRIPTION OF ACCIDENT (HOW AND WHERE)
DESCRIBE OCCUPATIONAL ILLNESS		

4. EMPLOYEE / PATIENT SIGNATURE AND RELEASE

I HEREBY APPLY FOR BENEFITS AND CERTIFY THAT THE ABOVE INFORMATION IS COMPLETE, TRUE AND CORRECT.
CLAIM CANNOT BE PROCESSED WITHOUT EMPLOYEE'S SIGNATURE.

EMPLOYEE SIGNATURE	DATE	DEPENDENT PATIENT SIGNATURE - IF NOT A MINOR	DATE

5. PHYSICIAN'S / SURGEON'S STATEMENT

DATE	DATE OF ILLNESS (FIRST SYMPTOM) OR INJURY (ACCIDENT) OR PREGNANCY	DATE PATIENT FIRST CONSULTED YOU FOR THIS CONDITION	HAS PATIENT EVER HAD SAME SYMPTOMS? ☐ YES ☐ NO
DATE PATIENT ABLE TO RETURN TO WORK	DATES OF TOTAL DISABILITY FROM THROUGH	DATES OF PARTIAL DISABILITY FROM THROUGH	
ADDRESS OF FACILITY WHERE SERVICES PROVIDED (IF OTHER THAN HOME OR OFFICE)	FOR SERVICES RELATED TO HOSPITALIZATION GIVE DATES ADMITTED DISCHARGED		
DIAGNOSIS OR NATURE OF ILLNESS OR INJURY			

PLEASE ATTACH ITEMIZED BILLS FOR ALL EXPENSES REPORTED ON THIS FORM.

AP picks up the costs of employee health insurance.

THE INDIRECT PASSIVE

"And there are employee stock purchase programs, in which employees **are given** the opportunity to buy shares of the company's stock ..."

The company **allows** *the employees* a choice of benefits.
→ *The employees* **are allowed** a choice of benefits.

Carol **gave** *me* information on benefits.
→ *I* **was given** information on benefits by Carol.

All secretarial applicants **are being given** word processing tests.
Ben and Steve **were assigned** a new project last week.
We **haven't been sent** a catalog by the sales representative yet.
You **will be notified** of any price changes.

Exercise 48

Examples: They showed us the plans for the new plant.
We were shown the plans for the new plant.

The customer asked the salesman many questions.
The salesman was asked many questions by the customer.

1. They offered Susan the position at the interview.

2. This company pays most employees a good salary.

3. We'll send you the information you requested.

4. My supervisor has just given me a raise.

5. The salesman was showing us the new AP product line.

6. They teach children to read in the first grade.

7. They will serve everyone coffee and doughnuts during the meeting.

8. The reporters asked the prime minister many questions regarding foreign policy.

9. Tom's boss practically guaranteed him a promotion within six months.

10. We'll interview you when you apply for a visa.

Exercise 49   SYNONYMS

Choose words from the box that are closest in meaning to those in italics.

Example: Several people were badly *(hurt)* **injured** in the fire.

1. A typing test is *(necessary)* _____ for all secretarial applicants.

2. An *(upgraded)* _____ benefits program would make AP more competitive in hiring.

3. The policy has been discussed, but it hasn't been *(put into effect)* _____ yet.

4. We'll have to *(postpone)* _____ our trip until after the holiday season.

5. Our major *(goal)* _____ is to cut labor costs by increasing efficiency.

6. A large *(fraction)* _____ of our profit is paid out in taxes.

7. Once the program is *(set up)* _____, it's difficult to make changes.

8. Employees are *(paid back)* _____ for all travel costs related to business trips.

merchandise
required
percentage
established
injured
reimbursed
provide
delay
implemented
objective
strategy
improved
role

9. Upgrading the benefits program is part of Crawford's long-term *(plan)* _____ to revitalize AP.

10. The advertising agency's plan included several proposals for increasing brand awareness of the company's *(products)* _____.

11. What *(part)* _____ will the plant manager play in developing the expansion plans?

12. Some companies *(offer)* _____ a range of benefits for employees to choose from.

USES OF *MATTER*

"[Peter] called Carol Nordstrom into his office to discuss the **matter** ..."

The English word *matter* is one you hear often. As a verb, it generally means "to be of importance." As a noun, it often means "the subject under consideration" (a *matter* for concern, or insurance *matters*). Here are more examples:

When learning a language, practice is what **matters**.
I have to speak to the director about a very important **matter**.
We know sales will improve; it's only **a matter of time**.
I'll give Tom your message; or **for that matter**, you can call him yourself.
No matter how difficult it is at times, bills have to be paid.

Exercise 50

Example: The decision to change careers is a __*serious*__ matter.

1. Paul loves coffee; as a matter of _____, he drinks six cups a day.	profits
	serious
2. After I called the front desk, it was only a matter of _____ before a waiter arrived at my door.	nothing
	money
3. There are many excellent brands of computers. It's a matter of _____ as to which is the best.	interest
	position
4. I'm sorry to hear you're closing the business. If it's a matter of _____, perhaps a loan could be arranged.	fact
	minutes
5. Sales are important, of course, but _____ are what really matter.	opinion

6.   A good résumé is important no matter what _____ you're applying for.

7.   The upgrades will be a matter of _____ to everyone at AP.

8.   Tim sounded worried, but he assured me that _____ was the matter.

MEMORANDUM

To: Peter Crawford

From: Carol Nordstrom

cc: Stan Waterman

Date: 5/11/90

Subject: Salary and benefit study

Per your request, I have investigated benefits and salary levels offered in comparable firms in the electronics industry. The results indicate that AP is competitive in salaries and medical insurance, but our position in the job market could be strengthened by adding some of the following to our benefits package:

- dental care
- reimbursement for job-related training costs
- profit-sharing
- employee stock purchase program
- day care subsidy for preschool children

I have detailed information about each of these programs, including cost and tax benefit to the company, means of implementation, and general appeal to employees.

I would like very much to meet with you to discuss the matter further.

CN:mdl

Peter asked Carol to put together a study of benefit programs being offered generally in the industry.

- The more workers get in terms of benefits and job security, the less inclined they are to give their best effort to the company. Discuss.

- Compare the benefits described in the text with those offered in your company.

revitalize

talented

turnover

stand (where we ~)

compensation

package (salary ~)

upgrade *(v)*

fringe benefits

pick up the costs

insurance (life ~)

coverage

premium (insurance ~)

share *(v)*

pension (~ benefits)

law (by ~)

Social Security

unemployment insurance

payroll

give thought to

reimbursement
– reimburse

day care

stock (~ in a corporation)

share (~ of stock)

implement *(v)*

range *(n, v)*

look into

deductible
– deduction

"I'll tell you what ..."

back up *(=support)*

willing (be ~ to)

10 STEVE BLAKE'S MARKET STUDY

Peter wanted his marketing people to follow up on the Tru-Tone sales problem before things got much worse. He set up a ten o'clock meeting in the conference room with Steve Blake and Ben Melnick, who had just completed the market study of the Tru-Tone line. He also invited Jane Collins and Jack Bell, who was in charge of the Audio Performance account at Creative Talents, the company's advertising agency.

"It looks as if we're all here," said Crawford. "Steve, why don't you start?"

Steve began by outlining the problems AP faced with the Tru-Tone line: declining market share, decreasing brand awareness, difficulties in getting discount and department stores to carry the line, and non-competitive pricing.

"First we prepared figures on total industry sales of stereo equipment for the past three years. We broke these numbers down into several categories: age, sex, income, and geographic distribution of the purchasers. We then broke the data down into the various categories of sales outlets: authorized dealers, discount houses, department stores, appliance stores, and so on. Then we compared the industry data with information we already had on our own products: where they were sold, who purchased them, and why. Then, to discover the factors that make buyers choose one brand over another, we prepared a questionnaire and did a mailing to 10,000 owners of stereo-related equipment."

An analysis of the results of the study reinforced what Crawford had already suspected. In addition to the problem of a limited distribution network, Tru-Tone hadn't kept pace with technological advances in the industry. The line lacked important features available in competing models.

Ben had been right about advertising, too. Emphasis was still being placed almost exclusively on print advertising, most of it misdirected. Tru-Tone had failed to attract the youth market, appealing mostly to middle- and upper-income people in the forty- to fifty-year range.

"Excuse me, Steve, may I say something?" said Melnick.

"Sure, Ben. Go ahead," replied Blake.

"You haven't mentioned why the line doesn't appeal to the youth market."

"I was just getting to that, Ben. The major complaint we hear is that Tru-Tone models are too big and bulky. Young people want the very latest technology in the most appealing package. They don't feel they're getting it from AP, and they're not impressed with the fact that we were innovators in the field 20 years ago. Beyond this, our advertising has never really been targeted toward young people. Their income level has risen sharply over the past few years, and we can't afford to ignore them any longer."

Peter was happy that the study had pinpointed the problem areas so clearly, but he was a little discouraged, too. He hadn't realized that the problems were so widespread. At that moment, turning things around seemed almost impossible. But he didn't dare let the others know what he was feeling.

"Jack," he said, "I'd like you to have your people prepare a detailed advertising plan. It should be more youth-oriented than our present plan, with substantial T.V. and radio support. I want costs and schedules submitted for each month over a one-year period. In the meantime I'll be working with Steve and Ben on a discount store strategy. Jane, could you check with the design people? I know they've been working on a way to eliminate the size problem, but I'm not sure how far along they are. Let's get together again in about a month."

"That sounds fine to me," said Bell. "We'll be ready with a complete presentation by the end of July."

Exercise 51   Vocabulary Check

Choose the correct words to complete the sentences.

1. AP's market share has been _____ for over a year.
   a) declining   b) lowering   c) breaking down

2. Steve's people _____ figures on sales in the industry as a whole.
   a) make   b) choose   c) prepare

3. The numbers were _____ into several categories.
   a) considered   b) compared   c) broken down

4. We want to find out what _____ influence people's purchases.
   a) reasons   b) factors   c) plans

5. The market study _____ Crawford's suspicions.
   a) reinforced   b) emphasized   c) told

6. The Tru-Tone line hadn't _____ technological advances.
   a) kept track of   b) kept looking for   c) kept pace with

7. AP needs to _____ their advertising toward the youth market.
   a) point   b) target   c) eliminate

8. The new advertising plan will have _____ T.V. and radio support.
   a) substantial   b) large   c) continued

INTERRUPTIONS

"Excuse me, Steve, may I say something?"
"Sure, Ben. Go ahead ..."

more formal

— Pardon me for interrupting, Mr. Crawford, but Mr. Burke is on the line.

— Thank you, Karen. Tell him I'll be right with him.

(in a meeting)
— Excuse me, Paul ... I have a question.

— Yes, Charles?

— Could you tell us how much these changes will affect the advertising budget?

— Certainly. I'll go into that in just a minute.

(in a meeting)
— Sorry to interrupt, Jane ... may I make a comment?

— If you could bear with me for just a minute, Ed, I'd appreciate it.

less formal

— I hate to interrupt, Jim, but this can't wait.

— That's all right, Sandra. What is it?

— This fax just came in from Mr. Fasano. He says he needs an immediate reply.

(at the door)
— Excuse me, Peter ... am I interrupting?

— Not at all, Ed. Come in. What's on your mind?

COMPARATIVES AND SUPERLATIVES

"Young people want the **very latest** technology in the **most appealing** package."

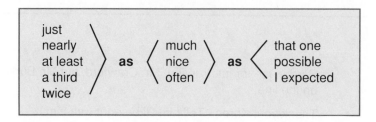

A room at the Plaza Hotel costs **at least as much as** one at the Imperial.
I don't get to travel **nearly as frequently as** I'd like to.
The new machine will be **almost twice as efficient as** the old one was.

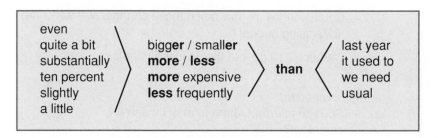

We've allowed for **quite a bit more** office space **than** we had before.
I'm **slightly less enthusiastic than** you are about the architect's plans.
Construction costs have risen **ten percent more than** we had budgeted for.

This country has **by far the most beautiful** beaches I've ever seen.
Texas is **the second largest** state in the United States.
The computer system we've installed is **one of the best** on the market.

Exercise 52

Examples: *(just / twice / by far)*
That exam was __*by far*__ the most difficult one I've ever taken!

(much / one of the / more)
The last exam was __*much*__ easier than this one.

1. *(at least / slightly / one of)*
We had dinner at _____ the most exclusive restaurants in London while we were there.

2. *(even / nearly / much)*
Most compact cars burn gas more efficiently than larger cars, but they aren't _____ as powerful.

3. *(at least / even / more)*
The World Trade Center is _____ taller than the Empire State Building.

4. *(by far / substantially / at least)*
This is _____ the most encouraging news we've had all year!

5. *(the second / a little / twice)*
The leading brand of coffee is _____ as expensive as our house brand.

6. *(one of the / quite a bit / at least)*
I didn't enjoy the movie. I thought the book was _____ more interesting.

7. *(the very / more / even)*
The weather is always bad in March, but this year it's _____ worse than usual.

8. *(twice / a little / by far)*
I can't understand you. Could you please speak _____ more slowly?

9. *(even / just / the second)*
Please send these orders out _____ as soon as possible.

10. *(the two / twice the / substantially the)*
These are _____ most detailed sketches we've had from the architect so far.

AUDIO PERFORMANCE
383 MADISON AVE., NEW YORK, NY 10017
TEL (212) 921-8500   FAX (212) 921-9449

May 15, 1990

Dear Consumer:

Could we ask you for a few minutes of your time? We at Audio Performance are proud of our reputation for quality products and would like to maintain this high standard. To do this, we need your help. We are conducting a survey to determine why people choose one brand of stereo system over another.

If you could take a moment to fill out and return the enclosed questionnaire, we would really appreciate it. Simply fold and seal the completed form and drop it in any mailbox. Thank you again for your help.

Cordially,

Steven Blake
Director of Marketing

SB/cb
Enc.

P.S. We really appreciate your input. As a way of saying thank you, we will send you a $10 gift certificate good toward the purchase of any AP product.

AP wanted to discover the factors that made buyers
choose one brand of stereo over another.

MARKET SURVEY

1. How long have you had your stereo system?

   ☐ 3 mos.　　☐ 6 mos.　　☐ 12 mos.　　☐ over 12 mos.

2. What brand is it?

   ☐ Philips　　☐ Magnavox　　☐ Panasonic　　☐ Akai

   ☐ Sony　　☐ Grundig　　☐ Tru-Tone　　☐ Other: _____

3. How much did you pay for it?

   ☐ Under $500　　　　☐ $1,000 - $2,000

   ☐ $500 - $1,000　　　☐ Over $2,000

4. Where did you buy it?

   ☐ Appliance store　　☐ Department store　　☐ Other: _____

   ☐ Stereo shop　　　☐ Discount store　　　_____

5. Did you buy it through an authorized dealer?

   ☐ Yes　　☐ No　　☐ Don't know

- -

6. Which factor most influenced your selection?

   ☐ Price　　　　☐ Friend's recommendation　　☐ Advertising

   ☐ Size/Weight　☐ General reputation　　　　☐ Other: _____

   ☐ Appearance　☐ Salesman's description　　　_____

7. Which of the following best describes your family income?

   ☐ Under $20,000　　　☐ $35,000 - $50,000

   ☐ $20,000 - $35,000　☐ Over $50,000

8. Your age _____　　Occupation _____

9. Who in your family uses the equipment the most?

   ☐ Self　　☐ Husband/Wife　　☐ Children

Thank you for your help. Please fold on the dotted
line, seal, and drop in any mailbox.

*AP prepared a questionnaire and did a mailing
to 10,000 owners of stereo equipment.*

PRESENT INFINITIVES

"Then, **to discover** the factors that make buyers choose one brand over another, we prepared a questionnaire and did a mailing ..."

They *ask* us **to speak** English in class.	They *ask* us **not to speak** any other language in class.
They *asked* us **to speak** English from the first lesson.	They *asked* us **not to speak** any other language from the first lesson.

Would you like **to learn** another language?
It's a disadvantage **not to speak** a second language.
I wanted **to be** proficient in a second language.

Careful!

They **don't** *tell us* to speak our own language in class.

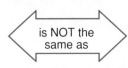
is NOT the same as

They tell us **not** to speak our own language in class.

Exercise 53

Examples: I heard about your accident.
I was sorry **_to hear about your accident_** .

Ed didn't leave early.
He was asked **_not to leave early_** .

1. John is doing well in his new job. He was determined _____.

2. I didn't get any mail yesterday. I was surprised _____.

3. We prepared the contract ourselves. We didn't ask an attorney _____.

4. Can we sign the contract soon? The best thing would be _____.

5. People don't park in this driveway. They've been warned _____.

6. Please don't mention this to anyone. I've also asked Phil _____.

7. Are you buying the suit? You can use your credit card _____.

8. I won't tell Bill about the party, but it'll be difficult _____.

NON-ESSENTIAL RELATIVE CLAUSES

"[Peter] also invited ... Jack Bell, **who was in charge** of the Audio Performance account at Creative Talents, the company's advertising agency."

The advertising plan will have T.V. and radio support. *(main sentence)*
It will be prepared by Jack Bell. *(extra information)*

→ The advertising plan, **which will be prepared by Jack Bell**, will have T.V. and radio support.

Discuss it with my assistant, *who'll be in charge while I'm away*.
Mrs. Wood, *whom we've known for years*, will be joining the firm.
I'd like to move to Miami, *where it's warm all year long*.
Mr. Bell, *whose agency handles our account*, will meet with us.
Gary was away last week, *which is why he didn't call*.

Exercise 54

Example: We're going to Europe in May. *(That's when the conference is.)*
   We're going to Europe in May, which is when the conference is.

1.   The land cost the company $400,000. *(That's expensive.)*

2.   We're planning a special retirement dinner for the director. *(He has been with the company for thirty years.)*

3.   In New York people use public transportation. *(Parking space is very limited.)*

4.   Judy is in charge of the secretarial pool. *(Her office is on the tenth floor.)*

5.   Mr. Hutchins is doing an excellent job. *(We just hired him last month.)*

6.   Labor costs in Baltimore have risen a lot. *(That's where we have a plant.)*

7.   Our benefits program is average for the industry. *(It represents thirty-five percent of total payroll costs.)*

8.   The advertising plan should have heavy T.V. support. *(The plan will be more youth-oriented.)*

Exercise 55   IDIOMS

Choose the correct words to complete the idioms.

Example: (make / do / put)
I don't know if I can make it to the meeting, but I'll **_do_** my best.

1. *(had / put / given)*
    Peter felt that some thought should be _____ to upgrading the AP benefits package.

2. *(front / look / face)*
    The first step toward finding a solution is to _____ the problem.

3. *(took / called / made)*
    Crawford _____ the meeting to announce some very important news.

4. *(hold / carry / take)*
    We should _____ advantage of the low interest rates while we can.

5. *(fill / do / put)*
    If the supplier can't _____ our order by the end of the month, we'll have to purchase the parts somewhere else.

6. *(feel / touch / hand)*
    Jack Bell has been in the advertising business for many years, so he has a good _____ for what appeals to consumers.

7. *(pick up / drop off / put away)*
    One way of upgrading our benefit program would be to _____ the cost of job-related training.

8. *(to / in / at)*
    Everyone was so helpful that I soon felt _____ home in my new job.

9. *(back / around / over)*
    Now that we've pinpointed the problem areas, we can begin working to turn the situation _____.

10. *(do / get / make)*
    Jim doesn't have much capital to start a business, but he's determined to _____ a go of it.

- Choose one T.V. commercial you feel is particularly effective and one you think is not. Describe each and explain your reasoning.

- With manufacturing techniques becoming more and more efficient, one would expect prices to fall. But manufacturers add needless "improvements" to products, which eat up any potential savings to the consumer. Discuss.

Vocabulary

account (advertising ~)	lack (n, v)
outline *(v)*	feature (n)
decline *(v)*	emphasis – emphasize
market share *(n)*	
break s.t. down	misdirected – direct (v)
income (middle, upper ~)	fail to
outlet (sales ~)	innovator
appliance store	target (n, v)
compare s.t. (with) – comparison	ignore
analysis – analyze	pinpoint (~ a problem)
	discouraged (~ with, by)
reinforce	widespread
suspect *(v)*	dare (v)
keep pace with	oriented (youth- ~)
advance *(n)*	in the meantime

11 RESEARCH PAYOFF FOR AUDIO PERFORMANCE

Peter Crawford sat and listened as Dr. Nicholas Kosloff, Audio Perform-ance's director of research and development, described his invention.

There were over 50 people in the room, including reporters from the local media and national trade publications. Bud Wilson, AP's public relations director, had arranged a press conference and cocktail party to celebrate the announcement of a new product. He had sent out a press release, made a lot of phone calls, and made all the necessary arrangements for the event. Now it was up to Dr. Kosloff.

Three years earlier, Crawford's predecessor had begun a major research project. The goal was to develop a device that would make home recording on CD's possible. The company had six full-time researchers working on the project, and spending had run into millions of dollars, but so far, there hadn't been any positive results. Peter had seriously considered cutting the program off completely, but there was something about Dr. Kosloff that inspired confidence. Peter decided to let the work go on for another six months.

One evening while having dinner at Kosloff's home, Crawford saw a strange device lying on top of the VCR next to the television, and he asked Kosloff what it was. Kosloff explained that it was "just a game machine" he had put together in his free time, using some of the technology developed during his work at AP. No larger than a CD player, the machine allowed the user, at the press of a button, to play up to 50 different games, all with full-motion video. The device had its own tiny video screen, but it could also be used with any television set.

"If you like games, you won't be able to put it down," Kosloff said. As Kosloff explained how it worked, Peter began to realize the toy's importance: a mass-market leisure product — something new, unique, with direct appeal to youth.

Peter and Kosloff got together the following Monday to talk in more detail about Kosloff's invention. Peter asked him if he would put some of his ideas down on paper, including a technical description. Peter wanted to get some idea of production costs from the engineering people. If commercial production turned out to be feasible, Peter didn't want to lose any time in getting the marketing people to work on exploring markets and distribution channels.

A month later the device had a name: the "Games Master." On the basis of market research, including a telephone survey, a marketing strategy was developed. Three months after that, the Games Master was in production at the Hartford plant, and tonight the public was going to find out about it from Kosloff himself.

"If it proves to be a success, the effect on sales and profits will be tremendous," thought Peter.

Peter was happy he had decided not to cut off Kosloff's work, even though the original objective hadn't been achieved. Now, he hoped, it was about to pay off. "If that investment hadn't been made," Peter thought, "this meeting never would have been possible."

Exercise 56　　　　Comprehension Check

Choose the best way to complete the sentences.

1. The press conference and party arrangements had all been made by ...
   a) Peter Crawford.
   b) Nicholas Kosloff.
   c) Bud Wilson.

2. The research project Kosloff had been working on for three years ...
   a) had produced the results originally hoped for.
   b) had indirectly led to the invention being introduced that night.
   c) was begun by Peter Crawford.

3. Kosloff had developed the game machine ...
   a) in his free time.
   b) using technology developed at AP.
   c) both of the above

4. At the press of a button, the user of the device could ...
   a) play CD's.
   b) play any one of fifty games.
   c) watch videos.

5. Peter realized the Games Master was important to AP because ...
   a) he loved to play games.
   b) it would appeal to large numbers of people.
   c) it used advanced technology.

6. The engineering people were asked to ...
   a) study the production process in order to determine costs.
   b) put together a report.
   c) explore possible distribution channels.

7. At the time of the press conference, ...
   a) Peter decided not to cut off Kosloff's work.
   b) AP was realizing a profit from the Games Master.
   c) Peter felt the Games Master would be a commercial success.

REQUESTING INFORMATION

"Crawford saw a strange device lying on top of the VCR ...
and he asked Kosloff what it was."

more formal

— Dr. Kosloff, could you possibly tell us how much has been spent on research for this project?

— I don't have the exact figures, but I believe it's around 50 million dollars.

— This is a little off the subject, Beth, but do you happen to know where the sales meeting is going to be held next year?

— It's been in Boston the last two years, but as far as I know, a location hasn't been chosen yet for next year.

— What I'm interested in finding out is when you plan to put the product on the market, Jim.

— Let's take a look at the timeline I've made up, Mary. That should answer your question.

less formal

— This device looks interesting, Tim. How does it work?

— Here, I'll show you, Robert. There's really nothing to it.

— Why didn't Kevin come to the meeting? Do you have any idea, Janet?

— Well, he said he had an appointment he couldn't change.

CONDITIONALS (1 and 2)

> **"If [the Games Master] proves** to be a success,
> the effect on sales ... **will be** tremendous."

---

1. **Future possible conditions:**

If the Games Master **is** a success, profits **will increase**.
If we **raise** our prices, sales **will** probably **decline**.
I'll let you **know if** I **need** more information.

2. **Present unreal conditions:**

I **would** buy a Games Master **if** I **enjoyed** games. *(But I don't enjoy them.)*
If Tom **didn't like** his job, he**'d look** for another one. *(But he does like it.)*
I **wouldn't buy** that car **if** I **were** you. *(But I'm not you.)*
If I **were going** to Paris, I **would be studying** French. *(But I'm not going.)*

Exercise 57

Examples: *(will / would)*
If we <u>take</u> an early train, we __***will***__ be in Paris by noon.

(take / took)
If we __***took***__ the 11:00 a.m. train, we <u>would arrive</u> at 5:00 p.m.

1. *(offered / offer)*
Do you think Mr. Taylor will accept the job if they _____ it to him?

2. *(would / will)*
If Joe got a haircut, he _____ make a better first impression.

3. *(Won't / Wouldn't)*
_____ my insurance rates increase if I have a car accident?

4. *(spends / spent)*
If the firm _____ more on advertising, it would pay off in the long run.

5. *(went / go)*
If I _____ to Australia, I would want to stay at least three weeks.

6. *(would / will)*
Ed _____ make a fortune if his invention is as practical as he says.

7. *(fly / flew)*
If we _____ to Majorca in the off-season, will the rates be cheaper?

PAST CONDITIONAL (3)

> "If that investment **hadn't been made**," Peter thought,
> "this meeting never **would have been** possible."

---

3. **Past unreal conditions:**

If we **had known** Peter was in town, we **could have stopped by** to see him. *(But we didn't know.)*
We **would have gone** bankrupt if we **hadn't closed** the plant. *(But we did close it.)*
Karen **wouldn't have been** late for work **if** she **hadn't missed** the bus. *(But she did miss it.)*

Exercise 58

Examples: I stayed late. I finished my report.
  If I <u>hadn't stayed</u> late, I <u>wouldn't have finished</u> my report.

  We didn't buy the car. We didn't have the money.
  We <u>would have bought</u> the car if we <u>had had</u> the money.

1.   There wasn't a mistake in the bill. I didn't notice it.

2.   We arrived at the theater late. We didn't see the first act of the play.

3.   You didn't call. I didn't tell you the big news.

4.   Jane flew business class. The firm was paying for the trip.

5.   The Burkes took the expressway. They didn't get caught in traffic.

6.   Peter trusted Kosloff. He continued funding the research.

7.   Tom and Mary enjoyed their sightseeing tour. It wasn't raining.

8.   I didn't have to use my credit card. I had enough cash.

"MIXED TIME" CONDITIONALS

"**Mixed time**" **conditionals** *(unreal past with results in the present)*:

If George **had attended** the meeting *(last week)*, he **would be** aware of the latest developments *(now)*.
We **wouldn't have** state-of-the-art products today if we **hadn't put** so much money into research years ago.
Mr. Hawkins **would** probably **be** head of the department by now if he **had stayed** with the company long enough.
If you **had received** the press release, you **would know** about our new product.

Exercise 59

Examples: Tom stayed out late last night, so he's tired today.
If he <u>hadn't stayed</u> out late last night, he <u>wouldn't be</u> tired today.

Costs have gone up 20 percent, so we aren't making a profit.
If costs <u>hadn't gone up</u> 20 percent, we <u>would be making</u> a profit.

1. We didn't have dinner, so we're hungry.

2. The Tru-Tone line hasn't kept pace with the industry, so it doesn't sell well.

3. You didn't take your medicine, so you don't feel better.

4. Peter has worked very hard, so he's a successful businessman.

5. Karen didn't have time to type the letters earlier, so she's doing them now.

6. It didn't rain hard, so the streets aren't very slippery now.

7. We made reservations two months in advance, so we're sitting at the best table in the restaurant.

8. I didn't learn English as a child, so I'm taking lessons now.

GAMES MASTER
TELEPHONE SURVEY

- Good morning (afternoon, evening.) My name is _____
  _____ . I'm gathering information for Audio
  Performance, a well-known producer of electronic equipment. I wonder if I
  could take a little of your time to ask you a few questions about video games.

- Do you presently own any home video games?   ☐ Yes   ☐ No
  If answer is "NO": Thank you very much for your time.

- How many do you own? _____

- Which ones? _____

- How many hours a week are video games played in your home? _____

- How many hours a week are the games used by. . .
  Yourself _____   Your Spouse _____   Your Children _____

- What age group(s) best describe the people who play the games most often?
  12 or under _____   13 - 19 _____   20 - 30 _____   31 - 50 _____   over 50 _____

- In your opinion, how important is the feature of portability?
  ☐ Very   ☐ Somewhat   ☐ Not very   ☐ Not at all

- Do you presently own a portable system?
  ☐ Yes   ☐ No

- Would you be interested in purchasing a portable game machine that had the
  capability to play 50 games?
  ☐ Yes   ☐ No

- Why or why not? _____

- How much would you be willing to pay for such a machine?
  ☐ Under $100   · ☐ $100 - $200   ☐ $200 - $300   ☐ Over $300

- Thank you very much for your time.

Form GMTS 2 No 1213

---

*On the basis of market research, including a telephone survey,
a marketing strategy for the Games Master was developed.*

Exercise 60   OPPOSITES

Choose the opposites from the words in the box.

Example: I had **made** an appointment to see Mr. Yates, but I ended up
having to ___*cancel*___ it at the last minute.

1. The new manager **succeeded** where the previous
    one had _____.

2. Peter was very _____ with Jack's presentation,
    but was **unhappy** that there were so many problems.

3. The new design **includes** many features that our
    present model _____.

4. I'd like to know why such a _____ increase in
    sales has had such a **slight** effect on profits.

5. The **rise** in demand during the holiday season was
    followed by a sharp _____ in January.

6. We have to **pay attention to** customer complaints.
    We can't afford to _____ them.

7. These papers are filed in a _____ manner. We
    should have a more **organized** filing system.

8. I told the salesman I wanted something **inexpensive**,
    but he still tried to sell me a _____ model.

9. As **successor** to the president of AP, Crawford decided
    to work with the team chosen by his _____.

10. While other manufacturers **raise** their prices, new
    production techniques will permit us to _____ ours.

11. Participation in the stock purchase program is **optional**, but Social
    Security payments are _____ by law.

12. The accounts **payable** department is well run, but accounts _____
    is taking too long to collect on invoices.

predecessor
cancel
substantial
lacks
required
failed
receivable
haphazard
premium
ignore
satisfied
decline
reduce

USES OF *RUN*

> "The company had six full-time researchers working on the project, and spending **had run into** millions of dollars ..."

By now you know that people can *run* across the street or *run* a business. The word *run* has many other uses as well. Here are some of them:

The trains don't **run** as often on weekends as on weekdays.
That was a great match. We lost, but we gave them a **run** for their money!
My car hasn't **run** well since I had an accident.
The cost of office space **runs** anywhere from $15 a square foot on up.

Exercise 61

Example: Our lease runs __*from*__ July first to June thirtieth.

1.   I ran _____ Ed Pearson at a party the other night.

2.   In Manhattan, streets run east _____ west;
     avenues run north to south.

3.   Many of my relatives have musical talent. It seems
     to run _____ the family.

4.   I would run _____ public office if I thought I could
     raise enough money for the campaign.

5.   Could you run _____ 200 more copies of the
     application form, please?

6.   This used to be a nice neighborhood, but now many of the buildings are
     old and run- _____ .

7.   The tape recorder can run _____ either batteries or electricity.

8.   We ran _____ quite a large bill at that expensive restaurant.

to
from
on
into
down
up
in
for
off

NEWS RELEASE

AUDIO PERFORMANCE, INC., 383 MADISON AVENUE, NEW YORK, NY 10017

CONTACT: Bud Wilson, Director of Public Relations
(212) 921-8500

FOR IMMEDIATE RELEASE:

AP LAUNCHES NEW VIDEO TOY

New York, June 18 - A new device that is expected to have a dramatic impact on the home entertainment market has been announced by Audio Performance, Inc., one of the nation's leading producers of home entertainment equipment.

The Games Master, the latest addition to AP's line, uses technology that could have far-reaching effects on the electronics industry. In simple terms, the device is a miniaturized computer that permits the user to play any one of 50 different games at the touch of a button. The Games Master is as easy to carry as it is to use, measuring only 1 x 4 x 5 1/2 inches and weighing less than one pound.

The device was developed by Dr. Nicholas Kosloff, AP's director of research and development. "The weight- and space-saving techniques used in the Games Master will eventually be incorporated into other AP products," Kosloff said, "although it could be years before we're able to develop all the possible applications."

"The Games Master is our first venture into the video market," said Peter Crawford, company president, "and we look forward to the exciting growth it will generate for AP over the coming years."

6/18/90

Bud Wilson, AP's public relations director, had sent out a press release to announce the introduction of the Games Master.

- In an age of rapidly changing technology, ongoing research is often essential to a company's survival. In which industries is this particularly true?

- As the inventor of the Games Master, Nicholas Kosloff should have a right to a share of any future profits from the toy even though the research behind it was funded by the company. Discuss.

Vocabulary

research and development
 ("R & D")
researcher

payoff *(n)*
pay off *(v)*

trade publication

public relations / "PR"

press conference
press release

celebrate

be up to s.o. to do s.t.

predecessor

device

run into millions

game

toy

mass market

leisure

put s.t. down on paper

get some idea of

– engineer
engineering

commercial(ly)

turn out (~ to be ...)

feasible

effect(s)
– have an effect on

12 CONSIDERING AN ACQUISITION

For some time Peter had been disturbed by the fact that almost all of Audio Performance's business was confined to a relatively narrow line of merchandise, most of which was quite vulnerable to foreign competition. The best way to protect corporate profits seemed to be diversification. He talked the matter over with Jim Burke, who encouraged him to explore the possibilities.

He and Burke also discussed the Games Master, which had been introduced a short time before. Burke felt that AP's distribution network wasn't adequate to exploit the full sales potential of such a mass-market product, at least not at that time. Peter had to agree with him.

Burke suggested finding a company that already had an established line of electronic games and toys and then negotiating a contract to market the Games Master through them by license arrangement. Following up on the suggestion, Peter had asked his assistant, Jane Collins, to look into the matter. She came up with a couple of possibilities, and they decided to approach a firm called Leisure Time Entertainment. LTE was a small but well-managed firm which manufactured a full line of toys, games, and sports equipment.

During negotiations on AP's proposal for a distribution arrangement, another idea occurred to Peter. He began to see in LTE a number of possibilities for the kind of diversification Audio Performance needed. With its proven record of performance and stability, it could offer AP greater access to the mass consumer market. Peter began to give serious consideration to the possibility of acquiring LTE.

"LTE could do a lot for us," thought Peter. "But would an acquisition be possible? How much would we have to pay? How much debt would we have to take on, and at what interest rate?" He made a few phone calls. The latest figures showed the firm had earned just under $6 million the year before. There were 2.5 million shares of stock outstanding, which put earnings per share at $2.40. The stock was currently trading on the New York Stock Exchange at $36 a share, giving a price-earnings ratio of 15.

The following morning, Peter phoned AP's controller, Stan Waterman. "Stan, I want you to find out a little more about Leisure Time Entertainment. I'm thinking about it as a possible acquisition. The company seems to be doing well, with good growth potential, but we'll never know what the truth is unless we dig a little deeper. See what you can find out."

"No problem," said Stan. "I have a couple of good contacts on Wall Street. I'll get hold of LTE's recent financial statements. I'll also run a credit check on them. Let's see what their rating is."

"It might also be worthwhile to see what you can learn about the management team: their backgrounds, experience, loyalty to the firm, and so on," Peter added.

"Then we can decide whether it still looks good in terms of acquisition. Oh, and one more thing — let's try to keep this confidential, just between you and me for the time being. If word gets out, it could drive the price of LTE stock up, which wouldn't be in our interest."

Exercise 62   Vocabulary Check

Choose the correct words to complete the sentences.

1. AP's product line was narrow and _____ foreign competition.
   a) helpful to
   b) vulnerable to
   c) protected from

2. _____ the product line was one way to make AP more competitive.
   a) Diversifying
   b) Protecting
   c) Confining

3. The Games Master had the _____ to be a mass-market product.
   a) features
   b) potential
   c) support

4. AP was _____ a distribution arrangement with LTE.
   a) taking
   b) exploring
   c) negotiating

5. He decided to _____ LTE because it was a manufacturer of toys and games.
   a) near
   b) approach
   c) attract

6. One of AP's objectives was to gain greater _____ to the mass consumer market.
   a) access
   b) opportunity
   c) stability

7. LTE was _____ at $36 a share on the NYSE.
   a) earning
   b) outstanding
   c) trading

8. Waterman, AP's controller, has _____ on Wall Street.
   a) loyalty
   b) contacts
   c) colleagues

9. Waterman can easily _____ LTE's financial statements.
   a) get hold of
   b) find out
   c) run

10. Please don't mention this to anyone. It's a _____ matter.
    a) loyal
    b) confidential
    c) worthwhile

PLACING AND RECEIVING CALLS

"The following morning, Peter phoned
AP's controller, Stan Waterman."

more formal

– Good morning. Apex Company. May I help you?

– Hello. May I speak to Mrs. Bennett, please?

– May I ask who's calling, please?

– This is Kenneth Farrell.

– One moment, please, Mr. Farrell. I'll put you through.

– Good afternoon. Crane Associates. Carla speaking.

– Yes. I'd like to speak to Mr. Stevens. This is Stan Waterman.

– Oh, hello, Mr. Waterman. I'll see if he's free ...
Mr. Waterman? Mr. Stevens will be right with you.

– Hello. Eberly Electronics.

– Yes. Can I speak to Mr. Eberly?

– May I have your name, please?

– It's Mary Kelly. He's expecting my call.

– Oh, yes, Miss Kelly. Just a minute, please.

less formal

– Derby Food Store. This is Terry.

– Hi. I'm trying to reach Tim Lane. Is he available?

– Yes, he's here. Hold on a minute and I'll get him.

– Hello?

– Hi. Is Barbara there?

– Sure. Hang on a second. I'll get her for you.

MODALS

- **can**, **be able to** *(ability)*

  I **can** meet with Mr. Parsons either today or tomorrow.
  I **couldn't** see him yesterday because I was out of town.
  We **haven't been able to** find a time convenient for both of us.
  Mr. Parsons **won't be able to** get here before 4 o'clock.

- **may**, **be allowed to**, **can** *(permission)*

  As a rule, employees **may not** leave early on Fridays.
  Last Friday they **were allowed to** leave at 4:15 p.m.
  May I leave early as long as my work is finished?
  You **can** go now if you like.

- **should**, **ought to**, **had better** *(advisability)*

  We **shouldn't** make any decision without careful consideration.
  Peter **ought to** give us each a copy of the proposal.
  We**'d better** consider all the facts before we begin negotiating a deal.

- **have to**, **must** *(obligation)*

  AP **has to** find a way to market the Games Master effectively.
  The acquisition **must** be approved by the Board.
  The plant expansion **had to** be approved by the Board, too.

- **might**, **may**, **could** *(possibility)*

  When do you think you **might** have time to meet with Mr. Burke?
  Stan **may not** be able to get all the information we need on LTE.
  If word of the acquisition gets out, it **could** drive the stock price up.

- **can't**, **couldn't** *(impossibility or disbelief)*

  I **can't** believe how much airfares have gone up since I last traveled by plane.
  It seems like we just arrived. It **couldn't** be time to leave already!
  A new phone **can't** cost that much. Why don't you go ahead and buy one?

Exercise 63

Example: *(might / should / must)*
You'd better take your raincoat; it looks like it __*might*__ rain.

1. *(may / can / must)*
To apply for a secretarial position, you _____ take a typing test.

2. *(can't / couldn't / might not)*
I _____ get through to Mr. Martin; his phone was busy all day.

3. *(have to / might / should)*
If the waiter gives you good service, you _____ leave a good tip.

4. *(had better / may / must)*
You _____ smoke, but only in designated areas.

5. *(may / can / had better)*
If we want to attract talented personnel, we _____ upgrade our
benefits package.

6. *(am able to / may / should)*
I'm not sure whether I'll be in tomorrow; I _____ take the day off.

7. *(can't / shouldn't / may not)*
You _____ tell me you won't be at the party! It won't be a party
without you!

8. *(has to / can / ought to)*
Jill _____ get her degree. She could get a better job if she did.

9. *(may not / can't / mustn't)*
Of course we _____ make any guarantees, but prime time
commercials usually get the best results.

10. *(can't / shouldn't / might not)*
This bill just _____ be right! Twenty dollars for two cups of coffee?

11. *(can / may / must)*
The meeting is very important. We really _____ be there on time.

12. *(should / won't be able to / has to)*
Bob _____ go to the party tonight because he _____ work late.

New York Ledger

July 3, 1990

Leisure Time Entertainment attributes rapid growth to hot new video games.

At LTE's annual meeting, Charles Brewster, president and CEO, reported sales up 17% over last year to $21.5 million, with a 23% increase in quarterly earnings. He said 1990 earnings would reach $3.12 per share, up from last year's $2.40.

Brewster announced that the Board of Directors had voted a $.20 per share increase in the quarterly dividend payable August 15, 1990 to shareholders of record on July 31, 1990.

Brewster attributed LTE's performance to the successful introduction of the company's new video games, "Interplanetary Wars" and "Space Cadet," which rank one and two in current industry sales ratings. He expressed optimism that LTE's future releases will be just as well-received.

LTE, a small but well-known player in the video game market, distributes its products under the brand name "22nd Century Videos." Leisure Time Entertainment, listed on the NYSE, closed yesterday at 36 3/4, and has a P/E ratio of 15.

S that Brewster went on a tion to a kn liv tr

Peter –
F.Y.I.
– Stan

LTE seems to be doing well, with good growth potential.

DIVIDENDS DECLARED

	Period rate	Stk of record	Pay-able
IRREGULAR			
Allied Irish Bk x	.7421	7-16	7-31
x - approx amount per ADR.			
Apex MuniFd	.0761	7-20	7-30
Colonial Intermarket	.105	7-16	8-1
Colonial InvGrd	.0775	7-16	8-1
Comstock Part	.0666	7-2	7-31
Montedison ADR x		7-1	8-6
x - approx .41 amount per Ordinary per Savings shares.	.574		
MuniEnhanced Fd	.0636	7-20	7-30
MuniVest Fd	.569	7-20	7-30
Sabine Royalty	.0977	7-16	7-30
Taurus MuniCalif	.06106	7-20	7-30
Taurus MuniNY	.06521	7-20	7-30
World Inco Fd	.1045	7-20	7-30

	Period rate	Stk of record	Pay-able
STOCK			
Luby's Cafe x		7-20	8-3
x - 3 for 2 split.			
Western Wasteland x		7-18	7-1
x - 2 for 1 split.			
SPECIAL			
MGM UA Commun x	4.00	7-10	7-21
x - previously reported as initial.			
Natl HealthLabs	1.52	7-19	7-24
Quest forVal Dual	.10	7-17	7-31
INITIAL			
ContinentalHomes	.05	7-19	8-17
Luby's Cafe n	.115	9-7	9-21
Taurus MuniNY	.06521	7-20	7-30
INCREASED			
Brenton Banks	Q .105	7-19	7-31
Brenton Banks	Q .52	7-31	8-15
Club Med Inc	S .15	8-30	9-14
Mercury Finance	Q .115	8-15	9-11

	Period rate	Stk of record	Pay-able
REGULAR			
Fst Amer Fncl	Q .10	7-12	7-16
Lomas Mtg Sec	M .105	7-16	7-26
Morrison Inc.	Q .06	7-17	7-31
New Am Hilnco	M .06	7-17	7-31
Putman DiversPrm	M .1025	7-20	8-1
Putman Div IncoFd	M .115	7-20	8-1
Putman HilncCvBd	M .071	7-20	8-1
Putman HiYldMuni	M .0675	7-20	8-1
Putman IntermGyt	M .08	7-20	8-1
Putman InvstGrade	M .074	7-20	8-1
Putman MngdMuni	M .0635	7-20	8-1
Putman MasterInco	M .0775	7-20	8-1
Putman Mastinterm	M .0725	7-20	8-1
Putman Perinco	M .0775	7-20	8-1
Quest forVal Dual	M .10	7-17	7-31
St Paul Bancorp	Q .10	7-31	8-14
g-Payable in Canadian Funds.			

> *LTE was currently trading on the New York Stock Exchange at $36 a share.*

MUSTN'T vs. DON'T HAVE TO

> You **have to** arrive on time.
> You **must** arrive on time.   ⟩ = *It's* **necessary** *for you to arrive on time.*
>
> You **don't have to** arrive early.   = *It's* **not necessary** *for you to arrive early.*
> You **mustn't** arrive late.   = *It's* **necessary** *for you* **not** *to arrive late.*

Exercise 64

Which is closest in meaning?

Example: You must be at work on time.   __*a*__
   a) You mustn't be late.   b) You don't have to be late.

1.   You must fill out the application here in the office. ___
   a) You mustn't take it with you.   b) You don't have to take it with you.

2.   Your attendance at the meeting tomorrow is optional. ___
   a) You mustn't attend.   b) You don't have to attend.

3.   We have to stay within our budget. ___
   a) We mustn't exceed it.   b) We don't have to exceed it.

4.   Regular customers may pay for purchases by check. ___
   a) They mustn't pay cash.   b) They don't have to pay cash.

5.   All car owners are required to have car insurance. ___
   a) You mustn't drive without it.   b) You don't have to drive without it.

6.   My supervisor insisted that I come to work tomorrow. ___
   a) I mustn't stay home.   b) I don't have to stay home.

7.   It's not important that this letter be typed today. ___
   a) It mustn't be typed today.   b) It doesn't have to be typed today.

8.   Payment can be made when the merchandise is delivered. ___
   a) You mustn't pay in advance.   b) You don't have to pay in advance.

Exercise 65   WORD FAMILIES

Complete these sentences using words from the same family.

Example: Berlitz **publishes** many books. This is one of their *__publications__* .

1. The company has **acquired** another subsidiary. The _____ cost nearly $12.5 million.

2. Recent ads have **emphasized** our low prices, but I believe we should start placing more _____ on our high quality.

3. At present AP is **negotiating** a license arrangement. The _____ could go on for several more weeks.

4. My professor **encouraged** me to major in business. Without his _____, I probably wouldn't have become a corporate executive.

5. Business travel is often a **deductible** expense. I had my accountant check to see if I qualified for a _____.

6. Anne studied _____ at Harvard University. Now she's a **lawyer** for a major international corporation.

7. Several people have **complained** about our latest models. The cost of repairs is one of the biggest _____.

8. You should _____ your investment portfolio. Greater **diversification** would lessen your risk of loss.

9. The firm has a very **stable** history. This _____ makes it attractive as an investment.

10. The president **announced** his decision at the staff meeting. Everyone was surprised at the _____ of so many budget cuts.

11. We are investigating the **feasibility** of using robotic technology in the plant. If it seems _____, we will allow for it in the budget.

12. The company's profit margin was in _____ of 18 percent last year, but it has never **exceeded** that figure.

USES OF *DO*

"The company seems to be **doing well**, with good growth potential ..."

The verb *do* is one of the most frequently used words in English. *Do* is often used to describe a process or an activity (*do* the dishes, *do* a good job) or as an auxiliary (Where *do* you work?). Here are some other examples:

The company **did** over $6 million **in sales** last year.
Fred drives an expensive car; his business must be **doing well**.
Would you **do me a favor** and drop this letter in the mail?
If you **do** your **homework**, your skills should improve.
I bought the car because I liked it; price **had nothing to do** with it.

Exercise 66

Example: AP would like to do more __***business***__ overseas.

1. I don't know if I can make it to the meeting, but I'll do my _____.

2. Mr. Jenkins is very quiet. His wife does most of the _____.

3. Since Mr. and Mrs. Paulsen both work, they have someone in once a week to do the _____.

4. The secretary finished typing everything, but she didn't have time to do the _____.

5. You can talk to Peter and try to change his mind, but it won't do any _____.

6. Tom and Mary remodeled an old house. It's lovely now; they've really done _____ with it.

7. The trains always run late. I wish _____ could be done about it.

8. What are you doing for _____? Would you like to go out?

lunch

best

housework

good

something

talking

business

wonders

filing

- What are the advantages and disadvantages of a company being acquired by a larger company?

- How common is it in your country to invest in the stock market? What other forms of investment are available?

Vocabulary

acquire
acquisition

vulnerable (to)

diversification
– diversify

encourage s.o. to do s.t.

exploit

negotiate (~ a contract)
negotiations

license arrangement

approach *(n, v)*

proposal
– propose

record *(n)*

stability
– stable

debt (take on ~)

outstanding *(= existing)*

earnings per share

trade *(v)*

New York Stock Exchange
– stock market

price-earnings (P/E) ratio

contacts (business ~)

Wall Street

statement (financial ~)

credit check (run a ~)

rating (credit ~)

worthwhile

background

drive up (~ a price)

interest (be in our ~)

13 JACK BELL'S ADVERTISING PRESENTATION

Steve Blake and Ben Melnick met Peter and Jane in the conference room to follow up on the Tru-Tone sales problem. Steve had presented the results of the market study about two months earlier. Since then, Jack Bell of Creative Talents had been working on an advertising campaign — one that he hoped would give new life to the Tru-Tone line. And today he was going to present his ideas. Jack walked into the room carrying a heavy briefcase and a large portfolio. Steve jumped to his feet, "Here, Jack, let me give you a hand with that."

"That's O.K., I've got it," said Jack. Everyone watched with interest as Jack set up the large full-color charts he had prepared. He then began his presentation.

"In the past most of our ads were placed in publications with a readership in the over-fifty age range, people with incomes over $40,000 a year. But that's not the market segment we should be targeting. Using what we learned from the market study, we've come up with a profile of the kind of people most likely to purchase a Tru-Tone product."

"As you can see," Jack continued, "they are young, between the ages of 18 and 28, and come from a family with a combined yearly income of $30 to $40,000 dollars. Our potential customers are likely to be interested in concerts, movies, and other leisure activities and have purchased at least one CD or cassette in the past three months. The entire focus of our campaign should be shifted to the younger market. To accomplish this we recommend using T.V., radio and print advertising, with special emphasis on T.V."

"Where do you propose running the print ads, Jack?" Melnick asked.

"Well, Ben, our media people have prepared a list of publications with a readership closely matching the profile of our potential buyers — youth-oriented magazines with a circulation guarantee of a million or more. That should give us just the kind of audience we want.

"But as I mentioned, a large portion of our advertising budget should go to television. As you may know, the average cost of reaching 1,000 households during prime time is around $10. That's not bad, particularly when you consider that each household usually has several viewers. The problem is, there are so many thousands of households that even at the $10 figure, the dollar outlay can be as high as $300,000 for a 30-second commercial in the 8 to 11 p.m. prime-time period. As a result, we propose purchasing only a limited number of 10-second spots initially, during programs that are most popular with young people."

Bell went on to describe the campaign in depth. He showed samples of proposed magazine ads and explained his ideas for the T.V. spots. Peter found the presentation very impressive. Jane Collins and Steve Blake were just as enthusiastic. Ben Melnick agreed, "With this kind of advertising support we should have no trouble turning things around!"

Peter then announced that in response to the pricing problem, while he fully understood the potential repercussions, he had decided to approve a 5 percent price cut on the entire Tru-Tone line, effective immediately.

The discussion then shifted to the advertising budget. The proposed campaign wouldn't be cheap and would mean doubling Tru-Tone's advertising expenditures over those of the previous year. Peter was taking a big risk — if either the ad campaign or the price cut failed to deliver substantial sales increases, the results could be disastrous. He asked Bell if it would be possible to run a test introducing the campaign on a limited scale; say, in New England, starting the fourth quarter. "No problem," said Bell, "I look forward to the challenge."

"If the combination of a price cut and the new advertising shows positive results in the test area," Peter said, "we can think about taking the campaign nationwide next year."

As the meeting ended, Peter complimented Bell on his excellent presentation. "I hope to see the results of our meeting reflected in the fourth quarter sales reports," he said.

Exercise 67   Comprehension Check

*Indicate whether the following statements are **True (T)** or **False (F)**.*

_____   1.   In the past, AP ads were targeted at readers under 50 years old.

_____   2.   Bell came up with a profile of Tru-Tone's potential buyers.

_____   3.   He recommended placing special emphasis on print advertising.

_____   4.   During prime time, the average per-household cost of television advertising is around $10.

_____   5.   The announcement Peter made during the meeting had to do with the advertising budget.

_____   6.   Everyone except Ben Melnick found Bell's presentation impressive.

_____   7.   Peter wants to introduce the ad campaign only in a certain area.

_____   8.   The ad campaign will be taken nationwide at the same time the price cut goes into effect.

OFFERING ASSISTANCE

"Here, Jack, let me give you a hand with that."
"That's O.K. I've got it ..."

more formal

— I'd be happy to write a letter of recommendation for you if you'd like, Charles.

— That's very kind of you, Mr. Burke. I appreciate it.

— Would you like me to drop these letters in the mail for you, Mr. Miller?

— Yes, please, John, if it wouldn't be too much trouble.

— I can stay late to work on the report if you really need me, Mr. Crawford.

— It's nice of you to offer, Karen, but it can wait till tomorrow.

— Why don't you let me take care of the arrangements for the meeting, Jane?

— That would be a big help, Karen. Thanks very much.

less formal

— I'm going out to pick up a sandwich, Carol. Can I get you something?

— No, I'm fine, Barbara. But thanks for the offer.

— Can I give you a hand with those packages, Mary?

— No, I can manage, Tom. Thanks anyway.

MODALS OF PROBABILITY

> "With this kind of advertising support we **should have** no trouble turning things around!"

Carol left the office at 5 o'clock. It takes her about an hour to get home.

It's now 5:50: She **may** / **might** be home by now.
6:15: She **should** be home by now.
7:45: She **must** be home by now.

Exercise 68

Complete the sentences using **may**, **should**, *or* **must**.

1. John worked until ten o'clock tonight; he _____ be very tired.

2. Peter hardly ever leaves the office before 6:00 in the evening. He _____ take his job very seriously.

3. My train leaves New York at 1:30 p.m., and the trip takes about three hours. I _____ be in Washington D.C. by 5:00 p.m.

4. I'm not sure whether I can finish this by 5:00 p.m. I _____ have to work late this evening.

5. Joe figured out how to operate the software program in a few hours. He _____ be very clever.

6. The market research was completed two weeks ago. We _____ be getting the results within a week.

7. We'd better check LTE's credit rating. They _____ have a lot of outstanding debt.

8. I only have one more page to type; I _____ be finished in a few minutes.

9. The manager doesn't know yet, but there _____ be an opening at the plant soon.

10. Kosloff invented the Games Master in his free time. He _____ enjoy games.

DEGREES OF PROBABILITY

> **Where's Peter?**
>
> He**'s definitely** in the building. *(= I know he is.)*
> He **must be** in his office. *(= I assume / I'm almost sure he is.)*
> He **should be** sitting at his desk. *(= He probably is.)*
> He **may** / **might be** on the phone. *(= Perhaps / It's possible he is.)*
> He **probably hasn't left** for lunch yet. *(= I don't think he has.)*

Exercise 69

Which is closest in meaning?

Example: **I know Jane is** at home now.
   a) She's definitely ...   b) She's probably ...   c) Maybe she's ...

1.   **It's possible Carol has** some résumés on file.
   a) She must have ...   b) She definitely has ...   c) She might have ...

2.   **The company will definitely** open a new plant next year.
   a) I'm sure they'll ...   b) I assume they'll ...   c) I think they'll ...

3.   **The manager should** be back by Tuesday.
   a) He'll definitely ...   b) I know he'll ...   c) He'll probably ...

4.   **Waterman knows we can** afford the research expenditure.
   a) We can definitely ...   b) We can probably ...   c) Maybe we can ...

5.   **We may** decide to go ahead with the LTE,acquisition.
   a) I'm sure we'll ...   b) I assume we'll ...   c) Perhaps we'll ...

6.   **A license arrangement is probably** the best distribution channel.
   a) I'm sure it's ...   b) I think it's ...   c) It might be ...

7.   **We may not** have the results before the end of the month.
   a) I know we won't ...   b) We shouldn't ...   c) We might not ...

8.   I haven't seen Ben all week. **He must be** on vacation.
   a) I assume he's ...   b) It's possible he's ...   c) I doubt he's ...

MODALS WITH SEVERAL MEANINGS

may:	You **may** smoke if you want. *(= You're allowed to.)*
	Ben **may** be in his office. *(= It's possible he's there.)*
should:	You **shouldn't** drive so fast. *(= You're not supposed to.)*
	You **should** apply for the job. *(= I advise you to.)*
	It's 7:15. Ed **should** be home by now. *(= He's probably there.)*
must:	Everyone **must** pay taxes. *(= It's an obligation.)*
	It's ten o'clock. Ed **must** be home by now. *(= I assume he is.)*

Exercise 70

Which is closest in meaning?

Example: **We should** transfer the money to a savings account.
    a)   I recommend that we ...   b)   We'll probably ...

1.   **This invoice must be** paid before the end of the month.
    a)   I'm sure we'll pay it ...   b)   We have to pay it ...

2.   **Employees may** take their lunch hour whenever they like.
    a)   They're allowed to ...   b)   It's possible that they ...

3.   I haven't seen Paul since this morning. **He must be** very busy.
    a)   I assume he's ...   b)   It's necessary that he be ...

4.   **You shouldn't** mention the budget discussions yet.
    a)   You probably won't ...   b)   It's better not to ...

5.   **You must** have a passport to enter the country.
    a)   I assume you have to ...   b)   You're required to ...

6.   **We may not** have enough time to go over the balance sheet.
    a)   It's possible we won't ...   b)   We're not allowed to ...

7.   The problem is minor. **It shouldn't** take long to repair.
    a)   It probably won't ...   b)   It's not supposed to ...

8.   It's 10 o'clock. **Ann must not be** coming today.
    a)   I assume she's not ...   b)   She can't be ...

150

TRU-TONE

Sounds too good to be true....

All the clarity, depth, and dynamics of a live performance.

From Michael Jackson to Mozart, from rap to jazz, Tru-Tone delivers the highest quality in sound.

For the Tru-Tone dealer nearest you, call toll-free 1-800-399-5545

Audio Performance

Jack Bell of Creative Talents described the ad campaign and showed samples of proposed magazine ads.

Exercise 71   OPPOSITES

Choose the opposites from the words in the box.

Example: The firm's **income** rose last year, but so did its ___*expenditures*___ .

1. I'm going to **withdraw** some money from my savings account and _____ it in my checking account.

2. The government has **failed to** slow inflation, but it has _____ winning people's confidence.

3. The radio I have is too big and **bulky**; I'd like to get something more _____.

4. Despite a decrease in **gross** revenues last year, the company showed an increase in _____ profits.

5. The results of the _____ survey were very similar to the **final** results.

6. The president was **in favor of** the proposal, but the Board was _____ it.

7. In spite of the firm's efforts to _____ with technological advances, they have **fallen behind**.

8. Everyone thought LTE was **protected** from takeover attempts, but it turned out to be _____ after all.

9. The plant manager feels that the equipment is **not good enough**, but management believes that it's _____.

10. So far the **actual** growth in sales of the Games Master is small compared to the _____ increases.

Box of words:

vulnerable

adequate

potential

opposed to

preliminary

deposit

compact

expenditures

succeeded in

keep pace

net

152

Exercise 72   **IDIOMS**

Fill in **up**, **down**, **over** *or* **out** *to complete the idioms.*

Example: Have you come __up__ with any ideas on how to reduce our collection
                 time on past due accounts?

1.   The past due accounts will all be turned _____ to a collection agency
     at the end of the month.

2.   It will only take the secretary a minute to call _____ the file on the
     computer.

3.   The report not only spelled _____ the problems, it mentioned possible
     solutions.

4.   We had a wonderful vacation. The hotel, the people, and the food all lived
     _____ to our expectations.

5.   Did Crawford talk _____ the idea of a price cut with Burke before
     making his decision?

6.   Before Tom got up to speak to the group, he put his thoughts _____
     on paper.

7.   The results of the market study backed _____ my theory on why sales
     were falling.

8.   Charles felt very let _____ when he found out his transfer request
     hadn't been approved.

9.   I wasn't able to attend the meeting. Did anything come _____ that I
     should know about?

10. There was a mix-up in Jane's reservations, but the travel agent was able to
     straighten things _____ before she left.

11. Since it was set _____ 20 years ago, the company has changed its
     product line substantially.

12. During his presentation, Jack Bell pointed _____ that much of Tru-
     Tone's advertising was misdirected.

MEMORANDUM

To: District Sales Managers

From: Ben Melnick

Date: 7/25/90

Subject: Price Reduction

cc: Peter Crawford
Stan Waterman
Steve Blake

Effective Monday, August 6, 1990, there will be an across-the-board price reduction of 5% on the entire Tru-Tone product line. In combination with our new ad campaign, we anticipate this action will result in a noticeable increase in sales over the coming months.

Please notify all your sales representatives of this change immediately. I am attaching a revised price list for distribution.

BM

BM:kl
Attachment

Peter had decided to approve a 5% price cut on the entire Tru-Tone line.

- What kinds of products and services do you consider best suited to T.V., magazine, newspaper, or radio advertising? Give your reasons.

- Concerns for the environment and a healthier lifestyle are growing. What effect will these concerns have on advertising?

Vocabulary

campaign *(n)*

segment (market ~)

likely (to)
– unlikely

shift *(v)*

accomplish

run (~ an ad / ~ a test)

guarantee *(n, v)*

audience

budget *(n)*

commercial (T.V. ~)

depth (in ~)

T.V. spot

find (~ s.t. impressive, boring, *etc.*)

repercussions

effective (~ immediately)

expenditure

nationwide (take ... ~)

compliment *(v)*

14 A REAL ESTATE PURCHASE

Five months after the original meeting regarding the possible expansion of AP's manufacturing facilities, Peter received the report written by Jeff Martinelli and Jane Collins. He called them into his office to go over their findings.

Peter had hoped they could find an existing facility to lease or purchase, but the recommendation was for new construction. "Due to AP's particular requirements and time limitations, it is unlikely that we will be able to locate an existing facility that will adequately meet our needs ..." were the words of the report. Also recommended was a location in either the southeastern or northwestern part of the country — both construction and labor costs in the Northeast, where Peter had wanted to locate, were just too expensive.

The general area of Greenville, South Carolina, had been chosen as the best location. The state of South Carolina had a special program to attract industry into the state. Under the program, the state issued special bonds, called industrial revenue bonds, to finance plant construction. The bonds were sold to regular investors throughout the country. The advantage to investors was that the interest received from state bonds was exempt from income tax. Because the bonds were tax-exempt, the state could sell them at a lower interest rate than the prevailing rate for corporate bonds, which were subject to tax. The state could then loan the proceeds of the bond issues to companies moving their operations into the state, at interest rates much lower than commercial banks could offer.

A number of potential properties in the Greenville area had already been identified and studied. Jeff explained that the best-suited site had already been sold before the report was even completed. "The buyers must have known someone else had expressed an interest. That's why they were in such a hurry to close the deal," said Jeff.

"We couldn't have done anything anyway," said Jane. "Even if we had gotten approval for the purchase right away, it would have been too late. But we'll have to move quickly if we don't want to miss out on our second choice as well."

"Which one is that?" asked Peter.

"This one here in the northern part of the state: 18 acres of unimproved land for $200,000," answered Jane.

"I've done a lot of searching, Peter, and if you ask me, it's a great location," added Jeff.

The three went over a number of other properties one by one, and Peter finally agreed that the site recommended by Jane and Jeff was indeed the best choice.

That afternoon Peter met with Jim Burke and got his approval to make an offer on the land. Jim said he had discussed the matter at a recent Board meeting and had received approval in principle to proceed with the overall expansion plan, including the purchase of land.

The next morning Peter contacted the real estate agent and put in a formal offer of $150,000 for the property, hoping to get it for about $175,000. The owner responded with a counteroffer of $190,000. Peter was a little disappointed the owner hadn't come down more, but he immediately responded with an offer of $160,000. He was pleased when the owner finally agreed to settle for $180,000.

Peter called Jim Burke and brought him up-to-date. Jim was happy to hear the news and congratulated Peter on the good price. As he put down the phone, Peter was beginning to feel more and more confident about the situation. He couldn't help feeling that Audio Performance was about to enter a new era.

Exercise 73   Comprehension Check

Choose the correct words from the box; then answer the questions.

Example: How long after the ___*original*___ meeting did Peter receive Jeff's report?
He received it five months after the original meeting.

1. Did AP find an existing facility that would be _____ for its needs?

2. Who were the _____ revenue bonds being issued by?

3. Which were _____ tax, state-issued or corporate bonds?

4. Was the interest rate on the state-issued bonds higher or lower than the _____ rate?

5. Who were the proceeds of these bond issues _____ to?

6. How many acres of _____ land was AP considering for purchase?

7. How much was Crawford's first _____ offer for the land?

8. Was Peter pleased or _____ with the deal he finally made?

prevailing
original
subject to
loaned
unimproved
disappointed
adequate
industrial
formal

ASKING AND GIVING OPINIONS

"I've done a lot of searching, Peter, and if you ask me, it's a great location."

more formal

— Let me ask you, Mrs. Stone, which do you consider to be the greater threat, foreign or domestic competition?

— In my judgment, foreign competition should be taken more seriously, Mr. Cole.

— In your opinion, Ed, why have production costs been rising so sharply?

— Well, Jeff, it seems to me that the plant may not be running as efficiently as it could.

— How do you feel about the government's plan to raise taxes, Carol?

— As far as I'm concerned, Philip, taxes are already too high.

less formal

— You've seen the résumés, Steve. Who do you think is the best for the job?

— I'd say Kurt Walker. He's got the education and the experience to do a great job.

— Hey, Tom. What did you think of the tennis tournament?

— I thought it was great! I saw some really exciting matches.

PAST FORMS OF MODALS

"We **couldn't have done** anything anyway," said Jane.

Present	Past
The report **should be** ready this Friday. *(It probably will be.)*	The report **should have been** ready last Friday. *(But it wasn't.)*
Tom **could get** here early. *(It's possible.)*	Tom **could have gotten** here early. *(But he didn't.)*

Exercice 74

*Write new sentences with **could(n't) have ...** or **should(n't) have** ...*

Example: You came in late. *(You weren't supposed to.)*
         You shouldn't have come in late.

1.   Ted took the money. *(He knew it wasn't his.)*

2.   Joan didn't buy the car. *(She had enough money.)*

3.   You didn't hear Steve's presentation. *(It was terrific.)*

4.   Mrs. Kane didn't wait for us. *(She had promised she would.)*

5.   Carol didn't drive to Boston. *(She doesn't have a car.)*

6.   I waited until yesterday to mail the letter to my client. *(It was urgent.)*

7.   We decided not to sell the property. *(We had several offers.)*

8.   The Chiltons didn't go to the party. *(They weren't invited.)*

9.   Fred stayed home from work. *(He wasn't really sick.)*

10.   The plane didn't land at Heathrow. *(It was an unscheduled flight.)*

11.   Paul didn't move to New York. *(He had a chance to.)*

12.   I didn't finish the report yesterday. *(I knew I was supposed to.)*

PAST FORMS OF MODALS

"The buyers **must have known** someone else had expressed an interest."

I'm almost sure that Jeff *knew* about the meeting.
→ He **must have known** about the meeting.

It's possible that he *didn't receive* the memo.
→ He **might not have received** the memo.

Maybe he *was called* out of town.
→ He **could have been called** out of town.

Mary isn't here yet. Do you think she **might have missed** her train?
Ken never called me. He **must not have gotten** my message.
Jeff **must have been told** about the land purchase by now.

Exercise 75

*Write sentences with **must have ...** or **might have ...***

Where's Bill? He's not usually late.

1.   He probably forgot about our appointment.

2.   Maybe he thought it was for tomorrow.

3.   But I'm sure someone told him.

4.   He definitely got the message.

5.   But it's possible he didn't get the message.

6.   I probably told him the wrong time.

7.   Maybe he misunderstood me.

8.   It's possible he got held up in traffic.

Exercise 76 *MIGHT HAVE* vs. *MUST HAVE*

*Complete the sentences using **might have (been) ...** or **must have (been) ...***

Example: *(rain)*
The roads are all wet; it **_must have rained_** last night.

1. *(transfer)*
I'm not sure if Ann still works in this department. She _____.

2. *(deliver)*
We sent that package two weeks ago, and it only takes four days to get there. It _____ by now.

3. *(submit)*
Our offer for the property wasn't accepted. A higher one _____.

4. *(misunderstand)*
Andrew says he's definitely not resigning. I _____ him.

5. *(fill)*
The job opening was posted only yesterday, but there's a chance it _____ since then.

6. *(phone)*
I don't know whether Joe has called, but I've been out of the office. He _____ during that time.

7. *(find)*
The car seems to be running perfectly since it was repaired. The mechanic _____ the problem.

8. *(give)*
Mr. Carlson left a very good job for a new company. He _____ a generous offer.

9. *(get)*
Peter _____ approval for the ad campaign already, but I doubt it.

10. *(make)*
The research department has been working on the design for months. They _____ some progress by now.

BROWN & WALKER
REAL ESTATE ASSOCIATES

535 Lee Ave. / Greenville, South Carolina 29601 / Tel. (803) 461-5308 / Fax (803) 461-7085

LISTING SHEET
Greenville Tract Industrial Site

ASKING PRICE: $200,000

SIZE: 18 acres

LOCATION: in the county of Greenville, South Carolina; nine miles north of the city of Greenville

ROAD FRONTAGE: 736 feet on U.S. Route 25

ZONING: commercial, industrial, or light manufacturing

PHYSICAL FEATURES: land is cleared and level

UTILITIES: public water; sewer connection available

TAXES: $985 est. (1990)

OTHER: 868 feet of railroad frontage; survey available

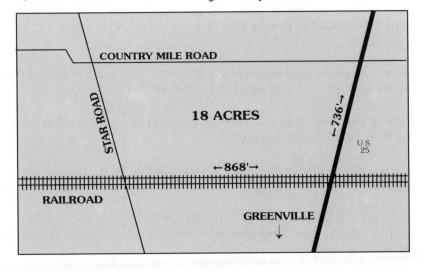

The property recommended by Jane Collins and Jeff Martinelli was in South Carolina. The owner was asking $200,000 for the 18-acre property.

163

Exercise 77   WORD FAMILIES

Complete these sentences using words from the same family.

Example: Profitable **investments** are what most ___*investors*___ are looking for.

1.   The firm's _____ position is strong, but it will still have to borrow
     money to **finance** the expansion.

2.   Mary Ann was hired as a **clerk**, but she's responsible for more than just
     _____ work.

3.   You're free to **choose** the person you want to hire, but the _____
     must be made by June 1.

4.   Sam's **enthusiasm** about his transfer was obvious, but his wife didn't
     speak as _____ about it.

5.   The present health plan **covers** only 70 percent of hospital expenses.
     Under the new plan employees will have much more extensive _____.

6.   If the firm decided to **proceed** with the acquisition, what would the
     _____ be?

7.   Several changes were **proposed** at the meeting. They should be written
     up in a formal _____ and submitted to the director.

8.   Peter is **confident** they can work out financing through the state, but he's
     not sure if the Board will share his _____.

9.   The real estate agent didn't know the exact **acreage**, but he said the
     property was at least 35 _____.

10. The man interested in buying the house hasn't _____ to our counter-
     offer. If I don't have a **response** from him tomorrow, I'll put it back on the
     market.

11. As importers, we_____ with many foreign countries. Our **dealings** are
     often affected by international events.

12. I thought Ms. Carlson's résumé was quite **impressive**. Were you as
     _____ with it as I was?

USES OF *PUT*

"The next morning Peter contacted the real estate agent
and **put in** a formal offer of $150,000 for the property ..."

The verb *put* usually means "to place" as in: "*Put* the book on the table." But there
are many other ways it can be *put to use*:

The owners **put** the business **up for sale** because they both wanted to retire.
We hope the new management will **put a stop to** the wasteful spending.
If you really want the job, I could **put in a good word** for you.

Exercise 78

Example: You'd better put the check __*away*__ in a safe place.

1. I'd like to put this purchase _____ my credit card.

2. The bike didn't come assembled; Joe had to put it
   _____.

3. When you're finished with the book, please put it
   _____ on the shelf.

4. The negotiators came close to settling, but nothing
   was put _____ writing.

5. Just a moment, please, I'll put you _____ to
   Mr. Burke.

6. Mary said the book was so interesting she couldn't
   put it _____.

7. Several investors put _____ the money to finance
   the remodeling of the hotel.

8. If you didn't understand, let me put it _____
   you a different way.

9. We missed out on the property because we put_____ making a decision.

10. I'm moving because I'm tired of putting up _____ noisy neighbors.

together
through
on
away
down
in
up
back
to
with
off

AUDIO PERFORMANCE
383 MADISON AVE., NEW YORK, NY 10017
TEL (212) 921-8500   FAX (212) 921-9449

Philip R. Hayes, Esq.
General Counsel

July 24, 1990

Mr. John Sutherland
Brown & Walker Real Estate Associates
535 Lee Avenue
Greenville, SC 29601

Dear Mr. Sutherland:

Following your telephone conversation today with Peter Crawford, I have been authorized to confirm our offer of $180,000 for the Greenville tract industrial site. It is our understanding that the offer has been accepted by the owner, Mr. Ian Carson.

I will forward a draft of the purchase contract this week for Mr. Carson's approval. We appreciate your continuing assistance in the speedy completion of this transaction.

Sincerely yours,

Philip R. Hayes

Philip R. Hayes

PRH/jd

The owner of the Greenville property finally agreed to settle for $180,000.

- Discuss property ownership vs. leasing in your area. How common is each? How do property transactions take place? How are they financed?

- Public bond issues should be used for public works projects and not to subsidize industry. Discuss.

Vocabulary

findings

due to

issue *(v)*

bond (corporate ~,
  industrial revenue ~)

finance *(v)*

exempt (~ from)

subject (be ~ to)

prevailing (~ rate)

proceeds *(n)*

close a deal

miss out on

acre

indeed

in principle

counteroffer
– counter *(v)*

disappointed

pleased

come down (~ in price)

settle for *(= accept)*

up-to-date (bring s.o. ~)

congratulate
– Congratulations!

can't help ...-ing

era

15 A COSTLY MISTAKE IN ACCOUNTING

It had been several months since Bob Smith, the manager of the Baltimore plant, had submitted his resignation. In the meantime, Jack Reilly had been named acting manager, but it was clear that a long-term solution had to be found.

After interviewing several candidates for the position, Ed Pearson had decided to turn the job over to Reilly on a permanent basis. Since Reilly had been assistant manager for several years, he was already thoroughly familiar with the mechanics of the operation. He also had the advantage of having already established a good working relationship with the employees at the plant. Besides, none of the other candidates could match Reilly's experience.

Shortly after Reilly assumed his new position, Pearson noticed what he thought might be a problem — it appeared that a serious accounting mistake had been made in the year-end report for the Baltimore plant. Ed had immediately asked Reilly to turn over all the accounting records for the period in question. After examining them closely, Pearson had ordered a complete audit of the books.

The error showed up clearly in the audit. The value of the inventory on hand at the close of the previous year had been overstated by $400,000, which meant that they had used up more inventory than they thought. As goods are taken out of inventory and shipped to customers, their value is reflected as a "cost of sales." The failure to reflect $400,000 in costs had, in turn, inflated the profit figure by the same amount, causing Audio Performance to pay about $200,000 in excess taxes.

Pearson knew he had to let Crawford know right away. Peter was having lunch at his desk reviewing some figures when Ed's call came in. Ed filled him in quickly.

Peter sounded annoyed. "I can't believe it! I thought you had said Reilly was working out well. That sounds like just plain sloppy bookkeeping."

"Well, Reilly has accepted the blame, but we can't really hold him responsible. The mistake dates back to when Smith was still in charge."

"If that's the case, then you're right," Peter said, calming down. "How do we go about recovering the $200,000?"

"We'll have to file an amended tax return and ask the Internal Revenue Service to credit the money to next year's tax liability. Of course, they might call for a complete audit of the return, but according to Stan Waterman, it's fairly obvious that the claim is legitimate. He doesn't foresee any real difficulty."

"That's encouraging," said Peter. "And when the IRS rules in our favor, it will improve this year's profit picture by $200,000."

Exercise 79   Comprehension Check

*Indicate whether the following statements are **True (T) or False (F)**.*

1. ____ Bob Smith resigned from his position as manager of the Baltimore plant several months ago.

2. ____ Jack Reilly was made permanent manager immediately after Smith resigned.

3. ____ Some of the other candidates for the position had just as much experience as Reilly did.

4. ____ Jack Reilly got along well with the plant employees and was very familiar with the operation.

5. ____ The first person to become aware of the accounting mistake was Ed Pearson.

6. ____ It was Peter who ordered a complete audit of the books.

7. ____ The value of the previous year's inventory had been understated by $400,000.

8. ____ The profit figure that was reported was greater than it should have been.

9. ____ Audio Performance had paid about $200,000 in taxes that they didn't actually owe.

10. ____ Pearson and Crawford agreed that Reilly should be held responsible for the error.

11. ____ Pearson planned to recover the excess taxes paid by filing an amended return.

12. ____ Stan Waterman was quite concerned by the possibility of an audit by the Internal Revenue Service.

EXPRESSING ANNOYANCE

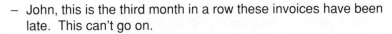

"I can't believe it! ... That sounds like just plain sloppy bookkeeping."

more formal

- John, this is the third month in a row these invoices have been late. This can't go on.

- I can certainly understand your annoyance, Mr. Parks. I assure you it won't happen again.

- The photocopier still hasn't been fixed, and I won't be able to make copies for the meeting. This is so frustrating!

- I don't blame you for being upset. The serviceman said he'd be here first thing in the morning, and it's after 11 now.

- I can't believe it! The drycleaner ruined my new suit. I'm absolutely furious about it!

- You have a right to be angry. But they'll replace it, won't they?

- Yes, but I just can't stand such incompetence!

less formal

- I give up! I just can't get this document to print out!

- Now calm down, Frank. Are you sure you entered the right command?

- I thought I did ... there! There it goes. That's better.

- That really kills me! I only parked there for five minutes, and I got a ticket. What a lot of nerve!

- Take it easy. There's nothing you can do.

PHRASAL VERBS

"The error **showed up** clearly in the audit."

Inseparable:

without object:
look up	He's *looking up* (from his desk).	—
look over	He's *looking over* (at me).	—

with object:
look for s.*	He's *looking for* his wallet.	He's looking **for it**.
look at s.	He's *looking at* the report.	He's looking **at it**.

Separable:

look s. up	He's *looking up* the word. *or:* He's *looking* the word *up*.	He's looking **it up**.
look s. over	He's *looking over* the car. *or:* He's *looking* the car *over*.	He's looking **it over**.

* s. = something or someone

Careful!

John is standing by the car; he's *looking* **it over**.
(= He's trying to decide whether to buy it.)

John is standing by the car; he's *looking* **over it**.
(He wants to see what's behind it.)

Separable	**Inseparable** *(with obj.)*	**Inseparable** *(without obj.)*
put together	speak to	go on
turn off	ask for	get up
open up	go into	get through
bring in	put up with	turn out
take out	look back on	come along

172

Exercise 80

Choose the words that best complete the phrasal verbs.

A. 1. I called several times, but I couldn't get _____.

    2. Ben got _____ from his chair and walked to the front of the conference room.

    3. If you state your ideas clearly, you'll be able to get your point _____.

    a) *across*
    b) *through*
    c) *up*

B. 1. Looking _____ on it, we made a wise decision.

    2. We looked _____ financing the expansion with industrial bonds, but decided against it.

    3. The Board looks _____ Peter to provide leadership.

    a) *into*
    b) *back*
    c) *to*

C. 1. Be sure to go _____ the figures once more before filing the tax return.

    2. The IRS has decided to go _____ with the audit.

    3. Ann didn't go _____ her reasons for resigning.

    a) *ahead*
    b) *into*
    c) *over*

Exercise 81

Choose the correct phrasal verbs to complete the following sentences.

A. 1. The desk was so big we couldn't _____ the door.

    2. May I use your pen when you _____?

    3. The report was long; it took me forever to _____.

    a) *get through*
    b) *get it through*
    c) *get through it*

B. 1. Here's a copy of the sales chart. Do you want a folder to _____?

    2. I have _____ a request for early retirement.

    3. I know Carol placed an ad for the job opening, but I have no idea what information she _____.

    a) *put in*
    b) *put in it*
    c) *put it in*

C. 1. The bus leaves soon; shouldn't you be _____?

    2. This shoe is too small. I'm having trouble _____.

    3. Now that he's _____ in years, Tom can't handle the job anymore.

    a) *getting on*
    b) *getting on it*
    c) *getting it on*

Exercise 82

Complete the sentences using phrasal verbs. Add pronouns where necessary.

Examples: (drive up)
Prices are already high, and an increase in labor costs would **_drive them up_** even higher.

(look into)
I don't know how good LTE's credit rating is, but I'll **_look into it_** .

(go on)
You haven't finished your explanation. Please **_go on_** .

1. *(get hold of)*
    Mr. Hill's line was busy all morning. When is the best time to _____?

2. *(break down)*
    Here are the latest sales figures. We'd like you to _____ by area.

3. *(break down)*
    With improved maintenance, the machinery wouldn't _____ so often.

4. *(put together)*
    The advertising plan looks excellent. Who _____?

5. *(go ahead with)*
    We had some doubts about the policy change, but decided to _____.

6. *(pay off)*
    The Collins have invested thousands of dollars in their daughter's education, but they know it will _____ someday.

7. *(turn out)*
    The contract negotiations are progressing smoothly. I'm sure everything will _____ the way we want.

8. *(rely on)*
    Our staff members are very loyal to the firm. You can _____ completely.

9. *(look over)*
    Several résumés have been submitted. Would you like to _____?

10. *(work through)*
    Ms. Nordstrom is head of personnel. If you need to hire a typist, you should _____.

AUDIO PERFORMANCE, INC.
INCOME STATEMENT
YEAR ENDED DECEMBER 31, 1989
(in millions of dollars)

Sales		164.8	
Cost of finished goods:			
Ending balance previous year		3.2	
Additions to inventory during year (includes raw materials and direct labor)		111.6	
Total		114.8	*corrected*
Deduct ending inventory	2.1 *2.5*	1*1*2.3 *112.7*	
Gross profit		5*2*.5 *52.1*	
Other operating expenses (includes general administrative costs, depreciation, debt payments, etc.)		15.3	
Net income from operations		3*7*.2 *36.8*	
Other income		5.0	
Net income before tax		4*2*.2 *41.8*	
Federal income tax		2*0*.2 *20.0*	
Net income		2*2*.0 *21.8*	

The value of inventory had been overstated by $400,000, resulting in an inflated profit figure, which caused AP to pay $200,000 in excess taxes.

Exercise 83   SYNONYMS

Choose words from the box that are closest in meaning to those in italics.

Example: When the equipment was first *(purchased)* __**acquired**__ , it was considered state-of-the-art.

1. We should follow our lawyer's advice. He's *(clearly)* _____ familiar with the tax laws.

2. After Reilly *(assumed)* _____ the position of plant manager, things started to improve.

3. Wage increases often *(bring about)* _____ price increases.

4. A close look at the books *(disclosed)* _____ a serious error in the gross earnings figure.

5. Mr. Pearson was very *(upset)* _____ about problems in the accounting department.

6. Mary was *(contacted)* _____ by two firms interested in her invention, but she turned both of them down.

7. The *(most common)* _____ attitude towards the government is one of uncertainty.

8. We were *(promised)* _____ our money back if we weren't satisfied with the product.

9. Paul felt very *(let down)* _____ when the deal he had been working on fell through.

10. The accounting supervisor discovered a *(mistake)* _____ on last month's balance sheet.

11. *(At first)* _____ we'd planned on purchasing a photocopier for the office, but it was more practical to lease one.

12. Martin *(said)* _____ that he might be in the cafeteria around noon.

---

revealed

prevailing

took over

originally

cause

guaranteed

mentioned

miscalculation

approached

acquired

disturbed

obviously

disappointed

USES OF *MAKE*

"... a serious accounting **mistake had been made** in the year-end report ..."

The verb *make* has a wide variety of uses. Here are some:

It's hard to hear in the plant because the machinery **makes** so much **noise**.
It's important to **make a good impression** during a job interview.
Tom had little formal education, but he **made a go of it** in the business world.
If we leave for the theater now, we'll **make it** there by seven.

Exercise 84

Example: Playing tennis always makes me __*thirsty*__ .

1.   Could I use your phone to make a local _____?

2.   If the _____ Reilly made were implemented,
     it could lead to greater efficiency.

3.   The benefits program can't stay as it is. Some
     _____ must be made.

4.   After several years of losses, the firm finally
     seems to be making a _____.

5.   Unless I make a _____ of the points I want
     to discuss, I won't remember them all.

6.   If a competing firm made you a better
     _____, would you quit your present job?

7.   Dr. Parker will be out of town all week, so I
     made an _____ for next Monday.

8.   Make a _____ at the corner and go three
     blocks. You'll see the subway station on your left.

9.   The restaurant is so popular you have to make _____ a month in
     advance.

10. Mr. Burke is in favor of the expansion plan, but it's up to the Board to
     make the final _____.

right
decision
changes
offer
call
profit
thirsty
reservations
suggestions
appointment
list

MEMORANDUM

To: Peter Crawford

From: Edward Pearson

Date: August 16, 1990

Subject: Audit Report: Baltimore Plant

With reference to my phone call of 8/12/90, I'd like to give you an update on the accounting situation at the Baltimore plant.

An independent audit of the books has confirmed that the value of inventory on hand at year-end was overstated by $400,000. This, in turn, resulted in a corresponding error in the reported cost of sales, which in turn inflated the profit figure for the year. As a result, AP paid about $200,000 in excess taxes.

As we discussed, I will have the tax department file an amended tax return requesting that the IRS credit the overpayment to next year's tax liability.

The audit report is attached. I intend to take action on this as soon as I have your approval.

EP:st
Attachment

cc: Stan Waterman

The accounting error showed up clearly in the audit.

- What is the tax situation, both corporate and individual, in your country? What changes would you like to see in the system?

- How could Peter justify the mistake in accounting to the UEI Board of Directors?

Vocabulary

acting (~ manager)

mechanics (the ~ of s.t.)

relationship (working ~)

assume (~ a position)

appear (~ that)

question (the ... in ~)

audit *(n, v)*
– auditor

books (company ~)

bookkeeping

show up

inventory (take ~)

close (~ of a year)

overstate
– understate

goods

cost of sales

failure (to)

fill s.o. in

work out (~ well)

sloppy

blame *(n, v)*

date back to

calm down

tax return

file (~ a tax return)

amend(ed)

Internal Revenue (Service)

liability (tax ~)

call for *(= ask for)*

claim *(n, v)*

16 EXPANDING THE USE OF COMPUTERS

Jane Collins was sitting in her office with Stan Waterman and Steve Blake. Peter had asked them to attend a presentation by Jeffrey Knowles, vice president of Data Masters, Inc. Data Masters was a well-known consulting firm in the data processing field. The firm specialized in advising companies on how computers could be used to make their operations more efficient.

At that time, AP's computer network was being used predominantly for payroll, which had already been automated to a great extent. Knowles, who had spent some time studying Audio Performance, asked whether Stan felt the system had performed satisfactorily.

"No doubt about it," Stan answered. "I can't imagine how we ever got along without it. Based on our favorable experience in payroll, I think the next areas worth looking into might be inventory and accounts receivable. We've been having problems controlling receivables for some time."

"I think you'll find many of these difficulties will become more manageable when you have accurate, up-to-date information to work with," said Knowles.

Knowles recommended setting up one overall system that would tie sales and production together with inventory and accounts receivable. Steve asked him how such a system would operate. Knowles explained that the data from each sales transaction would be fed into the computer: product code number, quantity sold and unit cost, as well as current pricing and any client information not already on file. At the same time, the system would also be receiving input regarding production and the movement of finished goods into inventory. Whenever a sale occurred, the finished goods inventory account would be reduced automatically. Simultaneously, the receivable account would be charged and an invoice issued to the customer.

The computer would also maintain a complete customer file containing information such as year-to-date purchases, amounts billed, and payment record. "All this feedback would be available in the form of daily and weekly printouts," Knowles explained. "In addition, if you chose to equip your salespeople in the field, they could have immediate access to the information via modem and laptop computer."

Knowles went on to talk about how the system could be used to improve efficiency from the standpoint of inventory control. The setting of production levels and the ordering of components from outside vendors could be fine-tuned by the computer. This would eliminate costly delays on the production line caused by a shortage of key components.

"Excuse me, Jeffrey, before we go any further, I have a question," said Jane. "This all sounds terrific, but I'm wondering if such a system would be affordable considering the size of our operation."

"Without question," Knowles replied. "The system will actually save money in the long run. The initial dollar outlay might seem high, but the savings resulting from increased control over inventory and receivables will more than make up for it," he said.

"Well, I know I'm sold," said Jane. "Why don't you put together a proposal along the lines we've discussed, and I'll submit it to Mr. Crawford. You can call on Stan for help with any of the details. I know Mr. Crawford would like to get moving on this as soon as possible."

Exercise 85   Vocabulary Check

Choose the correct words to complete the sentences.

Example: Jane, Stan, and Steve all __*c*__ Knowles' presentation.
a)   assisted   b)   participated in   **c)   attended**

1.   Knowles works for a well-known computer ___ firm.
a)   advising   b)   consulting   c)   accounting

2.   Should the ___ consideration in choosing a computer system be cost?
a)   predominant   b)   substantial   c)   customary

3.   A new system would make accounts receivable more ___.
a)   functional   b)   manageable   c)   operational

4.   The details of each sales ___ must be entered into the system.
a)   action   b)   data   c)   transaction

5.   AP purchases some of its components from outside ___.
a)   clients   b)   customers   c)   vendors

6.   Knowles said the system would be expensive, but still ___.
a)   affordable   b)   substantial   c)   terrific

7.   The system might seem costly but would ___ save the firm money.
a)   currently   b)   truly   c)   actually

8.   Jane told Knowles to ___ Stan for help with anything.
a)   tell   b)   call on   c)   offer

CERTAINTY AND UNCERTAINTY

"... I'm wondering if such a system would be affordable ..."

"Without question ... The system will actually save money in the long run."

Are you quite certain Mr. Bell is coming in today?

 – Yes, I can assure you he is. I spoke to him myself.

 – I believe he is. He usually comes in on Fridays.

 – I'm just not sure. Let me call his secretary for you.

more formal

How sure are you that the prices on this invoice are correct?

 – I'm absolutely positive. I got a new price list this morning.

 – I assume they are. They don't change very often.

 – I'm not at all sure. I'd better check them to make sure.

Are you positive we can afford to upgrade the equipment?

 – After looking at the figures, I'm convinced we can do it.

 – I really think so, but we'd better work out all of the numbers before making a decision.

less formal

 – At this point, it's hard to say. I'd like to look into it further.

I hear they might close the plant down. Is that for sure?

 – There's no doubt about it. They've announced it already.

 – I don't know it for a fact, but they've been talking about it for a long time.

 – Who knows? You can never tell what they'll do.

REPORTED SPEECH

> "Knowles **explained** that the data from each sales transaction **would be fed** into the computer ..."

Statements: "**I'm** very busy," said Stan.
                    → Stan said he **was** very busy.

He said:	He said (that):
– "I **am** busy."	– he **was** busy.
– "I **will be** busy."	– he **would be** busy.
– "I **can't** see Ed."	– he **couldn't** see Ed.
– "I **was** busy."	
– "I **have been** busy."	– he **had been** busy.
– "I **had been** busy."	

Karen **mentioned** she **was going** on vacation in May.
Who **told** you that buying a copier **would be** cheaper than leasing one?
Peter **said** that Data Masters **had installed** the original computer network.

Questions: "What time **is** it?" Stan asked (me).
                  → He asked (me) what time it **was**.

He asked (me):	He asked (me):
– "Who **are** you?"	– who I **was**.
– "Where **were** you?"	– where I **had been**.
– "How **have** you **been**?"	– how I **had been**.
– "Why **hadn't** you **called**?"	– why I **hadn't called**.
– "When **will** you **be** back?"	– when I **would be** back.
– "**Are** you free?"	– **whether** (or not) I was free.
	– **if** I was free.

Mr. Knowles **wanted to know** how well the system **was meeting** our needs.
I **questioned** whether we **could afford** such a large expenditure.
Tom **asked** when the copier **had** last **been serviced**.

Exercise 86   REPORTED STATEMENTS

Example: "Mr. Crawford is in a meeting."
Karen told me that Mr. Crawford ___**was in a meeting**___ .

1. "We have to make a decision on the advertising budget soon."
The marketing director said they _____.

2. "I can't make it to the meeting on time."
John informed us he _____.

3. "We have begun negotiating a three-year contract."
The labor leader said they _____.

4. "Our new product line will be introduced in the spring."
The public relations department announced that the line _____.

5. "We received your invoice on May fifteenth."
The company wrote us that they _____.

6. "The President arrived at the airport at 3:00 p.m."
The newspaper reported that the President _____.

7. "All of our products come with a full guarantee."
The ad claimed that all of the company's products _____.

8. "The delay in payment won't affect your credit rating."
The loan officer informed me that the delay _____.

9. "The sales manager hasn't been in since Tuesday."
The secretary told us the sales manager _____.

10. "The next annual conference will be held in Brussels."
Mr. Kahn mentioned that the next annual conference _____.

11. "Our inventory has been running low too often."
I complained that our inventory _____.

12. "We can't afford any large expenditures until our profit picture improves."
The Board decided the company _____.

Exercise 87 REPORTED QUESTIONS

Examples: "Is Mr. Collins in?"
Mr. Martin asked the secretary **_whether Mr. Collins was in_** .

"When will he be back?"
He asked **_when he would be back_** .

1. "Can we get a reservation for May first?"
   I asked the travel agent _____.

2. "How long ago did the Hartford plant open?"
   The reporter asked Peter Crawford _____.

3. "Does the company have problems keeping track of inventory?"
   Jeffrey Knowles wondered _____.

4. "When did the shipping supervisor submit his resignation?"
   I asked a colleague _____.

5. "Have you considered using the computer for forecasting?"
   Jeffrey asked Stan _____.

6. "What rate of production are you hoping for?"
   The production manager asked me _____.

7. "When will the fourth-quarter figures be available?"
   I wondered _____.

8. "Has the new equipment been running well?"
   The plant manager asked his assistant _____.

9. "Why was the production quota set so high?"
   The workers wanted to know _____.

10. "Will my performance be reviewed every six months?"
    Karen inquired _____.

11. "How soon can the new computer network be installed?"
    Crawford asked Knowles _____.

12. "Why is the company planning to expand its recruitment program?"
    The personnel director wanted to know _____.

AUDIO PERFORMANCE

383 MADISON AVE., NEW YORK, NY 10017
TEL (212) 921-8500   FAX (212) 982-9449

Date		Amount
08-13-90	Pay to the order of	$***443.43

Paul E. Jackson   314 M655 F1443
215 E. 67th Street
New York N.Y. 10022

Check No. **17254**

Detach and retain.

AUDIO PERFORMANCE

EARNINGS	HOURS		AMOUNT		DEDUCTIONS						YEAR TO DATE		
Regular	40	0	520	00	FICA	34	82	FED TAX	79	80	Gross Pay	18,824	00
Overtime	3	5	68	25	Disability	1	20	STATE TAX	20	20	F.I.C.A.	1,114	24
					Life Ins	1	50	CITY TAX	4	30	Fed. Tax	2,553	60
					Pension	3	00				State Tax	646	40
											City Tax	137	60

TOTAL EARNINGS			588	25		

FOR PERIOD ENDING
08-10-90

TOTAL DEDUCTIONS	144	82

NET PAY
443.43

PAUL E. JACKSON   Emp. No. **314 M655 F 1443**   Soc. Sec. No. **092-40-7320**

Check No. **17254**   STATEMENT OF EARNINGS AND DEDUCTIONS

AP's computer network was being used predominantly for payroll.

TIME EXPRESSIONS IN REPORTED SPEECH

Direct Speech	Reported Speech

"I'm leaving **tomorrow**," said Ed. → Ed said he was leaving **the next day**.

now	**then**
today	**that day**
tonight	**that night**
this morning	**that morning**
yesterday	**the day before (the previous day)**
the day before yesterday	**two days before (two days earlier)**
last week	**the week before (the previous week)**
two months ago	**two months before (earlier)**
tomorrow	**the next (following) day**
the day after tomorrow	**two days later (two days after that)**
next week	**a week later (the following week)**
a year from now	**a year from then (a year later)**

Exercise 88

Example: "I'm leaving for London today."
When I saw Tom, ___*he said he was leaving for London that day*___ .

1. "Would you like to have lunch with me tomorrow afternoon?"
   The last time I saw Ed, he asked me _____.

2. "How much did AP earn in profits last year?"
   I asked my stockbroker _____.

3. "Will the new policy be in effect a month from now?"
   At the last meeting, the employees wanted to know _____.

4. "How late does the store stay open tonight?"
   Several days ago, customers were calling to ask _____.

5. "Can we afford such a large expenditure at this time?"
   At the last quarter's meeting, I questioned _____.

NOUN SUFFIXES

" ... these **difficulties** will become more manageable when you
have accurate, up-to-date **information** to work with ..."

There are many suffixes that change verbs or adjectives into nouns. Here are
some examples:

-tion:	automation creation	**-ation:**	realization resignation	**-ition:**	proposition recognition
-cation:	notification qualification	**-sion:**	exclusion impression	**-al:**	approval proposal
-ment:	commitment requirement	**-ness:**	seriousness sloppiness	**-ity:**	generosity majority
-ance:	attendance importance	**-ence:**	existence insistence	**-y:**	inquiry recovery

Exercise 89

Use the suffixes from above to make nouns from the words in parentheses.

Example: Who is responsible for the *(promote)* __**promotion**__ of new products?

1.   The *(expand)* _____ of the facility began last month.

2.   Your input helped the group come to an *(agree)* _____.

3.   Better *(maintain)* _____ of the equipment would save us money.

4.   The report revealed the *(serious)* _____ of the firm's financial situation.

5.   Has there been any increase in the plant's *(productive)* _____?

6.   A *(minor)* _____ of shareholders expressed opposition to the merger.

7.   This expenditure will require Mr. Crawford's *(authorize)* _____.

8.   Your failure to respond to this offer by August 20th will be taken as a
     (refuse) _____.

AUDIO PERFORMANCE
383 MADISON AVE., NEW YORK, NY 10017
TEL (212) 921-8500   FAX (212) 921-9449

August 24, 1990

Mr. Jeffrey Knowles, Vice President
Data Masters, Inc.
313 West 39th Street
New York, NY 10018

Dear Mr. Knowles:

Audio Performance is interested in upgrading and expanding the capabilities of its data processing equipment at this time. We are very satisfied with the performance of the present system, which was installed by Data Masters four years ago.

I am enclosing a summary of the nature and volume of activity the present system is handling. I would like to meet with you to discuss the matter at your earliest convenience.

Sincerely yours,

Jane Collins

Jane Collins
Executive Assistant

JC/gb
Encl.

Data Masters, a well-known consulting firm in the data processing field, was going to upgrade AP's computer network.

- Computerized inventory and order tracking completely eliminate the need to perform these tasks manually. Discuss.

- The extension of computers into daily life represents the greatest threat to individual freedom in the future. Discuss.

Vocabulary

attend
– attendance

consulting firm

advise
– advice

extent (to a great ~)

get along without

base(d) on

worth (~ looking into)

manageable

tie

transaction

feed *(v)* (~ data)

feedback

field (salespeople in the ~)

modem

laptop computer

standpoint (from a ~ of ...)

vendor

fine-tune

run (in the long / short ~)

make up for

be sold on
– sell s.o. on s.t.

along ... lines

call on s.o. for s.t.

get moving (~ on s.t.)

17 THE SHOP-WAY BONANZA

It was around 7:30 in the evening, and Peter Crawford was sitting in his office going over UEI's most recent quarterly report. He was particularly interested in the parent company's consolidated balance sheet.

Peter loved this time of the day. With everyone else gone, the building was completely quiet. This gave him a chance to relax and concentrate without the constant interruptions of phone calls and appointments.

Peter was just beginning to pencil in a note next to the item "Inventory on Hand" when his phone rang. "Crawford here," he answered.

"Peter, I have some good news. Have you got a minute?" The voice was familiar.

"Ben? You're still here?" he said. "Sure, come on up!"

A few minutes later, Ben Melnick entered the office, holding a letter. He had a pleased, almost smug, look on his face. "Do you remember asking me to explore the possibility of marketing the Tru-Tone line in discount stores?" he asked.

"Sure I do. What've you got?"

"Well," Ben continued, "I've been in touch with some people at a number of the large chain stores, trying to put together some kind of deal. You know, a long-term, high-volume arrangement that would permit us to get our unit costs down."

"That's the kind of break we need, particularly with the new plant coming on line next year," said Peter. He sounded intrigued.

"About a month ago I spoke to Dave Williams, the director of purchasing for the Shop-Way stores," Melnick went on. "As you know, Shop-Way is one of the largest nationwide discount chains, with outlets in 56 cities. It's a two-billion dollar-a-year operation."

"And Shop-Way is interested in carrying the Tru-Tone line?" asked Crawford.

"*Interested* isn't the word. Just look at the letter!" answered Melnick. "Williams is talking about a five-year deal with minimum monthly orders, product by product. The contract is worth millions even if the orders never exceed the minimum!"

"What kind of discount are they looking for?" asked Crawford.

"They would insist on getting the units at 20 percent below our present wholesale rates. That's actually only about 6 percent above our current manufacturing cost, but as production and sales volume increase, our unit costs will begin to fall. Our profit margin may suffer temporarily, but if everything goes according to plan, it should eventually return to somewhere in the neighborhood of 12 percent."

"Where do we go from here?" asked Peter.

"They want us to draw up a contract for their review. Jane and I have started on it, but we're still working out the details: delivery schedules, terms of payment, guarantees, penalties, and so on."

"How soon do you think it'll be ready?" Peter asked.

"I'm sure we'll have completed a draft by the end of the week. Of course we'll have to run it past the legal department."

"Right, and be careful," warned Peter. "We don't want to commit ourselves to any unrealistic production schedules. You'd better talk to Jeff Martinelli about our expansion plans. Find out whether our capacity will have increased enough to meet the delivery schedules called for in the contract."

"I've already set up a meeting for tomorrow morning."

"Good! I'll be expecting to hear from you. And, Ben ... congratulations! It looks as if this may be the big one we've been waiting for!"

Exercise 90   Vocabulary Check

Choose the correct words from the box.

Example: Peter's office was quiet in the evening without the **_constant_** interruptions of the day.

1. Melnick looked _____ because he was pleased about the deal he had put together.

2. If AP could come up with a _____ sales arrangement, unit costs would go down.

3. Shop-Way is a large chain of _____ stores.

4. Shop-Way was insisting on a price lower than AP's current _____ rates.

5. The decrease in profits would be a _____ one.

6. The _____ department checks over all contracts.

7. Peter wanted to make sure Melnick's figures weren't _____ in view of AP's capacity.

8. AP's _____ would make production for the Shop-Way deal possible.

unrealistic
discount
constant
expansion
high-volume
smug
wholesale
legal
temporary

ANNOUNCING GOOD NEWS

"Peter, I have some good news. Have you got a minute?"

more formal

– Have you heard the latest news about the stock market?

– No, what happened?

– It went up 75 points today — and most of that was in the last hour of trading!

– That's quite a jump. Let's hope it continues.

– Did you know that Jim Stevens had gotten a promotion?

– No, I hadn't heard. So now he's a vice president?

– Yes. Isn't that something?

– It certainly is. He's worked hard enough. He's earned it.

– You'll never guess who I saw today. Bill Jensen.

– Really? That's great. How is Bill?

– He looks terrific. I guess retirement agrees with him.

– That's wonderful. I'm glad to hear he's doing so well.

less formal

– Guess what! They've started installing the new computer system.

– Is that right? That's going to be a big improvement.

– I can't wait to tell you about my vacation. It was fantastic!

– Really? That's great! I want to hear all about it.

THE FUTURE PERFECT

"I'm sure **we'll have completed** a draft by the end of the week."

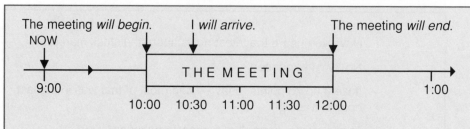

The meeting *will begin* at 10 o'clock. I *will arrive* at 10:30.

→ When I arrive, the meeting **will have** (already) **begun**.

→ When the meeting begins, I **won't have arrived** (yet).

In January, I **will have been** with the company for exactly a year.
By the time we get to the dinner, the food **will have** already **been served**.
When I meet Mary in Brussels, I'**ll have been traveling** for a month.

Exercise 91   **CONTRASTING TENSES**

A.   The Board meets in April, June, September, and December. It's May 1st.

   1.   *(has met, will have met)*
        So far this year, the Board _____ once.

   2.   *(will meet, will have met)*
        The Board _____ three more times this year.

   3.   *(will meet, will have met)*
        By year-end, the Board _____ four times.

B.   Tomorrow I'm going to Boston. My train leaves at 9:00 a.m. and gets
     in at 1:00 p.m.

   1.   *(will leave, will have left)*
        By 10:30 tomorrow morning, I _____ for Boston.

   2.   *(will be sitting, will have been sitting)*
        It's noon now. At this time tomorrow, I _____ on the train.

   3.   *(will meet, will have met)*
        My friend _____ me at the station when I arrive.

Exercise 92

Fill in the correct future tense.

Example: *(work)*
We can't meet for dinner tomorrow. I **_will be working_** late.

1. *(last)*
    Tomorrow's staff meeting _____ about 50 minutes.

2. *(leave)*
    By the time we get to the party, almost everyone _____ already.

3. *(go)*
    The construction contract _____ to the lowest bidder.

4. *(sit)*
    Meet me tomorrow at noon at the Riveria Restaurant; I _____ next to the window.

5. *(ask)*
    I _____ Tom and Mary to get moving on the market study right away!

6. *(begin)*
    By this time next year, they _____ to sell the Tru-Tone line in Shop-Way Stores.

7. *(be)*
    When Mr. Collins retires he _____ with the same firm over 30 years.

8. *(wait)*
    It's now 4:30 p.m. Two hours from now Ed _____ for your decision.

9. *(be)*
    The letter _____ ready for your signature in a few minutes.

10. *(check out)*
    By the time you speak to Carol, she _____ the applicants' references.

11. *(sign)*
    We _____ the contract as soon as the details have been worked out.

12. *(learn)*
    When you finish your course, you _____ a lot of useful words!

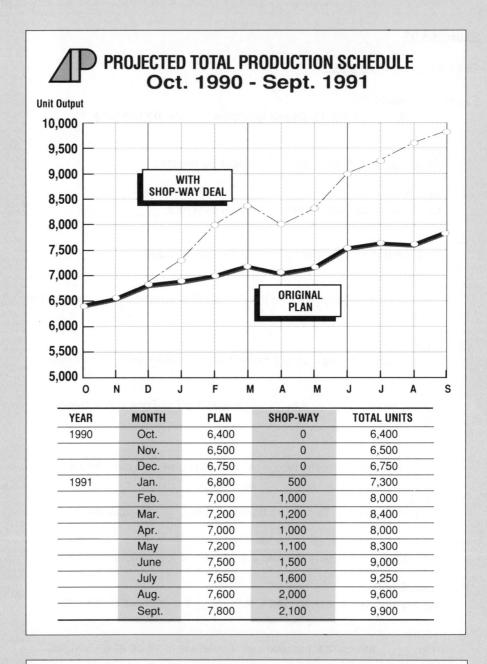

PROJECTED TOTAL PRODUCTION SCHEDULE
Oct. 1990 - Sept. 1991

Unit Output

WITH SHOP-WAY DEAL

ORIGINAL PLAN

YEAR	MONTH	PLAN	SHOP-WAY	TOTAL UNITS
1990	Oct.	6,400	0	6,400
	Nov.	6,500	0	6,500
	Dec.	6,750	0	6,750
1991	Jan.	6,800	500	7,300
	Feb.	7,000	1,000	8,000
	Mar.	7,200	1,200	8,400
	Apr.	7,000	1,000	8,000
	May	7,200	1,100	8,300
	June	7,500	1,500	9,000
	July	7,650	1,600	9,250
	Aug.	7,600	2,000	9,600
	Sept.	7,800	2,100	9,900

Peter warned Ben not to commit AP to an unrealistic production schedule.

AGREEMENT OF TENSES

Present:	We { know, believe, doubt, are aware, agree, assume, hope, etc. }	*(that)* the figures	{ **are, were, will be, can be** } accurate.

⇩

Past:	We { doubted, thought, felt, etc. }	*(that)* the figures	{ **were, had been, would be, could be** } accurate.

Exercise 93

Example: "The meeting will begin on time."
We all hoped ___**the meeting would begin on time**___.

1. "Mrs. Carlson is away on vacation this week."
   I wasn't aware that _____.

2. "The company will increase salaries before the end of the year."
   The employees hoped _____.

3. "Stanley Wells was transferred to London in May."
   Did you know that _____?

4. "Sales have increased ten percent since last month."
   Ed didn't realize _____.

5. "Unit costs can be reduced."
   Peter believed _____.

6. "Shop-Way is insisting on a substantial discount."
   Steve and Peter both knew _____.

7. "Mr. Knowles' presentation went over well."
   Everyone agreed that _____.

8. "All contracts are reviewed by the legal department."
   I assumed _____.

Exercise 94   **WORD FAMILIES**

Complete these sentences using words from the same family.

Example: There are nine **_accountants_** in the **accounting** department.

1.   The researchers **analyzed** the problem in detail and then submitted their
      _____ to the director.

2.   George had all the necessary _____ for the job. He was hired
      because he was the most **qualified** applicant.

3.   We were afraid the ad campaign would be a **disaster**, but it was anything
      but _____. It was a great success!

4.   The firm **failed** to withhold taxes from my salary. This _____ to take
      out taxes caused problems when I filed my tax return.

5.   The **accuracy** of the figures is all-important. If they aren't _____, the
      books won't balance.

6.   We will be **penalized** for breaking the agreement. Let's just hope the
      _____ won't be too great.

7.   When fax machines first went on the market, many small firms couldn't
      afford them. Since then, fax machines have become very _____.

8.   The lawyer tried to _____ that the driver was not responsible for the
      accident. His **proof** was conclusive.

9.   We need a **consultant** on this matter. Can you recommend a good
      _____ firm?

10.   I'd like to **congratulate** you on a job well done! Please give my
      _____ to the rest of the staff as well.

11.   The new president has done a lot to increase the company's **efficiency**.
      It's now operating more _____ than ever.

12.   This painting is **valued** at $3 million. It's the most _____ piece of art
      in the gallery.

Exercise 95   IDIOMS

Choose the corrects words to complete the idioms.

Example: *(on / to / for)*
You can take your vacation anytime — it's up **_to_** you.

1. *(for / on / in)*
The consultant assured us that the new computer network would pay off _____ the long run.

2. *(for / with / to)*
Mary doesn't mind working late, but she's not willing _____ work on Saturdays.

3. *(in / to / on)*
The personnel director told Sam she would be _____ touch with him if a position opened up.

4. *(for / on / about)*
I had my coat on and was _____ to leave when the phone rang.

5. *(for / by / in)*
I agree with you _____ principle, but I don't think your idea is practical.

6. *(for / to / from)*
The interest earned on corporate bonds is subject _____ tax.

7. *(of / from / to)*
Public bonds can offer lower interest rates because the bonds are exempt _____ taxes.

8. *(in / on / at)*
Audio Performance has been _____ business for over thirty-five years.

9. *(of / on / by)*
Both Burke and Crawford are sold _____ the idea of acquiring LTE — they think the company could do a lot for AP.

10. *(to / on / in)*
Janet works full-time and goes to school evenings. She's determined _____ get her degree.

Shop-Way Stores

1642 South Street, Philadelphia, PA 19107 Tel: (215) 735-5800 Fax: (215) 735-4990

September 7, 1990

Mr. Ben Melnick
Director of Sales
Audio Performance, Inc.
383 Madison Avenue
New York, NY 10017

Dear Mr. Melnick:

Following our discussion of August 20, I am writing to confirm Shop-Way's interest in concluding, at the earliest possible date, an agreement to carry the Tru-Tone line.

As we discussed, Shop-Way is willing to commit to a five-year program, with guaranteed minimum orders. We will, however, have to insist on the discount and delivery schedules discussed at our meeting, as well as a penalty clause to protect ourselves in the event the delivery schedule is not met.

I look forward to receiving a draft of the proposed agreement at your earliest convenience.

Sincerely,

David P. Williams
Director of Purchasing

DPW:sm

Melnick showed Crawford the letter from Shop-Way's director of purchasing, Dave Williams. The deal with Shop-Way would be worth millions of dollars.

- What are some of the risks AP is taking by signing a five-year contract with the Shop-Way stores? What provisions would you write into the contract to protect the company's interests?

- Chain stores make "big business" even bigger and force small "mom and pop" operations out of business because they are unable to compete. Discuss.

Vocabulary

bonanza

consolidated balance sheet

smug

look *(n)*

in touch (be ~ with)

chain (~ store)

volume (high ~, low ~)

on line (come, be, go ~)

intrigued (by)

billion

insist (on)

wholesale
– retail

profit margin

eventual(ly)

in the neighborhood of

draw up (~ a contract)

work out (~ details)

penalty

draft *(n)*

run s.t. past s.o.

commit oneself to (doing) s.t.

set up (~ a meeting)

18 EXCHANGE RATES CAUSE BUDGETING PROBLEMS

Peter Crawford had learned from long experience that control of a growing company was impossible without accurate, up-to-date financial planning. Much of the forecasting was the responsibility of AP's controller, Stan Waterman. Stan reviewed the company's sales forecasts and cost projections, which were broken down by product and geographic area. The information was then fed into a computer in order to come up with a consolidated budget for the corporation as a whole.

Peter wasn't normally involved in the details of the process, but today Stan wanted to discuss a problem regarding the exchange rate of the dollar against the British pound and how to allow for it in the financial plan for the coming year.

Export sales represented 16 percent of AP's total volume. The majority of the exports, about 60 percent, went to the United Kingdom. In four of the previous five years, the value of the dollar had fallen against the British pound. Each decrease in the value of the dollar meant a corresponding decrease in the price paid by British importers for AP goods. This, in turn, meant that AP's products had been getting more and more competitive on the British market. As a result, more units were being sold, and AP's revenues and profits from the U.K. were increasing steadily.

The problem facing Waterman at the moment was what assumption to make about the value of the dollar. The prevailing exchange rate was around $1.80 to the pound, but there was disagreement among economic experts as to whether the dollar would continue dropping, stabilize, or even start rising.

"Who knows," Waterman said, "if the dollar continues to fall, or even if it just levels off a little, our profit picture will continue to improve. On the other hand, we can't rule out a rise in the dollar, in which case the profit picture in the U.K. would be much less certain. We're just going to have to examine the data and make the best projection we can."

After talking things over, Peter and Stan came to the conclusion that the wisest thing to do would be to assume the current rate would remain relatively stable during the first part of the year, and then rise 3 percent in each of the next two quarters. "This allows for some fluctuation, and in any case," said Peter, "we'll be reforecasting on a quarterly basis, so we can keep an eye on the situation and make adjustments for whatever happens in the meantime."

Stan told him the plan for the coming year was almost complete. "The situation in Britain might be up in the air, but the picture here is clearly positive. If the projections for the U.S. are accurate, we might well see the largest single sales increase in the history of the company."

"But what about profits?" asked Peter.

"That's less certain, but I'm optimistic. As you well know, we're breaking a lot of new ground, which is expensive. Any dramatic profit increases might not be felt until a year or more from now. But I'm confident that our efforts will ultimately pay off."

"I agree," remarked Peter. I only hope the Board sees it that way."

Exercise 96　　　Comprehension Check

*Indicate whether the following statements are **True (T)** or **False (F)**.*

1. _____ After he joined AP, Crawford began to realize how important up-to-date financial planning was.

2. _____ It was Waterman's responsibility to come up with a consolidated budget for Audio Performance.

3. _____ Crawford was always closely involved in the financial planning process.

4. _____ Audio Performance exported 60 percent of all its products to the United Kingdom.

5. _____ The value of the dollar had fallen against the British pound in four out of the previous five years.

6. _____ When the value of the dollar fell, prices of goods imported to Britain also fell.

7. _____ The falling prices of AP's products made them more competitive in the U.K.

8. _____ The exchange rate at the time was $1.80 to the pound.

9. _____ Peter and Stan decided to assume that the current exchange rate would remain stable throughout the year.

10. _____ Necessary adjustments to the plan would be made when reforecasts were done.

11. _____ Stan's projections for the following year indicated there would be a slight increase in the volume of sales.

12. _____ Peter was sure the Board would trust Waterman's profit projections.

DISCUSSING ALTERNATIVES

"... there was disagreement among economic experts as to whether the dollar would continue dropping, stabilize, or even start rising."

more formal

— Do you think it'll be necessary to replace all of the old equipment, Mr. Pearson?

— We may have no choice, Jim. On the other hand, with repairs and better maintenance, we may be able to save some of it.

— Why do you suppose our turnover in the sales department is so high, George?

— I think it's either because the commission rate is too low or else our benefits program isn't competitive enough.

— What would you rather see first, Ed — the assembly line or the maintenance department?

— Let's look at the production area first, Bob. The maintenance department can wait.

less formal

— I can't think of a better alternative than raising prices, can you, Sam?

— It may be our only alternative, Mary. We've already cut costs everywhere we can.

— Barbara, I just can't decide whether to accept this job offer or not.

— Well, Sally, you have to look at the pros and cons. Why don't you make a list?

PRESENT PARTICIPLES USED AS ADJECTIVES

"Peter Crawford had learned from long experience that control of a **growing company** was impossible without accurate, up-to-date financial planning."

I saw the train; it was *moving*.
→ I saw the **moving train**. *(participle only)*

I saw the train. It was *moving slowly*.
→ I saw the **slowly moving train**. *(adverb + participle)*

I saw the train. It was *moving slowly down the track*.
→ I saw the **train moving slowly down the track**. *(participle + phrase)*

Exercise 97

Rewrite the sentences using present participles.

Examples: Hank is a salesman who travels.
Hank is a traveling salesman.

Do you know that man? He's standing at the podium.
Do you know that man standing at the podium?

1.   The prices concern me. They're rising steadily.

2.   What are the options that remain?

3.   The company's profits are increasing. We're happy to hear about it.

4.   Jobs are easy to find in an economy that's expanding rapidly.

5.   Customers who pay by check must show some identification.

6.   We heard frequent reports about the situation. It was changing constantly.

7.   People who travel on the weekend should make advance reservations.

8.   The labor problems continue. They will be discussed at the meeting.

Exercise 98 PRESENT OR PAST PARTICIPLE?

Examples: Here's a book that might **interest** you.
It was based on a very   ***interesting***   film.

The rains **damaged** many buildings.
It will be expensive to repair the   ***damaged***   property.

1. John **convinced** almost everyone.
   He offered a _____ argument.

2. Someone **broke** the window.
   The store owner had the _____ window replaced.

3. The election **surprised** many people.
   The _____ results were announced on the evening news.

4. We try to **satisfy** our customers.
   A _____ customer will come back again and again.

5. I asked the ticket agent to **estimate** what time our plane would arrive.
   Five o'clock was the _____ time of arrival.

6. The long drive to Baltimore **tired** us all.
   When the _____ trip was over, we took some time to rest.

7. Peter had to **revise** his proposal before submitting it to the Board.
   The Board then approved the _____ proposal.

8. The reports of declining profits **discouraged** everyone.
   Despite the _____ news, we expect to see improvement by year-end.

9. I wonder who will **win** the game.
   The _____ team will go on to play in the finals.

10. If the currency **stabilizes**, it will make our financial forecasts more accurate.
    A _____ currency would have other advantages, too.

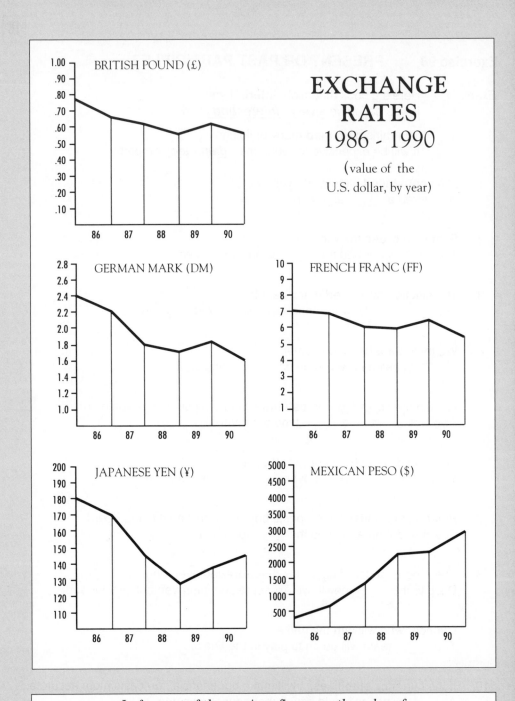

EXCHANGE RATES 1986 - 1990

(value of the U.S. dollar, by year)

BRITISH POUND (£)

GERMAN MARK (DM)

FRENCH FRANC (FF)

JAPANESE YEN (¥)

MEXICAN PESO ($)

In four out of the previous five years the value of the dollar had fallen against the British pound.

USING -*EVER* WORDS

"... we can keep an eye on the situation and make adjustments for **whatever** happens in the meantime."

Someone left a wallet in the office.
→ ***Whoever*** lost it must be looking for it.

It doesn't matter when you call. I'll be there.
→ I'll be there ***whenever*** you call.

You can do **whatever** you want; I don't care.
Walt seems to make friends **wherever** he goes.
Come today or tomorrow, **whichever** is more convenient.
Ship the goods **however** you like. It doesn't matter to me.
Please give the package to **whomever** you see.

Exercise 99

Rewrite the sentences using -*ever* *words.*

Example: You can come to the party with anyone you want.
You can come to the party with whomever you want.

1. I get disconnected every time I try to dial.

2. Someone broke the window. The one who did it should pay for it.

3. I don't have my own office. I use any office that happens to be free.

4. The drive to Berlin is long. It doesn't matter how you go.

5. Order anything you want for dinner — it's my treat!

6. Anywhere you go there's usually a pay phone nearby.

7. Who's in the office next door? He's making a lot of noise.

8. You can give the job to anyone you want.

Exercise 100   SYNONYMS

Choose words from the box that are closest in meaning to those in italics.

Example: Ohio was *(eliminated)* __**ruled out**__ from the list of possible plant sites.

1. There are many factors which must be *(taken into account)* _____ before a decision is made.

2. The fall in the value of the pound *(led to)* _____ a decrease in sales of imported goods.

3. If you don't feel better tomorrow, you should *(ask the advice of)* _____ a doctor.

4. The owners hoped the new products would *(give new life to)* _____ the business.

5. I don't feel our search for an export manager should be *(limited)* _____ to this area.

6. Stan was the one who *(developed)* _____ the consolidated budget.

7. Please feel free to *(ask)* _____ me for any assistance you need.

8. Economists have *(forecast)* _____ a slow but steady economic recovery.

9. The current exchange rate *(corresponds with)* _____ the finance department's earlier projections.

10. We *(believed)* _____ that the value of the dollar would hold steady.

11. After the engineers *(solve)* _____ a few small technical problems, the new model will be ready to go into production.

12. Mr. Crawford would like you to *(start)* _____ on the analysis as soon as possible.

resulted in
ruled out
confined
get moving
matches
revitalize
came up with
projected
call on
work out
considered
consult
assumed

THE PREFIXES *PRE-* AND *RE-*

" ... in any case, we'll be **reforecasting** [the budget] on a quarterly basis ..."

The prefixes *pre- (before* or *in advance)* and *re- (again)* are very common. A T.V. program recorded *in advance* is *pre*recorded. If the program isn't recorded correctly the first time, it has to be *re*recorded. Here are more examples:

prearrange	prejudge	preschedule
preassembly	prepackaged	presell
preheat	prepay	preview
reapply	redone	reorganize
rearrange	refill	resubmit
redesign	relocate	rewrite

Exercise 101

Example: Safety __*precautions*__ are important around any kind of machinery.

1. Most plant employees participated in a _____ program after the plant was modernized.

2. Tom's new health plan didn't cover medical bills for his injury because it was a _____ condition.

3. The company buys _____ application forms from an office supply store.

4. The invention of the automobile _____ the invention of the airplane.

5. If prices go up, can we _____ the contract?

6. Thanks for all your help. I don't know how I can _____ you.

premature
repay
precautions
reconsider
predated
retraining
pre-existing
renegotiate
preprinted

7. The Board has made its decision and will not _____.

8. Your disapproval of the new inventory system is _____. Give it three months, and you'll see how well it works.

Piccadilly Electronics Ltd.

250 Tottenham Court Road • London, WC2

13 September 1990

Mr Benjamin Melnick
Director of Sales
Audio Performance, Inc.
383 Madison Avenue
New York, NY 10017

Dear Mr Melnick

Thank you for sending me the catalogue I requested.

We are planning to expand our selection of imported electronic goods. We are particularly interested in your Tru-Tone line of CD players and changers.

I would appreciate it if you would send me the following information:

- price quotations
- terms of sale and payment
- discount policy
- availability and delivery schedules

I look forward to hearing from you.

Yours sincerely

John Smythe

John Smythe
Purchasing Manager

Telephone: 071-2734751 • Facsimile: 071-2735531

AP's products were becoming more competitive on the British market.

- Describe the positive and negative effects fluctuating exchange rates can have on a company's profitability.

- A company must spend money in order to make money. Discuss.

exchange rate	level off
forecast	rule out
reforecast	in which case...
projection – project *(v)*	conclusion (come to a ~)
involved in	wise – foolish
allow for	remain *(= stay)*
represent *(= stand for)*	fluctuation – fluctuate
majority – minority	up in the air
steadily – steady	might well see ...
assumption – assume	optimistic – pessimistic
economic – economy	break new ground
	ultimately

19 PLANS FOR ACQUIRING CONTROL OF LTE

Crawford had discussed the question of a possible LTE acquisition with Jim Burke over lunch one day. Burke had said he felt the idea was worth pursuing. He added that the Board was open to any reasonable proposal.

A few days later Crawford called a meeting of his top people to discuss the acquisition further. Stan Waterman and Jane Collins arrived in the conference room just before ten o'clock. They were accompanied by AP's general counsel, Phil Hayes, to whom all legal matters were referred. Peter had already examined the LTE financial data, most of which was very encouraging. He was convinced the company could make a major contribution to Audio Performance. In addition, he felt that LTE's distribution network would be ideal for a number of AP's products, beginning, of course, with the Games Master. Peter had asked Stan Waterman, AP's controller, to outline their options.

"There are basically three ways in which we could achieve control," Waterman began. "We could contact LTE's top management and propose a direct merger in which LTE shareholders would be given either cash or AP stock in exchange for their LTE shares. Whether they would approve it or not would depend on the size of our offer and how they felt such a merger would affect LTE."

"But with the company doing so well, how likely would they be to approve it?" asked Jane.

"It's hard to say," Stan answered. "But there's another way. It's also possible to control a company without owning it outright. We could approach several of the largest shareholders individually and try to purchase their shares privately. In the case of LTE there are only seven major shareholders, whose combined shares amount to almost 40 percent of the total stock outstanding. If we could find a way to acquire even half of those shares, we would have effective control."

"And if we can't acquire that many shares?" asked Peter.

"Then we always have the third option of making a tender offer, by which we'd announce publicly our offer to purchase LTE shares at a stated price until a certain date. It would be a little more complicated but would achieve the same objective in the end."

"What do you recommend?" asked Crawford.

"Phil and I have discussed it, and we both feel an approach to the private shareholders would be best," said Waterman, "particularly in this case. A Mrs. Lamb, whose LTE holdings amount to nearly 500,000 shares, has recently passed away. Almost all her holdings were in LTE stock, and her heirs are anxious to diversify the portfolio. Her block would go a long way toward giving us the control we need. Phil has already drafted a letter to the executors of her estate, stating our intentions and making a definite proposal with regard to the purchase of the shares. If this is the direction we decide to take and the proposal is accepted, this procedure would undoubtedly be the least complicated and the least expensive. And even if the offer is turned down, we can still approach the other six major shareholders."

What kind of money are we talking about, Stan?" asked Peter.

"Well, at the present market price of $36 a share and with future prospects for the company as good as they are, I would think an offer in the $42 range might be acceptable. No matter how we work it, we'll have to plan on acquiring at least 500,000 shares."

"So that would mean over $20 million for control. That's a lot of money, but it's not unreasonable," said Peter. "But before we make any offer, it'll have to be approved by the Board. Stan, I'd like you to write up a report of the options we've discussed today, including your recommendation. I'd like to submit it to Mr. Burke at next week's meeting, if at all possible."

Exercise 102   Vocabulary Check

Choose the correct words to complete the sentences.

1. We'd better _____ all the financial data before we approach LTE.
    a. find   b. examine   c. test

2. The Board seemed to be _____ any proposal from Crawford.
    a. open to   b. requiring   c. in favor of

3. We can control LTE even though we don't have _____ ownership of it.
    a. outright   b. correct   c. current

4. One _____ in acquiring LTE is to expand our distribution network.
    a. ideal   b. prospect   c. objective

5. AP will _____ have to offer more than $36 per share for the stock.
    a. usually   b. undoubtedly   c. quietly

6. Mrs. Lamb _____ recently.
    a. passed away   b. sold her stock   c. gave her money away

7. Mrs. Lamb's heirs are _____ make changes in the portfolio.
    a. anxious to   b. hurrying to   c. reluctant to

8. Everything _____ whether or not our offer is accepted.
    a. relies on   b. depends on   c. affects

CLARIFYING INFORMATION

"So that would mean over $20 million for control [of LTE]."

Clarifying meaning:

— What do you think Mr. Burke meant when he said the Board was open to any reasonable proposal?

— The way I understood it, Jeff, the Board would approve the acquisition if it weren't too costly.

— I gather you're not in favor of the acquisition, Ed. Is that what you're trying to tell me?

more formal

— Now, Jane, don't get me wrong. I just meant we should make sure of our own financial position before moving on it.

— There's one thing I'm not quite clear on, Stan. Would you mind explaining a little further?

— Of course not, Jane. What is it you don't understand?

— I don't think I follow you, Bill. Could you clarify what you mean?

— I guess I'm not making myself too clear. Let me put it another way.

less formal

Clarifying when you didn't hear / understand:

• I'm having trouble understanding you. Would you mind speaking a bit more slowly?

• I'm sorry, I can't hear you very well. Could you speak up a little?

• What did you say? I didn't catch it.

RELATIVE CLAUSES WITH PREPOSITIONS

"Then we always have the third option of making a tender offer, **by which** we'd announce publicly our offer to purchase LTE shares at a stated price ..."

Things:	This company is big. *I work* **for it**.
	→ The company *(which) I work* **for** is big. (1) The company **for which** *I work* is big. (2)
People:	That man is British. *I work* **for him**.
	→ The man *(who) I work* **for** is British. (1) The man **for whom** *I work* is British. (2)

(1) spoken form   (2) written form

Exercise 103

Rewrite the sentences using relative clauses with prepositions.

Example: This is the building. I live in it.
This is the building <u>in which</u> I live.

1.   Kathy is one of the people in the office. I can rely on her.

2.   The town is very old. Steve comes from it.

3.   Mr. Parsons is the accountant. You should direct your questions to him.

4.   We stayed at the hotel. You spoke so highly of it.

5.   I'd like you to meet someone. We've spoken about her often.

6.   The conference will be held at the hotel. It's very elegant.

7.   This is a piece of equipment. We can't operate the machine without it.

8.   The shareholders might be willing to sell. Stan was referring to them.

THAT'S *THE WAY* IT IS!

1960 is **the year in which** I was born.
→That's **when** I was born.
→ That's **the year** I was born.

That's **the way** I like my coffee. *(how)*
Tell me about **the time** you met the President! *(when)*
Was that **the reason** you were late? *(why)*
Is this **the place** you recommended we eat? *(where)*

Exercise 104

Rewrite the following sentences using the expressions in parentheses.

Example: My English improved when I traveled in the U.S. *(the year)*
My English improved the year I traveled in the U.S.

1. Manchester is where I'd really like to live. *(the place)*

2. Take the subway — that's how I usually go. *(the way)*

3. I had just returned from Paris when Phillip arrived. *(the day)*

4. Tell us why you decided to move to Montreal. *(the reason)*

5. Call me when you hear from the executor of the estate. *(the minute)*

6. Everyone was impressed with how the plant manager solved the problem. *(the way)*

7. I'll never forget when our car broke down on the highway. *(the time)*

8. I can't figure out why John resigned. *(the reason)*

9. The package arrived when we expected it. *(the afternoon)*

10. Cancun, Mexico, is where we went on vacation last year. *(the place)*

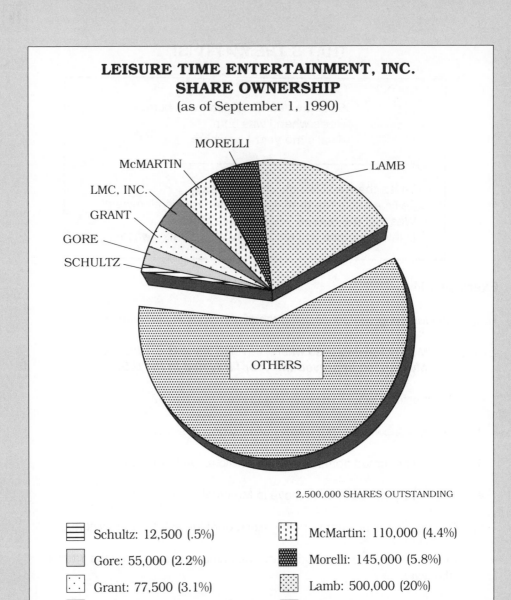

LEISURE TIME ENTERTAINMENT, INC. SHARE OWNERSHIP
(as of September 1, 1990)

MORELLI

McMARTIN

LMC, INC.

GRANT

GORE

SCHULTZ

LAMB

OTHERS

2,500,000 SHARES OUTSTANDING

Schultz: 12,500 (.5%)   McMartin: 110,000 (4.4%)

Gore: 55,000 (2.2%)   Morelli: 145,000 (5.8%)

Grant: 77,500 (3.1%)   Lamb: 500,000 (20%)

LMC, Inc.: 100,000 (4.0%)   Others: 1,500,000 (60%)

LTE had seven major shareholders whose combined shares amounted to almost 40% of the shares outstanding.

OF WHICH vs. OF WHOM

"Peter had already examined the LTE financial data, **most of which** was very encouraging."

Things:	The company has ten offices. Three **of them** are in New York. → The company has ten offices, three **of which** are in New York. The company has ten offices. I've visited three **of them**. → The company has ten offices, three **of which** I've visited.
People:	The company has five vice presidents. Two **of them** are women. → The company has five vice presidents, two **of whom** are women. The company has five vice presidents. I know most **of them**. → The company has five vice presidents, most **of whom** I know.

Exercise 105

*Rewrite the sentences using **of which** or **of whom**.*

Example: John sent me four books. I've already read two of them.
John sent me four books, two of which I've already read.

1. We have three children. All of them are married.

2. The plant is using outdated equipment. We're going to replace most of it.

3. The plant has 300 employees. Half of them work on the assembly line.

4. We saw two films. Neither of them was very interesting.

5. This year I have twenty students. I've taught two of them before.

6. Linda inherited some money. She's already spent half of it.

7. We interviewed four candidates. One of them is outstanding.

8. Tom owns three cars. One of them is a 1964 Jaguar.

Exercise 106   VERBS FOLLOWED BY PREPOSITIONS

Choose the correct prepositions to complete the sentences.

Example: *(in / on / for)*
         Prospects don't look very bright, but we're hoping __*for*__ the best.

1. *(from / to / in)*
    Dr. Kosloff's research resulted _____ the introduction of a popular
    video game.

2. *(on / at / for)*
    My boss complimented me _____ the way I had handled things while
    he was away.

3. *(with / on / to)*
    I've been close friends with George for twelve years now; I know I can rely
    _____ him.

4. *(from / in / against)*
    Harry is very ambitious. He won't let anything prevent him _____
    succeeding.

5. *(to / at / with)*
    I can't answer your question, but I'll refer you _____ someone who
    probably can.

6. *(of / in / to)*
    Mr. Sperry is a lawyer who specializes _____ real estate matters.

7. *(by / in / on)*
    Whether or not we raise prices depends _____ how much labor costs go up.

8. *(on / to / with)*
    Although he didn't agree entirely _____ company policy, the controller
    had to follow it.

9. *(for / at / by)*
    How much have you allowed _____ equipment maintenance in the budget?

10. *(on / in / at)*
    What terms and conditions might LTE insist _____?

USES OF *WAY*

"There are basically three **ways** in which we could achieve control ..."

The word *way* is one heard often and can be used in a variety of *ways*. Here are some examples:

Which way should I turn, right or left?
I met a friend **on my way** to work this morning.
Put the packages in the corner, where they'll be **out of the way**.
On conference calls, we sometimes have **four-way** conversations.
You can get to the center of town **by way of** Main Street.

Exercise 107

Example: Your table is ready. Come right **_this way_**.

1. Excuse me, is this _____ to the train station?

2. Please don't trouble yourself; don't go _____.

3. I have to go to the pharmacy. _____, do you know what time it closes?

4. Would you mind moving your car? It's _____.

5. Peter is very happy _____ you handled this project, Jim.

in some ways
in my way
on the way
by the way
this way
one way or another
out of your way
with the way
the right way

6. _____ to his office in the morning, Bill always stops for coffee.

7. I agree with you _____, but I still can't approve the expenditure.

8. Don't worry about how much it costs. We'll send Tommy to the university _____.

AUDIO PERFORMANCE
383 MADISON AVE., NEW YORK, NY 10017
TEL (212) 921-8500   FAX (212) 921-9449

Philip R. Hayes, Esq.
General Counsel

September 19, 1990

Mr. George R. Welk, Esq.
Phelps, Welk, Riley and Young
6 Montgomery Way
Greenwich, CT 06830

Dear Mr. Welk:

On behalf of Audio Performance, Inc., I have been authorized to submit a formal offer to purchase 499,500 common shares of Leisure Time Entertainment stock currently held in the estate of Mrs. A. H. Lamb.

The shares closed on the NYSE yesterday at $36 even. Audio Performance is prepared at this time to offer $42 a share, in cash, to acquire the entire block of shares.

This offer will remain in effect until midnight, September 30, 1990. Would you please convey the terms of the offer to the heirs of the Lamb estate? If they are interested in pursuing this matter, please contact me at the above address.

Yours truly,

Philip R. Hayes

PRH/jd

*Phil Hayes had already drafted a letter to the executors of
Mrs. Lamb's estate, offering to purchase LTE shares.*

- Great size in corporations is bad: it discourages innovation, limits competition, and eventually causes higher prices. Discuss.

- Why do companies acquire other companies?

pursue (~ an idea)	private(ly) – public(ly)
open (be ~ to)	amount to
counsel (general, legal ~)	tender offer
refer (~ s.t. / s.o. to ...)	holdings
convince s.o. to ... – convinced	portfolio (financial ~)
contribution – contribute	pass away
achieve (~ control)	heir – will *(n)*
merger	executor
shareholder	estate
block of shares	anxious to
depend on	intention(s)
affect	undoubtedly
outright (own s.t. ~)	prospect *(n)*

20 A MATTER FOR THE LAWYERS

Peter Crawford was returning from a sales meeting on the 23rd floor. "Any messages, Karen?" he asked, stopping in front of his secretary's desk.

"Yes, Mr. Martinelli called to say he wouldn't be free until at least 2:30," Karen answered. "He said he was supposed to join you for lunch. And Stan Waterman called too — he said he'd get back to you later. He mentioned that it was in reference to the LTE acquisition."

"Hmm ... That should be interesting. Is that all?"

"You asked me to remind you to call Mr. Hayes as soon as you got back from the meeting."

"Oh, yes. Would you get him for me now, please?" Peter walked into his office, sat down, and opened the newspaper lying on his desk.

A moment later, Karen had Hayes on the line. "Phil," Peter began, "have you seen the Play World ad in *News Today*? I'm no legal expert, but it looks to me as if we might have a patent infringement on our hands."

The ad showed a device called the Play Machine. Manufactured by a small Chicago-based firm called Play World, Inc., the machine's design appeared to have been copied directly from AP's Games Master.

"Yes, Peter, as a matter of fact, I've already gotten hold of one of the devices. I sent it over to our technical people and had it checked out. Play World seems to have used a very similar, though maybe not identical, design. The two are close enough that a good case for infringement could probably be made."

"This really worries me, Phil. We've got a lot riding on the Games Master," Peter said. "Do you think we should take legal action?"

"Well, patent litigation is known to be long and complicated, and can get very expensive. On the other hand, by suing, we would show the industry that we're aggressive and willing to fight for our rights. That could do a lot to prevent future infringement attempts. In addition, a successful lawsuit would help establish the patent's validity and encourage the industry to honor it."

"It seems to me," said Peter, "that since we're much larger, we could probably afford a court case more easily than Play World. But the last thing we need right now is a long, drawn-out court battle. Is there anything we can do short of taking them to court?"

"It may not go that far," Hayes replied. "In many cases, once legal action is threatened, an out-of-court settlement can be reached before suit is formally filed. Our best response at this point might be to send out a letter outlining the problem and advising them of our intentions. Then it'll be up to them to make the next move."

"All right, that sounds reasonable. But I'd like you to begin preparing our case anyway. If Play World doesn't back down, I want to be ready to go to court."

Exercise 108   Comprehension Check

Choose the best way to complete the sentences or answer the questions.

1. Waterman's phone call to Crawford was in reference to ...
    a)   a lunch appointment.
    b)   the LTE acquisition.
    c)   the sales meeting.

2. The first person to see Play World's advertisement in *News Today* was ...
    a)   Phil Hayes.
    b)   Peter Crawford.
    c)   Karen Lawrence.

3. The design of the Play Machine is _____ that of the Games Master.
    a)   identical to
    b)   very similar to
    c)   very different from

4. Which of the following is <u>not</u> true about patent litigation?
    a)   It's very expensive.
    b)   It can be settled fairly quickly.
    c)   It's a complicated process.

5. AP can probably afford a lawsuit better than Play World because ...
    a)   AP has its own corporate counsel.
    b)   the case against Play World is so strong.
    c)   AP is larger and has more resources than Play World.

6. Crawford asked Hayes to start preparing their case because ...
    a)   he wants to show that AP is willing to fight for its rights.
    b)   he doesn't believe an out-of-court settlement is possible.
    c)   he wants to be prepared just in case the case goes to court.

ON THE PHONE: MESSAGES

"And Stan Waterman called too — he said he'd get back to you later."

— Good morning. This is Mr. Williams at Shop-Way. I'd like to speak with Mr. Melnick, please.

— I'm sorry. I'm afraid Mr. Melnick is in a meeting at the moment. May I take a message, Mr. Williams?

— Yes, please. Would you have him call me? Tell him it's in reference to the delivery schedule.

— All right. I'll see that he gets the message as soon as he's free.

more formal

— Hello. Is Mr. Hawkins in? This is Mr. Richards.

— No, I'm sorry, he's out of town until Thursday. Is there something I can help you with?

— No, that's all right. I'll call back at the end of the week.

— Yes, can I speak to Tom Carlson, please?

— Sorry, he's out to lunch. Do you want to leave a message?

— This is Nancy Hart. Would you ask him to call me? The number is area code 703-394-2325.

less formal

— O.K. I'll give him the message when he comes in.

— Hi, this is Christine. Is Carol there?

— No, she's not. Can I take a message?

— Just tell her I called. I'll try her again later.

PRESENT *vs.* PERFECT INFINITIVES

> "[Mr. Martinelli] said he **was supposed to join** you for lunch."

Present Infinitive:	I *was* surprised **to hear** about Bill's illness. I *'m* not surprised **to hear** that he has resigned.
Perfect Infinitive:	Bill *is* lucky **to have found** such a good doctor. I *was* sorry **not to have been** here on Bill's last day.

Exercise 109

Examples: I didn't call you yesterday.
But I intended ___*to call you yesterday*___ .

Larry didn't get a promotion.
He's disappointed ___*not to have gotten a promotion*___ .

1. I'd like to leave for lunch in about an hour.
    I'll be ready _____ at 12:30 p.m.

2. You had us over for dinner last Saturday.
    It was very nice of you _____ us over.

3. Do you think we'll see an improvement in sales before year-end?
    We hope _____ some improvement by then.

4. I don't see Nick's name on the list.
    I'm surprised _____ it there.

5. The ad executive hasn't consulted anyone about the matter.
    He's foolish _____ someone.

6. I'm positive Ms. Jenkins has never paid this bill.
    But she claims _____ it a week ago.

7. The new accountant hasn't been trained on the computer.
    He's supposed _____ by now.

8. Our own lawyers will handle the case.
    We don't want anyone else _____ it.

INFINITIVES AFTER *SEEM* AND *APPEAR*

"... the machine's design **appeared to have been copied**
directly from AP's Games Master."

Present Infinitive:	I think Tom **is** very busy. → He *seems* **to be** very busy. → When I saw him yesterday, he *seemed* **to be** busy, too.
Perfect Infinitive:	I think Ann **enjoyed** her vacation. → She *appears* **to have enjoyed** her vacation. → Everyone agreed she *appeared* **to have enjoyed** it.

Exercise 110

Complete the following sentences using present or perfect infinitives.

Example: Mary said she wasn't tired, but she appeared **_to be tired_** .

1.   I think the economy has improved. At least it seems _____.

2.   Are you upset? You seem _____ about something.

3.   Ned said he hadn't gained weight, but he appeared to me _____.

4.   The labor problem wasn't serious. But at the time, it seemed _____.

5.   The lawyer's argument has convinced me, and it appears _____ the other members of the jury as well.

6.   Mr. Porter is making a good living in sales. At least he appears _____.

7.   We weren't sure whether news of the merger had been made public, but it appeared _____.

8.   The first applicant we interviewed had a positive attitude. At least she appeared _____.

USING INFINITIVES: GENERAL BELIEFS

> "... patent litigation **is known to be** long and complicated ..."

People *say* that George **is** this year's top salesperson.
→ George *is said* **to be** this year's top salesperson.

They *say* he **was** the top one last year, too.
→ He *is said* **to have been** the top one last year, too.

They *said* he **had sold** more than anyone else.
→ He *was said* **to have sold** more than anyone else.

The thief who broke into our house **is believed to** still **be** in the area.
That hotel **was said to be** one of the most luxurious on the coast.
Mr. Caldwell **is known to have made** millions in the stock market.
The lawsuit **was reported to have been settled** out of court.

Exercise 111

Rewrite the sentences using present or perfect infinitives.

Example:　Everyone knows smoking is dangerous to your health.
　　　　　Smoking is known to be dangerous to your health.

1.　Some think the higher accident rate is due to the increase in the speed limit.

2.　Most people believe that Lincoln was a great President.

3.　They say that *Emilio's* is the best restaurant in New York.

4.　Everyone knows the company has made some bad investments.

5.　We think that Henry is in line for an important assignment.

6.　The police assumed the embezzler had left the country.

7.　People believed that Columbus had discovered a new route to India.

8.　Some people think real estate is the best long-term investment.

To P.C.
Date 9/20   Time 10:35

While You Were Out

M R Jeff Knowles
of Data Masters
Phone 212-565-1244 2079
AREA CODE   NUMBER   EXTENSION

TELEPHONED		PLEASE CALL	
CALLED TO SEE YOU		WILL CALL AGAIN	
WANTS TO SEE YOU		**URGENT**	
RETURNED YOUR CALL	✓		

Message will be in the office anytime after 2pm.

KL
Operator

To P.C.
Date 9/20   Time 11:45

While You Were Out

M rs. Crawford
of
Phone
AREA CODE   NUMBER   EXTENSION

TELEPHONED		PLEASE CALL	
CALLED TO SEE YOU	✓	WILL CALL AGAIN	✓
WANTS TO SEE YOU		**URGENT**	
RETURNED YOUR CALL			

Message

To P.C.
Date 9/20   Time 11:20

While You Were Out

M Stan W.
of
Phone
AREA CODE   NUMBER   EXTENSION

TELEPHONED	✓	PLEASE CALL	
CALLED TO SEE YOU		WILL CALL AGAIN	✓
WANTS TO SEE YOU		**URGENT**	
RETURNED YOUR CALL			

Message Has some news from Phil Hayes about ITE shares.

KL
Operator

To P.C.
Date 9/20   Time 11:10

While You Were Out

M s. Martinelli
of
Phone 212   872-1420
AREA CODE   NUMBER   EXTENSION

TELEPHONED	✓	PLEASE CALL	
CALLED TO SEE YOU		WILL CALL AGAIN	
WANTS TO SEE YOU		**URGENT**	
RETURNED YOUR CALL			

Message must cancel 12:30 lunch appt - meeting with architect running longer than expected.

KL
Operator

When he returned from his sales meeting, Peter asked Karen if there were any messages.

Exercise 112   **OPPOSITES**

Choose the opposites from the words in the box.

Example: The inventory taken was inaccurate, so there was an **oversupply** of
some parts and a ___*shortage*___ of others.

1. You seem to be talking in **generalities**. Could
    we get down to _____?

2. I try not to **get angry** because it's hard for me
    to _____.

3. Many accidents are **caused** by careless drivers.
    These accidents could easily be _____.

4. Our attorney discussed the case with us **in brief**;
    we haven't had a chance to talk _____.

5. If the firm hadn't filed an amended return to
    _____ the money, they would have **lost** it.

6. The firm was **anxious** to buy the building, but the
    owners were _____ to sell.

7. We must **consider** both possibilities; neither of
    them can be _____ yet.

8. We thought Valerie was **foolish** to open her own
    agency, but it turned out to be a _____ move.

9. A **pessimist** would say that the glass is half empty;
    an _____ would say it's half full.

10. You should **stand up** for your rights. If you _____ now, the
    progress you've made will be lost.

11. When the value of the currency is _____, it is much easier to make
    forecasts than when it **fluctuates**.

12. The report of lower net profits was **discouraging**, but it was _____
    to hear that our margin had improved slightly.

back down
reluctant
recover
steady
specifics
shortage
optimist
in detail
wise
encouraging
calm down
prevented
ruled out

USES OF *HAVE*

"A moment later, Karen **had** Hayes on the line."

The verb *have* has a lot of uses. Let's look at a few of them:

If you don't **have time to** do it yourself, **have** your assistant do it.
It's getting late; we **had better** hurry.
We'd like to **have you over** for dinner sometime soon.
Did you **have trouble** finding a taxi?
I **have** Mr. Ritter **on the line**. Shall I **have** him hold for you?
Tom wants to see you. It **has something to do with** the lawsuit.

Exercise 113

Example: I'll see you next Monday. Have ___*a nice weekend*___!

1. Sales are down; expenses are up — we have _____ on our hands.

2. I'm very thirsty. Could I please have _____?

3. If you have _____, I'd like to discuss something with you.

4. I'm sorry to have missed your party. I had _____ and was in bed all weekend.

5. The report is urgent. Can you have _____ by tonight?

6. The driving conditions were terrible. We almost had _____.

7. I only had _____ at the balance sheet, but the situation seems to have improved.

8. Tom needs a new car, and he has _____ a sporty model.

9. I'd like to help you out, but I have _____ at the moment. Would tomorrow be all right?

10. If you're thinking of investing in the stock market, talk to Stan. He has _____ what's going on.

---

a quick look

a nice weekend

a terrible cold

a few minutes

a big problem

my hands full

an accident

it on my desk

a good feel for

something to drink

his eye on

AUDIO PERFORMANCE
383 MADISON AVE., NEW YORK, NY 10017
TEL (212) 921-8500   FAX (212) 921-9449

Philip R. Hayes, Esq.
General Counsel

October 18, 1990

Mr. Charles Campbell, President
Play World, Inc.
3365 Chestnut Street
Chicago, Illinois 60601

Dear Mr. Campbell:

Your company is presently manufacturing and selling a product you call the "Play Machine."

A recent analysis by our engineering staff has revealed that it makes use of technology, particularly in the area of micro-circuits, for which patents have been registered with the United States Patent Office in the name of Audio Performance, Inc.

We call on you to cease immediately any further manufacture and sale of "Play Machine" or any other product that makes use of this proprietary technology. Should you fail to comply with this request, we will have no alternative but to initiate legal action.

Sincerely,

Philip R. Hayes

Philip R. Hayes

Registered - Return
Receipt Requested

PRH/jd

The "Play Machine" appeared to have been copied from AP's Games Master.
Philip Hayes sent Play World, Inc. a letter threatening litigation.

- The U.S. has become known as a "litigating society," with individuals suing everyone from major corporations to next-door neighbors. How common are such lawsuits in your country? Under what circumstances might you sue someone?

- Trade names can become very valuable and have to be protected by the company which owns them. However, a company can lose the exclusive right to a name. How can this happen?

Vocabulary

in reference to	attempt *(n, v)*
patent *(n, v)* – infringe on	validity – valid
infringement	honor *(v)* (~ a patent)
have ... on one's hands	drawn-out *(= long)*
...-based (Chicago~)	battle *(n)*
have ... riding on ...	short of
litigation	once *(conj)* – threaten (to)
court (~ case)	be threatened
sue	settlement
lawsuit (file a ~)	reach
aggressive	make a move
rights (legal ~)	back down
fight for (one's rights)	

21 THE TRU-TONE PICTURE BEGINS TO CHANGE

It was one of those unusually mild days in late October. The sky was blue, the sun was shining, and the New York air was crystal clear. On mornings like this Peter would often take the time to walk the 20 blocks to his office.

Now as he stood at the window of the Audio Performance conference room, Peter recalled his morning walk and how pleasant it had been. But his thoughts soon returned to more practical matters, particularly since the day might prove to be a turning point in Tru-Tone's troublesome sales history. Peter had called a meeting to discuss the results of the new advertising and pricing policy in the New England test market. In fact, Ben Melnick, Steve Blake, Jeff Martinelli, and Jack Bell were due in the conference room any minute.

When everyone had arrived and coffee had been served, Peter opened the meeting. "Gentlemen, we have some good news," he said, "Ben, why don't you tell us what's been happening with Tru-Tone?"

"I'd be happy to," Melnick said, rising from his chair. He walked to the opposite end of the table and placed a transparency on the overhead projector. The numbers illustrated how Tru-Tone sales had been climbing in nearly all the major cities in the New England test area.

"As you can see, sales have nearly doubled since the campaign began," he said. "This means that our advertising is right on the mark. It's reaching just the segment of the population we targeted."

Ben went on to explain, however, that because of the price cut and the heavy advertising costs charged against Tru-Tone, profits on the increased sales were off about 13 percent from the previous year. "But if the upward trend in sales continues," Melnick concluded, "the profit picture should definitely improve."

"Thanks, Ben," Peter said as Melnick returned to his seat. "I'm glad to hear such encouraging news. But we're still left with an important question — will the trend continue, or will it level off over the next few months? Jack, what's your opinion?"

"Well, Peter," Bell began, "An advertising campaign takes time to become effective. I believe what we've been seeing in the past few weeks is only the beginning. By this time next month even more people will have been exposed to our T.V. and print media promotion. And remember, we still have the Christmas season ahead of us, when sales should really peak."

"I agree," said Blake. "Consumers are just beginning to respond to the younger image we're trying to project. And once the new, more compact models go on the market, sales should really start to climb."

"All right, gentlemen," said Peter. "It looks as if we're on the right track. And if sales do continue to increase, we might consider expanding the campaign to the rest of the country sooner than we'd planned." Peter turned to Martinelli. "And while we're on the subject, what about production schedules, Jeff? Would we be able to meet a substantial increase in demand at our present capacity?"

"We're actually operating at only 70 percent of capacity," said Jeff. "With the improvements we've been making at the plants, we could easily step up our rate of production to meet demand, particularly if we add extra shifts."

"And what about profits?" Peter asked.

"With a projected increase in sales of, say 30 percent, profits should return to last year's level within a few months of a nationwide campaign." Jeff continued, "And we can expect even greater profits once we start production at the new plant next year."

"That's what I like to hear!" Peter sounded confident. He was convinced that total profits would grow quickly after the full marketing program was introduced and the Greenville plant became operational. Yet he couldn't help but have second thoughts. Would the Board be equally encouraged by the New England test results? He had taken a serious risk, but it was too late to turn back.

Exercise 114   Vocabulary Check

Choose the correct words to complete the sentences.

1. Do you happen to _____ Jim Burke's phone number?
    a) tell   b) recall   c) call

2. The forecast was _____. We didn't have to make adjustments.
    a) on the mark   b) on time   c) on schedule

3. Profits are _____ over 10 percent due to falling sales.
    a) gone   b) off   c) out

4. Having borrowed to avoid a takeover, the firm _____ a large debt.
    a) was left with   b) took on   c) wanted

5. Sales _____ in December. It's always our best month.
    a) fall   b) peak   c) level off

6. I _____ about accepting the job, but I signed the contract anyway.
    a) considered   b) had second thoughts   c) was convinced

ADDING INFORMATION

"And while we're on the subject, what about
production schedules, Jeff?"

*more
formal*

– Should I send a copy of the letter to Mr. Burke, Mr. Crawford?

– That's a good idea, Karen. And now that you mention it, we'd better send copies to the other Board members as well.

– We're still looking for ways to lower production costs, Mr. Pearson.

– I know it's not easy, Jack. Oh, while we're on the subject, I meant to ask you for a copy of this month's production figures.

– Mrs. Hill, I wanted to remind you that I'm taking Thursday off.

– Oh, that's right, Amy. And incidentally, I won't be here on Friday.

– I haven't heard from Steven lately. Do you know what he's up to?

– As a matter of fact, I saw him a few days ago. He's doing well.

*less
formal*

– Did you hear that Mrs. Hart is finally going to retire?

– Yes, I did. That reminds me, I've been meaning to ask you what happened to Bill's secretary. Did she quit?

– Did you happen to see the T.V. program on Van Gogh last night?

– Yes. Wasn't it fascinating? By the way, there's an exhibit of his work coming to the art museum next month.

INTERROGATIVE NOUN CLAUSES

> "Ben, why don't you tell us **what's been happening** with Tru-Tone?"

Do you know ...?   **who that man is**
I don't remember ...   **where he came from**
I'm interested in ...   **how he got here**
I'm concerned about ...   **whether he's staying**

Who he is ...   doesn't matter
Where he came from ...   isn't important
How he got here ...   is not yet clear
What he's doing ...   doesn't concern us

Exercise 115

Example: What were Peter and Stan talking about?
              Everyone wondered ___*what they were talking about*___ .

1.   Where does the lawsuit go from here?
       _____ is up to the legal department.

2.   What did Bill do to offend you?
       Didn't he apologize for _____?

3.   Whom should I consult on this matter?
       Do you have any idea _____?

4.   Is Mr. Simpson going to accept the job offer?
       I'm not sure if _____.

5.   What time does Jill arrive? How much traffic is there?
       _____ depends on _____.

6.   Has the monthly balance sheet been prepared yet?
       I wonder if _____.

7.   Why did the company lose the contract?
       _____ is something no one can explain.

8.   Where will the meeting be held?
       We'd like to know _____.

USES OF *WILL* AND *WOULD*

> " ... Peter **would** often take the time to walk the 20 blocks to his office."

Future:	Malcolm **will** arrive at Heathrow at 9:00 a.m. tomorrow. At the time, I didn't know the flight **would** be delayed.
Habitual actions:	Ed is quiet; he'**ll** sit there for hours and **won't** say a word. My son **would play** outside all day when he was small.
Capability:	My new car **will** go 100 m.p.h., but it **won't** start in the cold. I thought it **wouldn't** start today, but it did.
Refusal / willingness:	I **will** help you with the report, but I **won't** type it for you. Ann **would** come in early, but she **wouldn't** work late.

Exercise 116

Which is closest in meaning?

Example: **Won't anyone** help me? __c__

    a) Doesn't   b) Can't   **c) Isn't anyone**
       anyone   anyone   **willing to**

1. This elevator **will hold** up to 20 people. ___

    a) often holds   b) can hold   c) is willing to hold

2. **We would** spend summers in the country when I was young. ___

    a) We used to   b) We could   c) We were willing to

3. Bill loves to read when he has time. **He'll sit** for hours without looking up. ___

    a) He can sit   b) He often sits   c) He's willing to sit

4. Terri's supervisor **wouldn't** let her have yesterday off. ___

    a) didn't use to   b) couldn't   c) wasn't willing to

5. Everyone believed sales **would** continue climbing. ___

    a) were able to   b) were going to   c) used to

Exercise 117

*Complete the following sentences using **will** or **would**.*

1. _____ you like something to drink?

2. _____ the results of the test marketing be ready by May?

3. When I was in school I _____ study hard every night.

4. Many people _____ rather live near their place of work.

5. The weather around here is unpredictable; it _____ rain one moment and be sunny the next.

6. If we relocated outside the city, our overhead _____ go down.

7. When I bought that house, I had no idea it _____ soon double in value.

8. I believe the judge _____ find the man guilty as charged.

Exercise 118

Fill in the words closest in meaning to those in italics.

Example: Before I go to Egypt I *(will)* __**am going to**__ learn some Arabic.

1. My last boss *(would)* _____ light up a cigar before making important announcements.

2. In general, compact cars *(will)* _____ get much better mileage than larger ones.

3. The manager *(will)* _____ listen to suggestions, but he has the final decision.

4. Philip said he *(would)* _____ leave a message, but I never heard from him.

5. The weatherman predicts it *(will)* _____ get milder before the weekend.

6. I *(wouldn't)* _____ sign the contract until I had read it.

was going to
am going to
is going to
used to
refused to
can
is willing to

OVERALL SALES: NEW ENGLAND
October 1990

Sales (in thousands of $)

WEEK: 1, 2, 3, 4

TRU-TONE SALES
NEW ENGLAND TEST MARKET
October 1990

	Oct 5	Oct 12	Oct 19	Oct 26
Boston, MA	130,400	163,500	273,200	311,000
Stamford, CT	32,600	39,600	59,000	71,000
Providence, RI	29,340	38,500	55,600	68,200
Hartford, CT	26,080	35,200	48,200	60,300
New Haven, CT	25,960	32,300	44,100	58,100
Worcester, MA	25,620	31,900	43,900	57,900
Springfield, MA	23,820	28,400	37,200	48,200
Manchester, NH	15,560	19,100	28,300	35,900
Portland, ME	11,040	10,700	10,900	10,600
Burlington, VT	6,500	8,200	11,300	13,600
Totals	326,920	407,400	611,700	734,800

Tru-Tone sales had been climbing in all the major cities in New England.

SUCH vs. SO

"I'm glad to hear **such** encouraging news."

so *(+ adjective / adverb)*	**such** *(+ noun)*
The food in the restaurant was **so** *bad (that)* we refused to pay the bill.	The restaurant served **such** *bad food (that)* we refused to pay the bill.
	They served **such** *a bad meal (that)* we refused to pay the bill.
Paul works **so** *efficiently (that)* he never wastes a moment.	Paul works with **such** *efficiency (that)* he never wastes a moment.
	His *efficiency* is **such that** he never wastes a moment.
I'm surprised the accident did **so much** *damage*.	I'm surprised the accident did **such** *a large amount of damage*.
How did the accident leave **so many** *marks* on the car?	How did the accident leave **such** *a large number of marks* on the car?

Exercise 119

*Complete the following sentences using **so** or **such**.*

1. The potential payoff was _____ low that the deal wasn't worth the risk.

2. I'm sorry to leave in _____ a hurry, but I have another appointment.

3. There was _____ much noise that I couldn't concentrate on my work.

4. His excitement was _____ that he couldn't hold it in.

5. Ed is _____ a pessimist! He never looks at the bright side of things.

6. The sky is crystal clear; we haven't had _____ nice weather in weeks.

7. If the house weren't _____ expensive, I'd seriously consider buying it.

8. I didn't expect the mechanic to charge me _____ much for _____ a simple job.

Exercise 120   **IDIOMS**

Choose the correct prepositions to complete the idioms.

Example: *(in / on / to)*
It's important that the new models go **_on_** the market well before the peak of the holiday season.

1. *(at / to / on)*
We asked our neighbors to keep an eye _____ the house while we were away.

2. *(of / with / on)*
If you could get hold _____ a copy of the report for me, I'd really appreciate it.

3. *(with / by / for)*
Your letter of application must be accompanied _____ a résumé.

4. *(out / on / up)*
The only way to step _____ our production in Baltimore would be to add another shift.

5. *(in / on / for)*
If two of the programmers quit at the same time, we would have a real problem _____ our hands.

6. *(for / on / in)*
Our first choice for the position didn't accept our offer, so we had to settle _____ our second choice.

7. *(on / over / out)*
A price increase will be a last resort, but it can't be ruled _____ completely.

8. *(to / up / over)*
Unless your outstanding balance is paid off by the end of the month, we'll have no choice but to take the matter _____ court.

9. *(for / through / up)*
Jane said she'd work late to make _____ for the time she missed when she was sick.

10. *(in / to / on)*
We must win this contract — the future of the firm is riding _____ it!

|||||||||||||HARBOR ELECTRONICS||||

October 29, 1990

Mr. Charles Cooper, Order Dept.
Audio Performance, Inc.
383 Madison Avenue
New York, NY 10017

Dear Mr. Cooper:

I am pleased to inform you that our sales of Tru-Tone products have been increasing steadily. Therefore we would like to modify our Purchase Order 5735 of October 11, 1990, as follows:

Item:	Original Qty.:	Increase to:
CD-1700 CD Players	30	50
CD-2300 Portable CD Players	30	50
SCD-75 Rack Systems	25	40
SP-5 Speakers	40	60

We would appreciate it greatly if you could arrange delivery by November 21st.

Sincerely yours,

Tom Burns

Tom Burns
Manager

Encl.: Purchase Order 5735

1437 BOYLSTON ST. • BOSTON, MA 02116 • TELEPHONE: (617) 266-1024 • FAX: (617) 266-7046

Tru-Tone sales had increased throughout the New England test area during the month of October.

- What factors should be considered when determining prices of products at wholesale and retail levels?

- Why don't increased sales always result in increased profits?

mild	be left with
recall	be exposed to
turning point	promotion (advertising ~)
troublesome	peak *(v, n)*
any minute	be on the right / wrong track
transparency	step up *(= increase)*
overhead projector	demand (meet the ~)
climb *(v) (= increase)*	shift *(n)*
on the mark	have second thoughts
be off *(= down)*	turn back
trend	

22 FOCUSING ON EXPORT SALES

"Alan, I'd like you to meet Stan Waterman, Ed Pearson, and Jane Collins. Ben, you and Alan already know each other."

Peter had called a meeting of his executive staff to introduce Alan Fischer, the man he had just named to head up the firm's new export department. Fischer had a great deal of experience in export sales, having worked in the electronics field for over 15 years as an overseas sales representative. During his years in the field he had acquired a good working command of several foreign languages, including German, French, and Spanish. He was currently working out of Los Angeles as West Coast sales manager for Crowe Products, one of AP's chief competitors. But he had been anxious to get back into a foreign environment, and the move to Audio Performance seemed ideal.

"Alan will be based in London and will be reporting to Ben," Peter began. "His first assignment will be to set up a sales office. He comes to us with extensive contacts in both Europe and Latin America, but he'll be focusing most of his attention on Europe for at least a year."

Crawford went on to mention further details on the specifics of Fischer's background in the industry and then asked him to say a few words about how he planned to handle his assignment.

"From the figures I've seen and from what Peter and Ben have told me, it's clear that export sales haven't been given the attention they deserve," Alan began. "The business you do abroad has developed more or less by itself. You've really only been filling orders, rather than selling aggressively. I believe there's tremendous potential for the AP line outside the United States, particularly in Europe, but we'll have to go after it carefully, systematically, and with a great deal of planning.

"AP's exports currently represent only 16 percent of sales, totaling around $26 million. As I've already told Mr. Crawford, I am confident I can double that figure over the next 24 months. In addition, I understand there are constant complaints about problems and delays encountered in getting goods out of Customs. Here, for example, is the bill of lading for a large shipment to the United Kingdom. The issue date is May 3rd, but I'm told the goods weren't released until last week. That's more than a six-month delay! This is just the kind of thing we can avoid by streamlining our procedures. One of my first priorities will be to set up warehousing facilities in the U.K. so each individual order won't have to be shipped out of the U.S."

Fischer was a hit with everyone. He spent most of that day and the next in meetings, familiarizing himself with the AP operation. He met with Stan Waterman to get a briefing on financial reporting procedures; Stan told him he would have to get to work right away on an administrative budget for the coming year.

Peter had asked Fischer to work with Jane Collins on the details of the relocation itself. Fischer was to submit a written estimate of the various costs involved, including airfare for himself and his family, shipment of his personal belongings, and temporary living expenses in London until he got settled.

By the end of the second day, Fischer had completed his talks and was ready to return to L.A. He had already given notice to his employers at Crowe and would leave them on December 15th. He planned to take a couple of weeks off and would return to New York on January 3rd for further discussions with Peter. He intended to leave for London on January 10th and hoped to be able to locate office space and be operational there by March.

As Crawford and Fischer shook hands at the elevator, it was clear that they had already established a good relationship. "Welcome aboard, Alan. I'm looking forward to working with you!"

Exercise 121   Comprehension Check

Choose the best way to complete the sentences.

1. Alan Fischer, whom Peter had named to head AP's export department, ...
    a) was originally from Europe.
    b) had been a sales representative in a number of fields.
    c) had over 15 years of experience.

2. One major reason Fischer accepted the position with AP was because ...
    a) he spoke several languages.
    b) he wanted to return to a foreign environment.
    c) he had become friends with Peter.

3. According to Fischer, AP's export sales ...
    a) could be doubled with aggressive selling.
    b) had been weak in spite of aggressive selling.
    c) had doubled in the past year.

4. At that time, AP ...
    a) had a small warehouse in the U.K.
    b) shipped each order from the U.S.
    c) had just finished streamlining existing procedures.

5. AP would <u>not</u> reimburse Fischer for ...
    a) purchase of personal belongings.
    b) airfare for himself and his family.
    c) temporary housing.

COMPLAINTS

"... I understand there are constant complaints about problems and delays encountered in getting goods out of Customs."

more formal

— I think there might be a problem with our dinner bill. The total doesn't seem to be correct.

— I'm terribly sorry, sir. Here, let me have it and I'll adjust it for you right away.

— Good morning. This is Mrs. Lee at UEI. I'm afraid the shipment of office supplies you delivered this morning wasn't complete.

— I'm very sorry, Mrs. Lee. Give me the order number and tell me what's missing. I'll take care of it for you.

— I'd like to return this VCR and get my money back. I bought it less than a month ago, and I'm just not satisfied with its performance.

— I'm sorry, but unless there's something actually wrong with it, I can't take it back.

— I think I'd better speak to the manager, if you don't mind.

less formal

— Hello ... PDQ? Listen, I sent an important package via your air express on Monday. It still hasn't arrived and I'm very unhappy about it. Delivery was guaranteed within two days.

— It's unusual, but it does happen. All I can do is put a trace on it for you. Do you have the airbill number?

— Is that the best you can do? Well, I guess I have no choice. But I certainly don't think I should have to pay for it.

REFLEXIVE PRONOUNS

"[Fischer] spent most of that day ... familiarizing **himself** with the AP operation."

My children are still too young to dress **themselves**.
The coffeepot turns **itself** off automatically.

Ann bought **herself** some new clothes.
Ed left **himself** a note so he'd remember our lunch date.

Einstein **himself** had trouble passing math in school.
My husband really enjoys football. I **myself** don't care for it.

There's a lot of food; **help yourself**!
My wife and I prefer to travel **by ourselves**.

Exercise 122

Fill in the correct reflexive or personal pronouns.

Examples: I hear that you're going to Mexico. Enjoy _**yourself**_ !

Did your teacher give _**you**_ a test today?

1. Mr. Crawford _____ answered my letter!

2. When the nurse weighed _____, I discovered I'd lost five pounds.

3. This product is so popular it practically sells _____.

4. Rita must have musical talent. She taught _____ to play the piano.

5. The guests weren't assigned to specific tables; they all seated _____.

6. Our suggestions made _____ unpopular with the other employees.

7. One seldom sees _____ as others do.

8. Charles looked so different that I almost didn't recognize _____.

REFLEXIVE vs. PERSONAL PRONOUNS
AFTER PREPOSITIONS

"Fischer was to submit a written estimate of the various costs involved, including airfare **for himself** and his family ..."

Personal: *(referring to location)*	Where is	your suitcase? the newspaper? the chair?	– I have it with **me**. – I put it beside **me**. – I pulled it toward **me**.
Reflexive: *(referring to subject)*	Most people like to talk about **themselves**. You're a great success! You must be proud of **yourself**! Having won the game, I was very pleased with **myself**.		

Exercise 123

Fill in the correct reflexive or personal pronouns.

Examples: I saw someone running toward _**me**_ .

You don't sound very sure of _**yourself**_ .

1.   Mary doesn't study hard, but she does well in spite of _____ .

2.   From inside the plane we could see clouds beneath _____ .

3.   Sam doesn't care about other people; he's only interested in _____ .

4.   I always keep my glasses on the desk next to _____ .

5.   When you travel abroad, you must carry your passport with _____ .

6.   The men saw the building in front of _____ .

7.   Instead of feeling sorry for _____ , you should try to improve things.

8.   Ed takes himself too seriously; he should learn to laugh at _____ .

9.   We don't believe the report; we'd like to see for _____ .

10.   You and your wife are very kind; it was nice of _____ to have us over.

REFLEXIVE PRONOUNS *vs. EACH OTHER*

"Ben, you and Alan already know **each other**."

Reflexive: **Reciprocal:**

Bill saw himself; Ann saw herself. → Bill and Ann saw *themselves*.

Bill saw Ann; Ann saw Bill. → Bill and Ann saw **each other**.

My son and I live in different cities, but we visit **each other** often.
During our lessons, we speak to **each other** only in English.
Tom and Mary don't agree with **each other** about politics.

Exercise 124

*Fill in a reflexive pronoun or **each other**.*

Examples: We found **_ourselves_** in a difficult situation.

Linda and I live within four miles of **_each other_** .

1.   The two vice presidents greeted _____ at the conference room door.

2.   During their training, new employees should familiarize _____ with as much of the operation as possible.

3.   My sister and I had an argument; we haven't spoken to _____ since.

4.   Turn that radio down! Neither Paul nor I can hear _____ think!

5.   I ran into an old friend last night; we hadn't seen _____ for years.

6.   If you and Kim would like drinks, please help _____.

7.   Janet and I have known _____ since we were in high school.

8.   The two drivers got into an argument; they accused _____ of being at fault in the accident.

Form No. G714D

Shipper: Audio Performance, Inc. 383 Madison Ave. New York, NY 10017	Document No. 71478

Consignee: Thomas Audio – Distribution Center
23 Stockley Road
W. Drayton, Middlesex, England U.K.

UNITED FREIGHT, INC.
12 Battery Place
New York, New York 10004

Notify Party *(only if not stated above)*:
Thomas Audio Ltd.
33 Red Lion Square
London WC29 SH 5

BILL OF LADING

Pier or Airport:
Maher Terminal, Elizabeth, NJ

Port of Loading: New York	Exporting Carrier: Trans Europa	Domestic Routing / Export Instructions: Our agent in
Port of Discharge: Felixstowe	Date of Departure: May 8, 1990	the U.K.: United Freight Ltd. Dunham Road, South Dagenham Essex RM10 8TX, England

PARTICULARS FURNISHED BY SHIPPER

Marks & Nos.	No. of Pkgs.	Description of Packages and Goods	Gross Weight	Measurement
Container #214-505	1	One 40' container said to contain: 75 cartons cassette tape decks 300 cartons stereo rack systems 100 cartons compact disc players	4,275 lbs. 13,500 lbs. 2,300 lbs.	300 cu. ft. 900 cu. ft. 200 cu. ft.
Container #128-714	1	One 40' container said to contain: 150 cartons amplifiers 200 cartons speakers	6,275 lbs. 7,225 lbs.	225 cu. ft. 1,550 cu. ft.
Container #235-633	1	One 20' container said to contain: 10 cartons headsets 50 cartons microphones 400 cartons cassette tapes 100 cartons misc. cables/adapters	150 lbs. 2,000 lbs. 12,000 lbs. 2,400 lbs. 50,125 lbs.	15 cu. ft. 100 cu. ft. 800 cu. ft. 100 cu. ft. 4,190 cu. ft.

SHIPPING AND HANDLING CHARGES

. . . . ———

. . . . ———

...Prepaid.... ———

. . . . ———

. . . . ———

. . . . ———

. . . . ———

Total ———

Shipper certifies that the information above is correct, agrees to the conditions on the reverse side, and accepts that carrier's liability is restricted as stated on the reverse.

Michael Adams

Signature of Shipper or Agent

Carrier certifies that the goods described above were received for transport, the goods then being in apparent good order and condition, except as noted above.

May 3, 1990   Elizabeth, NJ

Executed on *(Date)*   at *(Place)*

Marian Lee Johnson

by *(Signature of Issuing Carrier or Its Agent)*

Alan Fischer pointed to a bill of lading issued six months before the goods were released from Customs.

Exercise 125　　　　WORD FAMILIES

Complete these sentences using words from the same family.

Example:　Who will **represent** us at the conference this year? Last year's
　　　　 representative was Ms. Lee.

1.　The plant's quota was **reduced** again last month. A further _____
　　 could result in a shortage of merchandise.

2.　I wish we could develop a more organized filing **system**. If we could be
　　 more _____, it would be easier to find things.

3.　Several sales representatives will be **assigned** to work under Mr. Fischer.
　　 These _____ will be made by Fischer himself.

4.　The company hopes to **settle** the matter out of court. The sooner they can
　　 reach a _____, the better.

5.　You will be **briefed** when you start the job and will receive a regular
　　 monthly _____ after that.

6.　If you aren't **familiar** with the firm's accounting procedures, you should
　　 _____ yourself as soon as possible.

7.　I knew the storm had caused _____ damage, but I couldn't imagine
　　 the full **extent** of the damage until I saw the area.

8.　Who will be **managing** Eastern division sales after the present _____,
　　 Mr. Wilder, leaves?

9.　George didn't **intend** to offend anyone by bringing up the problem. His
　　 only _____ was to get things out in the open.

10.　Mr. Fischer's ideas sound **valid**, but we won't know how much _____
　　 they have until they're implemented.

USES OF *AS*

"**As** I've already told Mr. Crawford, I am confident
I can double that figure over the next 24 months."

The little word *as* is used in many different ways. You're already familiar with
some of its uses. Here are more examples:

> I'll finish this job **as fast as** I can.
> When in Rome, **do as** the Romans do.
> We all listened **as** Mr. Taylor explained the problem.
> **As** the guest speaker hasn't arrived, we can't begin the meeting.

Exercise 126

Example: Let me know **_as soon as_** you hear from Ed.

1. Our old house looked _____ I remembered it.

2. _____, Alan Fischer has recently joined AP.

3. The contract negotiations are proceeding
   smoothly _____ I know.

4. Just remember, if you buy a used car, it's
   _____; there's no guarantee it will run well.

5. It takes so long to find a cab; we _____ walk.

6. The new model will be more compact _____ lower in price.

7. You can leave early _____ you finish everything before you go.

8. Fischer will begin heading up exports _____ January 1, 1991.

as long as
as is
as soon as
as you know
might as well
as of
as far as
exactly as
as well as

MEMORANDUM

To: See Distribution

From: Peter Crawford

Date: 11/26/90

Subject: Alan B. Fischer

I am pleased to announce that effective January 1, 1991, Mr. Alan Baines Fischer will assume the position of Export Manager. Alan will be based in London, England, where he will be in charge of all European sales and distribution. He will be reporting to Ben Melnick, Director of Sales.

Alan has a BS in Electrical Engineering from the University of Rochester and an MBA in Marketing from the University of Chicago. He has extensive experience in export sales, and has lived with his wife and two daughters in Germany, France and Mexico. He comes to us from Crowe Products, where he held the position of West Coast sales manager.

I am sure you will all join me in welcoming Alan on board and wishing him the best of success in his new position.

Distribution:

S. Blake
J. Collins
P. Hayes
J. Martinelli
B. Melnick
S. Waterman

PC/kl

Alan Fischer had just been named to head up AP's new export department.

- What qualities would you look for in choosing an executive for a short-term or long-term foreign assignment? What are the risks involved in sending someone abroad?

- What are some of the problems a company faces shipping goods from one country to another?

Vocabulary

head (up)

working command (~ of a language)

work out of (~ L.A., home, *etc.*)

environment

go after something

systematic(ally)

a great deal (of)

bill of lading

avoid

streamline

warehousing *(adj)*
– warehouse *(n, v)*

hit (be a ~)

briefing *(n)*
– brief *(v)*

relocation
– relocate

settled (get ~)

give notice

"Welcome aboard!"

23 A PREVIEW OF THE NEW PLANT

Jeff Martinelli and Peter were looking over some architectural sketches and floor plans of the new Audio Performance plant, construction of which was scheduled to begin by early spring in Greenville, South Carolina. "The executive offices will be in this area, next to the main entrance. And over here, adjacent to the assembly line area, are the employee lounge and the cafeteria."

"As you can see," Jeff went on, "we'll have our own railroad siding and loading docks to serve the plant. Employee parking is over in this area. We've allowed space for more than 500 cars, although we estimate having only 400 employees at first. And you'll notice there's more than enough room for expansion — we could simply extend the building here on the right to increase the size as much as needed. We'll be creating about 40,000 square feet of manufacturing space, which will substantially increase our present capacity. As mentioned in our last meeting, I've also provided for over 34,000 square feet of warehouse space for storage of both raw materials and finished goods. It's going to be considerably larger than any of our present facilities."

"And more expensive, too," said Peter. "Just under $14 million!"

"We're trying to keep costs down as much as possible," Jeff pointed out. "And we've designed it in such a way that it would be possible to rent out up to 34,000 square feet of space, depending on our capacity requirements when the plant opens. The state requires that the building meet certain safety standards, and that has added a little to our original estimate of costs."

"Well, with the Shop-Way deal in the works, there's a good chance we'll be able to use as much capacity as we can get," commented Peter. "Our total production may have to be increased 25 percent over the next year or so. I'm only sorry the plant won't be in operation for another 11 months."

"There's just no way I know of to have it ready any sooner," Jeff said. "As you know, there have been a number of strikes recently. The steel workers went out on strike a week ago, and they're predicting serious shortages of structural steel unless it's settled soon. Last month it was the railroad workers, and now there's talk that the truckers might strike in February, depending on the results of negotiations that are currently under way. I've tried to allow for all this in setting up the construction schedules. We plan to break ground early next spring. Barring any unforeseen delays, we should have the building up by July, and they'll begin installing the equipment immediately. The plant should be in operation by late October."

"I know you've spent a lot of time on the plans, Jeff, and they look terrific. It looks as if all the work you've done is going to start paying off. You've done a great job!" Peter said.

"I appreciate the kind words, Peter. But we still haven't broken ground yet. Maybe you should save your congratulations for the ribbon-cutting ceremony!"

Exercise 127 Comprehension Check

*Indicate whether the following statements are **True (T)** or **False (F)**.*

1. _____ The assembly line area in the new plant will be adjacent to the executive offices.

2. _____ Construction of the new plant is scheduled to begin in the early spring.

3. _____ The plant will have its own railroad siding but no loading docks.

4. _____ Since the plant will have 400 employees, the plans include 400 parking spaces.

5. _____ The building could be enlarged, if necessary.

6. _____ The manufacturing area will be slightly smaller than the warehouse area.

7. _____ The new plant will be the largest of all of AP's facilities.

8. _____ They definitely plan to rent out 34,000 square feet of plant space.

9. _____ Plans are for the new plant to be operational within a year.

10. _____ Martinelli thinks he can find a way to have the plant ready sooner.

11. _____ Strikes could slow down the construction schedule.

12. _____ They will start to install the equipment in October.

COMPLIMENTS

"I know you've spent a lot of time on the plans, Jeff, and they look terrific. ... You've done a great job!"

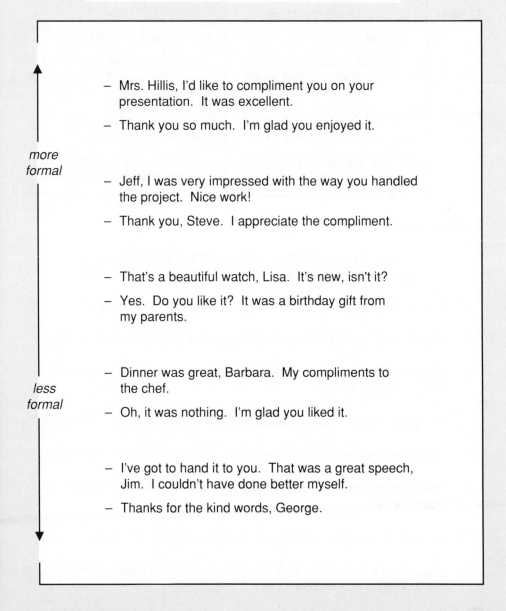

more formal

— Mrs. Hillis, I'd like to compliment you on your presentation. It was excellent.

— Thank you so much. I'm glad you enjoyed it.

— Jeff, I was very impressed with the way you handled the project. Nice work!

— Thank you, Steve. I appreciate the compliment.

— That's a beautiful watch, Lisa. It's new, isn't it?

— Yes. Do you like it? It was a birthday gift from my parents.

— Dinner was great, Barbara. My compliments to the chef.

— Oh, it was nothing. I'm glad you liked it.

less formal

— I've got to hand it to you. That was a great speech, Jim. I couldn't have done better myself.

— Thanks for the kind words, George.

SENTENCES INSIDE SENTENCES

"It looks as if **all the work you've done** is going to start paying off."

Things: I'm going to see the movie.

You said it was good. | *You said you enjoyed it.*

→ I'm going to see the movie *(that)* **you said was good.** | → I'm going to see the movie *(that)* **you said you enjoyed.**

People: The man left a message.

You said he would call. | *You said you'd call him.*

→ The man *(who)* **you said would call** left a message. | → The man *(whom)* **you said you'd call** left a message.

Exercise 128

Example: The book only cost $6.95. *(Tom said it would be expensive.)*
The book Tom said would be expensive only cost $6.95.

1. The flight will be delayed an hour. *(You said you were taking it.)*

2. The company went bankrupt recently. *(I thought it was doing so well.)*

3. The programmer was promoted to systems analyst. *(I remember being impressed with him.)*

4. The property was sold two weeks ago. *(Jeff thought it was still for sale.)*

5. I made an appointment with the doctor. *(You recommended I see him.)*

6. The woman is available tomorrow afternoon. *(Carol said she wanted to interview her.)*

7. Jill is interested in buying the car. *(I suggested she take a look at it.)*

8. Crawford wants to know more about the sales agreement. *(Melnick mentioned he was working on it.)*

VERBS USED WITH THE SUBJUNCTIVE

"The state **requires that** the building **meet** certain safety standards ..."

Karen **is** always at the office by 8:30 a.m.
→ Peter **insists that** she **be** there by 8:30 a.m. *

She didn't **go** to lunch while Peter was out.
→ He **suggested that** she **not go** while he was out.

The company's reports **are** always **typed**.
→ Company policy **requires that** they **be typed**.

_____

Other verbs commonly used with the subjunctive:
request   prefer   recommend
demand   ask   propose

Exercise 129

Example: Ann will confirm her flight reservation. The airline recommended
   ___*that she confirm her flight reservation*___ .

1.   You have to fill out an application form. Personnel requires _____.

2.   We didn't set the production level as high as last month. It was the plant manager who insisted _____.

3.   Stan and I will meet on a regular basis. Peter has requested _____.

4.   You must show two pieces of I.D. to cash a check. Our policy requires _____.

5.   I took a word processing course. My supervisor suggested _____.

6.   The driver got out of his car. The police officer demanded _____.

7.   The firm won't keep as much money in checking accounts. It has been proposed _____.

8.   We delay payment of certain invoices. The controller prefers _____.

---

*   The subjunctive is used more frequently in American English than in British English. In British English, *should* is often added: "He insists that she *should* be there by 8:30 a.m."

THE SUBJUNCTIVE AFTER ADJECTIVES

It is / was	important necessary required suggested **recommended** requested preferable advisable imperative	*that*	she **type** the report. the report **be typed**. the report **not be handwritten**.

Exercise 130

Example: The accounts payable department will hire additional staff.
It's necessary ___*that it hire additional staff*___ .

1. We would like to hire someone with at least two years' experience.
   It's advisable _____.

2. The meeting has been postponed until the end of the month.
   It was necessary _____.

3. Don't submit your report until you've re-checked all the figures.
   It's important_____.

4. The controller should keep a closer eye on our investments.
   It was suggested _____.

5. We must get production costs under control as soon as possible.
   It's imperative _____.

6. The marketing department won't make any decisions until the study is completed.
   It was recommended _____.

7. Melnick and Blake will work together on the market study.
   It's preferable _____.

8. Philip went in person to the consulate to apply for a visa.
   It was required _____.

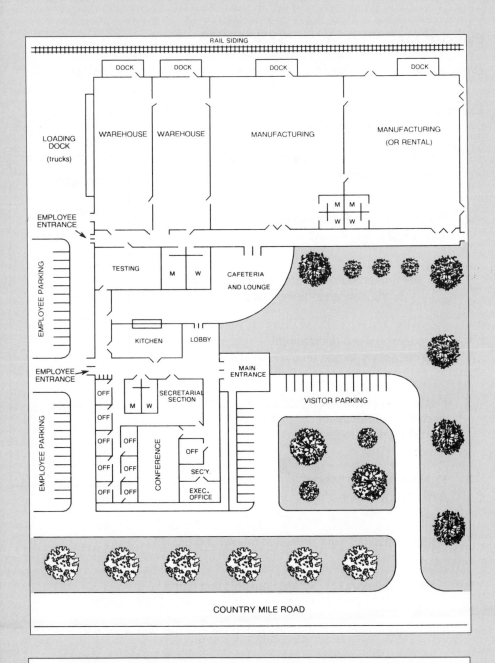

RAIL SIDING

DOCK   DOCK   DOCK   DOCK

LOADING
DOCK
(trucks)

WAREHOUSE   WAREHOUSE   MANUFACTURING   MANUFACTURING
(OR RENTAL)

M M
W W

EMPLOYEE
ENTRANCE

EMPLOYEE PARKING

TESTING   M   W   CAFETERIA
AND LOUNGE

KITCHEN   LOBBY

EMPLOYEE
ENTRANCE

MAIN
ENTRANCE

VISITOR PARKING

OFF   SECRETARIAL
SECTION
M   W

OFF   OFF
CONFERENCE
OFF

OFF   OFF
SEC'Y.

OFF   OFF
EXEC.
OFFICE

COUNTRY MILE ROAD

Jeff Martinelli and Peter Crawford looked over some architectural sketches and floor plans of the new Audio Performance plant.

271

Exercise 131   SYNONYMS

Choose words from the box that are closest in meaning to those in italics.

Example: The apartment building the Crawfords live in is *(next to)*
    __adjacent to__ Central Park.

1. I don't *(plan)* _____ to stay in New York
   longer than a week.

2. Do you think the European market is worth
   (pursuing) _____?

3. Mr. Bell presented some preliminary *(drawings)*
   _____ for the new advertising campaign.

4. If production were *(increased)* _____, would
   it be necessary to add an evening shift?

5. Researchers have been working on ways to
   (increase efficiency in) _____ the
   manufacturing process.

6. Profits have been *(rising)* _____ since the
   new president took office.

7. Congratulations! Your presentation was a great *(hit)* _____.

8. I don't *(remember)* _____ Mr. Jensen's first name.

9. The lawyer *(tried)* _____ to prove that the contract was invalid.

10. You shouldn't enter into the agreement unless you intend to *(respect)*
    _____ it.

attempted
recall
adjacent to
climbing
success
intend
honor
going after
streamline
sketches
stepped up

272

USES OF *KEEP*

"We're trying to **keep costs down** as much as possible ..."

We've seen that many words in English have a wide range of meanings. The verb *keep* is another word with very different uses. Here are some:

You don't have to give me back the newspaper; you can **keep** it.
Mr. Hall is ill and won't be able to **keep his appointment**.
You don't have to stop for a green light; you can **keep** *(on)* **going**.
I have to hurry; Mr. Duffy is here and I hate to **keep him waiting**.
A sign at the entrance said, "Private Property – **Keep Out**."

Exercise 132

Example: What I'm going to tell you is confidential. Can you keep a
___*secret*___ ?

1. Personnel keeps a _____ of sick and vacation days taken during the year.

2. I promised to be here on time, and I kept my _____.

3. I haven't played tennis in years. I don't even remember how to keep _____.

4. If we want to keep _____ with the rest of the industry, we must update our product line.

5. I haven't actually seen Jane in years, but we still keep in _____ over the phone.

6. With the new system, it's much easier to keep _____ of inventory on hand.

7. Who's going to keep an _____ on things while you're away?

8. Since I had my watch repaired, it has been keeping perfect _____.

time
touch
pace
record
track
secret
word
eye
score

Strikes Threaten Start of Construction

Workers at Matrix Steel Company walked off their jobs today in sympathy with the striking workers at Midland Steel. And matters may get more serious still. The employees at Gemco Steel are scheduled to take a strike vote tomorrow.

Should the strike spread throughout the entire industry, severe shortages of structural steel could result. This could stall plans by New York-based Audio Performance to begin construction of its new manufacturing plant here in Greenville. According to Peter Crawford, President of AP, 75,000 square feet of manufacturing and warehouse space is planned. The plant, which is currently scheduled to open next fall, will employ approximately 400 people.

At this time, no negotiations are going on between the Associated Steel Workers Union and Midland management. Though workers and management both claim they desire a speedy settlement, neither side has been willing to give on any of the major issues.

The ASWU is demanding hourly wage increases, a shorter workday, increased retirement benefits, and improved safety standards. Due to the availability of lower cost steel from abroad, Midland Steel claims that accepting union demands would force them to raise domestic steel prices to levels that would make them unable to compete in the world market. If the stalemate continues, AP and Greenville may have to wait.

There had been a number of strikes recently.
The steel workers had gone on strike a week before.

- Employees in critical occupations (police, nurses, etc.) should not be allowed to strike. Discuss.

- Do you recall a time when an important sector (transportation, public services, etc.) was on strike? What effects did it have on your life?

Vocabulary

– architect
architectural

sketch *(n)*

floor plan

adjacent to

railroad

siding (railroad ~)

loading dock

provide for

storage
– store

raw materials

keep costs down

in the works (be, have ~)

strike *(v, n)*

go out on strike

steel

settle a strike

break ground

barring *(= except)*

unforeseen

ceremony (ribbon-cutting ~)

24 TO THE FUTURE

The elevator doors opened slowly on the top floor of Peter's office building. He stepped out and walked towards the restaurant. It was just before noon on a Friday in late January. As the maître d' showed him to his table, Peter realized that it was at this same table over a year ago that Jim Burke had offered him the job at Audio Performance.

Burke, who was joining him for lunch again today, hadn't arrived yet, so Peter ordered a drink for himself. He was happy to have the chance to take a break from the hectic schedule he'd been keeping all week.

On Monday he and Carol Nordstrom, AP's director of personnel, had put the finishing touches on the new fringe benefits program. The original suggestions Carol had made in the spring regarding a more attractive benefits package had finally led to a number of changes in AP's compensation policies.

The week had also included a meeting to discuss the new Data Masters computer network, which had been installed three weeks before. Early reports indicated that the system was paying off handsomely. Although the cost of installation had exceeded the original estimate, the scope of the data which the computers could handle and the speed at which they operated left no doubt that the money had been well spent.

But the highlight of the week had been Peter's presentation at the year-end Board meeting on Thursday. Although he had appeared formally before the Board on earlier occasions, he was still nervous. But his fears turned out to be groundless. His presentation was a great success. He was able to report that with the nationwide advertising campaign for the Tru-Tone line in full swing, sales were up 10 to 15 percent. "The increased sales also indicate we're beginning to make inroads against foreign competition."

Then Peter turned to AP's successful purchase of LTE stock. Audio Performance had managed to acquire enough shares to ensure control of the firm and was already beginning to distribute some of its own products, including the Games Master, through LTE's broader distribution network.

"Hello, Peter! Sorry to have kept you waiting!" Crawford's thoughts were interrupted by the arrival of Jim Burke. "Say," Burke said as he took his seat, "that was quite a performance yesterday. The Board was really impressed with the Shop-Way deal. When do you begin shipping?"

"Next week," Crawford answered. "We've already received orders for half the minimum purchase for this year. And just this morning I got a call from Dave Williams about the possibility of producing a cheaper line to be marketed as a Shop-Way house brand."

"That's terrific," Burke replied. "The new plant will be coming along just in time."

"You said it!" Peter agreed. "We may even have to think about expanding it before long."

The waitress came to the table and took the lunch orders. As she took away the menus, Burke looked up at Crawford. "Peter, I'd like to congratulate you on the fine job you've done over the past year. It looks as if the man we hoped would save AP will end up making it one of our most successful profit centers."

"There's one other thing I've been meaning to talk to you about," Burke continued. "As you know, UEI is going through a period of growth and expansion. There are a number of very attractive opportunities in the organization for a man of your caliber. As you're aware, we've concluded several acquisitions recently, and we hope to be creating a number of new positions for vice presidents at the divisional level later in the year. It would mean assuming the responsibility for several operating companies, but I'm sure you could handle the challenge."

Peter could hardly find the words to express himself. "I appreciate your confidence, Jim, I ..."

Jim raised his glass "Don't say a word," he said. "You've earned it all. And now a toast ... to the future!"

"To the future!" replied Crawford.

Exercise 133　　　Vocabulary Check

Choose the correct words from the box.

Example:　My greatest **_fear_** is that the new product won't sell.

1. The full _____ of the damage from the earthquake won't be known for several weeks.

2. Don't take such a difficult job unless you enjoy _____.

3. The _____ of our trip to Japan was seeing Mt. Fuji.

4. The architect was given some _____, but the actual design was left up to her.

5. We can't attract high-_____ people with low salaries.

6. The length of the workday is a matter of company _____.

7. Our _____ into the European market is going well.

8. Peter couldn't have succeeded without a lot of self-_____.

> caliber
> policy
> **fear**
> guidelines
> challenges
> highlight
> scope
> confidence
> expansion

CONGRATULATIONS

"Peter, I'd like to congratulate you on the
fine job you've done over the past year."

*more
formal*

– Congratulations on your promotion, Mr. Carlson. I can't
think of anyone who deserves it more than you do.

– Thank you very much. I appreciate the kind words, Miss
Tibbs. I'm really looking forward to the challenge.

– Joe, on behalf of the department, I'd like to congratulate
you on your thirtieth anniversary with the company.

– Thank you, Ben, and thanks to everyone. It's wonderful to
be recognized like this.

– I just heard that your design won the top award from the
Architect's Society, Jill. Congratulations! You must be
very proud!

– Thank you. I can't quite believe it yet myself. I feel very
fortunate.

*less
formal*

– I've just heard that you and Tom are engaged to be
married, Jill. My congratulations! I wish you all the best.

– Thanks a lot, Sandra. We're both very happy about it.

– It looks like congratulations are in order, Tom. Vista
Company signed the contract! We couldn't have done it
without you!

– Thanks, James. But don't forget you had a hand in it, too.

Exercise 134   REVIEW OF VERB TENSES

Choose the verb forms that best complete the sentences.

Example: The phone __*b*__. Will you please answer it?
a) rings   **b) is ringing**   c) has rung   d) has been ringing

1. Where did you find those papers? ____ for them all day!
    a) I look   b) I'm looking   c) I've looked   d) I've been looking

2. The average American ____ about three cups of coffee a day.
    a) drinks   b) is drinking   c) drank   d) has been drinking

3. Mr. Hall was a lawyer for years before he ____ for public office.
    a) runs   b) has run   c) ran   d) had run

4. I can depend on Paul; as long as ____ him, he's never let me down.
    a) I know   b) I've known   c) I knew   d) I'd known

5. By the time I pay off the mortgage, I ____ $60,000 just in interest.
    a) pay   b) am paying   c) paid   d) will have paid

6. If payment isn't made by May 1, we ____ the matter over to a collection agency.
    a) turn   b) will turn   c) turned   d) will have turned

7. You're eligible for the group insurance plan, ____ you?
    a) do   b) don't   c) aren't   d) are

8. The meeting was very crowded; we ____ held it in a larger room.
    a) could   b) should have   c) may have   d) should

9. If you're not careful with that knife, you ____ cut yourself.
    a) could   b) should   c) could have   d) should have

10. In many countries, you ____ be at least 18 years old to vote.
    a) may   b) might   c) should   d) must

11. ____ so much money, the company went out of business.
    a) Losing   b) Being lost   c) Having lost   d) Having been lost

12. A passenger claims to ____ in the train accident yesterday.
    a) injure   b) have injured   c) be injured   d) have been injured

Exercise 135   REVIEW OF CONJUNCTIONS

Choose the correct conjunctions from the box.

Example: How long has it been __*since*__ you began this course?

1. Burke offered Crawford a position _____ he had
    performed so well as president of AP.

2. The flight attendant asked _____ we remain
    seated during takeoff.

3. Bill asked _____ installation was included in
    the price of the air-conditioning unit.

4. Our competitors spend a lot more on advertising
    _____ we do.

5. I mentioned the possibility of a strike _____
    I spoke to Ed Pearson on the phone last week.

6. _____ the job pays a low salary, it offers good
    opportunity for advancement.

7. Tom has his own keys, _____ he can lock up
    when he leaves.

that
but
whether
unless
so
since
as
because
until
as long as
than
although
when

8. We've just set up the business; we'll have to wait _____
    we're better established to start seeing a profit.

9. You're welcome to use my camera _____ you return it before the
    weekend.

10. Construction costs have risen tremendously, _____ the firm still
    insists on building a new office building.

11. The flight will take off on time _____ it starts snowing.

12. Earnings per share are now almost twice as high _____ they were
    before the advertising campaign.

PREPOSITIONAL ADVERBS

"[Peter] was able to report that with the nationwide advertising campaign ... in full swing, sales were **up** 10% to 15%."

- **in / out:**

    I'm sorry, Mr. Park isn't **in**. He'll be **out** the rest of the day.
    The results of the survey aren't **in** yet.
    The report will be **out** in a few weeks.
    We only have 100 units left; then we'll be **out** (of stock).

- **away / back:**

    The director is **away** this week. He'll be **back** on Monday.
    The report was **back** on my desk in two days.
    The conference is just a week **away**.

- **up / down:**

    It's nine o'clock; Bill should be **up** by now.
    Betty is upstairs. She'll be **down** in a minute.
    Sales are **up**, and costs are **down**.

- **on / off:**

    I'm still **on** the phone. I'll be **off** in a minute.
    Bert is **off** today; he took a personal holiday.
    Is the light in the storeroom usually **on** or **off**?
    The estimate was **off** *(= inaccurate)* by hundreds of dollars.
    The deal is **off** *(= cancelled)*.
    Stock prices are **off** *(= down)* this week.

- **over:**

    Bill left as soon as the meeting was **over**.
    You can't rent a car unless you're 21 or **over**.

- **through:**

    Are you **through** with that magazine yet?

- **around:**

    I'm not **around** much during the day. Try calling me in the evening.

Exercise 136

Use words from the opposite page to complete the sentences.

Example: Mr. Ross isn't __*in*__ at the moment. May I take a message?

1. I only have one more page to type; I'll be _____ in just a minute.

2. We ordered the supplies a month ago, and they aren't _____ yet.

3. The lights were _____ in your house, so I assumed you were home.

4. I'll only be gone a week. I have to be _____ at work May 5th.

5. The accountant was _____ in his calculations. The error cost the company a lot of money.

6. The hotel was so noisy that we were _____ half the night.

7. Mr. Carlson is _____ from his desk at the moment. Can he return your call?

8. Sheila can't input the data because the computer is _____.

9. The film had been _____ a month when it broke a box office record.

10. I have an appointment at two o'clock. Do you think the luncheon will be _____ by then?

11. It's supposed to rain. It looks like tomorrow's golf game is _____.

12. Your suits won't be _____ from the cleaners until tomorrow.

13. I thought I'd stop by your house on Saturday. Will you be _____?

14. I was _____ till 1:00 a.m. watching a movie.

15. Investors were disturbed to hear that profits were _____.

Exercise 137   REVIEW OF PRONOUNS

Choose the pronouns that best complete the sentences.

Example: *(which, who)*
               We sent a refund to a customer __*who*__ wasn't satisfied.

1. *(who, whom)*
   Those _____ survived the plane crash are now in critical condition.

2. *(whom, which)*
   The programmers, most of _____ have been with the company for some time, are happy with the new system.

3. *(what, whatever)*
   Tell me _____ you decided to do about the problem.

4. *(what, whatever)*
   Tracy is such an optimist; _____ happens, she always has something encouraging to say.

5. *(Who, Whoever)*
   _____ was on the line must have hung up.

6. *(who, whoever)*
   The police still don't know _____ committed the crime.

7. *(who, whom)*
   The sales representative, _____ I know as a personal friend, will give me a special discount.

8. *(that, who)*
   Your résumé was the one _____ impressed me the most.

9. *(us, ourselves)*
   Instead of going with a tour, we prefer to travel by _____.

10. *(ourselves, each other)*
    The station was so crowded that it took us ten minutes to find _____.

11. *(me, myself)*
    It was so noisy in the office I couldn't hear _____ think!

12. *(him, himself)*
    Although James had doubts about his decision, he convinced _____ he was doing the right thing.

Exercise 138   **IDIOMS**

Choose the correct words to complete the idioms.

Example: *(done / made / seen)*
               If the government could have __*made*__ inroads against inflation, the
               economy would have improved.

1.   *(break / turn / open)*
     The engineers estimate the bridge construction will be complete 18 months
     after they _____ ground.

2.   *(put / take / call)*
     Will the figures _____ into account the recent sale of the Baltimore
     facility?

3.   *(had / was / left)*
     The quarterly sales report _____ no doubt that the marketing
     promotion was on target.

4.   *(answer / propose / take)*
     I'd like to _____ a toast. Here's to our continued success!

5.   *(have / think / make)*
     I had all but decided to hire Ms. Stewart, but then I began to _____
     second thoughts.

6.   *(put / slow / keep)*
     Tell the children to _____ the noise down. I'm trying to concentrate!

7.   *(make / put / place)*
     When did they _____ the finishing touches on the benefits package?

8.   *(go / take / look)*
     If you have enough determination, you can achieve whatever you _____
     after.

9.   *(seen / run / gone)*
     The electronics industry has _____ through a period of rapid changes.

10. *(meant / managed / succeeded)*
     I tried to call Jane, but I never _____ to get hold of her.

11. *(level / slow / hold)*
     Will economic growth _____ off if the government imposes stricter
     trade restrictions?

12. *(give / take / tell)*
     Employees are asked to _____ at least two weeks notice when they
     resign.

UNITED ELECTRONIC INDUSTRIES, INC.

Minutes of the Regular Meeting
of the Board of Directors Held January 24, 1991

The Board of Directors o
the exec   **Minutes**

The me
sales al
loss, of
to imp
adver
line.
signif

Also
five
this

Mr
m

M
c
l

Minutes

acquisitions of Electro-Audio Systems, Inc. and National Electronics Distributors have been
successfully concluded.

Report on Audio Performance, Inc.

The president of Audio Performance, Peter F. Crawford, announced that after several months
of steady decline, sales of the Tru-Tone line of stereo equipment had begun to improve, with
sales for the current month up 12.3%. He attributed this rise largely to a
new advertising campaign but also to the addition of new models to the product line.
Mr. Crawford stated that although particularly heavy development costs had resulted in a
temporary net operating loss, the projected sales increases for the coming year would
result in significant overall profit increases.

Also announced was the successful conclusion of a five-year purchase agreement with
Shop-Way Stores for the Tru-Tone line. Crawford noted that this high-volume arrangement,
by permitting lower unit costs, would also contribute to increased profits in the future.

Mr. Crawford then reported that his company had acquired control of Leisure Time Entertainment, whose distribution network would be used for marketing Audio Performance products.

Mr. Crawford announced that construction of the new AP plant in Greenville, South Carolina
was scheduled to begin in early April, and be completed by year-end 1991. He stated that
the additional capacity would enable the company to meet anticipated increased production
levels as well as long-range expansion goals.

Mr. Paul T. Weaver introduced a resolution expressing the appreciation of the Board of
Directors for the leadership and new direction Mr. Crawford had given Audio Peformance
in his first year as president. The resolution was seconded and carried unanimously.

The Chair announced that the meeting was adjourned at 4:15 p.m.

MVB Marie V. Bennett, Recording Secretary

MVB/al

---

*The highlight of Peter's week had been his participation
in the UEI year-end board meeting .*

- Do you think it is a good idea for Peter Crawford to move on to another position at this time? Explain your reasoning.

- Describe the steps involved in preparing and making a business presentation. What aspects can make a difference between an effective and a poor presentation?

finishing touches (put the ~ on)	manage to do something
lead to	"You said it!"
handsomely	profit center
scope	go through *(= experience)*
doubt (leave ~)	caliber
highlight *(n)*	division(al)
groundless	operating company
in full swing	toast (make a ~, propose a ~)
make inroads against	"To ...!" *(toast)*

GLOSSARY

account *(n)* (Ch. 8): 1) a record of money paid and received. 2) any business relationship involving the exchange of money or credit. **checking account**: money placed in a bank, which may be taken out as needed by writing checks. *Ex.: Bill wasn't sure he had enough money left in his checking account to pay his electric bill.*

accounts payable (Ch. 8): money a company owes to suppliers and other businesses it deals with. *Ex.: Accounts payable made up the major part of the company's liabilities.*

accounts receivable (Ch. 8): money owed to a company by its customers. *Ex.: We check accounts receivable monthly to determine which collection steps should be taken.*

acquire *(v)* (Ch. 12): 1) to gain possession of. 2) to take over controlling interest in a company. **acquisition** *(n)*. *Ex.: Ajax Tool Co. rejected the acquisition proposal of Thor Manufacturing.*

acre *(n)* (Ch. 5, exhibit): a measure of land; 1 acre = 4,840 sq. yds. or 0.4047 hectares. (1 hectare = 2.47 acres.) *Ex.: Mr. Hillis recently purchased 5 acres of land in a rural area of Maryland.*

advertising agency (Ch. 10): a business that creates, produces and places advertising for other companies. *Ex.: The advertising manager discussed the company's objectives with several advertising agencies before choosing one.*

advertising campaign (Ch. 13): a plan detailing the type, scheduling, and cost of advertising over a given period of time. *Ex.: The advertising campaign was modified to meet the company's reduced advertising budget.*

amend *(v)* (Ch. 15): to add to or improve. *Ex.: The firm had to amend the profit figures because an error was discovered in the computations.*

annual (shareholders') meeting (Ch. 12, exhibit): a company meeting held once a year, at which management reports to shareholders on the year's activity, and the Board of Directors is elected. *Ex.: Mr. Keller always tries to attend the annual meetings of the companies in which he holds stock.*

applicant *(n)* (Ch. 4): a person who is seeking employment or admission to an organization or educational institution. **apply** *(v)*. *Ex.: The personnel department interviewed several applicants for the clerk-typist opening.*

arrears *(n)* (Ch. 8, letter): overdue debt. **in arrears**. *Ex.: Jack received notice from the department store that his account was in arrears and that he had 30 days to pay.*

assemble *(v)*: to put something together. **assembly line** (Ch. 3): a manufacturing system designed to assemble products; the parts are carried on a moving belt from worker to worker or from machine to machine until the final product is assembled. *Ex.: Working on the assembly line usually involves performing a small number of tasks over and over again.*

assets *(n)* (Ch. 8, exhibit): all real estate, equipment and money belonging to a person or company. **liquid assets**: those assets which can be converted to cash quickly. **fixed assets**: possessions of a business, such as real estate, equipment, furniture, etc. not quickly converted to cash. *Ex.: The accountants recalculated the value of the firm's fixed assets after the plant site was purchased.*

audit *(n)* (Ch. 15): in accounting, to check a financial account. **audit** *(v)*: to conduct such an examination. *Ex.: Janet keeps detailed records of her income and expenses to be prepared in case of a tax audit.*

automate *(v)* (Ch. 5): to create a system in which much of the production is done by equipment requiring a minimum of human labor. **automation** *(n)*. *Ex.: The production engineer said that new, automated equipment would not only improve product quality but also reduce production costs.*

average *(n, v)* (Ch. 7): a figure obtained when a set of numbers is added and then divided by the amount of numbers in the set. *Ex: Monthly sales have averaged 30 million dollars over the last two quarters.*

balance sheet (Ch. 8): a statement of the financial position of a company at a given time; includes assets, liabilities, and net worth. *Ex.: With current assets of $600 million and current liabilities of $30 million, the company's balance sheet appears in good health.*

benefits *(n)* (Ch. 9): compensation such as health or life insurance given to employees in addition to wages. **fringe benefits**: special benefits usually given to upper management executives. *Ex.: Mrs. Parker's company gave her the use of a company car as a fringe benefit.*

billion *(n)* (Ch. 17): a thousand million; 1,000,000,000. *Ex.: When ATZ Corp. was acquired by Thor Mfg., ATZ had assets of nearly 1.4 billion dollars.*

bill of lading (Ch. 22): a document which serves as both a receipt for merchandise and a shipping contract. It is issued by a transporter to the sender of goods. *Ex.: Bill was told that in order to claim his shipment he would have to present the original bill of lading as proof of ownership.*

block of shares (Ch. 19): a large number of a particular company's shares of stock (usually at least 10,000) held or traded at the same time. *Ex.: Mrs. Parker owns a block of 20,000 IBM shares.*

Board of Directors (Ch. 2): a group of persons elected by the shareholders to oversee the management of a corporation. *Ex.: The Board of Directors voted an increase in the quarterly dividend payment.*

bonanza *(n)* (Ch. 17): a source of great wealth or prosperity. *Ex.: The new product is a great success; no one thought it would be such a bonanza.*

bond *(n)* (Ch. 14): a certificate of debt issued by a corporation or public body; the issuer pays a fixed rate of interest and usually repays the face amount by a certain date (maturity date). *Ex.: To fund the plant expansion, the company issued $20 million worth of 20-year bonds.* **industrial revenue bonds**: in the U.S., debt issued by a local or state government to finance construction of industrial facilities. The interest on these bonds is either partially or completely exempt from taxes. *Ex.: Mr. Collins has over $100,000 invested in industrial revenue bonds issued by the state of California.*

bookkeeping *(n)* (Ch. 15): the keeping of records of a company's financial transactions. *Ex.: The manager of the accounting department is in the process of changing from manual to automated bookkeeping.*

books *(n)* (Ch. 15): the financial records of a company. *Ex.: The first thing the auditor did was to look over the company's books.*

boom *(n)* (Ch. 2): a spectacular increase in growth, wealth or sales. *Ex.: The stock market boom was believed to have been due to investors' confidence in the economy.*

brand *(n)* (Ch. 7): a name or trademark that identifies a product or manufacturer. *Ex.: The company is trying to increase brand awareness by giving away free samples of its food products.*

break down *(v)* (Ch. 3): 1) to fail to function. *Ex.: If the copier breaks down, the serviceman should be called immediately.* (Ch. 10): 2) to divide and subdivide into categories for purposes of analysis. *Ex.: Steve broke the sales figures down by type of sales outlet.*

break even *(v)* (Ch. 5): to reach a point where expenses equal costs; to show no profit or loss. *Ex.: Development costs of the new product were heavy; the company didn't expect to break even for at least five years.*

break ground *(v)* (Ch. 23): to begin excavation for a new building. *Ex.: The new facility will come on line one year after we break ground.*

broker *(n)* (Ch. 5): a person (**real estate broker**, **stockbroker**) who negotiates sales and purchases for a fee or commission. *Ex.: George used a real estate broker to help him find a house.*

budget *(n)* (Ch. 13): 1) a plan listing expected expenditures for a particular purpose or time period. *Ex.: We are about to submit the advertising budget for approval.* 2) a plan listing both expenditures and income for a future period of time. *Ex.: The government has announced a plan for balancing the nation's budget.*

cafeteria plan (Ch. 9): in personnel, a type of benefit package where a company offers a range of benefits from which each employee may select according to his needs. *Ex.: The cafeteria plan just adopted by the company has been extremely well-received by the employees.*

capacity *(n)* (Ch. 5): the maximum quantity a factory can produce in a given time. *Ex.: Paul reported that the plant was producing at 75 percent of capacity.*

capital *(n)* (Ch. 5): money for the operation or expansion of a business, or the total assets of a corporation. *Ex.: The company plans to raise additional capital by issuing 2 million additional shares of stock.*

capital stock (Ch. 8, exhibit): the total outstanding shares of a company's stock, chiefly common and preferred. *Ex.: Ajax Tool Co. acquired Maxtel Manufacturing by buying up 51 percent of its capital stock.* (see also *common stock; stock*.)

Chief Executive Officer (CEO) (Ch. 12, exhibit): the highest management official in a company. *Ex.: The CEO gave his report to the Board of Directors and stockholders at the annual meeting.*

chain store (Ch. 17): one of a group of nearly identical retail stores or businesses under the same ownership or management. *Ex.: Chain stores often have lower unit costs because they can order in large volume.*

circulation *(n)* (Ch. 13): the number of copies of a single issue of a publication, often a magazine or newspaper, sold or distributed to readers. *Ex.: The ad manager was looking for a magazine with a high circulation among teenagers.*

classified section (Ch. 4): the part of a newspaper in which advertisements are arranged into categories (employment, real estate, goods for sale, etc.). These advertisements are usually short, and use small print and abbreviations. *Ex.: When John was looking for a job, he read the employment ads in the classified section of the New York Times every day.*

clause *(n)* (Ch. 17, exhibit): a section of a contract or legal document. **penalty clause**: the part of a contract that states what will happen if one or both of the parties fail to fulfill any of the terms set out in the agreement. *Ex.: The penalty clause provided for a fine of $500 a day for late delivery of the merchandise.*

clerical *(adj)* (Ch. 4): of or relating to a clerk; clerical duties include typing, filing, etc. *Ex.: The personnel department usually places ads in the newspaper when trying to fill routine clerical positions.*

collection agency (Ch. 8): a company engaged by another company to collect on its past-due accounts. *Ex.: The department store turned Ed's account over to a collection agency because it was four months overdue.*

combined yearly income (Ch. 13): money earned during one year by more than one person, usually in the same household. *Ex.: John and his wife both have good jobs; their combined yearly income last year was $93,000.*

commercial *(n)* (Ch. 13): an advertisement on radio or television. *Ex.: The advertising agency scheduled the commercial to run on Saturday nights at 8 p.m. on national T.V.*

commercial bank (Ch. 14): a bank that accepts deposits and makes loans, primarily to businesses. *Ex.: Since the company does a lot of business abroad, it chose a commercial bank familiar with transactions involving foreign exchange.*

common stock (Ch. 19, letter): type of stock share which permits its owner to vote in the election of the Board of Directors; generally the type of stock required to control the company. *Ex.: Knowing that the prospects for a higher dividend were good, Bill bought 200 common shares of Intex Corp.* (see also *stock.*)

compensation *(n)* (Ch. 9): payment for work or services; wages, salary. *Ex.: Mr. Addison considered both the compensation and the benefits before accepting the position he was offered.*

component *(n)* (Ch. 1): a part of a whole, especially of something mechanical or electronic. *Ex.: Most of our products are assembled in this country, but many of the components are produced abroad.*

conglomerate *(n)* (Ch. 1): a group of companies, usually in different, diversified businesses, organized under a central management. *Ex.: Z-Tech is a conglomerate that includes several smaller electronics companies.*

consignee *(n)* (Ch. 22, exhibit): named on a bill of lading, the person or company to whom goods are to be sent. *Ex.: The consignee, Jones & Sons, Inc., hired an agent to take delivery of the goods at the port of discharge.*

consolidated balance sheet (Ch. 17): a financial statement that treats the accounts of a parent company and its subsidiaries as a single entity. *Ex.: Mr. Miller looked at the consolidated balance sheet of the corporation to get a picture of the company and its subsidiaries as a whole.* (see also *balance sheet.*)

consulting firm (Ch. 16): an outside company or individual hired to provide professional management or technical advice to organizations for a fee. *Ex.: The company hired a consulting firm to recommend ways to improve efficiency on the production line.*

consumer *(n)* (Ch. 10, letter): buyer or customer. *Ex.: The needs of consumers must be taken into account when developing new products.*

controller *(n)* (Ch. 8): the chief financial officer of a company. *Ex.: One of Mr. Carter's responsibilities as controller is to prepare the monthly balance sheets.*

corporate headquarters (Ch. 2): the main offices of a corporation. *Ex.: The president and other members of top management have their offices at the company's corporate headquarters.*

corporation *(n)* (Ch. 2): a business organization that can act as an individual but whose liabilities are separate from the persons who own it. *Ex.: The partners decided to form a corporation in order to protect their personal assets in case the business failed.*

cost of sales (Ch. 15): all costs associated with the production of goods over a given period of time. Includes cost of raw materials, labor and overhead items such as rent, electricity and supervision. *Ex.: The company decided to automate further because labor was becoming too large a component in its cost of sales.*

counteroffer *(n)* (Ch. 14): an offer made in response to an initial offer, with changes in some of the terms. *Ex.: I felt the owner's asking price of $95,000 for the house was too high, so I made an offer of $85,000. The owner refused my first offer, but made a counteroffer of $90,000.*

court *(n)* (Ch. 20): the place where legal cases are settled. **court case**, **take someone to court**: to sue. *Ex.: Mrs. Roberts warned Mr. Emerson that if he did not pay for the damage to her car, she would take him to court.*

credit check (Ch. 12): an examination of a person's or company's financial history and ability to pay bills. **credit rating**: an evaluation and report on a person's or company's financial position and business integrity. *Ex.: We run a credit check on all new customers to make sure they can pay their bills.*

credit *(v)* (Ch. 15): to add money to a financial account, reduce a liability. *Ex.: When funds are deposited electronically, the customer's bank account is credited immediately.*

cut *(v, n)* (Ch. 7): to reduce, as in **cut prices**. *Ex.: John suggested a price cut as the fastest way to increase sales.*

data processing (Ch. 16): the recording, classifying, sorting and retrieval of information electronically. *Ex.: The new data processing system will allow us very rapid access to a wide range of financial data.*

deal *(n)* (Ch. 14): a business sale, purchase, agreement or other transaction. **close a deal**: successfully conclude a business transaction. *Ex.: After we work out a few final details we should be able to close the deal quickly.*

dealer *(n)* (Ch. 7): a person or business which handles a certain type or brand of merchandise. **authorized dealer**: a dealer officially recognized by a manufacturer as qualified to sell its products and to provide warranty or repair services. *Ex.: To be sure of getting good repair service, Ken bought his stereo from an authorized dealer.*

debt *(n)* (Ch. 12): money or services owed to another party. *Ex.: Before deciding to take out a loan to remodel the office, we considered whether we would be able to handle the debt.*

deductible *(adj)* (Ch. 9): something which can be subtracted from the base on which income taxes are calculated. *Ex.: I asked my tax accountant whether the interest portion of my car payment was deductible.*

demand *(n)* (Ch. 21): desire, willingness, and ability to pay for goods or services. *Ex.: Since prices have gone down, there has been a rapid increase in the demand for car phones.*

deposit *(n)* (Ch. 8): money which has been put into a bank account. **on deposit**. *Ex.: The firm never has over a hundred thousand dollars on deposit at any one bank.*

depreciation *(n)* (Ch. 8, exhibit): 1) in accounting, spreading out the cost of an asset (such as plant and equipment) over its estimated life. **depreciate** *(v)*. *Ex.: The tax authorities did not permit the firm to deduct the entire cost of the copier in one year but did allow it to depreciate the cost over five years.*
2) a decrease in the value of something because of age, wear or deterioration. *Ex: The house has actually depreciated in value because it has been so poorly maintained.*

device *(n)* (Ch. 20): something, such as a machine, constructed for a particular purpose. *Ex.: The firm is marketing a new device which makes data transfer more efficient.*

disability insurance (Ch. 16, exhibit): a form of insurance that provides compensation to employees unable to work for physical or other reasons; the payments are based on a percentage of the insured's salary. **short-term / long-term disability**. *Ex.: When Mr. Hill was out of work with a broken hip, he received a disability check every month.*

discount store (Ch. 7): a store which regularly sells products at prices lower than the normal retail price. *Ex.: Laura saved over 20 percent by buying her stereo at a discount store instead of a department store.*

distribution *(n)* (Ch. 7): the system of supplying goods, especially to retailers. *Ex.: One major reason the business failed was because its system of product distribution was so inefficient.*

diversify *(v)* (Ch. 12): 1) to vary; to expand the range of products or areas of business, as in a conglomerate. 2) in investment, to spread assets among several categories of investment in order to reduce risks. **diversification** *(n). Ex.: As an investor, Mrs. Matthews decided to diversify her stock holdings further by adding oil and mining stocks to her portfolio.*

dividend *(n)* (Ch. 12, exhibit): the portion of a company's profits distributed to its shareholders. *Ex.: Mr. Farris is trying to maximize income, so he prefers to invest in companies whose stock pays a regular dividend.*

division *(n)* (Ch. 24): a relatively independent unit into which a company can be divided for purposes of management. *Ex.: The company had four major divisions, each responsible for a specific geographic area.*

earnings per share (Ch. 12): a company's profits (earnings) divided by the number of shares of common stock outstanding; e.g. if a company's profits are $20 million and there are 20 million shares outstanding, the earnings per share are $1. *Ex.: The Kelso Company reported an increase in earnings of $1, from $4 to $5 per share last year.*

engineering *(n)* (Ch. 11): the design, construction, and operation of structures, machinery, and systems. *Ex.: The city called in an engineering consultant to estimate the cost of repairing the bridge.*

equal opportunity employer (Ch. 6, exhibit): an employer who does not practice racial, religious, or other discrimination in hiring. *Ex.: As an equal opportunity employer, the company made an effort to hire as many women for management positions as possible.*

equity *(n)* (Ch. 8, exhibit): 1) the stock (as opposed to bonds) a company has issued to raise capital. 2) in finance, the value of a business or property in excess of the amount owed on it; net worth. *Ex.: Recent increases in the value of land owned by the company increased the shareholders' equity.*

estate *(n)* (Ch. 19): all the assets, in any form, a person owns. *Ex.: When Mr. Bancroft died, he left an estate worth over $500,000.*

exchange rate (Ch. 18): the price at which the currency of one country can be exchanged into currency of another country. *Ex.: The company tries to make its foreign investments at times when the exchange rates are most favorable.*

executive *(n)* (Ch. 1): a person at management level who makes policy decisions. *Ex.: The top executives met for a conference on the future of the industry.*
executive *(adj)*: belonging or relating to an executive, such as **executive parking area**.

executor *(n)* (Ch. 19): the person designated in a will to administer a person's estate after their death. *Ex.: Mrs. Collins has decided to name her attorney as executor of her estate.*

exempt from (Ch. 14): not subject to; free from a duty or obligation required of others. *Ex.: Some clothing products brought into the country are exempt from import duties.*

expenditure *(n)* (Ch. 13): an expense incurred in operating a business. *Ex.: We expect to have several large expenditures this year relating to the construction of the new retail outlet.*

facility *(n)* (Ch. 3): a place where business is conducted, often for manufac-turing. *Ex.: The Boston facility produces 20 percent of the company's output.*

Federal Insurance Contribution Act (FICA) (Ch. 16, exhibit): in the U.S., taxes withheld from an employee's salary or wages which support the Social Security system. *Ex.: The amount of money withheld from Helen's paycheck for FICA was nearly as much as for income tax.*

feedback *(n)* (Ch. 16): a return flow of information on the performance of someone or something. *Ex.: The president asked Jack to run tests on the new equipment in order to get feedback.*

figure *(n)* (Ch. 2): a number; a statistic; financial data giving information such as number of sales per month or per sales outlet. *Ex.: Jack was pleased that the sales figures for discount stores had improved.*

file *(v)* (Ch. 15): to record officially; to send in; file a tax return, a lawsuit, an application. *Ex.: The deadline for filing income tax returns is April fifteenth.*

finance *(v)* (Ch. 14): to obtain or provide money for some purpose or activity. *Ex.: Mr. and Mrs. Morgan financed their new car by taking out a loan.*

financial statement (Ch. 8): 1) a report showing the financial status or activity of a person or company. 2) a balance sheet showing assets and liabilities. *Ex.: Every public company is required to issue its financial statements to the public on a regular basis.*

finished goods (Ch. 15, exhibit): goods that have completed the manufacturing process and are ready for sale. *Ex.: The plant manager prepared an inventory of finished goods available for shipment to retail outlets.*

floor plan (Ch. 23): a scale diagram of a room, floor, or complete building, as seen from above. *Ex.: The architect prepared a floor plan showing the location of each of the offices.*

fluctuate *(v)* (Ch. 18): to continually change up and down. **fluctuation** *(n)*. *Ex.: The firm isn't concerned with daily currency fluctuations; the long-term trend is what matters.*

forecast *(n)* (Ch. 18): an estimate of future conditions, business results, or trends. *Ex.: The production manager needed an accurate sales forecast in order to set production levels.*

frontage *(n)* (Ch. 14, exhibit): a portion of a piece of land that faces a street, highway, railroad, river, etc. *Ex.: When we saw that the site had both highway and railroad frontage, we knew the location would be suitable.*

general counsel (Ch. 19): the chief legal representative of a company. *Ex.: Mr. Moore was chosen to be the company's general counsel because of his many years of experience in corporate law.*

give notice (Ch. 22): to notify in advance; as an employee, notify an employer of one's intent to leave the company. *Ex.: Employees in most companies are asked to give at least two weeks' notice, rather than leaving immediately.*

gross profit (Ch. 15, exhibit): the amount remaining after deducting the cost of goods sold from total sales. *Ex.: The firm's gross profits have improved, but net profits are down due to a large increase in corporate overhead.* (see also *profit*.)

holdings *(n)* (Ch. 19): the real or financial assets (real estate, stocks, etc.) owned by a person or corporation. *Ex.: Intertex is a large international firm with real estate holdings in many countries.*

house brand (Ch. 24): a product bearing the brand label of the store in which it is sold. *Ex.: Robert always buys the house brand of laundry detergent because it is cheaper and, in his opinion, just as good.*

image *(n)* (Ch. 7): the impression held by the public of a person, product, or company. **product image**. *Ex.: The company decided to change its product image to appeal more to middle-aged buyers.*

improved land (Ch. 5): land which has been prepared for construction or development on it, as by installing sewer connections, streets, etc. *Ex.: The company purchased a tract of improved land, since developing an unimproved piece of land would have been just as costly.*

income statement (Ch. 15, exhibit): a summary of the revenues and expenses of a company or organization. *Ex.: The accounting department is gathering figures from all the company departments in order to put together the year-end income statement.*

industrial park (Ch. 5, exhibit): an area developed as a location for a number of complementary companies and businesses. *Ex.: Rapid Line Trucking chose to locate their operation in an industrial park where several of their clients had facilities.*

infringement *(n)* (Ch. 20): violation of a protected right. *Ex.: The Sterling Co.'s new trademark turned out to be similar to that of another company, and the attorneys recommended it be changed in order to avoid an infringement lawsuit.*

input *(n)* (Ch. 3): information or data received. **computer input**: data put into a computer. *Ex.: Bill asked for the workers' input to help solve the production problems.*

intercom *(n)* (Ch. 4): a two-way communication system allowing people in different rooms or offices to talk to each other. *Ex.: Mary called her secretary on the intercom to let her know she was ready to dictate some letters.*

interest *(n)* (Ch. 8): 1) money charged to a borrower by a lender for money borrowed. *Ex.: The bank charged Chris 12 percent interest on his car loan.* 2) money paid to a lender for the use of his money. *Ex.: Mr. Harris chose the bank where his savings would earn the highest rate of interest.*

Internal Revenue Service (**IRS**) (Ch. 15): in the U.S., the government agency responsible for administering and enforcing federal tax laws. *Ex.: Robert called the local IRS office for help in filling out his tax forms.*

inventory *(n)* (Ch. 8, exhibit): in accounting, a summary of the quantity of goods or merchandise on hand. *Ex.: The store manager checks the inventory weekly to see if it's necessary to reorder.*

invest *(v)* (Ch. 8): 1) the purchase of some form of property in the hope that it will increase in value or produce a financial return. 2) to devote resources for future benefit. **investor**, **investment**. *Ex.: Bob invested his money wisely, so he now has enough to retire comfortably.*

invoice *(n)* (Ch. 8): an itemized bill. *Ex.: The company's invoice states that payment must be made within 30 days of receipt.*

issue *(n)* (Ch. 14): a block of stocks or other financial securities offered for sale by a corporation or government; *(v)* to offer such securities. *Ex.: The company's recent issue of 9-percent bonds was well-received by the financial community.*

labor costs (Ch. 1): the total cost of wages and benefits paid to a company's employees. *Ex.: Labor costs tend to rise when companies compete for workers.*

labor force (Ch. 5, exhibit): the total number of people who are employed or seeking employment. *Ex.: The percentage of women making up the nation's labor force has been increasing steadily.*

laptop computer (Ch. 16): a portable, battery-powered computer small enough to fit on a person's lap. *Ex.: When Arthur travels on business, he always takes his laptop computer so he can have access to the most recent customer data.*

lawsuit *(n)* (Ch. 20): a non-criminal legal action against an individual or group. **file a lawsuit**. *Ex.: When a neighbor's tree fell on his house, Joe filed a lawsuit for property damage.*

lease *(n, v)* (Ch. 5): a contract allowing use of property for a fixed time period in exchange for specified payments. *Ex.: The new company decided to lease rather than purchase its delivery trucks in order to keep initial costs down.*

leave of absence (Ch. 1, letter): authorized time away from work, usually without pay. *Ex.: Mary took a one-year leave of absence to finish an advanced degree in computer science.*

legal department (Ch. 17): the part of the company responsible for giving advice on all legal matters. *Ex.: It's company policy to forward all letters of complaint to the legal department.*

liability *(n)* (Ch. 8, exhibit): money owed, a debt. *Ex.: Everyone became concerned when the company's short-term liabilities began to increase sharply.*

license *(n)* (Ch. 12): a contract by which one company pays for the right to make or sell another company's products or services or to use its trade name. *Ex.: Wiltek Instruments markets the products of DKM Industries under a long-term license arrangement.*

listing sheet (Ch. 14, exhibit): a paper giving a description of a property being offered for sale, usually from a realtor's book which lists all properties currently for sale in an area. *Ex.: The realtor showed us the listing sheets for several houses; from those, we chose three to look at.*

litigation *(n)* (Ch. 20): legal action to settle a disagreement; a lawsuit. *Ex.: The firm's profits were negatively affected last quarter by high litigation costs.*

loading dock (Ch. 23): a platform outside a plant, warehouse, etc., often raised, where goods are picked up and delivered. *Ex.: All the loading docks are full at the moment, so the truck can't unload until after lunch.*

maintenance *(n)* (Ch. 3): the work of keeping something in good condition. *Ex.: The plant's efficiency has improved, but not without a large increase in maintenance costs.*

manage *(v)* (Ch. 1): to control or supervise, especially a business. **manager** *(n)*, **management** *(n)*. *Ex.: The president's management style was to set goals and let others work out the details.*

market *(n)* (Ch. 2): actual or potential customers; demand for a product or service. *Ex.: The market for home video products has been increasing steadily.*

marketing *(n)* (Ch. 2): the activities involved in developing and distributing goods and services to the consumer, including buying, packaging, transportation, and promotion. *Ex.: Even the best products won't sell unless they have the right kind of marketing.*

market share (Ch. 10): the percentage of total industry sales made by a company or product at a particular time. *Ex.: Our sales are down because of an industry-wide fall in sales, but our market share has actually gone up.*

market survey (Ch. 10): operation whereby data is collected on a given topic. *Ex.: The company conducted a market survey to determine the size of the market for a new line of teen cosmetics.*

market value (Ch. 19): 1) the price at which buyers and sellers agree that a product should be sold; market price. 2) on the stock exchange, the most recent price at which a stock traded. *Ex.: John wondered what the market value of his stamp collection would be.*

mass *(adj)* (Ch. 12): of or for large numbers of people. **mass market**. *Ex.: Our company produces an inexpensive line of men's shoes that appeals to the mass market.*

media *(n)* (singular: **medium**) (Ch. 11): a means of communication, especially in advertising, such as radio, T.V., or newspaper. *Ex.: Mr. Wilson sent a notice announcing the new product to all the local media representatives.*

merchandise *(n)* (Ch. 7): goods or products available for sale. *Ex.: Department stores carry all kinds of merchandise, from furniture to sports equipment.*

merger *(n)* (Ch. 19): the union of two or more independent companies into one. *Ex.: The two struggling companies decided a merger was the only way either could survive.*

micro-circuit *(n)* (Ch. 20, letter): a miniaturized electronic circuit. *Ex.: The radio was small and light because it used the most modern micro-circuits.*

minutes *(n)* (Ch. 24, exhibit): an official record, usually written, of matters discussed, action taken, and decisions made in a meeting. *Ex.: After the meeting was opened, the secretary read the minutes of the previous meeting.*

modem *(n)* (Ch. 16): a device that allows one computer to communicate with another computer via telephone lines. *Ex.: Tom has a computer and modem at home, so he can call up files from the office computer to work on.*

mortgage *(n)* (Ch. 8, exhibit): a contract in which a borrower uses property, usually real estate, to secure a loan. *Ex.: Mr. and Mrs. Lewis bought their house with a mortgage from a savings and loan bank.*

negotiate *(v)* (Ch. 12): to discuss or bargain in order to reach an agreement. **negotiations** *(n)*. *Ex.: The firm designated Mrs. White to negotiate the new contract with the supplier.*

net income (Ch. 15, exhibit): amount of money remaining after all expenses and taxes have been deducted; also called net profit. *Ex.: The proposed tax cut would mean a significant increase in net income for the company.*

network *(n)* (Ch. 7): a system in which the various parts connect or interact toward a common purpose. *Ex.: The company's distribution network is designed to move the merchandise quickly and efficiently from the plant to the stores.*

note *(n)* (Ch. 11, exhibit): an intermediate-term debt instrument, maturing in one to ten years. *Ex.: In order to finance its plant expansion, the company sold $7 million worth of notes maturing in 7 years, and paying 10 percent interest.*

NYSE (New York Stock Exchange) (Ch. 12, exhibit): oldest and largest stock exchange in the United States, where stocks, bonds and other securities are bought and sold. *Ex.: More than 2000 companies are listed on the NYSE.*

occupational illness (Ch. 9, exhibit): an illness directly caused by conditions at an employee's workplace. *Ex.: Unsafe working conditions can result in a wide range of occupational illnesses.*

on line (Ch. 17): able to function, operational. *Ex.: We expect to have more rapid access to financial data as soon as the new computer comes on line.*

operate *(v)* (Ch. 1): to manage a business or to run a piece of machinery or a vehicle. **operation** *(n)*: business. *Ex.: Joe started with a small business and then went on to run a much larger operation.*

operating company (Ch. 24): a company which produces revenue for a parent company. *Ex.: Parker Products has two major divisions, each of which supervises four separate operating companies.*

outlay *(n)* (Ch. 5): expenditure. *Ex.: The company's profits are down because of a huge outlay of cash for new equipment.*

outlet *(n)* (Ch. 10): a place where merchandise is sold to the public. *Ex.: The company sent notice of its price cut to all of its sales outlets.*

outline *(n, v)* (Ch. 19): to give the main points of; to summarize. *Ex.: Larry took a few minutes to go over the outline of his proposal before going into detail.*

output *(n)* (Ch. 3, exhibit): the amount produced during a given period of time. *Ex.: The new equipment will lower the plant's output of harmful pollutants.*

outstanding *(adj)* (Ch. 12): in effect, in existence (often stock or debt). **shares of stock outstanding**: the total number of shares of a company's stock in the hands of stockholders at any given time. *Ex.: At the present time, the company has 20 million dollars of long-term debt outstanding.*

overhead projector (Ch. 21): a device used to enlarge and display written or graphic material, from a horizontal surface such as a table, to a vertical surface. *Ex.: Jack uses an overhead projector in presentations to groups because it allows everyone to see.*

package *(n)* (Ch. 9): a number of items grouped together as a unit, such as **package tour**, **package deal**. *Ex.: The company offers its employees an excellent salary and benefits package.*

parent company *(n)* (Ch. 2): a company that owns or controls one or more subsidiary companies. *Ex.: After ten years as president of the largest subsidiary, Tom was named president of the parent company.*

patent *(n, v)* (Ch. 20): the exclusive right to produce or sell an invention. *Ex.: Before telling anyone about his invention, Tim applied for a patent.*

payroll *(n)* (Ch. 9): the total amount of money paid out to employees in wages and salary during a specific period of time. *Ex.: The company is trying to keep its payroll costs from increasing faster than the cost of living.*

pension *(n)* (Ch. 9): the income an employee receives from a company after retirement, usually paid at regular intervals. *Ex.: Mr. Kelly will retire next year but plans to find another job in order to supplement his pension.*

personnel *(n)* (Ch. 4): the employees who work in an organization. **personnel department**: company department responsible for administering matters relating to employees. *Ex.: Harry went to the personnel department to pick up a medical insurance claim form.*

plant *(n)* (Ch. 2): manufacturing facility, factory. *Ex.: The company plans to open two new assembly plants in the next year.*

pool *(n)* (Ch. 6): a grouping of people or resources for a common purpose. *Ex.: When Karen first joined the company, she worked in the secretarial pool and did work for many different executives.*

portfolio *(n)*: a collection or grouping of items. (Ch. 13): charts, drawings, etc. used for demonstration, or the case in which they can be carried. **investment portfolio** (Ch. 19): the entire collection of investments held by an investor. *Ex.: Mr. Edwards checked stock and bond prices every day to see if he needed to make any changes in his portfolio.*

premium *(n)* (Ch. 9): a payment or payments made to an insurance company for insurance coverage. *Ex.: Mrs. Wilson pays her life insurance premium at the beginning of each month.*

press *(n)* (Ch. 11): printed news publications such as newspapers and magazines. **press conference**: a meeting called to make an announcement to the news media. **press release**: a written statement given to radio and television stations, newspapers, etc. *Ex.: The bank sent out a press release to announce the opening of its new branch.*

price-earnings (PE) ratio (Ch. 12): the ratio obtained by dividing the market price of a share of stock by the company's earnings per share. For instance, a PE ratio of 15 means that the price of one share is 15 times the earnings per share. *Ex.: The company's stock was trading at a PE ratio of only 6, which Jean felt was a bargain.*

prime time (Ch. 13): the hours when television has its largest audience, from 8 to 11 in the evening. *Ex.: The firm decided it couldn't justify the high cost of advertising during prime time, but will run commercials in the 5 to 7 p.m. period.*

print advertising (Ch. 10): advertising of a product in newspapers, magazines, brochures, etc. *Ex.: Print advertising often permits a company to target its audience more precisely than radio does.*

printout *(n)* (Ch. 2): sheets of written information from a computer printer. *Ex.: The personnel director asked for a printout of the names and addresses of all employees.*

producer *(n)* (Ch. 1): manufacturer, maker, creator. **production** *(n)*: the act of making or manufacturing; the amount manufactured. *Ex.: The company will have to increase production in order to keep up with steadily increasing sales.*

product line (Ch. 2): the range of similar products offered for sale by a business. *Ex.: Our product line includes a variety of computers, monitors, printers, and related equipment.*

profile *(n)* (Ch. 13): a list of characteristics shared by a group of people or things. *Ex.: Today's teenagers don't fit the same profile as the teens of ten years ago, so our marketing strategies have had to change as well.*

profit *(n)* (Ch. 1): positive difference between the selling price and production price of a good or service. **gross profit** (Ch. 15, exhibit): revenue from sales minus the cost of the goods sold. **net profit**: the sum remaining after all costs and taxes have been met or deducted; also called net income. **profitable** *(adj)*: successful, producing a net gain. *Ex.: After two years of losses, the firm is now profitable once again.*

profit margin (Ch. 1, exhibit): the ratio obtained by dividing profit by sales. *Ex.: The controller attributed the improved profit margin to increased efficiency in the manufacturing area.*

profit-sharing plan (Ch. 9): a program where a firm distributes a part of its profits to its employees each year as a form of incentive. *Ex.: The personnel director felt that the introduction of a profit-sharing plan would help lower employee turnover.*

project *(v)* (Ch. 18): to estimate future performance. **projection** *(n)*. *Ex.: The production manager projects the quantities of raw materials needed for the year.*

promote *(v)* (Ch. 4): to raise a person to a higher or better job or rank. **promotion** *(n)*. *Ex.: Joe received a promotion because of the consistently high quality of his work.*

promotion *(n)* (Ch. 21): efforts to increase the sales of a product through advertising or other forms of publicity. **promote** *(v)*. *Ex.: The use of the firm's name in connection with the golf tournament was one of the ways it promoted its products.*

public relations (PR) (Ch. 11): communication that is directed toward creating a positive image and relationship of a person, product or company with the public. *Ex.: Through the efforts of our public relations agency, several of our products have been favorably reviewed in a number of recent publications.*

purchase agreement (Ch. 17, letter): a contract stating the terms of sale for specified goods or services. *Ex.: According to the terms of the purchase agreement, payment must be made within 45 days of the receipt of the goods.*

purchase order (Ch. 21, exhibit): a written document giving authorization to a vendor or supplier to provide a certain quantity of specified goods. *Ex.: The company from whom we purchase office supplies requires a purchase order before they will process any order over $100.*

quarter *(n)* (Ch. 7): a division of the financial year; a three-month period.
Ex.: The controller gave the president the sales figures for the first quarter, that is, sales from January through March.

questionnaire *(n)* (Ch. 10, letter): a printed form asking a set of questions designed to get certain information to be used for statistical purposes. *Ex.: The company learned a lot about consumer preferences from its recent questionnaire, which was mailed out to 5,000 people.*

quota *(n)* (Ch. 3): The number of units scheduled to be produced by a group or by each member of a group. *Ex.: Each sales representative has a monthly quota of calls he must make on new clients.*

quotation *(n)* (Ch. 18, letter): an offer to sell goods or services at a specified price. *Ex.: John wanted to be sure he got the lowest price on the merchandise, so he called several suppliers to get quotations.*

railroad siding (Ch. 23): a short section of railroad track connecting to the main track. *Ex.: The company is investigating the cost of building a railroad siding so that goods don't have to be trucked to the main rail terminal.*

raise *(n)* (Ch. 4): an increase in salary. *Ex.: Mr. Spencer received a 20 percent raise when he was promoted to assistant manager.*

raw material (Ch. 15, exhibit): a natural substance or semi-finished product from which industrial or manufactured products are made. *Ex.: Iron is a raw material used in making steel, and steel is a raw material in the manufacture of motor vehicles.*

readership (Ch. 13): all the readers of a publication taken as a group.
Ex.: Mr. Nelson examined the readership profiles of several magazines before deciding where to place the firm's advertisements.

real estate (Ch. 5): land, including the improvements on it; the business of buying, selling, and leasing properties. *Ex.: Before the firm decided where to open a branch office, it checked out the prices of real estate in several areas.*

record *(n)* (date of ~) (Ch. 12, exhibit): date on which a shareholder must officially own the stock in order to receive a dividend. *Ex.: Dividends can only be paid to shareholders of record as of March thirty-first.*

recover *(v)* (Ch. 8): to regain or get something back, especially money or other investments. *Ex.: The firm spent $20 million developing the product, but expects to recover the entire amount within four years.*

recruiter *(n)* (Ch. 6): a person whose business it is to locate and screen potential employees or members of an organization. **recruit** *(v)*. *Ex.: Baseball teams spend a lot of time recruiting new players from colleges around the country.*

reference *(n)* (Ch. 6): a statement, usually written, recommending someone for a job and giving information on the person's character, abilities, experience, etc. *Ex.: When applying for jobs, people are often asked to supply both personal and professional references.*

reimbursement *(n)* (Ch. 9): repayment of money paid out. **reimburse** *(v)*. *Ex.: When Mrs. Carlton returned from her trip she filled out an expense report to have her expenses reimbursed.*

release *(n)* (Ch. 9, exhibit): in law, the giving up of a benefit or claim to the person or organization the claim could be used against. *Ex.: When the insurance company reimbursed me for the medical expenses resulting from my injury in a car accident, they asked me to sign a release form freeing them from further responsibility.*

relocate *(v)* (Ch. 6, exhibit): to move to another place. *Ex.: During the interview, Paul asked Fred if he would be willing to relocate to Los Angeles.*

report to *(v)* (Ch. 2): to provide information to; to be accountable to. *Ex.: As an accounting clerk, Tom reports to the chief accountant, Mr. Parker.*

research and development (R & D) (Ch. 11): the part of a company devoted to the systematic development, especially by engineers and scientists, of new products and processes. *Ex.: Companies in new industries tend to spend heavily on research and development.*

resign *(v)* (Ch. 6): to quit one's job, usually turning in a written statement. **resignation** *(n)*. *Ex.: Because Henry's work was so poor, Phillip was forced to ask for his resignation.*

résumé *(n)* (Ch. 6): a formal statement summarizing an applicant's experience and qualifications (employment record, education, interests, etc.); curriculum vitae (CV). *Ex.: Amy sent her résumé to many companies, but was only called to interview with a few.*

retained earnings (Ch. 11): the profits of a company which remain after dividends to shareholders have been paid. *Ex.: A large portion of our retained earnings will be used to fund our research project.*

retire *(v)* (Ch. 1): to stop working, usually when one has reached 60–65 years of age. **retirement** *(n)*. *Ex.: Bill is 64 and he's looking forward to retirement.*

return *(n)* (Ch. 8): profit or payback from an investment. *Ex.: Mr. Black invested in a company that promised returns as high as 35 percent.*

revenue *(n)* (Ch. 2): total amount of income, as from sales. *Ex.: The improvements in the economy resulted in steady increases in sales revenue.*

ribbon-cutting ceremony (Ch. 23): a ceremony marking the first use or opening of a building, road, etc., when a ribbon is often cut to commemorate the event. *Ex.: The vice president spoke at the ribbon-cutting ceremony of the new library.*

robot *(n)*: a computer-controlled machine that can do repetitive tasks automatically. *Ex.: Robots are used for a wide range of tasks in the automobile industry.* **robotize** *(v)* (Ch. 3): to introduce the use of robots into a process, such as manufacturing. *Ex.: The engineers estimate that efficiency could be increased by 15 percent if the plant robotizes its packing process.*

security *(n)* (Ch. 8): a financial instrument such as stock, bonds, etc. **short-term securities**: investments that mature within one year. *Ex.: Because of the uncertain economic climate, the company preferred to invest in short-term rather than long-term securities.*

settlement *(n)* (Ch. 20): an agreement reached through negotiation. *Ex.: Neither Mr. Crane nor Mr. Thomas wanted the expense of a court trial, so they agreed to an out-of-court settlement.*

share *(n)* (Ch. 9): one unit of stock, representing partial ownership in a corporation. *Ex.: Mr. Collins owned hundreds of thousands of shares of Amtex stock.*

shareholder *(n)* (Ch. 19): a person who owns shares of stock in a company; a stockholder *Ex.: Mr. Irwin was not only president of the company, he was also its major shareholder.*

shift *(n)* (Ch. 21): a specified period of time, usually 8 hours, during which a group of employees works, often in a factory. *Ex.: The plant has only a day shift right now, but it would add a second shift if business improved.*

shorthand *(n)* (Ch. 6): a method of writing using symbols in place of words; used by secretaries, stenographers, etc. *Ex.: Bill's secretary takes shorthand at 120 words a minute.* (see also *steno.)*

Social Security (Ch. 9): a U.S. government program funded by employer and employee contributions that provides payments to persons for disability, unemployment and retirement. *Ex.: Mrs. Pierce was eligible for Social Security benefits when she retired.*

specifications *(n, plural)* (Ch. 7): a detailed description, especially of something to be built or manufactured. *Ex.: Before Steve assembled his computer, he checked the specifications to make sure he had all the parts.*

spot *(n)* (Ch. 13): in advertising, a short commercial on radio or television. *Ex.: The advertising budget was divided between 15-second prime-time spots and cheaper, but longer, spots after 11 p.m.*

stalemate *(n)* (Ch. 23, news article): a position reached by two opponents in which neither is able to move without loss. *Ex.: The negotiations reached a stalemate when both the company and the strikers refused to yield in their demands.*

standard(s) (Ch. 23): a level of behavior or quality agreed upon as acceptable. **safety standards**: standards referring to safety. *Ex.: The new government regulations have forced the plant to review all of the safety standards at its facility.*

state-of-the-art *(adj)* (Ch. 5): having the most recent technical developments; very advanced. *Ex.: When the company automated the plant, it installed only state-of-the-art equipment.*

steno *(n, adj)* (Ch. 4): shorthand; short for stenography. **steno pad**: a special notebook used for taking shorthand or notes. *Ex.: Fred's secretary noted down in her steno pad the names of the people he wanted her to contact. (see also shorthand.)*

stock *(v, n)* (Ch. 7): to carry a product; to keep a supply of. *Ex.: The bookstore didn't have the book Phyllis wanted in stock, but they were able to order it for her.*

stock (share of ~) *(n)* (Ch. 9): a share in the ownership of a corporation. *Ex.: Tom bought 200 shares of stock in Atlas Mining Co. at 59½. (see also common stock.)*

stock option (Ch. 22): a form of compensation giving an employee, usually an executive, the right to buy shares of the company's stock at a specified price for a specified period of time. *Ex.: Because of the company's stock option plan, Mrs. Lane was able to buy 2,000 shares of stock at five dollars below the market price.*

stock purchase program (Ch. 9): a program in which employees may buy shares of the company's stock, often at a discounted price, as a type of benefit. *Ex.: Al invests 2 percent of his monthly salary in the firm's stock purchase program.*

stockholder *(n)* (Ch. 8, exhibit): a person who owns shares of stock in a company, a shareholder. *Ex.: The company's annual meeting was well attended by stockholders as well as by other potential investors.*

streamline *(v)* (Ch. 22): to make more efficient; modernize. *Ex.: Roy's ideas for streamlining distribution saved the company $50,000 in the first year.*

strike *(n)* (Ch. 23): a work stoppage called by labor to force management to agree to certain demands. *Ex.: When management rejected a demand for increased benefits, the plant workers went out on strike.*

subsidiary *(n)* (Ch. 2): a company which is owned or controlled by another (parent) company. *Ex.: Mantex Corp. is a subsidiary of Prime Manufacturing, which owns 55 percent of Mantex Corp.'s common stock.*

subsidy *(n)* (Ch. 9, memo): money given to a person, company or organization to reduce the price of a specified good or service. **subsidize** *(v)*. *Ex.: The food in the employee cafeteria is very reasonably priced because it's subsidized by the company.*

sue *(v)* (Ch. 19): to bring legal action against someone in order to obtain compensation, usually money, for some loss, damage, injury or offense. *Ex.: Manufacturers are careful about product safety, knowing that they can easily be sued if a defective product causes injury or damage.*

supplier *(n)* (Ch. 1): a person or company that provides something to another company, especially goods or materials. **supply** *(v)*. *Ex.: The store manager orders most of his small electronics products from the same supplier.*

survey *(n)* (Ch. 14, exhibit): in real estate, a map showing boundary measurements and topographical features of a piece of land. *Ex.: Mr. Bowes ruled out purchasing the land when the survey showed a large area of wetlands not suitable for construction.*

target *(v)* (Ch. 10): to aim at, orient toward. *Ex.: The company has decided to target teen-age consumers more closely in its new ad campaign.*

tax return (Ch. 15): report of income, deductions, and taxes due which must be submitted to the tax authorities annually by taxpayers. *Ex.: Mr. Hall always has an outside accountant prepare his tax return, which must be filed by April 15.*

temporary help (Ch. 6): workers who are hired for limited periods of time. *Ex.: Arthur didn't have enough people to finish the construction job on schedule so he hired several temporary workers.*

tender offer (Ch. 19): a public offer, valid until a specific date, to buy a specified number of shares of stock in a company, at a stated price. *Ex.: Ed has decided to submit his stock for sale under the terms of the company's tender offer.*

terms of payment (Ch. 17): the specific details of how and when payment is to be made. *Ex.: Our terms of payment include a 2 percent discount for payments received within 10 days, 2 percent interest per month after 60 days, and a 5 percent penalty after 90 days.*

tract *(n)* (Ch. 14, exhibit): a large piece of land often subdivided into smaller plots. *Ex.: The owner advertised his tract as suitable for a single industrial site or for several smaller ones.*

trade *(v)* (Ch. 12): to buy or sell a stock, bond or other type of financial security. *Ex.: Chris owns several stocks that trade on the New York Stock Exchange.*

trade publication (Ch. 11): a magazine or newsletter dealing only with subjects of interest to a particular industry. *Ex.: Mrs. Morton had many articles printed in computer trade publications and was well-known within the industry.*

transaction *(n)* (Ch. 16): a business operation involving the transfer of assets from one person or company to another. *Ex.: The store cashier recorded the number of cash and credit transactions each day.*

transparency *(n)* (Ch. 21): a clear sheet of plastic used in connection with an overhead projector. *Ex.: Mary prepared a series of transparencies to be used during her presentation on changing market trends. (see also overhead projector.)*

unemployment insurance (Ch. 9): a government program funded by employer, and sometimes employee, that provides payments for a limited time to people who are unemployed. *Ex.: When Larry lost his job, he collected unemployment insurance for two months, then he found another job.*

unimproved land (Ch. 5): land which has not been prepared for construction. *Ex.: The property taxes on Ted's land are low because it's unimproved; he knows they'll go up when he has utility connections installed. (see also improved land.)*

unit *(n)* (Ch. 5): a single, individual item. **unit sales**, **unit cost**. *Ex.: With increasing sales, the unit cost of VCR's has dropped, permitting the company to lower its prices.*

utilities *(n)* (Ch. 5): public services such as gas, water and electricity. *Ex.: Ann's monthly apartment rent includes water, but she is responsible for paying all other utilities.*

vendor *(n)* (Ch. 16): a seller, often a supplier. *Ex.: The firm keeps a list of all the vendors it regularly does business with.*

venture *(n)* (Ch. 11, exhibit): a new business project undertaken with some risk involved. *Ex.: Timothy is trying to get people to invest in his latest venture, an import/export business.*

volume *(n)* (Ch. 17): total number or amount. *Ex.: The manufacturer offered a substantial discount on high-volume orders.*

Wall Street (Ch. 12): term usually used to refer to the financial district of New York City, and the financial community based there. *Ex.: Wall Street reacted favorably to the news that interest rates were about to drop.*

warehouse *(n)* (Ch. 22): a building used for storage. *(v)*: to place goods in storage. *Ex.: In an effort to shorten delivery time to retailers, the company has recently set up warehouses in various regions around the country.*

wholesale *(adj)* (Ch. 17): the sale of goods in large quantities, usually to a "middleman," not directly to the public; not retail. *Ex.: The company decided to approach the manufacturer directly in order to get the merchandise at wholesale prices.*

word processing (Ch. 4): the production of typewritten documents by the use of a specially programmed computer which allows the user to format and edit documents before they are printed. *Ex.: Mary is anxious to get the upgraded version of her word processing program because it will have many new features.*

worker's compensation (Ch. 9): a program providing payments to workers who are injured on the job or who contract employment-related illnesses. These payments usually cover hospital expenses, medical expenses and loss of wages. *Ex.: When Jack was injured by a fall at work, his expenses were covered by worker's compensation.*

zoning *(n)* (Ch. 14, exhibit): the legal dividing of a town or area into districts where only certain types of activities are permitted (industrial, commercial, and residental zoning). **zone** *(v)*. *Ex.: Mr. Williams wanted to open a bookstore, but when he checked the city's zoning regulations, he found out the location he was interested in wasn't zoned for commercial use.*

WRITING PRACTICE

Chapter 1

Write a short review of the performance report on page 6. Try to use these words and phrases:

quarter	profitable
tax	growth rate
profit margin	year to date
increase / decrease	improving

You're Jim Burke. Write a response to Bill Jensen's letter on page 10. Try to use these words and phrases:

sorry to hear	request
doctor's advice	retirement benefits
unexpected	appreciate
approve	take it easy

Chapter 2

You're resigning from your job. Write a letter of resignation. Try to use some of these words and phrases:

inform you	find a replacement
difficult decision	appreciate
advancement	learning experience
pass up the opportunity	future

You're the editor of AP's newsletter. Write an article announcing Crawford's appointment as president of AP. Try to use some of these words and phrases:

named to the position	capable
corporate headquarters	energy
management experience	lead the company
comes to us from	wish him the best

Chapter 3 You're Bob Smith. Write a memo to your boss, Ed Pearson, to let him know that you're working to improve production, and to reassure him that things will get better. Use these words and phrases:

meet the quota	maintenance
production reports	do my best
delivery schedule	turn things around
efficiently	look forward to

Write a response to Mr. Daley's letter on page 34. Try to use these words and phrases:

apologize	equipment problems
inconvenience	hope
delay	future orders
expect delivery	valuable customer

Chapter 4 You've been assistant manager of production in a small manufacturing firm for two years. Because of production quota increases you've been working a lot of overtime, and it will continue. Write a letter to your supervisor asking for a raise. Use some of the words below:

from the start	additional responsibilites
satisfied with	no alternative
request a raise	give consideration to
because of	get back to someone

You're the personnel manager. You've received a résumé and application from an underqualified individual and you must inform him/her that the application has been rejected. Write a letter of rejection, using some of these words:

receive	regret
in response to	hire
application	interest
experience	a later date

Chapter 5   You're a real estate agent at DKP Associates. You received a letter of inquiry from Jeff Martinelli. Using the information in DKP's ad on page 58, write a letter describing the property. Try to use some of these words:

eager to	take advantage of
expansion plans	city utilities
industrial site	get back to me
improved land	appointment

You've just finished a study of labor costs in another area of the country. According to the results, labor costs there are quite low and the area's population is still growing. Write a memo to your manager reporting the results of the study. Use some of the words below:

results	labor supply
labor costs	in terms of
labor climate	increase capacity
take advantage of	available

Chapter 6   You're Peter Crawford. Write a letter to Bob Smith, asking for his resignation. Use some of these words:

as a result of	submit
incapable of	letter of resignation
turn things around	effective date
regret	appreciate

You've been an assistant department manager for three years. Your boss, the department manager, is being promoted. You feel that you are the best one to take over his position as department manager. Write a letter to him expressing interest in the position. Use some of these words:

regarding	experience
opportunity	enthusiastic
capable of	under consideration
fill the position	in the near future

Chapter 7   Write a letter in response to Mr. Aronson's letter on page 82, showing concern about the decrease in sales. Use some of these words:

appreciate	in the future
inventory report	product image
sorry	offer "pre-sold" items
overstocked	increase

You're an advertising representative from Creative Talents Agency. Write a letter to Peter expressing your ideas on how AP's sales and profits could be improved through advertising. Use some of these words:

in my opinion	put together a study
advertising support	get to work
brand awareness	long-term
household word	strategy

Chapter 8   You work in the accounts receivable section. Your company has recently increased the early-payment discount from 1 percent to 2 percent. Write a form letter to tell your customers about the higher discount, using some of these words:

inform you	take advantage of
collection policy	discount
in the past	maintain a good relationship
prompt payment	appreciate yourbusiness

Your company has excess cash it wants to invest in low-risk, short-term securities. Write a letter to your broker explaining the company's cash situation and its investment goals. Use some of these words and phrases:

at this time	keep an eye on
on deposit	recommend
no-interest accounts	short-term securities
available	higher return

Chapter 9

You're the personnel director. Your company has just added a stock purchase plan to its benefit package. Write a memo to all employees, explaining the program. Try to use some of these words and phrases:

pleased to announce   shares of company stock
addition of   discount
fringe benefit   as of March 15, 19--
stock purchase plan   investment

You fell at work and broke your leg. To receive worker's compensation, you must write aletter to the personnel department explaining your condition and formally requesting the benefit. Use some of these words and phrases:

injured on the job   health coverage
unable to work   according to the doctor
eligible for   stay in hospital
in addition   return to work

Chapter 10

Your firm's sales have fallen recently. Your boss asked you to write a letter to a market research firm asking them to do a survey. Write the letter stating the problems, and request a meeting. Use some of these words:

well-knownfirm   analyze
suspect   compare
misdirected   break down data
survey   results

You bought an AP "personal stereo" last week. When you got it home, you realized the headphones only had sound on one side. You exchanged it for a different brand, one which had more features for the same price. Write a letter of complaint to AP's consumer relations department, expressing your dissatisfaction. Use some of these words:

not functioning   as a result
poor quality   exchange
lack features   different brand
not impressed with   reputation

Chapter 11　　You work for a public relations firm and you've been asked to write a press release for a new computerized dictionary. Using some of these words, write the release announcing the product's arrival on the market.

launch	look up words
years of research	will be available
have an impact on	computer disk
easy to use	features

You're a reporter for a small newspaper and you have just interviewed the local inventor, Dr. Kosloff. Write a brief article about him and his invention, using some of these words:

research	release
technology	success
device	pay off
unique	feasible

Chapter 12　　You are Charles Brewster, CEO of Leisure Time Entertainment. Using the information reported in the New York Journal article on page 139, prepare a report for your Board of Directors outlining your company's current financial position and future prospects. Use some of these words:

growth	success
P/E ratio	optimistic
New York Stock Exchange	diversification
trade	credit rating

As a representative of AP, write to Charles Brewster to propose a license arrangement to market the Games Master. Try to use these words and phrases:

well-established	access to
product line	profits
of mutual benefit	negotiate
in your interest	hear from you

Chapter 13   You're Peter Crawford. Write a letter praising Jack Bell on his advertising presentation and let him know that you are planning to implement his ideas in the future. Try to use these words:

compliment you on	look forward to
impressive	strategy
presentation	turn around
full-color	results

Write a letter to a local newspaper inquiring about advertising in the publication. Be sure to ask about rates, reader profile, and circulation of the paper. Use some of the words below:

think about	size
run advertisements	readership
rates	figures
design	match a profile

Chapter 14   You've been asked to find office space to rent. You came across a good location at a good price, but the offices are going quickly and you're afraid that you might miss the opportunity. Write a memo to your boss describing your discovery and expressing the need for quick action. Use some of these words:

up-to-date	miss out on
locate	first choice
to meet s.o.'s needs	settle for
a good deal	reply

Write a brief article for AP's company newsletter. Describe the site chosen in South Carolina. Try to use some of these words:

location	space
choose / choice	increase
bond issue	production
attract	move

Chapter 15

You're Ed Pearson. Write a memo to Jack Reilly, acting manager of the Baltimore plant. Inform him you have decided to offer him the position on a permanent basis. Use some of the words below:

make up my mind	the mechanics of
turn over (job)	well-qualified
permanent	candidate
realize	confident

As a result of an accounting error, your firm paid too much in taxes. Write a letter to the IRS stating why you are filing an amended return. Ask them to credit the overpayment against next year's tax liability. Try to use some of these words:

due to	if possible
accounting error	tax liability
amended return	information
year 19--	don't hesitate to

Chapter 16

Write a proposal for your company to buy a new, updated computer system. Use some of these words:

look into	laptop computers
update	printout
efficiency	get along without
state-of-the-art	in conclusion

Make a list of the major tasks that your current computer system is used for in the office. Use some of these words:

on file	payroll
keep track of	marketing
inventory	standpoint
invoice	organization

Chapter 17   You're director of sales for a large company. Write a memo to the legal department informing them that you are working on a purchase agreement, and that you will be needing advice on the contract. Use some of these words:

work on	terms of payment
rough draft	penalties
enter into	details
purchase agreement	be in touch

Write a brief article about the Shop-Way deal for AP's company newsletter. Be sure to mention Ben Melnick, and use some of the words below:

deal	production
chain	at the same time
interested in	profit picture
contract	congratulations

Chapter 18   You're Ben Melnick. Reply to John Smythe's letter on p. 214. Tell him that you're sending the requested information, but that the price quotes are not fixed due to the fluctuation of the dollar. Use some of these words:

enclosed	price quotes
information	depend on
fluctuation	current rates
assume	look forward to

Write a brief report about the value of your country's currency against the dollar. Explainhow it might affect AP's financial and production situation should AP decide to sell its products in your country. Use some of these words:

fluctuation	prevailing
steady	imports
value	sales projections
increase (decrease)	climate

Chapter 19   You're George Welk and have just received the letter on page 226. Respond to Mr. Hayes, accepting or rejecting the offer, or making a counteroffer. Use some of these words:

in response to	market value
heirs	however
at this time	get back to
(not) interested in	within

You're Peter Crawford. Write a memo to Jim Burke. Bring him up-to-date on the LTE situation and request a meeting in the next week. Try to use some of these words:

encouraging	effective control
contribution	recommendation
go ahead with	take action
stock outstanding	as soon as possible

Chapter 20   You're Mr. Campbell. You've received the letter from Mr. Hayes on page 238. Respond, letting him know what you've decided to do: either cease or continue production. Use some of the words below:

patent	aware of
investigate	lawsuit
R & D department	legal action
design	be in touch with

Play World did not stop production of the device and AP took legal action to defend its patent by filing a lawsuit. Write an article for the local newspaper about AP's lawsuit against Play World. Use some of these words:

legal action	patent infringement
manufacture	willing to
defend	in court
as a result	protect (the patent)

Chapter 21   You're Peter Crawford. Write a memo to Jack Reilly, the manager of the Baltimore plant. Inform him of the increase in production that will be necessary to meet increased demand due to the successful ad campaign. Try to use some of these words:

test area	extra shifts
demand	capacity
trend	confident
step up	accomodate

You're Jim Burke. You have many questions about the new ad campaign, the sales trend, and the pricing policy. Write some of these questions down so that you can raise them at the next meeting with Peter Crawford. Use some of the words below:

profit	respond to
level off	on the market
anticipate	production plan
consumers	competitors

Chapter 22   You're Alan Fischer and you've just accepted the job with AP. Write a letter of resignation to your superior at Clay Products, Mr. Greystone, explaining the reasons for your decision to change jobs. Try to use some of these words and phrases:

serious consideration	challenge
give notice	foreign environment
relocate	work out of ...
head up	appreciate

You're Jane Collins and you've been working with Alan Fischer on his relocation package. Write a memo to him outlining AP's policies on relocation expenses, using some of these words:

Welcome aboard!	living expenses
reimburse	written estimate
airfare	receipts
personal belongings	further assistance

Chapter 23   Peter Crawford has been asked to give the Board an update on the expansion of AP's facilities. Make notes for his presentation. Include a description, cost estimates and a timetable. Use some of the following words and expressions:

square feet	warehouse space
keep costs down	provide for
capacity requirements	break ground
rail transportation	in operation

You need a definite timetable from the construction site manager in Greenville. Write a letter asking him to give you a detailed schedule. Use some of the following expressions:

need to know	state standards
specific concerns	non-essential items
structural steel	keep me informed
truckers' strike	definite dates

Chapter 24   You're Jim Burke. Write a letter to Peter Crawford complimenting him on AP's performance and on his presentation to the Board. Use some of the following words and expressions:

appreciate	impressive
put down in writing	consolidated
turn things around	division
team	challenge

Write a press release for AP announcing its takeover of LTE. Mention the effect this will have on the distribution of the Games Master and other AP products. Use some of the following:

effective date	investment
cooperation	partnership
management	confident
potential	optimistic

Answer Key

ANSWER KEY

Exercise 1	1. c 2. b 3. c 4. a 5. b 6. c
Exercise 2	1. read; am reading 2. 's calling; do ... call 3. take it easy; is taking it easy 4. are ... doing; does ... do 5. is growing; grow 6. requests; 's requesting 7. are including; include
Exercise 3	1. saw; were eating 2. were talking; arrived 3. was going; ran into 4. took; was earning 5. had to; was leaving
Exercise 4	1. ago 2. until 3. now 4. for 5. at 6. on 7. during 8. in 9. from ... to 10. during 11. ago 12. for
Exercise 5	1. retirement age 2. production manager 3. springtime 4. workday 5. sales report 6. business card 7. nightclubs 8. desk clerk
Exercise 6	1. c 2. c 3. c 4. a 5. b 6. b
Exercise 7	1. has met 2. signed 3. checks out 4. has ... hired 5. dictates 6. has been 7. keep in touch 8. took 9. has had 10. have been
Exercise 8	1. for 2. yet 3. since 4. already 5. since 6. for 7. yet 8. already 9. since; yet 10. since 11. for 12. already; yet
Exercise 9	1. because of 2. in order to 3. due to 4. in order to 5. Since 6. for 7. so 8. That's why
Exercise 10	1. industries 2. supplier 3. competition 4. retirement 5. leadership 6. expand 7. profitable 8. approval
Exercise 11	1. three-week tour 2. 50,000-word dictionary 3. five-course meals 4. $25,000-car 5. eighteen-passenger plane 6. eight-person committee 7. six-foot fence 8. nine-month computer course
Exercise 12	1. a 2. b 3. b 4. c 5. b 6. c
Exercise 13	1. I've just had dinner with a friend (whom) I haven't seen in years. 2. We have twenty new trainees who were hired last month. 3. I went over the paperwork (that) you put on my desk. 4. Ted works for a firm that has offices all over the

country. 5. The Board chose a president who has had many years of experience. 6. Mr. Crawford was on the flight that left at one o'clock. 7. The client who called about an order would like you to return her call. 8. The expansion (that) we're planning should increase the company's profits. 9. There are some problems at the plant (that) the manager is concerned about. 10. The passenger who lost her ticket will have to pay another fare. 11. The book that was recommended to me is now a best seller. 12. I'm having lunch with some people (whom) I met at the meeting.

Exercise 14   1. is going over 2. was ... leaving 3. have been talking 4. were having 5. will ... be raining 6. has been meeting 7. is working 8. are waiting 9. were walking 10. has been teaching

Exercise 15   1. keeps 2. spoken with 3. be wearing 4. was doing 5. come 6. been expecting 7. been waiting 8. dictates 9. be lying 10. is making 11. was raining 12. been going over

Exercise 16   1. underpriced 2. underproduced 3. oversupply 4. overcharged 5. undertaxed 6. overreacted 7. overdressed 8. underrated

Exercise 17   1. located; It's located just outside Peter's office. 2. urgent; No, it wasn't. 3. practical; She hadn't had any. 4. secretarial; Yes, she had. 5. enthusiastic; She was so enthusiastic about becoming Mr. Crawford's secretary because it was a good opportunity. 6. additional; Some of her additional responsibilities were going to be keeping Crawford's files in order, keeping track of all of his appointments, and making travel arrangements when necessary. 7. satisfied; He was more than satisfied with her performance. 8. latest; He was going to discuss them with Ed Pearson.

Exercise 18   1. I had already eaten 2. the plane hadn't left yet 3. Bill had already requested retirement 4. she hadn't found another job yet 5. I had already gone over the figures

Exercise 19   1. When Peter Crawford gave Jim Burke his decision, he had already talked it over with his wife. 2. When Janet went to work for AP, it had just become a subsidiary of UEI. 3. When I left work at 6:30 p.m., I still hadn't finished going over the sales figures. 4. When your representative contacted us, we had just signed a contract with another firm. 5. When Mr. Park left the meeting, we had already discussed foreign competition. 6. When the sales manager retired, they still hadn't found a replacement for her. 7. When the computer technician arrived after lunch, we had already solved the problem ourselves. 8. When we drove through the intersection, the accident had just taken place. 9. When I spoke to Sally last week, she still hadn't found an apartment. 10. When Jim arrived at the garage, they had just finished repairing his car. 11. When Stephen invited me to dinner, I had already made other plans. 12. When we saw our friends in August, we had just come back from vacation the week before.

Exercise 20 1. revenues 2. break down 3. professional 4. domestic 5. raise 6. picked up 7. joined 8. in order 9. accept 10. sharply 11. major 12. increase

Exercise 21 1. signed 2. has met 3. had gone out 4. drove 5. hadn't finished 6. has been 7. stopped 8. hadn't talked 9. have watched 10. hadn't left

Exercise 22 1. get 2. made 3. have 4. took 5. in 6. take 7. meet 8. place 9. of 10. chance

Exercise 23 1. action 2. option 3. facility 4. assistant 5. capacity 6. transportation 7. proximity 8. outlay 9. project 10. objectives 11. results 12. construction

Exercise 24 1. traveling all over the world on business 2. working as a real estate agent 3. Learning to use a word processor 4. analyzing the study on May fifteenth 5. Leasing an existing plant 6. put off writing up the report 7. Discussing the expansion plans 8. Looking at properties

Exercise 25A 1. Mr. Crawford didn't mind her leaving the office early. 2. Don't you remember their agreeing to consider our suggestion? 3. I appreciate your giving me the information. 4. Susan told me about his finding a new job. 5. My getting up late caused a lot of problems at work.

Exercise 25B	1. The plant can increase production by buying new equipment. 2. As a result of speaking with several brokers, Jeff became aware of the options. 3. After reading the reports, the sales director made his decision. 4. Kurt got a bonus for being the company's top salesperson. 5. While waiting for the elevator, I talked to the receptionist. 6. Ed talked it over with his wife before accepting the offer. 7. Steve signed the memo without reading it. 8. Since moving to St. Moritz, Paul has learned to ski well. 9. In spite of being young, George has had a lot of practical experience. 10. We bought an existing facility instead of building a new one.
Exercise 26	1. b 2. a 3. a 4. a 5. b 6. a 7. a 8. b 9. b 10. b 11. a 12. b
Exercise 27	1. about 2. for 3. with 4. to 5. with 6. of 7. about 8. for 9. of 10. about 11. in 12. for
Exercise 28	1. unimpressed 2. incapable 3. impossible 4. nontaxable 5. irreplaceable 6. inexpensive 7. dislike 8. unlimited
Exercise 29	1. a 2. b 3. a 4. c 5. b 6. c
Exercise 30	1. All appointments are scheduled by the secretary. 2. Their top managers are paid high salaries. 3. Our quota had been filled by the end of last month. 4. This stereo component is manufactured by AP. 5. Important decisions are made by the Board of Directors. 6. These reports will be discussed at the next meeting. 7. Capacity was finally increased by adding extra shifts. 8. An increase in the production quota has been recommended. 9. Our obsolete equipment will be replaced by modern machines. 10. Twenty-five new employees have been trained over the past six months. 11. A meeting was being planned by the director of sales. 12. This product is only distributed through department stores. 13. Detailed résumés have been submitted by all of the applicants. 14. Many questions were asked by the interviewer. 15. Many products are imported by the firm I work for.
Exercise 31	1. This project must be completed by the first of August. 2. Some factory workers can be replaced by machines. 3. Business letters should always be typed. 4. This product can't

be bought in department stores yet. 5. The machines should be delivered by the same company that sold them. 6. That copier can't be carried by one person alone. 7. Personal calls shouldn't be made from the office. 8. The proposal must be reviewed by Mr. Burke before we proceed.

Exercise 32   1. reviewed   2. handles 3. purchase   4. position   5. recommended 6. requested 7. submit 8. assembled 9. consider 10. frank 11. responsibilities 12. opportunity

Exercise 33   1. together 2. through 3. ahead 4. down 5. going 6. interesting 7. across 8. point

Exercise 34   1. apologize; Yes, he did. 2. fallen; They had fallen over the past year. 3. distributed; Seventy-one percent of Tru-Tone products was being distributed through authorized dealers. 4. falling; It was falling off because Tru-Tone received far less advertising support than the competing products on the market. 5. priced; He felt it was priced too high. 6. cutting; No, he wasn't. 7. review; He wanted to review the situation with Steve Blake. 8. hold; He held the sales department responsible for the falling sales. 9. put together; He wants them to put together a complete market study in order to get a better picture of their present position. 10. develop; They needed data on pricing, advertising, and distribution.

Exercise 35   1. We buy our equipment from a well-known company. 2. The applicant chosen for the job had ten years of experience. 3. A maintenance person replaced the broken window. 4. Increasing competition was one topic discussed at the meeting. 5. The purchasing agent ordered some badly-needed supplies. 6. The personnel director interviewed four well-qualified applicants. 7. The ad placed in the newspaper got immediate results. 8. Our line is as good as other similarly-priced lines.

Exercise 36   1. unless 2. in spite of 3. depending on 4. still 5. Even though 6. without 7. if 8. If so 9. If not 10. still

Exercise 37   1. hasn't it; No, it hasn't. 2. shouldn't we; Yes, we should. 3. does it; No, it doesn't. 4. do they; Yes, they do. 5. will she;

No, she won't. 6. aren't I; No, you aren't (you're not). 7. didn't she; Yes, she did. 8. haven't they; Yes, they have.

Exercise 38	1. have 2. does 3. do 4. didn't 5. can 6. does 7. did 8. has 9. will 10. could
Exercise 39	1. of 2. as 3. to 4. in 5. for 6. on 7. At 8. behind 9. In 10. on
Exercise 40	1. F 2. T 3. T 4. T 5. F 6. T 7. T 8. F 9. F 10. T 11. T 12. F
Exercise 41	1. c 2. b 3. c 4. a 5. b 6. c 7. a 8. c 9. c 10. a 11. b 12. c
Exercise 42	1. a 2. c 3. b 4. b 5. c 6. a 7. b 8. c 9. b 10. a
Exercise 43	1. item 2. competitive 3. resignation 4. supervising 5. promotion 6. collection 7. inherited 8. consideration 9. specifications 10. responsibilities 11. reduce 12. authorized
Exercise 44	1. felt 2. sound 3. looks 4. felt 5. sounds 6. felt 7. sounds 8. looks
Exercise 45	1. package 2. insurance 3. pension 4. required 5. reimbursement 6. day care 7. cafeteria 8. willing
Exercise 46	1. Working for an advertising agency, Robert has the opportunity to meet many interesting people. 2. Not having a good benefits program, the firm has trouble attracting top people. 3. Traveling so much, I don't have a lot of time to spend with my family. 4. Not being familiar with the city, Helen may have trouble finding her way around. 5. Not believing the sales figures, Carl will check them over himself. 6. Using the computer, I finished my report in less than an hour. 7. Spending two years in Sweden, the Martins would learn a lot about the country. 8. Not remembering that Jill and Frank were out of town, we stopped to visit them. 9. Being head of personnel, Carol must make difficult decisions. 10. Not knowing where you were, I couldn't return your call.

Exercise 47	1. Having seen the movie twice, Anita isn't going to see it again. 2. Not having studied a language in school, I'm finding German very difficult. 3. Having read the newspaper, we knew about the accident. 4. Never having flown in a plane before, Mrs. Perkins was a little nervous. 5. Having done a thorough study on benefits, Carol was able to make recommendations. 6. Not having had a vacation for two years, my wife and I are really looking forward to this one. 7. Having worked in accounts payable for many years, Tom was a good candidate for department head. 8. Never having lived in a large city, I don't know if I would like it.
Exercise 48	1. Susan was offered the position at the interview. 2. Most employees are paid a good salary by this company. 3. You will be sent the information you requested. 4. I have just been given a raise by my supervisor. 5. We were being shown the new AP product line by the salesman. 6. Children are taught to read in the first grade. 7. Everyone will be served coffee and doughnuts during the meeting. 8. The prime minister was asked many questions regarding foreign policy by the reporters. 9. Tom was practically guaranteed a promotion within six months by his boss. 10. You will be interviewed when you apply for a visa.
Exercise 49	1. required 2. improved 3. implemented 4. delay 5. objective 6. percentage 7. established 8. reimbursed 9. strategy 10. merchandise 11. role 12. provide
Exercise 50	1. fact 2. minutes 3. opinion 4. money 5. profits 6. position 7. interest 8. nothing
Exercise 51	1. a 2. c 3. c 4. b 5. a 6. c 7. b 8. a
Exercise 52	1. one of 2. nearly 3. even 4. by far 5. twice 6. quite a bit 7. even 8. a little 9. just 10. the two
Exercise 53	1. to do well in his new job 2. not to get any mail yesterday 3. to prepare the contract 4. to sign the contract soon 5. not to park in this driveway 6. not to mention this to anyone 7. to buy the suit 8. not to tell Bill about the party

Exercise 54	1. The land cost the company $400,000, which is expensive. 2. We're planning a special retirement dinner for the director, who's been with the company for thirty years. 3. In New York, where parking space is very limited, people use public transportation. 4. Judy, whose office is on the tenth floor, is in charge of the secretarial pool. 5. Mr. Hutchins, whom we just hired last month, is doing an excellent job. 6. Labor costs in Baltimore, where we have a plant, have risen a lot. 7. Our benefits program, which represents thirty-five percent of total payroll costs, is average for the industry. 8. The advertising plan, which will be more youth-oriented, should have heavy T.V. support.
Exercise 55	1. given 2. face 3. called 4. take 5. fill 6. feel 7. pick up 8. at 9. around 10. make
Exercise 56	1. c 2. b 3. c 4. b 5. b 6. a 7. c
Exercise 57	1. offer 2. would 3. Won't 4. spent 5. went 6. will 7. fly
Exercise 58	1. If there had been a mistake in the bill, I would have noticed it. 2. If we hadn't arrived at the theater late, we would have seen the first act of the play. 3. If you had called, I would have told you the big news. 4. Jane wouldn't have flown business class if the firm hadn't been paying for the trip. 5. If the Burkes hadn't taken the expressway, they would have gotten caught in traffic. 6. If Peter hadn't trusted Kosloff, he wouldn't have continued funding the research. 7. Tom and Mary wouldn't have enjoyed their sightseeing tour if it had been raining. 8. I would have had to use my credit card if I hadn't had enough cash.
Exercise 59	1. If we had had dinner, we wouldn't be hungry. 2. If the Tru-Tone line had kept pace with the industry, it would sell well. 3. If you had taken your medicine, you would feel better. 4. If Peter hadn't worked very hard, he wouldn't be a successful businessman. 5. If Karen had had time to type the letters earlier, she wouldn't be doing them now. 6. If it had rained hard, the streets would be very slippery now. 7. If we hadn't made reservations two months in advance, we wouldn't be

sitting at the best table in the restaurant. 8. If I had learned English as a child, I wouldn't be taking lessons now.

Exercise 60	1. failed 2. satisfied 3. lacks 4. substantial 5. decline 6. ignore 7. haphazard 8. premium 9. predecessor 10. reduce 11. required 12. receivable
Exercise 61	1. into 2. to 3. in 4. for 5. off 6. down 7. on 8. up
Exercise 62	1. b 2. a 3. b 4. c 5. b 6. a 7. c 8. b 9. a 10. b
Exercise 63	1. must 2. couldn't 3. should 4. may 5. had better 6. may 7. can't 8. ought to 9. can't 10. can't 11. must 12. won't be able to; has to
Exercise 64	1. a 2. b 3. a 4. b 5. a 6. a 7. b 8. b
Exercise 65	1. acquisition 2. emphasis 3. negotiations 4. encouragement 5. deduction 6. law 7. complaints 8. diversify 9. stability 10. announcement 11. feasible 12. excess
Exercise 66	1. best 2. talking 3. housework 4. filing 5. good 6. wonders 7. something 8. lunch
Exercise 67	1. F 2. T 3. F 4. F 5. F 6. F 7. T 8. F
Exercise 68	1. must 2. must 3. should 4. may 5. must 6. should 7. may 8. should 9. may 10. must
Exercise 69	1. c 2. a 3. c 4. a 5. c 6. b 7. c 8. a
Exercise 70	1. b 2. a 3. a 4. b 5. b 6. a 7. a 8. a
Exercise 71	1. deposit 2. succeeded in 3. compact 4. net 5. preliminary 6. opposed to 7. keep pace 8. vulnerable 9. adequate 10. potential
Exercise 72	1. over 2. up 3. out 4. up 5. over 6. down 7. up 8. down 9. up 10. out 11. up 12. out
Exercise 73	1. adequate; No, it didn't. 2. industrial; They were being issued by the state of South Carolina. 3. subject to; Corporate bonds

were subject to tax.   4. prevailing; It was lower than the prevailing rate.   5. loaned; They were loaned to companies moving their operations into the state.   6. unimproved; AP was considering 18 acres of land for purchase.   7. formal; His first formal offer was $150,000.   8. disappointed; He was pleased with the deal he finally made.

Exercise 74   1. He shouldn't have taken the money.   2. She could have bought the car. 3. You should have heard Steve's presentation. 4. She should have waited for us. 5. She couldn't have driven to Boston.   6. I shouldn't have waited until yesterday to mail the letter to my client. 7. We could have sold the property. 8. They couldn't have gone to the party.   9. He shouldn't have stayed home from work. 10. It couldn't have landed at Heathrow. 11. He could have moved to New York. 12. I should have finished the report yesterday.

Exercise 75   1. He must have forgotten about our appointment.   2. He might have thought it was for tomorrow. 3. Someone must have told him.   4. He must have gotten the message.   5. He might not have gotten the message.   6. I must have told him the wrong time.   7. He might have misunderstood me.   8. He might have gotten held up in traffic.

Exercise 76   1. might have been transferred 2. must have been delivered 3. must have been submitted   4. must have misunderstood   5. might have been filled 6. might have phoned 7. must have found 8. must have been given 9. might have gotten 10. must have made

Exercise 77   1. financial 2. clerical 3. choice 4. enthusiastically 5. coverage 6. procedure 7. proposal 8. confidence 9. acres 10. responded 11. deal 12. impressed

Exercise 78   1. on 2. together 3. back 4. in 5. through 6. down 7. up 8. to 9. off 10. with

Exercise 79   1. T 2. F 3. F 4. T 5. T 6. F 7. F 8. T 9. T 10. F 11. T 12. F

Exercise 80   A. 1. b 2. c 3. a B. 1. b 2. a 3. c C. 1. c 2. a 3. b

Exercise 81	A. 1. b 2. a 3. c B. 1. c 2. a 3. b C. 1. b 2. c 3. a
Exercise 82	1. get hold of him 2. break them down 3. break down 4. put it together 5. go ahead with it 6. pay off 7. turn out 8. rely on them 9. look them over 10. work through her
Exercise 83	1. obviously 2. took over 3. cause 4. revealed 5. disturbed 6. approached 7. prevailing 8. guaranteed 9. disappointed 10. miscalculation 11. originally 12. mentioned
Exercise 84	1. call 2. suggestions 3. changes 4. profit 5. list 6. offer 7. appointment 8. right 9. reservations 10. decision
Exercise 85	1. b 2. a 3. b 4. c 5. c 6. a 7. c 8. b
Exercise 86	1. had to make a decision on the advertising budget soon 2. couldn't make it to the meeting on time 3. had begun negotiating a three-year contract 4. would be introduced in the spring 5. had received our invoice on May fifteenth 6. had arrived at the airport at 3:00 p.m. 7. came with a full guarantee 8. wouldn't affect my credit rating 9. hadn't been in since Tuesday 10. would be held in Brussels 11. had been running low too often 12. couldn't afford any large expenditures until its profit picture improved
Exercise 87	1. whether we could get a reservation for May first 2. how long ago the Hartford plant had opened 3. whether the company had problems keeping track of inventory 4. when the shipping supervisor had submitted his resignation 5. whether he had considered using the computer for forecasting 6. what rate of production I was hoping for 7. when the fourth-quarter figures would be available 8. whether the new equipment had been running well 9. why the production quota had been set so high 10. whether her performance would be reviewed every six months 11. how soon the new computer network could be installed 12. why the company was planning to expand its recruitment program
Exercise 88	1. whether I would like to have lunch with him the next (following) afternoon 2. how much AP had earned in profits the year before (the previous year) 3. whether the new policy would be in effect a month later (a month from then) 4. how

late the store would stay open that night 5. whether we could afford such a large expenditure at that time

Exercise 89	1. expansion 2. agreement 3. maintenance 4. seriousness 5. productivity 6. minority 7. authorization 8. refusal
Exercise 90	1. smug 2. high-volume 3. discount 4. wholesale 5. temporary 6. legal 7. unrealistic 8. expansion
Exercise 91	A. 1. has met 2. will meet 3. will have met B. 1. will have left 2. will be sitting 3. will meet
Exercise 92	1. will last 2. will have left 3. will go 4. will be sitting 5. will ask 6. will have begun 7. will have been 8. will be waiting 9. will be 10. will have checked out 11. will sign 12. will have learned
Exercise 93	1. Mrs. Carlson was away on vacation this week 2. the company would increase salaries before the end of the year 3. Stanley Wells had been transferred to London in May 4. sales had increased ten percent since last month 5. unit costs could be reduced 6. Shop-Way was insisting on a substantial discount 7. Mr. Knowles' presentation had gone over well 8. all contracts were reviewed by the legal department
Exercise 94	1. analysis 2. qualifications 3. disastrous 4. failure 5. accurate 6. penalty 7. affordable 8. prove 9. consulting 10. congratulations 11. efficiently 12. valuable
Exercise 95	1. in 2. to 3. in 4. about 5. in 6. to 7. from 8. in 9. on 10. to
Exercise 96	1. F 2. T 3. F 4. F 5. T 6. T 7. T 8. T 9. F 10. T 11. F 12. F
Exercise 97	1. The steadily rising prices concern me. 2. What are the remaining options? 3. We're happy to hear about the company's increasing profits. 4. Jobs are easy to find in a rapidly expanding economy. 5. Customers paying by check must show some identification. 6. We heard frequent reports about the constantly changing situation. 7. People traveling on

the weekend should make advance reservations. 8. The continuing labor problems will be discussed at the meeting.

Exercise 98

1. convincing 2. broken 3. surprising 4. satisfied 5. estimated 6. tiring 7. revised 8. discouraging 9. winning 10. stabilized

Exercise 99

1. I get disconnected whenever I try to dial. 2. Whoever broke the window should pay for it. 3. I use whichever office happens to be free. 4. The drive to Berlin is long however you go. 5. Order whatever you want for dinner — it's my treat! 6. Wherever you go there's usually a pay phone nearby. 7. Whoever's in the office next door is making a lot of noise. 8. You can give the job to whomever you want.

Exercise 100

1. considered 2. resulted in 3. consult 4. revitalize 5. confined 6. came up with 7. call on 8. projected 9. matches 10. assumed 11. work out 12. get moving

Exercise 101

1. retraining 2. pre-existing 3. preprinted 4. predated 5. renegotiate 6. repay 7. reconsider 8. premature

Exercise 102

1. b 2. a 3. a 4. c 5. b 6. a 7. a 8. b

Exercise 103

1. Kathy is one of the people in the office on whom I can rely. 2. The town from which Steve comes is very old. 3. Mr. Parsons is the accountant to whom you should direct your questions. 4. We stayed at the hotel of which you spoke so highly. 5. I'd like you to meet someone about whom we've spoken often. 6. The hotel at which the conference will be held is very elegant. 7. This is a piece of equipment without which we can't operate the machine. 8. The shareholders to whom Stan was referring might be willing to sell.

Exercise 104

1. Manchester is the place I'd really like to live. 2. Take the subway — that's the way I usually go. 3. I had just returned from Paris the day Phillip arrived. 4. Tell us the reason you decided to move to Montreal. 5. Call me the minute you hear from the executor of the estate. 6. Everyone was impressed with the way the plant manager solved the problem. 7. I'll never forget the time our car broke down on the highway. 8. I can't figure out the reason John resigned. 9. The package

arrived the afternoon we expected it. 10. Cancun, Mexico, is the place we went on vacation last year.

Exercise 105   1. We have three children, all of whom are married. 2. The plant is using outdated equipment, most of which we're going to replace. 3. The plant has 300 employees, half of whom work on the assembly line. 4. We saw two films, neither of which was very interesting. 5. This year I have twenty students, two of whom I've taught before. 6. Linda inherited some money, half of which she's already spent. 7. We interviewed four candidates, one of whom is outstanding. 8. Tom owns three cars, one of which is a 1964 Jaguar.

Exercise 106   1. in 2. on 3. on 4. from 5. to 6. in 7. on 8. with 9. for 10. on

Exercise 107   1. the right way 2. out of your way 3. By the way 4. in my way 5. with the way 6. On the way 7. in some ways 8. one way or another

Exercise 108   1. b 2. a 3. b 4. b 5. c 6. c

Exercise 109   1. to leave 2. to have had 3. to see 4. not to see 5. not to have consulted 6. to have paid 7. to have been trained 8. to handle

Exercise 110   1. to have improved 2. to be upset 3. to have gained weight 4. to be serious 5. to have convinced 6. to be making a good living in sales 7. to have been made public 8. to have a positive attitude

Exercise 111   1. The higher accident rate is thought to be due to the increase in the speed limit. 2. Lincoln is believed to have been a great President. 3. *Emilio's* is said to be the best restaurant in New York. 4. The company is known to have made some bad investments. 5. Henry is thought to be in line for an important assignment. 6. The embezzler was assumed to have left the country. 7. Columbus was believed to have discovered a new route to India. 8. Real estate is thought to be the best long-term investment.

Exercise 112	1. specifics 2. calm down 3. prevented 4. in detail 5. recover 6. reluctant 7. ruled out 8. wise 9. optimist 10. back down 11. steady 12. encouraging
Exercise 113	1. a big problem 2. something to drink 3. a few minutes 4. a terrible cold 5. it on my desk 6. an accident 7. a quick look 8. his eye on 9. my hands full 10. a good feel for
Exercise 114	1. b 2. a 3. b 4. a 5. b 6. b
Exercise 115	1. Where it goes from here 2. what he did to offend you 3. whom I should consult on this matter 4. he's going to accept the job offer 5. What time she arrives; how much traffic there is 6. it has been prepared yet 7. Why it lost the contract 8. where it will be held
Exercise 116	1. b 2. a 3. b 4. c 5. b
Exercise 117	1. Would 2. Will 3. would 4. would 5. will 6. would 7. would 8. will
Exercise 118	1. used to 2. can 3. is willing to 4. was going to 5. is going to 6. refused to
Exercise 119	1. so 2. such 3. so 4. such 5. such 6. such 7. so 8. so; such
Exercise 120	1. on 2. of 3. by 4. up 5. on 6. for 7. out 8. to 9. up 10. on
Exercise 121	1. c 2. b 3. a 4. b 5. a
Exercise 122	1. himself 2. me 3. itself 4. herself 5. themselves 6. us 7. oneself 8. him
Exercise 123	1. herself 2. us 3. himself 4. me 5. you 6. them 7. yourself 8. himself 9. ourselves 10. you
Exercise 124	1. each other 2. themselves 3. each other 4. ourselves 5. each other 6. yourselves 7. each other 8. each other

Exercise 125	1. reduction 2. systematic 3. assignments 4. settlement 5. briefing 6. familiarize 7. extensive 8. manager 9. intention 10. validity
Exercise 126	1. exactly as 2. As you know 3. as far as 4. as is 5. might as well 6. as well as 7. as long as 8. as of
Exercise 127	1. F 2. T 3. F 4. F 5. T 6. F 7. T 8. F 9. T 10. F 11. T 12. F
Exercise 128	1. The flight you said you were taking will be delayed an hour. 2. The company I thought was doing so well went bankrupt recently. 3. The programmer I remember being impressed with was promoted to systems analyst. 4. The property Jeff thought was still for sale was sold two weeks ago. 5. I made an appointment with the doctor you recommended I see. 6. The woman Carol said she wanted to interview is available tomorrow afternoon. 7. Jill is interested in buying the car I suggested she take a look at. 8. Crawford wants to know more about the sales agreement Melnick mentioned he was working on.
Exercise 129	1. that you fill out an application form 2. that we not set the production level as high as last month 3. that Stan and I meet on a regular basis 4. that you show two pieces of I.D. to cash a check 5. that I take a word processing course 6. that the driver get out of his car 7. that the firm not keep as much money in checking accounts 8. that we delay payment of certain invoices
Exercise 130	1. that we hire someone with at least two years' experience 2. that it be postponed until the end of the month 3. that you not submit your report until you've re-checked all the figures 4. that he keep a closer eye on our investments 5. that we get production costs under control as soon as possible 6. that it not make any decisions until the study is completed 7. that they work together on the market study 8. that he go in person to the consulate to apply for a visa

Exercise 131	1. intend 2. going after 3. sketches 4. stepped up 5. streamline 6. climbing 7. success 8. recall 9. attempted 10. honor
Exercise 132	1. record 2. word 3. score 4. pace 5. touch 6. track 7. eye 8. time
Exercise 133	1. scope 2. challenges 3. highlight 4. guidelines 5. caliber 6. policy 7. expansion 8. confidence
Exercise 134	1. d 2. a 3. c 4. b 5. d 6. b 7. c 8. b 9. a 10. d 11. c 12. d
Exercise 135	1. because 2. that 3. whether 4. than 5. when 6. Although 7. so 8. until 9. as long as 10. but 11. unless 12. as
Exercise 136	1. through 2. in 3. on 4. back 5. off 6. up 7. away 8. down 9. out 10. over 11. off 12. back 13. in 14. up 15. down (off)
Exercise 137	1. who 2. whom 3. what 4. whatever 5. Whoever 6. who 7. whom 8. that 9. ourselves 10. each other 11. myself 12. himself
Exercise 138	1. break 2. take 3. left 4. propose 5. have 6. keep 7. put 8. go 9. gone 10. managed 11. level 12. give

TAPESCRIPTS

UNEXPECTED NEWS

Peter Crawford had lunch with Jim Burke an hour ago. Peter and Jim are old friends
from college days. But at lunch today they had other things to discuss. When Peter
got back to the office, he called his wife, Helen.

Helen: *Hello?*

Peter: *Hi! It's me.*

Helen: *Peter! What's up? Anything wrong?*

Peter: *No, everything's fine. I just got back from lunch with Jim Burke. He's
president of United Electronics. You know ... the big conglomerate?*

Helen: *United Electronics! Hmm ... Jim always hoped to become president of a
big company someday. The two of you sure have come a long way since
your college days together.*

Peter: *Well, we didn't talk about college today. We had a long business
discussion, and Jim came up with some very surprising news.*

Helen: *Oh?*

Peter: *Well, one of United Electronics' subsidiaries is Audio Performance — a
company that specializes in stereo systems.*

Helen: *I didn't know they were a part of United Electronics.*

Peter: *Anyway, the president of Audio Performance, Bill Jensen, hasn't been
well. It's his heart. He's going to have to take early retirement.*

Helen: *Oh, dear, that's too bad. But what does all this have to do with you?*

Peter: *That was the unexpected part of our discussion. Audio Performance is
looking for a replacement, and who do you suppose Jim has in mind?*

Helen: *You?! As president of Audio Performance? Oh, Peter, that's terrific! Did
Jim say anything else?*

Peter: *Only that he and the Board have looked at my management experience
and everything I've done at ESI since becoming president, and they think
I'm the right person to take charge of things at Audio Performance.*

Helen: *How soon does Jim expect a decision?*

Peter: *He'd like me to give him an answer in the next few days.*

Helen: *I see. Well, Peter, we have a lot to talk about!*

Peter: *We sure do, starting tonight. I should be home around 6:30.*

Helen: *All right. And, Peter, we still have some time, so let's take it easy and
make the right decision.*

Now, let's listen to the conversation once again. And then ... answer the questions.
Peter's wife, Helen, has just picked up the phone.

Helen: *Hello?*

Peter: *Hi! It's me.*

Helen: *Peter! What's up? Anything wrong?*

Peter: No, everything's fine. I just got back from lunch with Jim Burke. He's president of United Electronics. You know ... the big conglomerate?

Helen: United Electronics! Hmm ... Jim always hoped to become president of a big company someday. The two of you sure have come a long way since your college days together.

Peter: Well, we didn't talk about college today. We had a long business discussion, and Jim came up with some very surprising news.

Answer!

Did Peter call his wife before or after his lunch meeting?	He called her after his lunch meeting.
He didn't have lunch alone today, did he?	No, he didn't have lunch alone today.
Who did he have lunch with, Jim Burke?	Yes, he had lunch with Jim Burke.
What's Jim president of, a small firm or a big conglomerate?	He's president of a big conglomerate.
He always hoped to become president of a big company, right?	That's right, he always hoped to become president of a big company.
Did Peter and Jim have a long or short discussion over lunch?	They had a long discussion over lunch.
They didn't talk about their old college days, did they?	No, they didn't talk about their old college days.
They discussed business, right?	That's right, they discussed business.

Very good!

Repeat!

Jim wants to find a replacement.	He hasn't found a replacement yet.
Peter wants to tell Helen about the job offer.	He hasn't told her about the job offer yet.
Answer! He hasn't told her ...	
Helen wants to hear the surprising news.	She hasn't heard the surprising news yet.
She hasn't ...	
Peter may become Audio Performance's new president.	He hasn't become Audio Performance's new president yet.
He ...	
Peter and Helen are going to discuss the offer.	They haven't discussed the offer yet.
They ...	

Very good! Peter is still talking to his wife, Helen. Listen!

Peter: Well, we didn't talk about college today. We had a long business discussion, and Jim came up with some very surprising news.

Helen: Oh?

Peter: Well, one of United Electronics' subsidiaries is Audio Performance — a company that specializes in stereo systems.

Helen: I didn't know they were a part of United Electronics.

Peter: Anyway, the president of Audio Performance, Bill Jensen, hasn't been well. It's his heart. He's going to have to take early retirement.

Helen: Oh, dear, that's too bad. But what does all this have to do with you?

Peter: That was the unexpected part of our discussion. Audio Performance is looking for a replacement, and who do you suppose Jim has in mind?

Helen: You?! As president of Audio Performance? Oh, Peter, that's terrific!

Answer!

Is United Electronics a subsidiary of Audio Performance?	No, it isn't a subsidiary of Audio Performance.
AP is the subsidiary, right?	That's right, AP is the subsidiary.
Does it specialize in stereo systems or televisions?	It specializes in stereo systems.
AP is the subsidiary of United Electronics that specializes in stereo systems, right?	That's right, AP is the subsidiary of United Electronics that specializes in stereo systems.
What's Bill Jensen, president or vice president of AP?	He's president of AP.
Has he been feeling well lately?	No, he hasn't been feeling well lately.
That's why he's requested early retirement, isn't it?	Yes, that's why he's requested early retirement.
I beg your pardon? Who's requested early retirement, Peter Crawford or Bill Jensen?	Bill Jensen has requested early retirement.
Will Audio Performance need a replacement for Bill?	Yes, they'll need a replacement for Bill.
AP will need a replacement for Bill Jensen, who's requested early retirement, right?	That's right, they'll need a replacement for Bill Jensen, who's requested early retirement.
Who does Jim Burke have in mind to be president of AP?	He has Peter Crawford in mind to be president of AP.

Very good! Now you ask the questions. *Repeat!*
Do you suppose Jim and Peter had a serious discussion over lunch?
Where do you suppose they went for lunch?
Why do you suppose Bill Jensen has requested early retirement?
How much do you suppose Peter is presently earning?
Which company do you suppose he'll decide on?
How long do you suppose it'll take him to make a decision?
Good! Now let's listen again to Peter and Helen speaking on the phone.

Helen: *You?! As president of Audio Performance? Oh, Peter, that's terrific! Did Jim say anything else?*

Peter: *Only that he and the Board have looked at my management experience and everything I've done at ESI since becoming president, and they think I'm the right person to take charge of things at Audio Performance.*

Helen: *How soon does Jim expect a decision?*

Peter: *He'd like me to give him an answer in the next few days.*

Helen: *I see. Well, Peter, we have a lot to talk about!*

Peter: *We sure do, starting tonight. I should be home around 6:30.*

Helen: *All right. And, Peter, we still have some time, so let's take it easy and make the right decision.*

Answer!

Have Jim and the Board looked at Peter's management experience?	Yes, they've looked at his management experience.
Do they think Peter's the right or wrong person for the job?	They think he's the right person for the job.
The Board has looked at Peter's management experience and they think he's the right person for the job, right?	That's right, the Board has looked at Peter's management experience and they think he's the right person for the job.
They'd like him to take charge of AP, wouldn't they?	Yes, they'd like him to take charge of AP.
Does Jim expect Peter's answer in the next few months or in the next few days?	He expects Peter's answer in the next few days.
I beg your pardon? When does Jim hope to have Peter's decision?	He hopes to have Peter's decision in the next few days.
Who's Peter going to discuss his decision with, his wife or his secretary?	He's going to discuss his decision with his wife.

Very good! Peter and Helen have an important decision to make. Let's hope that together they make the right decision. Well, that's all for now. This is the end of Tape 1.

Tape 2   THE PRESIDENT

It was late in the afternoon when Peter Crawford stopped by Ben Melnick's office to discuss a recent drop in the sales figures. Ben is director of sales at Audio Performance.

Peter: Hi, Ben! Got a minute?

Ben: Sure, Peter. Come in. I was just finishing up for the day.

Peter: Ben, as you know, I requested a review of our sales figures. I haven't finished studying it yet, but I must say, what I've seen so far doesn't look good.

Ben: I know, Peter. It's the competition. That's our problem, and I agree — it's serious.

Peter: We all know about the growing competition from abroad. But I really hadn't expected domestic competition to be expanding as fast as the report shows.

Ben: But our main problem is still our inability to compete with foreign manufacturers, Peter. It's putting us at a real disadvantage.

Peter: Uh-huh. Labor costs abroad are lower, so foreign companies are becoming more and more competitive. And they can sell in the U.S. at prices Audio Performance can't meet.

Ben: As I see it, Peter, unless we find a solution, we can expect both our sales and profits to continue dropping.

Peter: I'll tell you what. Jane Collins has been going over the sales report, too. And I know she would want to discuss it with us. Why don't the three of us set up a meeting for sometime next week?

Ben: Sounds good.

Peter: O.K. I'll talk it over with her. In the meantime, I know the two of you will come up with ideas that'll lead us in the right direction.

Ben: We'll get to work on it right away, Peter.

Now, let's listen to the conversation again. And then ... answer some questions. Peter has just entered Ben's office.

Peter: Hi, Ben! Got a minute?

Ben: Sure, Peter. Come in. I was just finishing up for the day.

Peter: Ben, as you know, I requested a review of our sales figures. I haven't finished studying it yet, but I must say, what I've seen so far doesn't look good.

Ben: I know, Peter. It's the competition. That's our problem, and I agree — it's serious.

Answer!

Was Ben just starting work when Peter came in?	No, he wasn't just starting work when Peter came in.
He was just finishing up for the day, wasn't he?	Yes, he was just finishing up for the day.
Did he and Peter have a discussion about taxes or sales figures?	They had a discussion about sales figures.
The sales figures don't look too good, do they?	No, they don't look too good.
I beg your pardon? What doesn't look too good?	The sales figures don't look too good.
What does Ben think the problem is, the competition or taxes?	He thinks the problem is the competition.
Do Peter and Ben agree the problem is serious?	Yes, they agree the problem is serious.
A review of the sales figures was made recently, right?	That's right, a review of the sales figures was made recently.
Who had requested the review, Ben or Peter?	Peter had requested it.
Has he finished studying it yet?	No, he hasn't finished studying it yet.
Peter had requested the review, but he hasn't finished studying it yet, right?	That's right, Peter had requested the review, but he hasn't finished studying it yet.
Very good!	

Repeat!

Peter requested a review a month ago. Jim Burke had requested it before that.	
Ben Melnick received the report last week.	
Answer! Peter had received it ...	Peter had received it before that.
Ben read the report last Monday. Peter had read ...	Peter had read it before that.
Peter discovered serious problems after getting the report. Ben had ...	Ben had discovered them before that.
Domestic manufacturers were competitive last year. Foreign manufacturers ...	Foreign manufacturers had been competitive before that.

Jane inquired about the problems yesterday.
Jim and Peter ...

Jim and Peter had inquired about them before that.

Very good! Now, listen again. Ben is telling Peter about the problem Audio Performance is facing.

> Ben: *I know, Peter. It's the competition. That's our problem, and I agree — it's serious.*
>
> Peter: *We all know about the growing competition from abroad. But I really hadn't expected domestic competition to be expanding as fast as the report shows.*
>
> Ben: *But our main problem is still our inability to compete with foreign manufacturers, Peter. It's putting us at a real disadvantage.*
>
> Peter: *Uh-huh. Labor costs abroad are lower, so foreign companies are becoming more and more competitive. And they can sell in the U.S. at prices Audio Performance can't meet.*

Answer!

Does Peter want to know exactly what kinds of problems AP is facing?

Yes, he wants to know exactly what kinds of problems AP is facing.

What's increasing, sales or competition as a whole?

Competition as a whole is increasing.

Did the report show that both domestic and foreign competition were expanding?

Yes, it showed that both domestic and foreign competition were expanding.

But Peter hadn't expected domestic competition to be expanding as fast as the report showed, had he?

No, he hadn't expected domestic competition to be expanding as fast as the report showed.

Have foreign manufacturers been putting AP at an advantage or disadvantage?

They've been putting them at a disadvantage.

I beg your pardon? Who's been putting them at a disadvantage?

Foreign manufacturers have been putting them at a disadvantage.

Does this mean that foreign companies are becoming more and more competitive?

Yes, it means that foreign companies are becoming more and more competitive.

Is this because labor costs abroad are higher or lower?

It's because labor costs abroad are lower.

Labor costs abroad are lower, so foreign companies are becoming more and more competitive, right?

That's right, labor costs abroad are lower, so foreign companies are becoming more and more competitive.

Can AP meet the present prices of foreign companies?	No, they can't meet the present prices of foreign companies.

Very good!

Repeat!

Peter hasn't finished studying the report yet, but he will finish it soon.

Recent sales figures don't look too good now, but they will begin to look better soon.

Ben doesn't have any specific solutions in mind yet, but he will have some soon.

Ben and Jane Collins haven't discussed the sales report yet, but they will discuss it soon.

Peter doesn't expect to find a solution right away, but he will expect one soon.

Good! Now let's listen again as Peter and Ben finish their discussion.

> Peter: *Labor costs abroad are lower, so foreign companies are becoming more and more competitive. And they can sell in the U.S. at prices Audio Performance can't meet.*
>
> Ben: *As I see it, Peter, unless we find a solution, we can expect both our sales and profits to continue dropping.*
>
> Peter: *I'll tell you what. Jane Collins has been going over the sales report, too. And I know she would want to discuss it with us. Why don't the three of us set up a meeting for sometime next week?*
>
> Ben: *Sounds good.*
>
> Peter: *Okay. I'll talk it over with her. In the meantime, I know the two of you will come up with ideas that'll lead us in the right direction.*
>
> Ben: *We'll get to work on it right away, Peter.*

Answer!

Have Peter and Ben agreed on a final solution yet?	No, they haven't agreed on a final solution yet.
Can AP expect sales to continue dropping if a solution isn't found?	Yes, they can expect sales to continue dropping if a solution isn't found.
Will profits go up or down if sales continue dropping?	They'll go down if sales continue dropping.
Jane Collins has also been going over the sales report, right?	That's right, Jane Collins has also been going over the sales report.
Do Peter and Ben hope to set up a meeting for next week?	Yes, they hope to set up a meeting for next week.
Does Peter think Jane would want to be at the meeting or not?	He thinks she would want to be at the meeting.

Very good! There are some serious problems facing Audio Performance, but Peter and Ben are determined to lead the company in the right direction. We'll have to wait to find out what happens next, because this is the end of Tape 2.

Tape 3   PRODUCTION PROBLEMS

Peter Crawford and his production manager, Ed Pearson, have just finished visiting the Audio Performance manufacturing plant in Baltimore. They're very concerned about the plant, and they're discussing it on the flight back to New York.

Peter: Well, Ed, let's hear it. How do you feel about what we've just seen?

Ed: Peter, I think we're in serious trouble. As I see it, we're facing two problems ... in the technical area and in management.

Peter: Go on.

Ed: Well, as for the technical, I've been concerned about the equipment for some time. Most of it is over twenty years old, and it's always breaking down. Every repair costs us time, money, and production. At the rate it's operating now, the plant will never fill its production quota, and we won't be able to meet delivery schedules on several of our large contracts.

Peter: What kind of an increase would we need in our production rate to meet those schedules?

Ed: According to reports that I've checked, production will have to increase by at least fifteen percent.

Peter: That much, huh? Well, I had a chance to talk with a number of the people working on the assembly line. And I really got the impression they're trying to do their best. They have a very good attitude.

Ed: I've known most of them for years, Peter. And I agree, they don't want to see production decreased any more than we do.

Peter: However, they did make some comments that we should think about. First, they said they were understaffed and that members of the maintenance department weren't properly trained.

Ed: And as a result, they feel overworked.

Peter: Exactly. They also feel that management just waits for equipment to break down and then repairs it, when they should be training the maintenance staff to prevent breakdowns.

Ed: Right. But, that's the responsibility of the plant manager, Bob Smith. Are you suggesting he may be part of the problem?

Peter: Well, we know that something's wrong, Ed, and we've got to find out what. It's clear the equipment is old, but another factor could be poor management.

Ed: *Maybe. What do you think we should do?*

Peter: *We don't have a choice. I'd like you to study the situation carefully, then talk with Smith, and let him know he's got two months to turn things around.*

Ed: *And if he doesn't?*

Peter: *We may have to consider a replacement.*

Now, let's listen to the conversation again. And then ... answer some questions. Peter's about to ask Ed about their tour of the AP manufacturing plant.

Peter: *Well, Ed, let's hear it. How do you feel about what we've just seen?*

Ed: *Peter, I think we're in serious trouble. As I see it, we're facing two problems ... in the technical area and in management.*

Peter: *Go on.*

Ed: *Well, as for the technical, I've been concerned about the equipment for some time. Most of it is over twenty years old, and it's always breaking down. Every repair costs us time, money, and production. At the rate it's operating now, the plant will never fill its production quota, and we won't be able to meet delivery schedules on several of our large contracts.*

Peter: *What kind of an increase would we need in our production rate to meet those schedules?*

Ed: *According to reports that I've checked, production will have to increase by at least fifteen percent.*

Answer!

AP has a manufacturing plant, doesn't it?	Yes, it has a manufacturing plant.
Are Peter and Ed making a tour of it right now?	No, they're not making a tour of it right now.
They've already visited the plant, haven't they?	Yes, they've already visited it.
What does Ed think, that the plant is all right or that it's in serious trouble?	He thinks it's in serious trouble.
He's concerned about the equipment, right?	That's right, he's concerned about the equipment.
Does the equipment operate well or is it always breaking down?	It's always breaking down.
I beg your pardon? What's always breaking down?	The equipment is always breaking down.
The plant isn't currently filling its production quota, is it?	No, it isn't currently filling its production quota.

Good!

Now, listen ... and *repeat*!

AP manufactures stereo equipment.

AP is a company that manufactures stereo equipment.

Ed visited the plant.

Ed's the person who visited the plant.

The quota has to be filled.

Answer! The plant has a quota that ...

The plant has a quota that has to be filled.

Peter made a tour of the plant.
Peter's the one ...

Peter's the one who made a tour of the plant.

The equipment is always breaking down.
Ed checked the equipment ...

Ed checked the equipment that's always breaking down.

Peter and Ed are concerned about repairs.
They're the ones ...

They're the ones who are concerned about repairs.

The reports showed a production problem.
Peter reviewed the reports ...

Peter reviewed the reports that showed a production problem.

Good work! Now, let's go back to the conversation. Ed was telling Peter about the production increase. Listen!

> Ed: According to reports that I've checked, production will have to increase by at least fifteen percent.

> Peter: That much, huh? Well, I had a chance to talk with a number of the people working on the assembly line. And I really got the impression they're trying to do their best. They have a very good attitude.

> Ed: I've known most of them for years, Peter. And I agree, they don't want to see production decreased any more than we do.

> Peter: However, they did make some comments that we should think about. First, they said they were understaffed and that members of the maintenance department weren't properly trained.

> Ed: And as a result, they feel overworked.

> Peter: Exactly. They also feel that management just waits for equipment to break down and then repairs it, when they should be training the maintenance staff to prevent breakdowns.

Answer!

Was Peter shown the assembly line at the plant?

Yes, he was shown the assembly line at the plant.

He also had a chance to talk with the people working on the assembly line, right?	That's right, he also had a chance to talk with the people working on the assembly line.
What do they want, to see production increase or decrease?	They want to see production increase.
But they are trying to do their best, aren't they?	Yes, they are trying to do their best.
Is the maintenance staff properly trained?	No, they aren't properly trained.
They should be trained to prevent breakdowns, right?	That's right, they should be trained to prevent breakdowns.

Very good! Let's return to the conversation. Peter thinks the plant manager may be part of the problem. Listen!

Peter: *They also feel that management just waits for equipment to break down and then repairs it, when they should be training the maintenance staff to prevent breakdowns.*

Ed: *Right. But, that's the responsibility of the plant manager, Bob Smith. Are you suggesting he may be part of the problem?*

Peter: *Well, we know that something's wrong, Ed, and we've got to find out what. It's clear the equipment is old, but another factor could be poor management.*

Ed: *Maybe. What do you think we should do?*

Peter: *We don't have a choice. I'd like you to study the situation carefully, then talk with Smith, and let him know he's got two months to turn things around.*

Ed: *And if he doesn't?*

Peter: *We may have to consider a replacement.*

Answer!

Did Peter suggest the problem could be poor management?	Yes, he suggested the problem could be poor management.
He really wants to find out what's wrong at the plant, right?	That's right, he really wants to find out what's wrong at the plant.
I beg your pardon? Is he or isn't he determined to find out what's wrong?	He is determined to find out what's wrong.
Who's the plant manager, Ed Pearson or Bob Smith?	Bob Smith is the plant manager.
Will Smith be given a chance to turn things around?	Yes, he'll be given a chance to turn things around.

How much time will he have to get the job done, two months or two years?

He'll have two months to get the job done.

Very good! Now, listen carefully ... and *repeat*!

Peter and Ed are concerned about AP's manufacturing plant in Baltimore.

They're concerned about the plant's technical problems and its management.

Peter told Ed he was concerned about the possibility of poor management.

He's concerned about having to find a replacement for the plant manager.

Good! Well, it's clear that Peter and Ed have a lot to be concerned about. However, their trip to Baltimore is over, and so is this tape. This is the end of Tape 3.

Tape 4   THE PRESIDENT'S SECRETARY

At the time Peter Crawford was named president of Audio Performance, Karen Lawrence had been working as a secretary in AP's legal department. When Karen heard of an opening "at the top" as the new president's executive secretary, she had applied immediately.

Peter: *I was given your file by the personnel department, Karen, and I must say, what you've done since joining AP is really impressive.*

Karen: *Thank you, Mr. Crawford. As you know, when I first joined AP three years ago, I was hired as a receptionist.*

Peter: *But I see you had already completed several secretarial courses when you applied.*

Karen: *That's right. But I didn't have any practical experience at the time.*

Peter: *I understand. In going over your file, I've also noticed how quickly you were promoted. Let's see, from receptionist to clerk typist and then to secretary. And your supervisors consider your job performance and efficiency excellent. They've also been very impressed with your pleasant personality — especially when things go wrong, as we know they sometimes do.*

Karen: *My supervisors have helped me a lot, too, Mr. Crawford. I've always been able to get help when something wasn't clear.*

Peter: *I'm glad to hear it. That's the kind of supervision our managers are supposed to provide. Now let's see, in this position you'd be assisting me in a number of areas — typing, scheduling appointments, greeting clients, making travel arrangements — in general, keeping track of just about everything. It's a big job.*

Karen: *It sure is. However, before submitting my application, I considered the additional duties and responsibilities, and I think I can manage them.*

> You see, Mr. Crawford, I really feel this position will offer me an oppor-
> tunity to use my abilities to the fullest. And I would do my best to be
> successful.

Peter: *Well, together with your qualifications and experience, that's good enough*
for me! Karen, I'd like to offer you the position — a promotion to
executive secretary, effective immediately!

Karen: *Oh, Mr. Crawford, I don't know what to say. I accept, of course, and*
thank you!

Peter: *I'll notify the personnel department right away, so they can get started on*
the paperwork. They'll make all the necessary arrangements including, of
course, the raise that comes with your new position.

Karen: *Oh, yes, the raise — I almost forgot!*

Let's listen to the interview again. And then ... answer some questions. Peter is
speaking to Karen.

Peter: *I was given your file by the personnel department, Karen, and I must say,*
what you've done since joining AP is really impressive.

Karen: *Thank you, Mr. Crawford. As you know, when I first joined AP three years*
ago, I was hired as a receptionist.

Peter: *But I see you had already completed several secretarial courses when*
you applied.

Karen: *That's right. But I didn't have any practical experience at the time.*

Answer!

Was Peter given Karen's file?	Yes, he was given her file.
Was it sent to him by the personnel department or the sales department?	It was sent to him by the personnel department.
Karen first joined AP three years ago, didn't she?	Yes, she first joined AP three years ago.
She had already completed several secretarial courses before that, right?	That's right, she had already completed several secretarial courses before that.
But she hadn't had any practical experience, had she?	No, she hadn't had any practical experience.
What was she first hired as, a receptionist or a secretary?	She was first hired as a receptionist.
I beg your pardon? She was or she wasn't first hired as a secretary three years ago?	She wasn't first hired as a secretary three years ago.

Good!

And now, listen carefully ... and *repeat*!

Karen didn't retire from a job three years ago; she applied for one.

She didn't turn down the receptionist's job; she accepted it.

At first Karen's salary didn't go up sharply; it went up gradually.

Her job qualifications haven't decreased; they've increased.

The secretarial courses weren't a disadvantage; they were an advantage.

Karen wasn't nervous during her interview; she was relaxed.

Very good! Now, let's go back to the interview. Karen was explaining to Peter why she wasn't hired as a secretary when she first joined AP. Listen!

Peter: *But I see you had already completed several secretarial courses when you applied.*

Karen: *That's right. But I didn't have any practical experience at the time.*

Peter: *I understand. In going over your file, I've also noticed how quickly you were promoted. Let's see, from receptionist to clerk typist and then to secretary. And your supervisors consider your job performance and efficiency excellent. They've also been very impressed with your pleasant personality — especially when things go wrong, as we know they sometimes do.*

Karen: *My supervisors have helped me a lot, too, Mr. Crawford. I've always been able to get help when something wasn't clear.*

Peter: *I'm glad to hear it. That's the kind of supervision our managers are supposed to provide. Now let's see, in this position you'd be assisting me in a number of areas — typing, scheduling appointments, greeting clients, making travel arrangements — in general, keeping track of just about everything. It's a big job.*

Answer!

What did Peter notice, how quickly or how slowly Karen was promoted?

He noticed how quickly she was promoted.

Have Karen's supervisors considered her job performance poor?

No, they haven't considered her job performance poor.

They've considered her performance and efficiency excellent, right?

That's right, they've considered her performance and efficiency excellent.

Karen wouldn't be assisting Peter in just one area, would she?

No, she wouldn't be assisting him in just one area.

She'd be keeping track of just about everything, right?

That's right, she'd be keeping track of just about everything.

Does that include scheduling appointments and greeting clients?

Yes, that includes scheduling appointments and greeting clients.

Her duties would also include making travel arrangements, wouldn't they?

Yes, her duties would also include making travel arrangements.

Good!

Now ... *repeat!*
They didn't hire Karen as a secretary at first.
Karen wasn't hired as a secretary at first.

Audio Performance offered her another position.
She was offered another position by Audio Performance.

They quickly promoted her to clerk typist.
Answer! She was quickly ...

She was quickly promoted to clerk typist.

Her supervisor considered Karen's work excellent.
Karen's work was ...

Karen's work was considered excellent by her supervisor.

They then offered her a secretarial position.
She ...

She was then offered a secretarial position.

Karen's pleasant personality impressed everyone.
Everyone ...

Everyone was impressed by Karen's pleasant personality.

They told her to apply for executive secretary.
She ...

She was told to apply for executive secretary.

Very good! That wasn't so difficult, was it? Now, let's continue with the interview. Peter was telling Karen what duties were included in her new position. Let's listen!

Peter: It's a big job.

Karen: It sure is. However, before submitting my application, I considered the additional duties and responsibilities, and I think I can manage them. You see, Mr. Crawford, I really feel this position will offer me an oppor-tunity to use my abilities to the fullest. And I would do my best to be successful.

Peter: Well, together with your qualifications and experience, that's good enough for me! Karen, I'd like to offer you the position — a promotion to executive secretary, effective immediately!

Karen: Oh, Mr. Crawford, I don't know what to say. I accept, of course, and thank you!

Peter: I'll notify the personnel department right away, so they can get started on the paperwork. They'll make all the necessary arrangements including, of course, the raise that comes with your new position.

Karen: Oh, yes, the raise — I almost forgot!

Answer!
Karen didn't submit her application after the interview, did she?

No, she didn't submit her application after the interview.

She submitted it before applying, right?	That's right, she submitted it before applying.
Has she considered the additional duties and responsibilities?	Yes, she has considered the additional duties and responsibilities.
And what does she think? Does she think she can manage them or not?	She thinks she can manage them.
Did Peter offer Karen a promotion or ask her to apply again?	He offered her a promotion.
He considered her qualifications and experience, didn't he?	Yes, he considered her qualifications and experience.
Did Karen accept the promotion or turn it down?	She accepted the promotion.
Who will notify the personnel department about the promotion, Peter or Karen?	Peter will notify the personnel department about the promotion.
Is that so they can get started on the paperwork?	Yes, that's so they can get started on the paperwork.
Karen's salary won't be the same as before, will it?	No, her salary won't be the same as before.
A raise is included, right?	That's right, a raise is included.

Very good! Things went very well for Karen during the interview. She got a promotion to executive secretary and, of course, a raise, too. Peter made the right decision, don't you think? Well, the interview is over, and so is this tape. This is the end of Tape 4.

Tape 5   BUY, BUILD, OR LEASE

Peter Crawford is determined to find a solution to the production problems at the Baltimore plant, so he asked his executive assistant, Jane Collins, to meet with Jeff Martinelli, AP's vice president of planning. They met the next day.

Jeff: *I read your report on labor costs in our plants, Jane. It was well-written.*

Jane: *Thanks, Jeff. I put it together at Peter's request. He's very concerned about the Baltimore plant in particular.*

Jeff: *I know. I met with him yesterday to report on the options we have available in terms of expansion. In fact, it was your data on the rising labor costs in Baltimore that gave Peter the idea of phasing out our unprofitable operation there and opening a new and bigger facility somewhere else.*

Jane: *How much of an expansion are we talking about?*

<table>
<tbody>
<tr><td>Jeff:</td><td>I'm recommending a facility of about 200,000 square feet, which will more than double our present capacity. Besides, it'll permit us to lower unit costs and give us a much better profit picture.</td></tr>
<tr><td>Jane:</td><td>Hmm ... but we still have an important choice to make. Do we find an existing facility that meets our needs and lease it? Do we buy an existing facility? Or do we build our own plant from the ground up?</td></tr>
<tr><td>Jeff:</td><td>Well, I've spoken to a few real estate brokers already. And the problem is there just don't seem to be that many facilities available, either for buying or leasing.</td></tr>
<tr><td>Jane:</td><td>In that case, we may have no alternative but to find a suitable piece of property and build our own plant.</td></tr>
<tr><td>Jeff:</td><td>As I see it, whether we buy, build, or lease, the most important thing is locating a favorable labor climate, but also a site that will meet our needs in terms of taxes, labor supply, construction costs, proximity to transportation, and so on.</td></tr>
<tr><td>Jane:</td><td>And don't forget labor costs!</td></tr>
<tr><td>Jeff:</td><td>Right! You know, I just had an idea. There's been a lot of economic growth in South Carolina. I went to school in Greenville and have a couple of friends in the real estate business down there. One of them's a broker. He might be able to recommend something suitable.</td></tr>
<tr><td>Jane:</td><td>You never know. Well, why don't we make that the first step in our plan of action?</td></tr>
<tr><td>Jeff:</td><td>I'll get started on it right away. Who knows? I may get a chance to see some old school friends again.</td></tr>
</tbody>
</table>

Let's listen to the beginning of the discussion again. And then ... answer a few questions.

<table>
<tbody>
<tr><td>Jeff:</td><td>I read your report on labor costs in our plants, Jane. It was well-written.</td></tr>
<tr><td>Jane:</td><td>Thanks, Jeff. I put it together at Peter's request. He's very concerned about the Baltimore plant in particular.</td></tr>
<tr><td>Jeff:</td><td>I know. I met with him yesterday to report on the options we have available in terms of expansion. In fact, it was your data on the rising labor costs in Baltimore that gave Peter the idea of phasing out our unprofitable operation there and opening a new and bigger facility somewhere else.</td></tr>
</tbody>
</table>

Answer!

Did Jane write a report evaluating labor costs in AP's plants?	Yes, she wrote a report evaluating labor costs in AP's plants.
Who had requested the evaluation, Jeff Martinelli or Peter Crawford?	Peter Crawford had requested the evaluation.
The data didn't show that labor costs in Baltimore were going down, did it?	No, the data didn't show that labor costs in Baltimore were going down.

It pointed out that labor costs were rising, right?

That's right, it pointed out that labor costs were rising.

Is the Baltimore plant a profitable or unprofitable operation?

It's an unprofitable operation.

Has Peter turned down the idea of phasing out the Baltimore operation?

No, he hasn't turned down the idea of phasing out the Baltimore operation.

Does that mean he might replace it with a new facility?

Yes, that means he might replace it with a new facility.

Would it be bigger or smaller than the current plant?

It would be bigger than the current plant.

Very good!

Listen ... and *repeat*!
Peter wants to open a new plant.
He's thinking of opening a new plant.

Jane likes to work with data.
She's experienced in working with data.

Now, it's your turn. *Repeat.*

Peter wants to improve production.
Answer! He's concerned about ...

He's concerned about improving production.

He wants to find a solution.
He insists on ...

He insists on finding a solution.

Jane tried to evaluate labor costs.
She succeeded in ...

She succeeded in evaluating labor costs.

Jeff needs to study the available options.
He's in charge of ...

He's in charge of studying the available options.

Everyone wants to make the right choice.
They're working hard at ...

They're working hard at making the right choice.

They may move the plant to a new location.
What will Jane say about ...?

What will Jane say about moving the plant to a new location?

Very good! Now let's get back to the conversation. Jeff had just told Jane about the possibility of opening a new and bigger plant. Listen!

Jane: *How much of an expansion are we talking about?*

Jeff: *I'm recommending a facility of about 200,000 square feet, which will more than double our present capacity. Besides, it'll permit us to lower unit costs and give us a much better profit picture.*

> Jane: Hmm ... but we still have an important choice to make. Do we find an existing facility that meets our needs and lease it? Do we buy an existing facility? Or do we build our own plant from the ground up?
>
> Jeff: Well, I've spoken to a few real estate brokers already. And the problem is there just don't seem to be that many facilities available, either for buying or leasing.
>
> Jane: In that case, we may have no alternative but to find a suitable piece of property and build our own plant.

Answer!

Is Jeff recommending a facility of three hundred thousand or two hundred thousand square feet?	He's recommending a facility of two hundred thousand square feet.
Will that double present capacity or decrease it?	It'll double present capacity.
Will unit costs go up if expansion takes place?	No, unit costs won't go up if expansion takes place.
I beg your pardon? Will expansion raise or lower unit costs?	It'll lower unit costs.
Will that mean a favorable or unfavorable profit picture?	It'll mean a favorable profit picture.
Jeff has already spoken to a few real estate brokers, hasn't he?	Yes, he's already spoken to a few real estate brokers.
There aren't many existing facilities available for either buying or leasing, are there?	No, there aren't many existing facilities available for either buying or leasing.
AP may have to build a new plant from the ground up, right?	That's right, they may have to build a new plant from the ground up.

Good!

And now, listen and *repeat*!

By increasing production capacity, AP can lower unit costs.

By lowering unit costs, the overall profit picture should improve.

By talking with real estate brokers, Jeff got a description of available facilities.

By evaluating the options, Jane became aware that there was no point in leasing or buying.

Very good! Now, let's go back to the discussion and see what Jeff and Jane decide to do. Listen!

> Jane: In that case, we may have no alternative but to find a suitable piece of property and build our own plant.
>
> Jeff: As I see it, whether we buy, build, or lease, the most important thing is locating a favorable labor climate, but also a site that will meet our needs

> in terms of taxes, labor supply, construction costs, proximity to
> transportation, and so on.
>
> Jane: And don't forget labor costs!
>
> Jeff: Right! You know, I just had an idea. There's been a lot of economic
> growth in South Carolina. I went to school in Greenville and have a
> couple of friends in the real estate business down there. One of them's a
> broker. He might be able to recommend something suitable.
>
> Jane: You never know. Well, why don't we make that the first step in our plan
> of action?
>
> Jeff: I'll get started on it right away. Who knows? I may get a chance to see
> some old school friends again.

Answer!

Are we sure yet whether AP will buy, build, or lease?	No, we aren't sure yet whether they'll buy, build, or lease.
Does Jeff recommend finding a favorable or unfavorable labor climate?	He recommends finding a favorable labor climate.
What does this mean? Does it mean things like construction costs and labor supply?	Yes, it means things like construction costs and labor supply.
Taxes and proximity to transportation are also included, right?	That's right, taxes and proximity to transportation are also included.
Did Jeff go to school in Florida?	No, he didn't go to school in Florida.
I beg your pardon? Did he go to school in Florida or South Carolina?	He went to school in South Carolina.
And one of his friends down there is a real estate broker, right?	That's right, one of his friends down there is a real estate broker.
Is he the one who might be able to recommend a suitable site?	Yes, he's the one who might be able to recommend a suitable site.
Have Jeff and Jane finally agreed on a plan of action?	Yes, they've finally agreed on a plan of action.

Very good! Yes, Jeff Martinelli and Jane Collins have taken the first step in their
plan of action, and Jeff might even be flying to South Carolina soon to look at real
estate. We'll be keeping track of what develops. But for now, this is the end of Tape
5.

Tape 6 A BUSY DAY FOR PERSONNEL

The situation at the Baltimore plant did not improve, and Bob Smith, the plant
manager, was asked to submit his resignation. Now, Ed Pearson, AP's production

manager, is looking for a replacement. He's discussing the matter with Carol Nordstrom, director of personnel.

Ed: Carol, I need some advice on the situation at the Baltimore plant. Have you heard any of the details?

Carol: Only that Bob Smith's resignation had been requested and that it was submitted yesterday. I am sorry about Bob.

Ed: It was a hard decision, but we had no choice. I personally made sure Bob was given every opportunity to turn things around, but the situation went from bad to worse. In the end, I really had no alternative but to ask for his resignation.

Carol: I know you did your best, Ed. Will Jack Reilly be serving as temporary replacement?

Ed: Yes, and we think he may have the right qualifications for the position.

Carol: I went through Jack's résumé and his employment record since joining AP. He started out on the assembly line, was named supervisor, then went on to become assistant manager. All that in addition to finishing up a management program at the university!

Ed: Peter's impressed, too. However, there's another consideration. Of course, we're all aware of how important it is to give our own personnel every chance to move up in the company. But Peter also wants us to consider qualified applicants from outside the company, and he's asked me to work through you on this decision.

Carol: All right. I'll see to it that our recruiter is given a detailed job descrip-tion. Then we'll go ahead and do the screenings, arrange interviews, check out references, and so on.

Ed: It sounds very thorough. How long will it take to come up with some candidates?

Carol: Well, we have an excellent recruitment agency. We'll get started on it right away. I'll send you an update every couple of days.

Ed: Fine. In the meantime, at least I know that Reilly is looking after the plant. You know, Carol, in a way I hope he turns out to be the best applicant.

Carol: Of course each one will be given equal consideration, but between you and me, Ed, I hope Jack's the best qualified, too!

Now, let's listen to the first part of the discussion again. And then ... answer some questions.

Ed: Carol, I need some advice on the situation at the Baltimore plant. Have you heard any of the details?

Carol: Only that Bob Smith's resignation had been requested and that it was submitted yesterday. I am sorry about Bob.

Ed: It was a hard decision, but we had no choice. I personally made sure Bob was given every opportunity to turn things around, but the situation went from bad to worse. In the end, I really had no alternative but to ask for his resignation.

Carol: I know you did your best, Ed. Will Jack Reilly be serving as temporary replacement?

Ed: Yes, and we think he may have the right qualifications for the position.

Answer!

Whose resignation had been requested recently, Peter Crawford's or Bob Smith's?	Bob Smith's resignation had been requested recently.
Wasn't he the manager of the Baltimore plant?	Yes, he was the manager of the Baltimore plant.
He was the one who was asked to submit his resignation, right?	That's right, he was the one who was asked to submit his resignation.
He was given every opportunity to turn things around, wasn't he?	Yes, he was given every opportunity to turn things around.
Did the situation improve?	No, the situation didn't improve.
There was no alternative but to ask for his resignation, right?	That's right, there was no alternative but to ask for his resignation.
Who will be serving as temporary replacement, Carol Nordstrom or Jack Reilly?	Jack Reilly will be serving as temporary replacement.

Very good!

Now, listen and *repeat*!

Bob Smith had been given every opportunity to turn things around at the plant.

All results were evaluated and every detail was thoroughly checked.

In the end, Ed Pearson had no alternative but to ask for Smith's resignation.

As soon as Smith resigned, Jack Reilly was selected as a temporary replacement.

Very good! Now, let's go back to the conversation. Ed is telling Carol that Jack Reilly will be temporarily managing the Baltimore plant. Listen!

Carol: Will Jack Reilly be serving as temporary replacement?

Ed: Yes, and we think he may have the right qualifications for the position.

Carol: I went through Jack's résumé and his employment record since joining AP. He started out on the assembly line, was named supervisor, then went on to become assistant manager. All that in addition to finishing up a management program at the university!

Ed: Peter's impressed, too. However, there's another consideration. Of course, we're all aware of how important it is to give our own personnel every chance to move up in the company. But Peter also wants us to *consider qualified applicants from outside the company, and he's asked me to work through you on his decision.*

Answer!

Jack Reilly is currently managing the Baltimore plant, isn't he?	Yes, he's currently managing the Baltimore plant.
So far he's only a temporary replacement, right?	That's right, so far he's only a temporary replacement.
Has Carol gone through Jack's résumé and employment record?	Yes, she's gone through his résumé and employment record.
Jack didn't start out as a manager at AP, did he?	No, he didn't start out as a manager at AP.
How did he start out, working in management or on the assembly line?	He started out working on the assembly line.
Jack attended the university while working at AP, didn't he?	Yes, he attended the university while working at AP.
What did he finish up at the university, a management program or a real estate program?	He finished up a management program at the university.
Should employees be given a chance to move up in their company?	Yes, they should be given a chance to move up in their company.

Very good! That was excellent!

Now, listen and *repeat*!

Carol should give the recruiter a full job description.	
The recruiter should be given a full job description.	
She has to consider all applicants equally.	
All applicants have to be considered equally.	
Personnel will set up interviews immediately.	
Answer! Interviews will be ...	Interviews will be set up immediately.
All applicants must submit detailed résumés.	
Detailed résumés must ...	Detailed résumés must be submitted.
They should include references.	
References ...	References should be included.
AP can request recommendations.	
Recommendations ...	Recommendations can be requested.
The company may choose an applicant from the outside.	
An applicant ...	An applicant from the outside may be chosen.

But they would give Jack Reilly
every consideration.
But Jack Reilly ...

But Jack Reilly would be given
every consideration.

Very good! Now, let's go back to the conversation. Carol and Ed are discussing how the new manager at the Baltimore plant will be selected. Listen!

Ed: But Peter also wants us to consider qualified applicants from outside the company, and he's asked me to work through you on this decision.

Carol: All right. I'll see to it that our recruiter is given a detailed job descrip-tion. Then we'll go ahead and do the screenings, arrange interviews, check out references, and so on.

Ed: It sounds very thorough. How long will it take to come up with some candidates?

Carol: Well, we have an excellent recruitment agency. We'll get started on it right away. I'll send you an update every couple of days.

Ed: Fine. In the meantime, at least I know that Reilly is looking after the plant. You know, Carol, in a way I hope he turns out to be the best applicant.

Carol: Of course each one will be given equal consideration, but between you and me, Ed, I hope Jack's the best qualified, too!

Answer!

Peter hasn't decided yet who the new plant manager will be, has he?

No, he hasn't decided yet who the new plant manager will be.

Will applicants from the outside also be considered?

Yes, applicants from the outside will also be considered.

Carol is going to work through a recruitment agency, right?

That's right, she's going to work through a recruitment agency.

Will the applicants' references be checked out?

Yes, the applicants' references will be checked out.

They'll be checked out and evaluated thoroughly, won't they?

Yes, they'll be checked out and evaluated thoroughly.

All applicants will be thoroughly checked out and given equal consideration, right?

That's right, all applicants will be thoroughly checked out and given equal consideration.

Who does Ed hope the best applicant will be, himself or Jack Reilly?

He hopes the best applicant will be Jack Reilly.

Very good! Well, it'll be interesting to see who's finally chosen as the new plant manager. As for us, we have no choice but to wait for the results, because this tape has ended. This is the end of Tape 6.

Tape 7 A SALES MEETING

Sales of AP's Tru-Tone stereo equipment have fallen sharply over the past year. As a result, Peter Crawford arranged for Ben Melnick, his director of sales, to meet with Steve Blake, AP's marketing director. Steve, as we'll see, has a strong personality.

Steve: *Look, Ben, I don't believe our problem with Tru-Tone is low brand awareness. Tru-Tone has a well-established and highly respected name. So why aren't people buying the product? To me, it suggests something's wrong with the strategy your salespeople are using.*

Ben: *Now, Steve, there's no point in trying to hold any one department responsible for what's happening. Maybe Tru-Tone is overpriced, maybe our competition is better technically. We should look at the overall picture, don't you think?*

Steve: *I have looked at the overall picture, Ben. And what I see is that sales of our merchandise are falling an average of over 3 percent per quarter. At that rate, it won't be long before we're cut out of the market completely!*

Ben: *I'm aware of all that, Steve. In fact, Peter and I have agreed to develop a broader distribution — more outlets. We'll be selling through more department stores and discount houses, too.*

Steve: *I'm certainly glad to hear that!*

Ben: *But that may account for only a part of the problem. Steve, I personally feel advertising could be improved, but that's really the responsibility of you and your marketing people.*

Steve: *Well, uh, I'm willing to look at it, of course. But I still think distribution is our problem, not advertising. On the other hand, I told Peter I was ready to help in any way I can, so I'll have my staff put together as broad a market study as possible.*

Ben: *It would help us get a better picture of what's wrong and how to boost sales ... and profits. What we need is an industry-wide study, and you're the one to do it, Steve.*

Steve: *OK, here's what we'll do. I'll have my people proceed with a complete review of the Tru-Tone image, brand-name awareness, advertising strategies, and so on. I'll need your help with this, Ben.*

Ben: *You'll have the full support of the sales department, Steve. I'll autho-rize my managers to give you any information you request — their opinions on pricing, the competition — anything you need. I'll also get them to send you a report on how and where each of our products is distributed and sold.*

Steve: *I really appreciate it, Ben. With that kind of help, my people in market-ing should be able to get us back on the right track in no time at all.*

Now, let's listen to the meeting again. And then ... answer some questions.

Steve: Look, Ben, I don't believe our problem with Tru-Tone is low brand awareness. Tru-Tone has a well-established and highly respected name. So why aren't people buying the product? To me, it suggests something's wrong with the strategy your salespeople are using.

Ben: Now, Steve, there's no point in trying to hold any one department responsible for what's happening. Maybe Tru-Tone is overpriced, maybe our competition is better technically. We should look at the overall picture, don't you think?

Steve: I have looked at the overall picture, Ben. And what I see is that sales of our merchandise are falling an average of over 3 percent per quarter. At that rate, it won't be long before we're cut out of the market completely!

Ben: I'm aware of all that, Steve. In fact, Peter and I have agreed to develop a broader distribution — more outlets. We'll be selling through more department stores and discount houses, too.

Answer!

Who's Steve Blake, AP's president or AP's marketing director?	He's AP's marketing director.
Have sales been rising over the past year?	No, they haven't been rising over the past year.
Merchandise sales have been falling, right?	That's right, merchandise sales have been falling.
What's Ben Melnick, director of marketing or sales?	He's director of sales.
He thinks the competition might be better technically, right?	That's right, he thinks the competition might be better technically.
Does he feel Tru-Tone should be sold only through authorized dealers?	No, he doesn't feel Tru-Tone should be sold only through authorized dealers.
He feels more department stores and discount houses should be included, right?	That's right, he feels more department stores and discount houses should be included.

Very good!

Now you ask the questions. *Repeat!*

Ben and Steve should be looking at the overall picture.

Ben and Steve should be looking at the overall picture, shouldn't they?

Tru-Tone's sales haven't risen.
Tru-Tone's sales haven't risen, have they?

There's a marketing director at AP.
Question? There's a marketing director ...

There's a marketing director at AP, isn't there?

Steve Blake was named marketing director years ago.
Question? Steve Blake ...

Steve Blake was named marketing director years ago, wasn't he?

He doesn't believe Tru-Tone's problem is low brand awareness.
Question? He doesn't ...

He doesn't believe Tru-Tone's problem is low brand awareness, does he?

Ben Melnick hasn't been sales director very long.
Question? Ben Melnick ...

Ben Melnick hasn't been sales director very long, has he?

Ben and Steve knew that merchandise sales were falling.
Question? Ben and Steve ...

Ben and Steve knew that merchandise sales were falling, didn't they?

They'll try to find out what's wrong.
Question? They'll ...

They'll try to find out what's wrong, won't they?

Tru-Tone should be sold in department stores and discount houses.
Question? Tru-Tone ...

Tru-Tone should be sold in department stores and discount houses, shouldn't it?

AP couldn't be cut out of the market completely.
Question? AP ...

AP couldn't be cut out of the market completely, could it?

Very good! Now let's go back to the conversation. Listen!

Ben: *I'm aware of all that, Steve. In fact, Peter and I have agreed to develop a broader distribution — more outlets. We'll be selling through more department stores and discount houses, too.*

Steve: *I'm certainly glad to hear that!*

Ben: *But that may account for only a part of the problem. Steve, I personally feel advertising could be improved, but that's really the responsibility of you and your marketing people.*

Steve: *Well, uh, I'm willing to look at it, of course. But I still think distribution is our problem, not advertising. On the other hand, I told Peter I was ready to help in any way I can, so I'll have my staff put together as broad a market study as possible.*

Ben: *It would help us get a better picture of what's wrong and how to boost sales ... and profits. What we need is an industry-wide study, and you're the one to do it, Steve.*

Answer!

It's possible that advertising could be improved, isn't it?	Yes, it's possible that advertising could be improved.
Developing an advertising strategy isn't the responsibility of Ben's sales department, is it?	No, developing an advertising strategy isn't the responsibility of Ben's sales department.
Who's responsible for advertising, Ben's salespeople or Steve's marketing department?	Steve's marketing department is responsible for advertising.
Steve's going to have his marketing staff do an industry-wide study, right?	That's right, he's going to have his marketing staff do an industry-wide study.
That should give a better picture of how to boost sales and profits, shouldn't it?	Yes, that should give a better picture of how to boost sales and profits.

Good!

Now *repeat!*

AP is a major corporation.
It has been a major corporation for some time now.

Tru-Tone sales aren't going up.
They haven't gone up for some time now.

Steve Blake specializes in marketing. *Answer!* He has specialized ...	He has specialized in marketing for some time now.
Ben Melnick is director of sales. He ...	He has been director of sales for some time now.
Tru-Tone doesn't have a premium image. It ...	It hasn't had a premium image for some time now.
Ben is determined to improve sales. He ...	He's been determined to improve sales for some time now.

Very good! Now, let's return to the meeting as Steve agrees to work on a market study. Listen!

Steve: *OK, here's what we'll do. I'll have my people proceed with a complete review of the Tru-Tone image, brand-name awareness, advertising strategies, and so on. I'll need your help with this, Ben.*

Ben: *You'll have the full support of the sales department, Steve. I'll autho-rize my managers to give you any information you request — their opinions on pricing, the competition — anything you need. I'll also get them to send you a report on how and where each of our products is distributed and sold.*

Steve: I really appreciate it, Ben. With that kind of help, my people in market-ing should be able to get us back on the right track in no time at all.

Answer!

Steve's going to proceed with a complete review of the Tru-Tone image, right?	That's right, he's going to proceed with a complete review of the Tru-Tone image.
He'll include brand-name awareness and advertising strategies, won't he?	Yes, he'll include brand-name awareness and advertising strategies.
Did Ben say he wouldn't authorize his salespeople to help with the review?	No, he didn't say he wouldn't authorize his salespeople to help with the review.
He said he'll get them to offer Steve their full support, right?	That's right, he said he'll get them to offer Steve their full support.

Good! Well, Steve will be proceeding with a market study, and Ben's salespeople are going to give him their full support. Meanwhile, like the meeting, this tape has ended, too. This is the end of Tape 7.

Tape 8   A PROBLEM IN CASH MANAGEMENT

AP's controller, Stan Waterman, manages the company's finances. Peter Craw-ford dropped by Stan's office one afternoon to go over last month's balance sheet.

Peter: I'm sorry I wasn't able to get together with you sooner, Stan. In the future, however, I suggest we meet regularly.

Stan: Right! How do the figures look to you, Peter?

Peter: Overall, they look good. But I also think we're at a point where we need to make a few improvements.

Stan: What did you have in mind?

Peter: I'm referring primarily to cash management. It's important that we take a careful look at the cash being held on deposit in checking accounts. And, according to the balance sheet, there's some $600,000 on deposit in various banks. Isn't that a lot to be holding in checking accounts?

Stan: It is a rather large amount, yes.

Peter: OK, here's what we'll do. I suggest you move more funds out of those checking accounts and into short-term securities. Leave in the checking accounts only what's required for day-to-day expenses. Oh, and Stan, be careful that those short-term securities aren't selected in a haphazard way. Invest wisely.

Stan: Of course. In fact, those excess funds could provide us with returns of eight or nine percent.

Peter: *Exactly! OK, point number two. I'm also concerned about accounts receivable and payable. It's taking much too long to collect from our customers. On the other hand, we're paying our bills right on time. I think we should start delaying payments on certain of our accounts. That'll give us more cash on hand.*

Stan: *Will do. As for accounts receivable, I'll ask our people to make a special effort to collect on past due accounts. We do offer a one percent discount on invoices paid within ten days, but it's still taking an average of four months to collect.*

Peter: *Let's increase the invoice discount to two percent. That might get more customers to pay sooner. Oh, and Stan, I'm going to establish a year-end goal — to cut the average collection time on accounts receivable from four months to two.*

Stan: *We'll do our best, Peter. In fact, I'm already confident the balance sheets will soon be showing a far different picture.*

Peter: *A brighter one, I hope.*

Let's listen now to the first part of the meeting again. And then ... answer some questions.

Peter: *I'm sorry I wasn't able to get together with you sooner, Stan. In the future, however, I suggest we meet regularly.*

Stan: *Right! How do the figures look to you, Peter?*

Peter: *Overall, they look good. But I also think we're at a point where we need to make a few improvements.*

Stan: *What did you have in mind?*

Peter: *I'm referring primarily to cash management. It's important that we take a careful look at the cash being held on deposit in checking accounts. And, according to the balance sheet, there's some $600,000 on deposit in various banks. Isn't that a lot to be holding in checking accounts?*

Stan: *It is a rather large amount, yes.*

Answer!

Peter's meeting with his controller, Stan Waterman, right?	That's right, he's meeting with his controller, Stan Waterman.
Overall, how do the figures look, good or bad?	Overall, they look good.
Peter doesn't think this is the time to take it easy, does he?	No, he doesn't think this is the time to take it easy.
I beg your pardon? Did he suggest this was the time to take it easy or to make some improvements?	He suggested this was the time to make some improvements.

| Did he recommend that personnel management or cash management be improved? | He recommended that cash management be improved. |
| Did he say there was a lot of cash being held on deposit in various banks? | Yes, he said there was a lot of cash being held on deposit in various banks. |

That was very good!

Now *repeat!*

Overall, the figures on the balance sheet look good, but some precautions need to be taken.

Overall, improvements are needed in the area of cash management.

Very good! Now, let's return to the meeting. Peter just told Stan that there seemed to be a lot of money on deposit in various banks. Listen!

Peter: *Isn't that a lot to be holding in checking accounts?*

Stan: *It is a rather large amount, yes.*

Peter: *OK, here's what we'll do. I suggest you move more funds out of those checking accounts and into short-term securities. Leave in the checking accounts only what's required for day-to-day expenses. Oh, and Stan, be careful that those short-term securities aren't selected in a haphazard way. Invest wisely.*

Stan: *Of course. In fact, those excess funds could provide us with returns of eight or nine percent.*

Peter: *Exactly! OK, point number two. I'm also concerned about accounts receivable and payable. It's taking much too long to collect from our customers. On the other hand, we're paying our bills right on time. I think we should start delaying payments on certain of our accounts. That'll give us more cash on hand.*

Answer!

Peter's recommending that excess cash be moved out of checking accounts, right?	That's right, he's recommending that excess cash be moved out of checking accounts.
Is that so the excess cash can be invested?	Yes, that's so the excess cash can be invested.
He also suggested that Stan invest in short-term securities, right?	That's right, he also suggested that Stan invest in short-term securities.
Stan shouldn't select securities in a haphazard way, should he?	No, he shouldn't select securities in a haphazard way.
Peter feels the securities should be invested wisely, right?	That's right, he feels they should be invested wisely.

Is he concerned because AP's paying its bills too late or too promptly?	He's concerned because AP's paying its bills too promptly.
I beg your pardon? Why is Peter concerned?	He's concerned because AP's paying its bills too promptly.
He's not satisfied with the way accounts receivable are being handled, is he?	No, he's not satisfied with the way accounts receivable are being handled.
It's taking AP too long to collect from their customers, right?	That's right, it's taking them too long to collect from their customers.

Very good!

Now *repeat!*

AP's bills shouldn't be paid too promptly.
It's suggested that AP's bills not be paid too promptly.

Peter asked Stan about the balance sheet.
It was important that Peter ask Stan about the balance sheet.

Stan provides Peter with all financial documents. *Answer!* It's required that Stan ...	It's required that Stan provide Peter with all financial documents.
Every detail is thoroughly checked. It's important that ...	It's important that every detail be thoroughly checked.
Excess cash shouldn't be left in checking accounts. It's recommended ...	It's recommended that excess cash not be left in checking accounts.
Excess funds must be invested wisely. It's required ...	It's required that excess funds be invested wisely.

Very good! Now, let's listen again as Peter and Stan work on a plan.

Peter: *I think we should start delaying payments on certain of our accounts. That'll give us more cash on hand.*

Stan: *Will do. As for accounts receivable, I'll ask our people to make a special effort to collect on past due accounts. We do offer a one per-cent discount on invoices paid within ten days, but it's still taking an average of four months to collect.*

Peter: *Let's increase the invoice discount to two percent. That might get more customers to pay sooner. Oh, and Stan, I'm going to establish a year-end goal — to cut the average collection time on accounts receivable from four months to two.*

Stan: *We'll do our best, Peter. In fact, I'm already confident the balance sheets will soon be showing a far different picture.*

Peter: *A brighter one, I hope.*

Did Peter suggest that AP pay its bills sooner or delay payments?	He suggested that AP delay payments.
Isn't that so the company will have more cash on hand?	Yes, that's so the company will have more cash on hand.
A lot of customers' accounts are past due, right?	That's right, a lot of customers' accounts are past due.
What's past due, the accounts payable or the accounts receivable?	The accounts receivable are past due.
Does AP offer its customers a discount on invoices paid promptly?	Yes, they offer them a discount on invoices paid promptly.
Is that in order to get more customers to pay sooner?	Yes, that's in order to get more customers to pay sooner.
Peter wants to cut the average collection time of accounts receivable, right?	That's right, he wants to cut the average collection time of accounts receivable.

Very good! Well, it sounds as if Stan has a lot of work ahead of him. And you've had a lot of work on this tape, too. This is the end of Tape 8.

Tape 9   DISCUSSING FRINGE BENEFITS

Peter Crawford recently suggested that his executive assistant, Jane Collins, speak with Carol Nordstrom, AP's personnel director, about employee benefits. Jane and Carol are on the phone now.

Carol: *So you see, Jane, in order to attract talented personnel, we've got to start to upgrade AP's employee benefits.*

Jane: *Upgrade them!? Don't we already equal and, in most cases exceed, what other companies are paying their employees?*

Carol: *Well, in salaries, yes. But we won't have a real competitive advantage in the job market unless we offer more and better fringe benefits.*

Jane: *But, Carol, according to my estimate, current fringe benefits already account for better than thirty percent of AP's total payroll costs, which is a lot!*

Carol: *That's true. But it's only average when you consider benefits in many other companies. And, employees are also aware that a good part of the benefits package is required by law anyway.*

Jane: *I know — Social Security, workmen's compensation for injuries suffered on the job, and so on. On the other hand, AP does pick up all costs for an excellent health plan and a retirement plan, too. And then there's our* optional life insurance coverage, with AP and the employee sharing the premiums. What else could you possibly add? A dental plan, I suppose.

Carol: As a matter of fact, yes.

Jane: Hmm, either that or a stock purchase program permitting employees to buy shares of AP's stock at a discounted price.

Carol: Why not profit sharing and a stock purchase program? Jane, dollar-for-dollar fringe benefits are a good investment. Because they're not taxed, many employees consider them almost as important as salary. And, of course, those same benefits are tax deductible for the company.

Jane: Well, Carol, you certainly have given this all a good deal of thought. Knowing how determined Peter is to revitalize AP, your ideas on benefits could become an important factor in his overall plan.

Carol: That's what I'm hoping, Jane. Oh, and thanks for calling. I'm glad to have been able to go over everything with both you and Peter.

Now, let's listen to the conversation again. And then ... answer some questions.

Carol: So you see, Jane, in order to attract talented personnel, we've got to start to upgrade AP's employee benefits.

Jane: Upgrade them!? Don't we already equal and, in most cases exceed, what other companies are paying their employees?

Carol: Well, in salaries, yes. But we won't have a real competitive advantage in the job market unless we offer more and better fringe benefits.

Jane: But, Carol, according to my estimate, current fringe benefits already account for better than thirty percent of AP's total payroll costs, which is a lot!

Answer!

Carol wants to upgrade AP's fringe benefits, doesn't she?	Yes, she wants to upgrade AP's fringe benefits.
Does that mean she wants to provide more or fewer benefits?	That means she wants to provide more benefits.
AP doesn't want to lose their competitive advantage on the job market, do they?	No, they don't want to lose their competitive advantage on the job market.
By staying competitive, AP can attract talented personnel, right?	That's right, by staying competitive, they can attract talented personnel.
Don't AP's salaries equal or exceed most other companies'?	Yes, their salaries equal or exceed most other companies'.
Did Carol say fringe benefits were or weren't included in payroll costs?	She said fringe benefits were included in payroll costs.

Very good! Let's go back to the conversation now. Jane is telling Carol how much AP already pays in fringe benefits. Listen!

Jane: But, Carol, according to my estimate, current fringe benefits already account for better than thirty percent of AP's total payroll costs, which is a lot!

Carol: That's true. But it's only average when you consider benefits in many other companies. And, employees are also aware that a good part of the benefits package is required by law anyway.

Jane: I know — Social Security, workmen's compensation for injuries suffered on the job, and so on. On the other hand, AP does pick up all costs for an excellent health plan and a retirement plan, too. And then there's our optional life insurance coverage, with AP and the employee sharing the premiums. What else could you possibly add? A dental plan, I suppose.

Answer!

Carol considers AP's current fringe benefits only average, right?

That's right, she considers AP's current fringe benefits only average.

I beg your pardon? What's only average, the salary package or the fringe benefits package?

The fringe benefits package is only average.

Aren't some employee benefits required by law?

Yes, some employee benefits are required by law.

What do they include, things like Social Security or life insurance?

They include things like Social Security.

Workmen's compensation is also required by law, isn't it?

Yes, workmen's compensation is also required by law.

What's it for, injuries suffered at home or on the job?

It's for injuries suffered on the job.

Is life insurance coverage optional or required?

It's optional.

I beg your pardon? What's optional?

Life insurance coverage is optional.

And payment of the premiums is shared by AP and the employee, right?

That's right, payment of the premiums is shared by AP and the employee.

Very good!

Repeat!

Carol studied the benefit program.
Then she made her recommendations.
Having studied the benefit program, she made her recommendations.
She made her recommendations.
Then she wrote a report.
Answer! Having made her recommendations, she wrote ...

Having made her recommendations, she wrote a report.

She wrote her report.
Then she sent it to Peter.
Having written ...

Having written her report, she sent it to Peter.

She sent her report to Peter.
Then she called him up.
Having ...

Having sent her report to Peter, she called him up.

She discussed her report with Peter.
Then she spoke to Jane.
Having ...

Having discussed her report with Peter, she spoke to Jane.

Very good! Now let's go back to the conversation. Jane seems to think AP's benefits package already offers a lot. Listen!

Jane: *What else could you possibly add? A dental plan, I suppose.*

Carol: *As a matter of fact, yes.*

Jane: *Hmm, either that or a stock purchase program permitting employees to buy shares of AP's stock at a discounted price.*

Carol: *Why not profit sharing and a stock purchase program? Jane, dollar-for-dollar fringe benefits are a good investment. Because they're not taxed, many employees consider them almost as important as salary. And, of course, those same benefits are tax deductible for the company.*

Answer!

Would a stock purchase program offer shares to employees at a discounted price?

Yes, it would offer shares to employees at a discounted price.

I beg your pardon? Would the employees be paying the normal share price or a discounted share price?

They'd be paying a discounted share price.

Do fringe benefits provide tax advantages?

Yes, they provide tax advantages.

I beg your pardon? What provides tax advantages?

Fringe benefits provide tax advantages.

Are most of them taxable or nontaxable for the employee?

Most of them are nontaxable for the employee.

And they're tax deductible for the company, right?

That's right, they're tax deductible for the company.

Very good! Now let's go back to the conversation. Jane may be willing to give Carol's ideas some serious thought. Listen!

Jane: *Well, Carol, you certainly have given this all a good deal of thought. Knowing how determined Peter is to revitalize AP, your ideas on benefits could become an important factor in his overall plan.*

Carol: That's what I'm hoping, Jane. Oh, and thanks for calling. I'm glad to have been able to go over everything with both you and Peter.

Answer!

Jane doesn't think Carol has given fringe benefits too little thought, does she?	No, she doesn't think Carol has given fringe benefits too little thought.
Carol has given this all a good deal of thought, right?	That's right, she's given this all a good deal of thought.
Could her ideas become important in revitalizing AP?	Yes, her ideas could become important in revitalizing AP.
None of her ideas have been turned down so far, have they?	No, none of her ideas have been turned down so far.
She's hoping they'll be accepted, right?	That's right, she's hoping they'll be accepted.

Very good! Well, Carol and Jane have finished their discussion. And you've finished this tape. Congratulations! This is the end of Tape 9.

Tape 10   STEVE BLAKE'S MARKET STUDY

AP's marketing director, Steve Blake, has just finished a market study of AP's Tru-Tone line of stereo equipment. Before presenting the results to AP's management, Steve met with sales director, Ben Melnick.

Steve: Well, Ben, Tru-Tone sales have been declining because AP hasn't kept pace with modern technology.

Ben: Oh, really? I've been hearing that complaint from my sales staff for about three years now. Tru-Tone has a weight problem, it's bulky, and its overall design lacks appeal.

Steve: Well, what your salespeople have been saying definitely reinforces the information that's in the study. There is something wrong with Tru-Tone's design. It's failing to attract the youth market, Ben.

Ben: That's for sure! So, it's almost exclusively the middle and upper income people who buy Tru-Tone. They're what ... in the 40- to 50-year range?

Steve: Exactly. And, in general, they seem to be satisfied with Tru-Tone's quality. But — and listen to this, Ben — we've discovered that even older purchasers are deciding against Tru-Tone more and more. Let me tell you, this analysis breaks down figures and data into a lot of categories — age, sex, income, geographic distribution.

Ben: What about advertising, Steve? Has it been misdirected in any way?

Steve:	Well, ... yes, as a matter of fact, it has. I'm afraid my marketing people have been relying too much on print advertising. Don't people read anymore, Ben?
Ben:	Sure they do. But we also need heavy advertising on radio and, especially, T.V. Remember? ... youth-oriented.
Steve:	Sounds good to me. But I must say, Ben, in the meantime you've got to change your sales outlet strategy. Your sales staff needs to get Tru-Tone into more department stores, appliance stores, discount houses ... not just the same old dealership network.
Ben:	I've told you before, Steve, Peter and I have already agreed on that.
Steve:	That's good to hear. Of course, I can't eliminate your sales outlet problem from my presentation in the conference room tomorrow. But you can rely on me, Ben. I won't spend too much time on it. No reason to make you suffer more than necessary.
Ben:	That's kind of you, Steve. I hope I can do the same for you sometime.

Let's listen to the conversation once again. And then ... answer some questions.

Steve:	Well, Ben, Tru-Tone sales have been declining because AP hasn't kept pace with modern technology.
Ben:	Oh, really? I've been hearing that complaint from my sales staff for about three years now. Tru-Tone has a weight problem, it's bulky, and its overall design lacks appeal.
Steve:	Well, what your salespeople have been saying definitely reinforces the information that's in the study. There is something wrong with Tru-Tone's design. It's failing to attract the youth market, Ben.

Answer!

Ben's sales staff have had a complaint about Tru-Tone, haven't they?

Yes, they've had a complaint about Tru-Tone.

Is Tru-Tone's overall design appealing?

No, its overall design isn't appealing.

I beg your pardon? What lacks appeal, Tru-Tone's name or its overall design?

Its overall design lacks appeal.

Very good!

Now *repeat!*

Steve Blake, who's marketing director at AP, has just finished a market study.

Tomorrow morning Steve will be in the conference room, where he'll be presenting his study.

Steve's presentation is important, which is why AP's directors were invited.

They were invited by Peter Crawford, who is determined to revitalize sales.

Good! That was very good! Now, let's go back to the conversation. Steve hasn't given his presentation yet. He's still meeting with Ben. Listen!

Steve:	There is something wrong with Tru-Tone's design. It's failing to attract the youth market, Ben.
Ben:	That's for sure! So, it's almost exclusively the middle and upper income people who buy Tru-Tone. They're what ... in the 40- to 50-year range?
Steve:	Exactly. And, in general, they seem to be satisfied with Tru-Tone's quality. But — and listen to this, Ben — we've discovered that even older purchasers are deciding against Tru-Tone more and more. Let me tell you, this analysis breaks down figures and data into a lot of categories — age, sex, income, geographic distribution.
Ben:	What about advertising, Steve? Has it been misdirected in any way?
Steve:	Well, ... yes, as a matter of fact, it has. I'm afraid my marketing people have been relying too much on print advertising.

Answer!

Is it mostly lower income people who are still buying Tru-Tone?	No, it's not mostly lower income people who are still buying Tru-Tone.
They're almost exclusively middle and upper income people, right?	That's right, they're almost exclusively middle and upper income people.
Are they in the 20- to 30-year range or the 40- to 50-year range?	They're in the 40- to 50-year range.
But even the older purchasers have begun deciding against Tru-Tone, haven't they?	Yes, even the older purchasers have begun deciding against Tru-Tone.
Steve's data wasn't broken down into just a few categories, was it?	No, it wasn't broken down into just a few categories.
Did the categories include age, sex, and income?	Yes, they included age, sex, and income.
Have Steve's marketing people been relying too much or too little on print advertising?	They've been relying too much on print advertising.
Their advertising has been misdirected, hasn't it?	Yes, it's been misdirected.

Very good! Yes, Steve had his marketing staff ask customers a lot of questions about Tru-Tone. And they discovered that advertising had been misdirected. Listen!

Steve:	I'm afraid my marketing people have been relying too much on print advertising. Don't people read anymore, Ben?
Ben:	Sure they do. But we also need heavy advertising on radio and, especially, T.V. Remember? ... youth-oriented.

Steve: Sounds good to me. But I must say, Ben, in the meantime you've got to change your sales outlet strategy. Your sales staff needs to get Tru-Tone into more department stores, appliance stores, discount houses ... not just the same old dealership network.

Ben: I've told you before, Steve, Peter and I have already agreed on that.

Steve: That's good to hear. Of course, I can't eliminate your sales outlet problem from my presentation in the conference room tomorrow. But you can rely on me, Ben. I won't spend too much time on it. No reason to make you suffer more than necessary.

Ben: That's kind of you, Steve. I hope I can do the same for you sometime.

Answer!

Have Steve's marketing people relied too much on T.V. advertising?	No, they haven't relied too much on T.V. advertising.
They've been relying too much on print advertising, right?	That's right, they've been relying too much on print advertising.
What's needed, more or less youth-oriented advertising?	More youth-oriented advertising is needed.
Ben's sales outlet strategy doesn't sound too good, does it?	No, his sales outlet strategy doesn't sound too good.
He needs to get Tru-Tone into more appliance stores and discount houses, doesn't he?	Yes, he needs to get Tru-Tone into more appliance stores and discount houses.
He's been relying too much on the same old dealership network, right?	That's right, he's been relying too much on the same old dealership network.

Very good!

Repeat!

Steve had his staff prepare a report. He had the report prepared.	
He had them check the facts. *Answer!* He had the facts ...	He had the facts checked.
He had someone type the report. He had the ...	He had the report typed.
He had his secretary make ten copies. He had ...	He had ten copies made.
He had someone distribute the copies. He had ...	He had the copies distributed.

Very good. Well, it looks as if Ben has a lot of work ahead of him in improving his sales network. On the other hand, Steve will have to do something about AP's misdirected advertising. In the meantime, their meeting is over, and so is this tape. This is the end of Tape 10.

Tape 11   RESEARCH PAYOFF FOR AUDIO PERFORMANCE

Public relations director, Bud Wilson, is meeting with Peter Crawford to plan the announcement of AP's new product, the Games Master.

Bud: *What's this Games Master I've been hearing about, Peter? It's not a toy, is it?*

Peter: *No, it's not, Bud. What it is, is a very small computer that lets you play games using a normal T.V. set.*

Bud: *You don't mean another one of those electronic game machines? Peter, the leisure market is filled with them.*

Peter: *That was my feeling, too, at first. However, the Games Master is unique, Bud. It really is. It's going to prove a tremendous success, especially in the youth market.*

Bud: *Peter, if I didn't have confidence in your judgment, I'd say the word "unique" was rather strong. I'm thinking of our public announcement, and the questions we'll be facing from the press. I can just hear them asking what it is that makes our Games Master unique.*

Peter: *Well, for one thing, it's capable of playing over 50 different games, all at the press of a button.*

Bud: *Hmm, that does seem like a lot of games for one machine. If our objective is to make this product appeal to younger people, just the number of games it can play should be a positive factor.*

Peter: *Exactly. However, the feature that really places the Games Master in a special category is a computer-controlled audio system that can be used with stereo speakers. I'm telling you, Bud, I've never heard anything like it. You really get a strange feeling playing this machine in stereo. If you didn't know it was right there in front of you, you'd think you were playing against real people.*

Bud: *Peter, from what you've just said, this talking game machine is going to have a real effect on the market. Our public relations department will be working full-time on this project, that's for sure. In fact, I'm going right over to talk to the research staff who put this device together.*

Peter: *Start with Dr. Kosloff. The Games Master is his invention.*

Bud: *What?! But Kosloff is director of research and development. He's always so serious. Are you saying he came up with a game machine?*

Peter: *He sure did. And I'd like to let him make the announcement personally to the press. Tell you what ... why don't we make the announcement at a cocktail party? Let's really celebrate the occasion. After all, it's*

Kosloff's research that's going to pay off for AP. I'll leave all the details up to you, Bud.

Bud: *OK. I'll handle all the preliminary work. We'll invite reporters from the local media and national trade publications. We'll have press releases sent out and, of course, I'll arrange everything for the big party. Nicholas Kosloff and a game machine — I still don't believe it!*

Let's listen once again to the beginning of Bud Wilson's discussion with Peter Crawford. And then ... answer some questions.

Bud: *What's this Games Master I've been hearing about, Peter? It's not a toy, is it?*

Peter: *No, it's not, Bud. What it is, is a very small computer that lets you play games using a normal T.V. set.*

Bud: *You don't mean another one of those electronic game machines? Peter, the leisure market is filled with them.*

Peter: *That was my feeling, too, at first. However, the Games Master is unique, Bud. It really is. It's going to prove a tremendous success, especially in the youth market.*

Answer!

Is the Games Master a toy?	No, it's not a toy.
It's a small computer, right?	That's right, it's a small computer.
Does it let you play electronic games or cassette tapes?	It lets you play electronic games.
Isn't the leisure market already filled with electronic game machines?	Yes, the leisure market is already filled with electronic game machines.
Does Peter think the Games Master is unique or not?	He thinks the Games Master is unique.
He feels it'll prove to be a tremendous success, right?	That's right, he feels it'll prove to be a tremendous success.

Very good! Now, let's go back to the conversation. Listen!

Peter: *However, the Games Master is unique, Bud. It really is. It's going to prove a tremendous success, especially in the youth market.*

Bud: *Peter, if I didn't have confidence in your judgment, I'd say the word "unique" was rather strong. I'm thinking of our public announcement, and the questions we'll be facing from the press. I can just hear them asking what it is that makes our Games Master unique.*

Peter: *Well, for one thing, it's capable of playing over 50 different games, all at the press of a button.*

Bud: Hmm, that does seem like a lot of games for one machine. If our objective is to make this product appeal to younger people, just the number of games it can play should be a positive factor.

Answer!

Did Bud say he had confidence in Peter's judgment?

Yes, he said he had confidence in Peter's judgment.

There'll be a public announcement of the Games Master, right?

That's right, there'll be a public announcement of the Games Master.

What was Bud concerned about, the questions he'd face from Peter or from the press?

He was concerned about the questions he'd face from the press.

Do Peter and Bud expect the Games Master to appeal to younger or older people?

They expect the Games Master to appeal to younger people.

That's their objective, isn't it?

Yes, that's their objective.

Does the Games Master play just a few games?

No, it doesn't play just a few games.

It's capable of playing a lot of games at the press of a button, right?

That's right, it's capable of playing a lot of games at the press of a button.

Very good!

Repeat!

Peter played the Games Master.
He realized it was unique.
If he hadn't played the Games Master, he wouldn't have realized it was unique.

Peter was impressed.
He gave his approval.
Answer! If he hadn't been impressed ...

If he hadn't been impressed, he wouldn't have given his approval.

Peter needed a press conference.
He called Bud Wilson.
If he hadn't ...

If he hadn't needed a press conference, he wouldn't have called Bud Wilson.

Bud had experience.
He knew about press conferences.
If he ...

If he hadn't had experience, he wouldn't have known about press conferences.

Bud had confidence in Peter.
He was willing to proceed.
If ...

If he hadn't had confidence in Peter, he wouldn't have been willing to proceed.

Very good! Excellent! Let's go back now to the conversation. Bud was beginning to agree with Peter that the Games Master will prove to be a success. Listen!

Bud: *If our objective is to make this product appeal to younger people, just the number of games it can play should be a positive factor.*

Peter: *Exactly. However, the feature that really places the Games Master in a special category is a computer-controlled audio system that can be used with stereo speakers. I'm telling you, Bud, I've never heard anything like it. You really get a strange feeling playing this machine in stereo. If you didn't know it was right there in front of you, you'd think you were playing against real people.*

Bud: *Peter, from what you've just said, this talking game machine is going to have a real effect on the market. Our public relations department will be working full-time on this project, that's for sure. In fact, I'm going right over to talk to the research staff who put this device together.*

Peter: *Start with Dr. Kosloff. The Games Master is his invention.*

Answer!

The Games Master has an audio system that's controlled by a computer, right?	That's right, it has an audio system that's controlled by a computer.
Did Peter get a strange feeling playing the game in stereo?	Yes, he got a strange feeling playing the game in stereo.
He'd never heard anything like it before, had he?	No, he'd never heard anything like it before.

Good, very good! Peter has just told Bud that the Games Master is Dr. Kosloff's invention. Listen!

Peter: *Start with Dr. Kosloff. The Games Master is his invention.*

Bud: *What?! But Kosloff is director of research and development. He's always so serious. Are you saying he came up with a game machine?*

Peter: *He sure did. And I'd like to let him make the announcement personally to the press. Tell you what ... why don't we make the announcement at a cocktail party? Let's really celebrate the occasion. After all, it's Kosloff's research that's going to pay off for AP. I'll leave all the details up to you, Bud.*

Bud: *OK. I'll handle all the preliminary work. We'll invite reporters from the local media and national trade publications. We'll have press releases sent out and, of course, I'll arrange everything for the big party. Nicholas Kosloff and a game machine – I still don't believe it!*

Answer!

Was Bud aware that the Games Master had been Dr. Kosloff's invention?	No, he wasn't aware that it had been Dr. Kosloff's invention.
Dr. Kosloff is director of research and development, right?	That's right, he's director of research and development.

Will Peter be the one to make the announcement to the press?	No, he won't be the one to make the announcement to the press.
He'd like to let Dr. Kosloff make the announcement, right?	That's right, he'd like to let Dr. Kosloff make the announcement.
What does Peter have in mind, a small press conference or a big cocktail party?	He has a big cocktail party in mind.
He's leaving all the details up to Bud, isn't he?	Yes, he's leaving all the details up to Bud.

Very good! Well, thanks to Dr. Kosloff's research, AP has come up with a new product. And we've come to the end of another tape. This is the end of Tape 11.

Tape 12   CONSIDERING AN ACQUISITION

Peter Crawford is deciding whether AP should purchase a company called Leisure Time Entertainment. He's on the phone speaking with his controller, Stan Waterman.

Stan: *But, Peter, the Games Master is a terrific product. There shouldn't be any problem marketing it.*

Peter: *That's right. But the fact is, Stan, AP's sales distribution network is too narrow. We won't be able to exploit the full sales potential of the Games Master, and that disturbs me.*

Stan: *Hmm, it may be worthwhile to explore the possibility of a license arrangement with another company. That would give us access to a bigger market, don't you think?*

Peter: *Licensing is one possibility, yes. In fact, I've already made a proposal to Leisure Time Entertainment, and they seem interested. Have you ever heard of them?*

Stan: *Leisure Time Entertainment? Sure. LTE manufactures toys, electronic games, and sports equipment. They're small, but well managed, with a proven record of performance and stability. And they've done very well in the video game market. Who knows, they may just be the company we need to market the Games Master for us.*

Peter: *Why do you say they're well managed?*

Stan: *Well, it's strange you should be considering LTE. I've got a friend who's been encouraging me to buy LTE stock for a long time. She bought a lot of it a few years ago relatively cheap. Now it's trading for just under $40 a share.*

Peter: *$36 to be exact, with a price-earnings ratio of 15. Stan, I haven't discussed this with anyone else, but I'm seriously considering an acquisition.*

Stan: Buying LTE? But, Peter, we can't afford that kind of acquisition. It would leave us too vulnerable financially.

Peter: Maybe ... maybe not. LTE is a young company with what might be a lot of growth potential. I think both companies would benefit by joining forces.

Stan: Well, it would certainly give us more diversification. And that should help increase profits. How can I help, Peter?

Peter: Get a hold of your contacts on Wall Street. Have them run a thorough credit check on LTE and its management. Let's find out if the company is really doing well and has growth potential. Maybe its stock is simply overpriced. Oh, and Stan, do be careful who you talk to about this. I haven't spoken to LTE about a possible acquisition, and I wouldn't want them to hear any announcements about it on the evening news!

Stan: No problem, Peter. You can rely on me.

Now, listen to the first part of the conversation again. And then ... answer some questions.

Stan: But, Peter, the Games Master is a terrific product. There shouldn't be any problem marketing it.

Peter: That's right. But the fact is, Stan, AP's sales distribution network is too narrow. We won't be able to exploit the full sales potential of the Games Master, and that disturbs me.

Stan: Hmm, it may be worthwhile to explore the possibility of a license arrangement with another company. That would give us access to a bigger market, don't you think?

Peter: Licensing is one possibility, yes. In fact, I've already made a proposal to Leisure Time Entertainment, and they seem interested.

Answer!

Isn't it a fact that AP's sales distribution network is too narrow?	Yes, it's a fact that their sales distribution network is too narrow.
It wouldn't be able to exploit the full sales potential of the Games Master, would it?	No, it wouldn't be able to exploit the full sales potential of the Games Master.
Is that what disturbs Peter?	Yes, that's what disturbs him.
Would licensing give AP a bigger or smaller share of the market?	It would give them a bigger share of the market.
Peter has already made a proposal to Leisure Time Entertainment, right?	That's right, he's already made a proposal to Leisure Time Entertainment.
Did he propose a license arrangement or a real estate purchase?	He proposed a license arrangement.

Very good! Let's go back to the conversation now. Peter and Stan are exploring the possibility of a license arrangement. Listen!

Peter: *In fact, I've already made a proposal to Leisure Time Entertainment, and they seem interested. Have you ever heard of them?*

Stan: *Leisure Time Entertainment? Sure. LTE manufactures toys, electronic games, and sports equipment. They're small, but well managed, with a proven record of performance and stability. And they've done very well in the video game market. Who knows, they may just be the company we need to market the Games Master for us.*

Peter: *Why do you say they're well managed?*

Stan: *Well, it's strange you should be considering LTE. I've got a friend who's been encouraging me to buy LTE stock for a long time. She bought a lot of it a few years ago relatively cheap. Now it's trading for just under $40 a share.*

Answer!

LTE's products aren't confined to sports equipment, are they?	No, their products aren't confined to sports equipment.
They also manufacture toys and electronic game machines, right?	That's right, they also manufacture toys and electronic game machines.
LTE doesn't look as if it's been poorly managed, does it?	No, it doesn't look as if it's been poorly managed.
It seems to have a proven record of performance and stability, doesn't it?	Yes, it seems to have a proven record of performance and stability.
Stan has a friend who's been encouraging him to purchase LTE stock, right?	That's right, he has a friend who's been encouraging him to purchase LTE stock.
Were shares of LTE relatively cheap or expensive a few years ago?	They were relatively cheap a few years ago.

Very good!

Repeat!

The acquisition will probably work out.
It should work out.

It probably won't be a problem.
Answer! It shouldn't be a ...   It shouldn't be a problem.

It will probably be profitable.
It should ...   It should be profitable.

It probably won't take long.
It shouldn't ...   It shouldn't take long.

It will probably increase sales.
It ...   It should increase sales.

Very good! Now, let's go back to the conversation. Stan is telling Peter how much LTE shares are selling for. Listen!

Stan: *Now it's trading for just under $40 a share.*

Peter: *$36 to be exact, with a price-earnings ratio of 15. Stan, I haven't discussed this with anyone else, but I'm seriously considering an acquisition.*

Stan: *Buying LTE? But, Peter, we can't afford that kind of acquisition. It would leave us too vulnerable financially.*

Peter: *Maybe ... maybe not. LTE is a young company with what might be a lot of growth potential. I think both companies would benefit by joining forces.*

Answer!

Is LTE doing well or not so well on the stock market?	It's doing well on the stock market.
Is Peter thinking of buying LTE?	Yes, he's thinking of buying it.
Did Stan say that AP could afford the acquisition?	No, he didn't say they could afford the acquisition.
He feels an acquisition would leave AP too vulnerable financially, right?	That's right, he feels an acquisition would leave them too vulnerable financially.

Very good! Well, Stan certainly didn't expect Peter to be considering an acquisition. Let's go back to the conversation and see what else Peter has in mind. Listen!

Peter: *I think both companies would benefit by joining forces.*

Stan: *Well, it would certainly give us more diversification. And that should help increase profits. How can I help, Peter?*

Peter: *Get a hold of your contacts on Wall Street. Have them run a thorough credit check on LTE and its management. Let's find out if the company is really doing well and has growth potential. Maybe its stock is simply overpriced. Oh, and Stan, do be careful who you talk to about this. I haven't spoken to LTE about a possible acquisition, and I wouldn't want them to hear any announcements about it on the evening news!*

Stan: *No problem, Peter. You can rely on me.*

Answer!

Peter hasn't bought LTE yet, has he?	No, he hasn't bought it yet.
But if he did, it would give AP more diversification, right?	That's right, if he did, it would give them more diversification.
Does Stan have contacts on Wall Street that he can get a hold of?	Yes, he has contacts on Wall Street that he can get a hold of.

Does Peter want them to run a credit check on LTE or Audio Performance?	He wants them to run a credit check on LTE.
LTE's stock could be overpriced, couldn't it?	Yes, their stock could be overpriced.
Peter doesn't want any public announcement of a possible acquisition, does he?	No, he doesn't want any public announcement of a possible acquisition.
Is that why Stan should be careful who he talks to on Wall Street?	Yes, that's why he should be careful who he talks to on Wall Street.

Good, very good! Well, Peter and Stan are considering the possibility of an acquisition, but they don't want this known by the public just yet. In the meantime, we know that this tape has just ended. This is the end of Tape 12.

Tape 13   JACK BELL'S ADVERTISING PRESENTATION

Jack Bell works for Creative Talents Advertising Agency. He's just given a presentation on how to improve sales of AP's Tru-Tone line. Jack's discussing his proposals with AP's executive assistant, Jane Collins, sales director, Ben Melnick, and marketing director, Steve Blake.

Jane: *Jack, my compliments to you and your staff at Creative Talents. Your advertising strategy may be just the thing to boost Tru-Tone sales.*

Jack: *Thanks, Jane. Of course, I can't guarantee immediate results. But I'm going to follow up on every detail of the campaign personally. We'll be sending you in-depth information and samples of the kinds of ads we think will prove effective. ... Yes, Ben?*

Ben: *I just wanted to mention, Jack, that we'll be making some changes in distribution. Up to now, we've been focusing on authorized dealers. From now on, we're going to start using other kinds of outlets as well.*

Jack: *Good. I didn't include it in my presentation, but I am aware of the problem, Ben. Steve put a lot of emphasis on it in his market study.*

Ben: *I knew the sales department would be at the top of Steve's list of problems. Were we really the first on the list, Steve?*

Steve: *Now, Ben, you mustn't take these things personally ...*

Jack: *Well, uh ... to get back to the point, Ben. When we begin testing the ad campaign in the New England area ... Oh, you wanted to add something, Steve?*

Steve: *Just to say, Jack, that your presentation today confirms what I pointed out in the market study. Young people are more likely to shop at discount stores than at authorized dealers. How long have I been*

Jane: *telling you, Ben? Your people in sales have been selling Tru-Tone in the wrong places.*

Jane: *There you go again, Steve! Maybe you should take a closer look at Jack's charts. To me, they show the problem has been misdirected advertising. AP hasn't been reaching the right audience. That involves marketing, Steve.*

Steve: *You mustn't forget, Jane, up to now the marketing budget has been very limited. But now that Peter seems willing to increase advertising expenditures, there shouldn't be a problem. Right, Jack?*

Jack: *It'll still be a challenge, Steve.*

Steve: *Well, we in marketing look forward to doing all we can to make the new campaign a success. I'll work on this with Ben and his sales staff, too.*

Ben: *Thanks, Steve. I was just about to say ... I don't know what I'd do without your backup in these situations.*

Now, listen to the first part of the conversation again. And then ... answer some questions.

Jane: *Jack, my compliments to you and your staff at Creative Talents. Your advertising strategy may be just the thing to boost Tru-Tone sales.*

Jack: *Thanks, Jane. Of course, I can't guarantee immediate results. But I'm going to follow up on every detail of the campaign personally. We'll be sending you in-depth information, and samples of the kinds of ads we think will prove effective. ... Yes, Ben?*

Ben: *I just wanted to mention, Jack, that we'll be making some changes in distribution. Up to now, we've been focusing on authorized dealers. From now on, we're going to start using other kinds of outlets as well.*

Answer!

Does Jack Bell work for AP or Creative Talents?	He works for Creative Talents.
What is Creative Talents, a travel agency or an advertising agency?	It's an advertising agency.
Did Jane compliment Jack on his presentation?	Yes, she complimented him on his presentation.
She thinks his advertising strategy will help Tru-Tone sales, doesn't she?	Yes, she thinks his advertising strategy will help Tru-Tone sales.
She said she thought it might be just the thing to boost Tru-Tone sales, right?	That's right, she said she thought it might be just the thing to boost Tru-Tone sales.
Jack didn't say he could guarantee immediate results, did he?	No, he didn't say he could guarantee immediate results.

| But he's going to follow up on every detail personally, isn't he? | Yes, he's going to follow up on every detail personally. |
| Jack said he couldn't guarantee results immediately, but he was going to follow up on every detail personally, right? | That's right, he said he couldn't guarantee results immediately, but he was going to follow up on every detail personally. |

Very good! Now, let's go back to the meeting. Listen!

> Ben: *From now on, we're going to start using other kinds of outlets as well.*
>
> Jack: *Good. I didn't include it in my presentation, but I am aware of the problem, Ben. Steve put a lot of emphasis on it in his market study.*
>
> Ben: *I knew the sales department would be at the top of Steve's list of problems. Were we really the first on the list, Steve?*
>
> Steve: *Now, Ben, you mustn't take these things personally ...*
>
> Jack: *Well, uh ... to get back to the point, Ben. When we begin testing the ad campaign in the New England area ... Oh, you wanted to add something, Steve?*

Answer!

Did Jack include the sales outlet problem in his presentation?	No, he didn't include the sales outlet problem in his presentation.
But he was aware of the problem, wasn't he?	Yes, he was aware of the problem.
Steve's market study included a list of problems, right?	That's right, Steve's market study included a list of problems.
His study included a list of problems, and the sales department was at the top of the list, right?	That's right, his study included a list of problems, and the sales department was at the top of the list.
Where will the advertising test be run, in the South or in the New England area?	It'll be run in the New England area.

Very good!

Repeat!

Maybe they're using the wrong advertising.	
They could be using the wrong advertising.	
Maybe they're selling to the wrong market.	
Answer! They could be selling ...	They could be selling to the wrong market.
Maybe they're focusing on the wrong people.	
They could be ...	They could be focusing on the wrong people.

Maybe they're reaching the wrong audience.
They could ...

They could be reaching the wrong audience.

Maybe they're making the wrong decisions.
They ....

They could be making the wrong decisions.

Very good! Now, let's go back to the meeting. Listen!

> Jack: ... you wanted to add something, Steve?
>
> Steve: *Just to say, Jack, that your presentation today confirms what I pointed out in the market study. Young people are more likely to shop at discount stores than at authorized dealers. How long have I been telling you, Ben? Your people in sales have been selling Tru-Tone in the wrong places.*
>
> Jane: *There you go again, Steve! Maybe you should take a closer look at Jack's charts. To me, they show the problem has been misdirected advertising. AP hasn't been reaching the right audience. That involves marketing, Steve.*

Answer!

Did Jane agree with Steve's analysis of the situation?

No, she didn't agree with Steve's analysis of the situation.

Did she feel the problem had been misdirected sales or misdirected advertising?

She felt the problem had been misdirected advertising.

She said that was what was really reflected in Jack's charts, didn't she?

Yes, she said that was what was really reflected in Jack's charts.

Has AP been reaching the right audience?

No, they haven't been reaching the right audience.

I beg your pardon? They have or haven't been reaching the right audience?

They haven't been reaching the right audience.

They haven't been reaching the right audience, and that's a problem that involves marketing, right?

That's right, they haven't been reaching the right audience, and that's a problem that involves marketing.

Very good! Well, Jane seems to agree with Ben that the problem is with advertising, not sales. Let's hear Steve's response.

> Steve: *You mustn't forget, Jane, up to now, the marketing budget has been very limited. But now that Peter seems willing to increase advertising expenditures, there shouldn't be a problem. Right, Jack?*
>
> Jack: *It'll still be a challenge, Steve.*

Steve: *Well, we in marketing look forward to doing all we can to make the new campaign a success. I'll work on this with Ben and his sales staff, too.*

Ben: *Thanks, Steve. I was just about to say ... I don't know what I'd do without your backup in these situations.*

Answer!

Has Steve's marketing budget been limited up to now?	Yes, his marketing budget has been limited up to now.
He told Jane she mustn't forget that, didn't he?	Yes, he told her she mustn't forget that.
Peter hasn't proposed decreasng AP's advertising budget, has he?	No, he hasn't proposed decreasing it.
What has he proposed?	He's proposed increasing it.
Steve's looking forward to making the new campaign a success, isn't he?	Yes, he's looking forward to making the new campaign a success.

Very good! Well, AP's new ad campaign for its Tru-Tone recorders is about to start ... and this tape, Tape 13, is about to end. This is the end of Tape 13.

Tape 14   A REAL ESTATE PURCHASE

Jeff Martinelli, vice president of planning, has spent two weeks in South Carolina looking for a site suitable for the expansion of Audio Performance's production facilities. AP's executive assistant, Jane Collins, flew down to check out a piece of property that Jeff was recommending.

Jane: *We were surprised by your recommendation, Jeff. Peter and I felt there should have been at least one facility we could buy or lease, rather than our having to build a new plant.*

Jeff: *Jane, I inspected every facility in the area, and not one of them was adequate. They were either too small, too old, or poorly located. The real estate broker I've been working with agrees that it's highly unlikely we'll find one suited to our needs.*

Jane: *All right, then why don't you bring me up-to-date on this piece of property you wanted me to check out.*

Jeff: *O.K. It's 18 acres in the northern part of the state, near Greenville. It's unimproved land, but the location is perfect — with excellent access to main roads as well as to a railroad line that extends the full length of one side of the property. At $200,000, it's by far our best buy.*

Jane: *$200,000 for unimproved land? That's a little high, Jeff. And 18 acres? That's almost double what we originally had in mind. We'll never get the Board's approval on it.*

Jeff: Well, I think it's worth it, even at that price. But I did contact the owner, and he may be willing to lower his price to $180,000 ... maybe less.

Jane: Hmm ... Let's put in a bid of $150,000. The owner may counterbid and we may be able to settle for something between $160 and $170,000.

Jeff: I'll leave everything regarding bids and counterbids up to you and Peter. But there's another important factor to keep in mind. In order to attract new industry, South Carolina issues industrial revenue bonds. The proceeds from the bonds would be made available to us at a very low interest rate to help finance the construction.

Jane: Let's be sure to include that in our report to Peter. Who knows, Jeff? If this property is as good as you say, we may be on the way to a real estate purchase.

Jeff: I'm sure of it, Jane, but we've got to move fast. A lot of private investors are buying up land around here. In fact, that's how I lost my first choice. An investor must have heard I was interested, and before I could even contact you and Peter, he had already signed a deal with the owner.

Jane: Well, in that case, let's go inspect the property — all 18 acres of it ...

Now, listen to the first part of the conversation again. And then ... answer some questions.

Jane: We were surprised by your recommendation, Jeff. Peter and I felt there should have been at least one facility we could buy or lease, rather than our having to build a new plant.

Jeff: Jane, I inspected every facility in the area, and not one of them was adequate. They were either too small, too old, or poorly located. The real estate broker I've been working with agrees that it's highly unlikely we'll find one suited to our needs.

Jane: All right, then why don't you bring me up-to-date on this piece of property you wanted me to check out.

Answer!

Were Peter and Jane surprised by Jeff's recommendation?

Yes, they were surprised by his recommendation.

Did Jeff recommend leasing an existing plant or building a new one?

He recommended building a new one.

I beg your pardon? What did he recommend doing?

He recommended building a new plant.

Did Jeff inspect the facilities that were available?

Yes, he inspected the facilities that were available.

He inspected the facilities, but none of them was suitable, right?

That's right, he inspected the facilities, but none of them was suitable.

Does Jeff think it's likely or unlikely a suitable facility will be found?	He thinks it's unlikely a suitable facility will be found.
Jeff's located a piece of land that's suitable for construction, hasn't he?	Yes, he's located a piece of land that's suitable for construction.
Jane wants to be brought up-to-date on it, right?	That's right, she wants to be brought up-to-date on it.

Very good! Well, it looks like Jeff has located a piece of property that might be suitable. Let's return to the conversation. Listen!

> **Jane:** All right, then why don't you bring me up-to-date on this piece of property you wanted me to check out.
>
> **Jeff:** O.K. It's 18 acres in the northern part of the State, near Greenville. It's unimproved land, but the location is perfect — with excellent access to main roads as well as to a railroad line that extends the full length of one side of the property. At $200,000, it's by far our best buy.
>
> **Jane:** $200,000 for unimproved land? That's a little high, Jeff. And 18 acres? That's almost double what we originally had in mind. We'll never get the Board's approval on it.
>
> **Jeff:** Well, I think it's worth it, even at that price. But I did contact the owner, and he may be willing to lower his price to $180,000 ... maybe less.
>
> **Jane:** Hmm ... Let's put in a bid of $150,000. The owner may counterbid and we may be able to settle for something between $160 and $170,000.

Answer!

Has Jeff located a piece of property that's 18 acres or 80 acres?	He's located a piece of property that's 18 acres.
Is it improved or unimproved land?	It's unimproved land.
The owner isn't asking 200 million dollars for the land, is he?	No, the owner isn't asking 200 million dollars for the land.
How much is he asking for the land, 200 million or 200 thousand dollars?	He's asking 200 thousand dollars for it.
That's the asking price, right?	That's right, that's the asking price.
Jane doesn't think getting the Board's approval will be easy, does she?	No, she doesn't think getting their approval will be easy.
And what does Jeff think? Does he think the owner might be willing to lower his asking price?	Yes, he thinks the owner might be willing to lower his asking price.
That's why Jane's considering putting in a formal bid, isn't it?	Yes, that's why she's considering putting in a formal bid.

Very good!

Repeat!
They didn't want to lease a plant.
They could have leased one if they had wanted to.

They didn't want to pay a lot.

Answer! They could have paid a lot if ...	They could have paid a lot if they had wanted to.
They didn't want to expand the old plant. They could have ...	They could have expanded the old plant if they had wanted to.
They didn't want to buy an existing plant. They could ...	They could have bought an existing plant if they had wanted to.
They didn't want to raise their bid. They ...	They could have raised their bid if they had wanted to.

Very good! Let's go back to the conversation. Listen!

> Jane: The owner may counterbid and we may be able to settle for something between $160 and $170,000.
>
> Jeff: I'll leave everything regarding bids and counterbids up to you and Peter. But there's another important factor to keep in mind. In order to attract new industry, South Carolina issues industrial revenue bonds. The proceeds from the bonds would be made available to us at a very low interest rate to help finance the construction.
>
> Jane: Let's be sure to include that in our report to Peter. Who knows, Jeff? If this property is as good as you say, we may be on the way to a real estate purchase.
>
> Jeff: I'm sure of it, Jane, but we've got to move fast. A lot of private in-vestors are buying up land around here. In fact, that's how I lost my first choice. An investor must have heard I was interested, and before I could even contact you and Peter, he had already signed a deal with the owner.
>
> Jane: Well, in that case, let's go inspect the property — all 18 acres of it ...

Answer!

Does the state of South Carolina issue industrial revenue bonds?	Yes, the state of South Carolina issues industrial revenue bonds.
The state of South Carolina issues the bonds in order to attract new industry, right?	That's right, the state of South Carolina issues the bonds in order to attract new industry.
Are the proceeds of the bonds made available at high or low interest rates?	The proceeds of the bonds are made available at low interest rates.

Are a lot of private investors buying up land in the area?	Yes, a lot of private investors are buying up land in the area.
Jane and Jeff should move fast if they want to close the deal, right?	That's right, they should move fast if they want to close the deal.
Did Jeff already lose one deal?	Yes, he already lost one.
Another investor closed the deal before Jeff could contact Peter, right?	That's right, another investor closed the deal before Jeff could contact Peter.

Good! Very good! Well, it looks as if AP is on its way to making a real estate purchase. And you're on your way to finishing up another tape. This is the end of Tape 14.

Tape 15   A COSTLY MISTAKE IN ACCOUNTING

AP's production manager, Ed Pearson, had reason to believe there had been a serious accounting mistake at the Baltimore plant. He's on the phone now speaking with Jack Reilly, the plant's new manager.

Jack: *Ed, am I glad to hear from you! I've been at it day and night ... looking over the records. But I can't find anything that points to a mistake in our year-end report. I turned over all our books to the accounting department as you requested. Have you heard anything?*

Ed: *Yes, Jack. A call just came in from the controller's office. The audit revealed the plant's inventory was overstated by $400,000 at the close of last year.*

Jack: *$400,000? How could I have missed that? And a mistake like this coming so soon after being named plant manager. I don't know what to say, Ed. I'm really sorry about this.*

Ed: *The mistake was made at the close of last year, Jack. Whatever the problem was, it happened long before you became plant manager. We're certainly not going to hold you responsible.*

Jack: *Whew! That makes me feel a lot better. I'm glad you alerted me when you did, Ed. What happens now?*

Ed: *Well, for one thing, the accountants are looking into how the error affected the taxes we paid last year. The overstatement of $400,000 in inventory caused us to understate our cost of sales by the same amount. And this naturally inflated our profit figure.*

Jack: *In other words, our net income was $400,000 less than we reported to Internal Revenue.*

Ed: *Precisely. And the accountants estimate we paid $200,000 too much in taxes for the period.*

Jack: I'm not that familiar with the mechanics of the tax system, Ed, but can't we file an amended tax return to get the money back?

Ed: We sure can, and will. We'll explain the situation to Internal Revenue and ask them to credit the $200,000 to this year's tax liability. If they agree, it'll improve our profit picture for the current year.

Jack: It's a legitimate claim. They'll approve it, don't you think?

Ed: They should. They may order a complete audit — and you can be sure our accountants won't like that part of it one bit. But, yes, I'm confident we can prove our case. Who knows, Jack, we may still be able to turn this mistake to our advantage.

Jack: And I may be able to start getting some sleep again!

Now let's listen to the first part of the conversation again.

Jack: Ed, am I glad to hear from you! I've been at it day and night ... looking over the records. But I can't find anything that points to a mistake in our year-end report. I turned over all our books to the accounting department as you requested. Have you heard anything?

Ed: Yes, Jack. A call just came in from the controller's office. The audit revealed the plant's inventory was overstated by $400,000 at the close of last year.

Jack: $400,000? How could I have missed that? And a mistake like this coming so soon after being named plant manager. I don't know what to say, Ed. I'm really sorry about this.

Answer!

Did Ed Pearson tell Jack there had been a mistake in the year-end report?

Yes, he told him there had been a mistake in the year-end report.

Has Jack been able to find the mistake?

No, he hasn't been able to find it.

He's been looking over the records day and night, hasn't he?

Yes, he's been looking them over day and night.

He's been looking over the records day and night, but he hasn't found the mistake yet, right?

That's right, he's been looking them over day and night, but he hasn't found the mistake yet.

Had an audit been ordered?

Yes, an audit had been ordered.

Did Jack refuse to turn over his books to the accounting department?

No, he didn't refuse to turn them over to the accounting department.

He agreed to turn them over, didn't he?

Yes, he agreed to turn them over.

Did the audit reveal that the inventory had been overstated or understated?

It revealed that the inventory had been overstated.

The audit revealed that the plant's inventory had been overstated by $400,000, right?

That's right, it revealed that the plant's inventory had been overstated by $400,000.

Good.   Very good!

Now, *repeat!*

Jack's been looking over the figures.

He's been looking them over.

He turned over the books.

Answer! He turned ...   He turned them over.

They're going to write up the report.

They're going to ...   They're going to write it up.

They're looking over the books.

They're looking ...   They're looking them over.

They may call in the controller.

They may ...   They may call him in.

They're going to check out the problem.

They're ...   They're going to check it out.

Then the auditors will send back the
records.

Then they'll ...   Then they'll send them back.

Very good! Now let's go back to the conversation.

> Jack: *I don't know what to say, Ed. I'm really sorry about this.*
>
> Ed: *The mistake was made at the close of last year, Jack. Whatever the
> problem was, it happened long before you became plant manager. We're
> certainly not going to hold you responsible.*
>
> Jack: *Whew! That makes me feel a lot better. I'm glad you alerted me when
> you did, Ed. What happens now?*
>
> Ed: *Well, for one thing, the accountants are looking into how the error affected
> the taxes we paid last year. The overstatement of $400,000
> in inventory caused us to understate our cost of sales by the same
> amount. And this naturally inflated our profit figure.*

Answer!

Did the error take place before Jack
became plant manager?

Yes, it took place before he
became plant manager.

He won't be held responsible for
the error, will he?

No, he won't be held responsible
for it.

Are the accountants looking into the
effects of the error?

Yes, they're looking into the effects
of the error.

They're looking into how the mistake
affected AP's taxes last year, right?

That's right, they're looking into
how it affected AP's taxes last
year.

Did the error deflate or inflate the
profit figure?

It inflated the profit figure.

Very good! Listen again.

> Ed: The overstatement of $400,000 in inventory caused us to understate our cost of sales by the same amount. And this naturally inflated our profit figure.

> Jack: In other words, our net income was $400,000 less than we reported to Internal Revenue.

> Ed: Precisely. And the accountants estimate we paid $200,000 too much in taxes for the period.

> Jack: I'm not that familiar with the mechanics of the tax system, Ed, but can't we file an amended tax return to get the money back?

> Ed: We sure can, and will. We'll explain the situation to Internal Revenue and ask them to credit the $200,000 to this year's tax liability. If they agree, it'll improve our profit picture for the current year.

Answer!

Did AP pay too much in taxes last year?	Yes, they paid too much in taxes last year.
Did they pay a million dollars too much in taxes?	No, they didn't pay a million dollars too much in taxes.
Did they pay $100,000 or $200,000 too much in taxes?	They paid $200,000 too much in taxes.
Can AP get this money back?	Yes, they can get it back.
They can get it back by filing an amended tax return, can't they?	Yes, they can get it back by filing an amended tax return.
They want to credit the money to this year's tax liability, don't they?	Yes, they want to credit the money to this year's tax liability.
That would improve AP's profit picture for this year, wouldn't it?	Yes, it would improve AP's profit picture for this year.

Good! Now let's go back to the conversation.

> Ed: We'll explain the situation to Internal Revenue and ask them to credit the $200,000 to this year's tax liability. If they agree, it'll improve our profit picture for the current year.

> Jack: It's a legitimate claim. They'll approve it, don't you think?

> Ed: They should. They may order a complete audit — and you can be sure our accountants won't like that part of it one bit. But, yes, I'm confident we can prove our case. Who knows, Jack, we may still be able to turn this mistake to our advantage.

> Jack: And I may be able to start getting some sleep again!

Answer!

Does Jack think they have a legitimate claim?	Yes, he thinks they have a legitimate claim.

Ed thinks Internal Revenue will approve it, doesn't he?	Yes, he thinks they'll approve it.
Does he also think they may order a complete audit?	Yes, he also thinks they may order a complete audit.
How will AP's accountants feel about the audit? Will they like it?	No, they won't like it.
They won't like that part of it one bit, will they?	No, they won't like that part of it one bit.

Excellent! Well, it looks like everything may work out all right for AP in the end. And speaking of the end, we have now come to the end of this tape, Tape 15. This is the end of Tape 15.

Tape 16 EXPANDING THE USE OF COMPUTERS

Jeffrey Knowles is vice president of a well-known computer consulting firm. AP's executive assistant, Jane Collins, recently met with him. She's now discussing the results of the meeting with Peter Crawford.

Peter: *So, Jane, what did Jeffrey say about expanding our use of computers?*

Jane: *He said he was surprised we hadn't contacted him sooner. He remembered when we first introduced computers in the payroll department ... how some of our staff hadn't been sure the system would perform satisfactorily.*

Peter: *And now those same people insist the department wouldn't be manageable without it.*

Jane: *I told Jeffrey that the payroll system had proven to be one of our wisest investments, and that he'd been right about the time and money saved.*

Peter: *Can he help us do the same for accounts receivable?*

Jane: *Yes, but he wouldn't limit automation to accounts receivable alone — as we originally had in mind. Instead, he advises us to put in a data processing system that would tie inventory and accounts receivable together with sales and production.*

Peter: *Hmm ... did he give any specifics?*

Jane: *Well, every sales transaction would be fed into the computer ... product identification number, quantity sold, unit cost, plus customer information and pricing. This sales data would then be matched with input on production and inventory.*

Peter: *Which means the inventory account is automatically reduced each time a sale takes place. The next logical step would be for the computer to issue customer invoices and keep track of all payments received from customers, including overdue accounts.*

Jane: And that would solve our problems with accounts receivable. I asked Jeffrey whether a system like this was affordable. He said yes, but he warned that it might seem a little expensive at the beginning. But in the long run, the savings in efficiency will more than make up for the cost.

Peter: O.K., I'm sold ... on the idea at least. Did you ask how much time he needed to write up a proposal?

Jane: He said he had one already prepared.

Peter: You know, Jane, I get the feeling Jeffrey knows more about AP's operations than we do.

Let's listen to the first part of the conversation again ... and then answer some questions.

Peter: So, Jane, what did Jeffrey say about expanding our use of computers?

Jane: He said he was surprised we hadn't contacted him sooner. He remembered when we first introduced computers in the payroll department ... how some of our staff hadn't been sure the system would perform satisfactorily.

Peter: And now those same people insist the department wouldn't be manageable without it.

Jane: I told Jeffrey that the payroll system had proven to be one of our wisest investments, and that he'd been right about the time and money saved.

Answer!

Did Jane speak to Jeffrey about expanding the use of computers?	Yes, she spoke to him about expanding the use of computers.
AP was already using computers, weren't they?	Yes, they were already using computers.
Were they first introduced in the sales department or in the payroll department?	They were first introduced in the payroll department.
In the beginning, had they been sure the system would perform satisfactorily?	No, in the beginning they hadn't been sure the system would perform satisfactorily.
Has the computer system proven to be a bad investment?	No, it hasn't proven to be a bad investment.
It's saved AP time and money, hasn't it?	Yes, it's saved them time and money.

Very good!

Repeat!
It's been a good investment.
Jane said it had been a good investment.
They introduced the system in the payroll department.

Answer! She said they had introduced the system ...

She said they had introduced the system in the payroll department.

It's saved the company time and money. She said it had ...

She said it had saved the company time and money.

The system has performed satisfactorily. She said ...

She said the system had performed satisfactorily.

It didn't cost too much. She said it hadn't ...

She said it hadn't cost too much.

It hasn't been a bad investment. She said it ...

She said it hadn't been a bad investment.

Very good! Let's go back now to the conversation.

Jane: *I told Jeffrey that the payroll system had proven to be one of our wisest investments, and that he'd been right about the time and money saved.*

Peter: *Can he help us do the same for accounts receivable?*

Jane: *Yes, but he wouldn't limit automation to accounts receivable alone — as we originally had in mind. Instead, he advises us to put in a data processing system that would tie inventory and accounts receivable together with sales and production.*

Peter: *Hmm ... did he give any specifics?*

Jane: *Well, every sales transaction would be fed into the computer ... product identification number, quantity sold, unit cost, plus customer information and pricing. This sales data would then be matched with input on production and inventory.*

Answer!

What did Jeffrey advise, hiring more personnel?

No, he didn't advise hiring more personnel.

He advised putting in a data processing system, didn't he?

Yes, he advised putting in a data processing system.

Would he limit the new system to accounts receivable?

No, he wouldn't limit it to accounts receivable.

He'd also include inventory, wouldn't he?

Yes, he'd also include inventory.

What about sales and production? Would he tie them in, too?

Yes, he'd tie them in, too.

The sales data would be matched with production and inventory, wouldn't it?

Yes, the sales data would be matched with production and inventory.

Good! Very good!

Repeat!

Does the computer handle accounts receivable?

Peter asked whether the computer handled accounts receivable.

Does it tie accounts receivable with sales?	He asked whether it tied accounts receivable with sales.
Answer! He asked whether it ...	
Is the payroll department satisfied with it?	He asked whether the payroll department was satisfied with it.
He asked whether ...	
Will it perform satisfactorily?	He asked whether it would perform satisfactorily.
He asked...	

Very good! Let's go back to the conversation.

> Jane: *This sales data would then be matched with input on production and inventory.*
>
> Peter: *Which means the inventory account is automatically reduced each time a sale takes place. The next logical step would be for the computer to issue customer invoices and keep track of all payments received from customers, including overdue accounts.*
>
> Jane: *And that would solve our problems with accounts receivable. I asked Jeffrey whether a system like this was affordable. He said yes, but he warned that it might seem a little expensive at the beginning. But in the long run, the savings in efficiency will more than make up for the cost.*

Answer!

Did Peter say the computer would issue customer invoices?	Yes, he said it would issue customer invoices.
He said it would issue customer invoices and keep track of all payments received, right?	That's right, he said it would issue customer invoices and keep track of all payments received.
Jane wanted to know whether the system was affordable, didn't she?	Yes, she wanted to know whether it was affordable.
Did Jeffrey warn that the initial cost might seem low or high?	He warned that it might seem high.
But there would be savings in efficiency, wouldn't there?	Yes, there would be savings in efficiency.
The savings in efficiency should more than make up for the initial cost, right?	That's right, the savings in efficiency should more than make up for the initial cost.

Very good! Let's listen again.

> Peter: *O.K. I'm sold ... on the idea at least. Did you ask how much time he needed to write up a proposal?*
>
> Jane: *He said he had one already prepared.*

Peter:	You know, Jane, I get the feeling Jeffrey knows more about AP's operations than we do.

Answer!

Peter's sold on the idea of a new computer system, isn't he?	Yes, he's sold on the idea of a new computer system.
Does Jeffrey need time to write up a proposal?	No, he doesn't need time to write up a proposal.
He told Jane he had already written up a proposal, right?	That's right, he told her he had already written up a proposal.

Good! Very good! Well, it looks like the new computer project is about to begin. But this tape, Tape 16, is about to end. This is the end of Tape 16.

Tape 17 THE SHOP-WAY BONANZA

Ben Melnick, AP's director of sales, is trying to close a deal with Shop-Way, a very large nationwide discount chain. He's now in a meeting with Jane Collins, Peter Crawford's executive assistant, and Jeff Martinelli, vice president of planning.

Jeff:	*Congratulations, Ben! From what I've heard, your deal with Shop-Way could turn into a real bonanza for AP. How did you get one of the largest chain stores in the country to carry Tru-Tone? They must have heard of the problems we've been having.*
Ben:	*Let's just say that I was able to convince them that Tru-Tone's quality will have been greatly improved by the time they get their first delivery.*
Jane:	*We're still writing up a first draft of the contract, Jeff. But I agree — Ben's done a terrific job. This deal is definitely the big one we've been hoping for. Just think ... Shop-Way has outlets in almost 60 cities.*
Ben:	*But that's what we're concerned about, Jeff. Jane and I have been working out the details, and we have to be very careful how we word the conditions of the contract. It's important not to commit ourselves to any unrealistic production figures or delivery schedules.*
Jeff:	*I'm going to have to know what kind of sales volume we're talking about here.*
Ben:	*It'd be a 5-year agreement worth somewhere in the neighborhood of $10 million.*
Jane:	*And that's even if they don't purchase anything beyond the minimum. The actual figure could go as high as $15 million.*
Jeff:	*Wow! How much of a discount are they asking for?*
Ben:	*They want to get the units at 20 percent below our present wholesale rate.*

Jane: Which is only 6 percent above our manufacturing cost. And that worries me.

Jeff: But as production increases, unit costs will drop significantly. With a contract this big, there shouldn't be a problem getting our profit margin back up to where we want it.

Ben: That's the question, Jeff. Can you guarantee the production needed on a deal this big?

Jeff: Well, we're now operating at only 70 percent of full capacity. But we could increase production by about 25 percent in a very short time. And in a year or so, we'll have completed the new plant in South Carolina. Yes, we'll have enough capacity.

Ben: Then congratulations are in order to you, Jeff. Your answer may have just made the Shop-Way "bonanza," as you call it, a reality.

Now, let's listen to the beginning of the conversation again. Jeff Martinelli is just about to offer his congratulations to Ben Melnick.

Jeff: Congratulations, Ben! From what I've heard, your deal with Shop-Way could turn into a real bonanza for AP. How did you get one of the largest chain stores in the country to carry Tru-Tone? They must have heard of the problems we've been having.

Ben: Let's just say that I was able to convince them that Tru-Tone's quality will have been greatly improved by the time they get their first delivery.

Jane: We're still writing up a first draft of the contract, Jeff. But I agree — Ben's done a terrific job. This deal is definitely the big one we've been hoping for. Just think ... Shop-Way has outlets in almost 60 cities.

Answer!

Is Shop-Way a chain store?	Yes, it's a chain store.
It's one of the largest chain stores in the country, isn't it?	Yes, it's one of the largest chain stores in the country.
Is Ben trying to close a big deal with Shop-Way?	Yes, he's trying to close a big deal with Shop-Way.
He's been trying to close a deal, but he hasn't closed the deal yet, right?	That's right, he's been trying to close a deal, but he hasn't closed the deal yet.
He and Jane are still writing up a first draft of the contract, aren't they?	Yes, they're still writing up a first draft of the contract.
The deal hasn't turned into a bonanza for AP yet, has it?	No, it hasn't turned into a bonanza for AP yet.
But if all goes well, it could turn into a real bonanza, right?	That's right, if all goes well, it could turn into a real bonanza.
Very good!	

Repeat!
The deal hasn't turned into a bonanza yet.
By this time next year, it will have turned into a bonanza.

They haven't signed the deal yet.

Answer! By this time next year, they will have ...	By this time next year, they will have signed the deal.
They haven't sold the products yet. By this time next year, they ...	By this time next year, they will have sold the products.
They haven't made the deliveries yet. By this time next year ...	By this time next year, they will have made the deliveries.
They haven't increased production yet. By this time ...	By this time next year, they will have increased production.
They haven't improved the quality yet. By this time ...	By this time next year, they will have improved the quality.

Very good! Let's go back to the meeting.

Jane: *Shop-Way has outlets in almost 60 cities.*

Ben: *But that's what we're concerned about, Jeff. Jane and I have been working out the details, and we have to be very careful how we word the conditions of the contract. It's important not to commit ourselves to any unrealistic production figures or delivery schedules.*

Jeff: *I'm going to have to know what kind of sales volume we're talking about here.*

Ben: *It'd be a 5-year agreement worth somewhere in the neighborhood of $10 million.*

Jane: *And that's even if they don't purchase anything beyond the minimum. The actual figure could go as high as $15 million.*

Answer!

Have Ben and Jane been working out the details of the contract?	Yes, they've been working out the details of the contract.
They have to be careful how they word the conditions of the contract, right?	That's right, they have to be careful how they word the conditions of the contract.
They don't want to commit themselves to unrealistic production figures, do they?	No, they don't want to commit themselves to unrealistic production figures.
They've also got to be careful not to commit themselves to unrealistic delivery schedules, don't they?	Yes, they've also got to be careful not to commit themselves to unrealistic delivery schedules.
How much would the Shop-Way deal be worth, somewhere in the neighborhood of $100 million?	No, it wouldn't be worth somewhere in the neighborhood of $100 million.

414

It'd be worth somewhere in the neighborhood of $10 million, wouldn't it?

Yes, it'd be worth somewhere in the neighborhood of $10 million.

The deal would be a 5-year agreement worth somewhere in the neighborhood of $10 million, right?

That's right, it would be a 5-year agreement worth somewhere in the neighborhood of $10 million.

Very good! Listen again!

> Jeff: Wow! How much of a discount are they asking for?
>
> Ben: They want to get the units at 20 percent below our present wholesale rate.
>
> Jane: Which is only 6 percent above our manufacturing cost. And that worries me.
>
> Jeff: But as production increases, unit costs will drop significantly. With a contract this big, there shouldn't be a problem getting our profit margin back up to where we want it.

Answer!

Shop-Way is asking for a discount, aren't they?

Yes, they're asking for a discount.

They don't want to buy the units at the present wholesale rate, do they?

No, they don't want to buy them at the present wholesale rate.

They want to get them at 20 percent below the present wholesale rate, right?

That's right, they want to get them at 20 percent below the present wholesale rate.

Is production expected to increase with a contract this big?

Yes, it's expected to increase with a contract this big.

Will unit costs go up or drop as production increases?

They'll drop as production increases.

As production increases, AP's profit margin should improve, right?

That's right, as production increases, AP's profit margin should improve.

Good! Very good! Let's go back to the conversation.

> Jeff: But as production increases, unit costs will drop significantly. With a contract this big, there shouldn't be a problem getting our profit margin back up to where we want it.
>
> Ben: That's the question, Jeff. Can you guarantee the production needed on a deal this big?
>
> Jeff: Well, we're now operating at only 70 percent of full capacity. But we could increase production by about 25 percent in a very short time. And in a year or so, we'll have completed the new plant in South Carolina. Yes, we'll have enough capacity.

Ben: Then congratulations are in order to you, Jeff. Your answer may have just made the Shop-Way "bonanza," as you call it, a reality.

Answer!

Will the Shop-Way deal require AP to increase production?

Yes, it'll require them to increase production.

Are their plants operating at full capacity now?

No, they aren't operating at full capacity now.

They aren't operating at full capacity now, but they could increase production in a short time, right?

That's right, they aren't operating at full capacity now, but they could increase production in a short time.

Has construction of the new plant in South Carolina been completed?

No, it hasn't been completed.

But it will have been completed in a year or so, won't it?

Yes, it will have been completed in a year or so.

Very good! Well, it looks like the deal with Shop-Way may be off to a good start. Their deal is about to start, and our tape, Tape 17, is about to end. This is the end of Tape 17.

Tape 18   EXCHANGE RATES CAUSE BUDGETING PROBLEMS

AP's controller, Stan Waterman, is meeting with Peter Crawford to go over some last minute details concerning the budget forecast.

Karen: Yes, Mr. Crawford?

Peter: Would you hold my calls, Karen? Mr. Waterman and I are going over the budget, and I'd like not to have any interruptions.

Stan: Well, Peter, I'm happy to say the budget forecast is almost finished.

Peter: Good. Can we assume AP will still be in business next year?

Stan: I think that's a safe assumption. I'm very optimistic, Peter. If our estimates are correct, the increase in next year's sales volume will be the largest AP has ever had.

Peter: Now that is good news! We've been committing ourselves to a tremendous outlay of dollars for capital improvements ... more automation, new products and marketing strategies — not to mention the new plant we'll have in operation this time next year. What does the profit picture look like when you take all these expenditures into account?

Stan: Our profit margin may drop just a bit at first. But in about a year's time, we should begin to see a dramatic improvement.

Peter: Sounds good to me. What about the foreign market? It's 16 percent of our total sales volume right now.

Stan: That's true. And as you know, the majority of our export sales revenue comes from the U.K. The falling dollar has made us more competitive in the British market.

Peter: But will the downward trend in the value of the dollar continue? You're a better judge of that than I am, Stan. What do you think will happen to the exchange rate?

Stan: It's difficult to make forecasts. Not even the experts agree as to whether the dollar will continue its fall, stabilize, or even begin rising.

Peter: In any case, Stan, the only thing we can do is keep an eye on the situation abroad and reforecast on a quarterly basis. ... Oh, before I forget — I'm thinking of opening a sales office in Europe. It might be just what we need to increase that export sales figure.

Stan: Now that really would be breaking new ground! Does it mean I might have to learn French or Spanish ...

Peter: ... or German! Well, I wouldn't rule it out, Stan.

Now, let's listen to the first part of the discussion again ... and then answer some questions.

Karen: Yes, Mr. Crawford?

Peter: Would you hold my calls, Karen? Mr. Waterman and I are going over the budget, and I'd like not to have any interruptions.

Stan: Well, Peter, I'm happy to say the budget forecast is almost finished.

Peter: Good. Can we assume AP will still be in business next year?

Stan: I think that's a safe assumption. I'm very optimistic, Peter. If our estimates are correct, the increase in next year's sales volume will be the largest AP has ever had.

Answer!

Are Peter and Stan going over the budget forecast?

Yes, they're going over the budget forecast.

Peter told Karen he didn't want any interruptions, didn't he?

Yes, he told her he didn't want any interruptions.

He told her he didn't want any interruptions because he and Stan were going over the budget forecast, right?

That's right, he told her he didn't want any interruptions because he and Stan were going over the budget forecast.

What does the forecast show? Will there be a decrease in sales volume next year?

No, there won't be a decrease in sales volume next year.

If the estimates are correct, there'll be an increase in sales volume, won't there?

Yes, if the estimates are correct, there'll be an increase in sales volume.

If the estimates are correct, the increase will be the largest AP has ever had, right?

That's right, if the estimates are correct, the increase will be the largest AP has ever had.

Very good! Let's listen again.

> Stan: I'm very optimistic, Peter. If our estimates are correct, the increase in next year's sales volume will be the largest AP has ever had.
>
> Peter: Now that is good news! We've been committing ourselves to a tremendous outlay of dollars for capital improvements ... more automation, new products and marketing strategies — not to mention the new plant we'll have in operation this time next year. What does the profit picture look like when you take all these expenditures into account?
>
> Stan: Our profit margin may drop just a bit at first. But in about a year's time, we should begin to see a dramatic improvement.
>
> Peter: Sounds good to me.

Answer!

Has AP spent a lot of money on capital improvements?

Yes, they've spent a lot of money on capital improvements.

Did Stan take capital improvements into account when he made his forecast?

Yes, he took capital improvements into account when he made his forecast.

Does he expect a big increase in the profit margin right away?

No, he doesn't expect a big increase in the profit margin right away.

He said it might drop just a bit at first, didn't he?

Yes, he said it might drop just a bit at first.

When should they begin to see an improvement, in a month's time or a year's time?

They should begin to see an improvement in a year's time.

Good. Very good!

Repeat!

Profits will improve.
They'll see improving profits.

Sales will rise.
They'll see rising sales.

Costs will decrease.
Answer! They'll see ...

They'll see decreasing costs.

Conditions will change.
They'll see ...

They'll see changing conditions.

Interest rates will fluctuate.
They'll see ...

They'll see fluctuating interest rates.

Markets will expand.

They'll ...   They'll see expanding markets.

Growth will continue.

They'll ...   They'll see continuing growth.

Very good! Let's go back to the conversation.

> *Peter:*   *What about the foreign market? It's 16 percent of our total sales volume right now.*
>
> *Stan:*   *That's true. And as you know, the majority of our export sales revenue comes from the U.K. The falling dollar has made us more competitive in the British market.*
>
> *Peter:*   *But will the downward trend in the value of the dollar continue? You're a better judge of that than I am, Stan. What do you think will happen to the exchange rate?*
>
> *Stan:*   *It's difficult to make forecasts. Not even the experts agree as to whether the dollar will continue its fall, stabilize, or even begin rising.*

Answer!

Does the majority of export sales revenue come from the U.K.?	Yes, the majority of export sales revenue comes from the U.K.
Has the dollar been rising or falling in the U.K.?	It's been falling in the U.K.
Has the falling dollar had an effect on AP?	Yes, it has had an effect on AP.
Has it made AP less competitive or more competitive in the British market?	It's made AP more competitive in the British market.
Who does Peter think is a better judge of what will happen to exchange rates, himself or Stan?	He thinks Stan is a better judge of what will happen to exchange rates.

Very good! Now listen again.

> *Stan:*   *It's difficult to make forecasts. Not even the experts agree as to whether the dollar will continue its fall, stabilize, or even begin rising.*
>
> *Peter:*   *In any case, Stan, the only thing we can do is keep an eye on the situation abroad and reforecast on a quarterly basis. ... Oh, before I forget — I'm thinking of opening a sales office in Europe. It might be just what we need to increase that export sales figure.*
>
> *Stan:*   *Now that really would be breaking new ground! Does it mean I might have to learn French or Spanish ...*
>
> *Peter:*   *... or German! Well, I wouldn't rule it out, Stan.*

Answer!

Do the experts agree as to whether the dollar will keep falling or stabilize?	No, they don't agree as to whether it will keep falling or stabilize.

The dollar could begin rising, too, couldn't it?	Yes, the dollar could begin rising, too.
Does Peter want Stan to forget about the situation abroad or keep an eye on it?	He wants him to keep an eye on it.
He told him he should reforecast on a quarterly basis, didn't he?	Yes, he told him he should reforecast on a quarterly basis.
He told him he should keep an eye on the situation abroad and reforecast on a quarterly basis, right?	That's right, he told him he should keep an eye on the situation abroad and reforecast on a quarterly basis.
Peter is thinking of opening a sales office abroad, isn't he?	Yes, he's thinking of opening a sales office abroad.
Is he thinking of opening an office in Latin America or Europe?	He's thinking of opening an office in Europe.
It looks like Stan may have to start learning a foreign language, right?	That's right, it looks like Stan may have to start learning a foreign language.

Very good! That was excellent! Well, it looks like AP may have some good opportunities in export sales. Their plans are about to begin. But this tape, Tape 18, is about to end. This is the end of Tape 18.

Tape 19   PLANS FOR ACQUIRING CONTROL OF LTE

Controller Stan Waterman is meeting with Philip Hayes, AP's legal counsel. They're discussing ways for Audio Performance to acquire a company called Leisure Time Entertainment.

Stan: So, Phil, I'd like to pursue the possibility of acquiring Leisure Time Entertainment. I thought maybe you could outline our options.

Phil: Well, Stan, the ideal way would be a direct merger. If a merger is acceptable to both sides, AP would end up owning Leisure Time Entertainment outright.

Stan: Ideally, we would simply give LTE's stockholders AP stock in exchange for their shares in LTE. Yes, I agree ... a merger would be ideal. But I'm afraid it's out of the question, Phil.

Phil: You're probably right. It would be expensive.

Stan: Not only that. But LTE's prospects look so good, why would they want to sell out? I wouldn't if I were in their place.

Phil: O.K. In that case, we could simply contact their largest stockholders individually. We could buy their blocks of shares privately. If we can get 20 percent of the total shares outstanding, we'll have control of the company.

Stan: Well, there are seven major stockholders whose combined shares amount to 40 percent of LTE's total stock.

Phil: Who's the largest of the stockholders?

Stan: A Mrs. Lamb. Almost all of her holdings are in LTE stock ... over 500,000 shares. Just that block alone would give us almost the entire 20 percent we need to acquire control of the company. But, I'm sorry to say, she recently passed away.

Phil: I see. Well, you never know in a situation like this, Stan. Her heirs might still be willing — even anxious — to sell off some of the shares.

Stan: I think an offer of $6 over the present market price of $36 a share would be attractive. That would amount to over 20 million dollars!

Phil: That's a bargain, Stan. Why don't we get Peter Crawford's approval to draft a letter to the executors of Mrs. Lamb's estate? We should submit an offer to them in writing.

Stan: We can approach the other six major stockholders, too. Peter's called a meeting of our top people for next Tuesday. I'd like you to be there, Phil. When he hears about the 20 million dollar offer, I may need to hire you as my legal counsel!

Now let's listen to the beginning of the conversation once again ... and then answer some questions.

Stan: So, Phil, I'd like to pursue the possibility of acquiring Leisure Time Entertainment. I thought maybe you could outline our options.

Phil: Well, Stan, the ideal way would be a direct merger. If a merger is acceptable to both sides, AP would end up owning Leisure Time Entertainment outright.

Stan: Ideally, we would simply give LTE's stockholders AP stock in exchange for their shares in LTE. Yes, I agree ... a merger would be ideal. But I'm afraid it's out of the question, Phil.

Answer!

Are Stan and Phil discussing the possibility of acquiring LTE?	Yes, they're discussing the possibility of acquiring LTE.
A direct merger was one of their options, wasn't it?	Yes, a direct merger was one of their options.
A merger hasn't taken place yet, has it?	No, a merger hasn't taken place yet.
A merger hasn't taken place yet, but it's one of the options they're discussing, right?	That's right, a merger hasn't taken place yet, but it's one of the options they're discussing.
But if a merger took place, AP would end up owning LTE outright, wouldn't it?	Yes, if a merger took place, AP would end up owning LTE outright.
Stan and Phil think a direct merger would be ideal, don't they?	Yes, they think a direct merger would be ideal.

Very good! Now let's go back to the conversation.

> Stan: Yes, I agree ... a merger would be ideal. But I'm afraid it's out of the question, Phil.
>
> Phil: You're probably right. It would be expensive.
>
> Stan: Not only that. But LTE's prospects look so good, why would they want to sell out? I wouldn't if I were in their place.
>
> Phil: O.K. In that case, we could simply contact their largest stockholders individually. We could buy their blocks of shares privately. If we can get 20 percent of the total shares outstanding, we'll have control of the company.
>
> Stan: Well, there are seven major stockholders whose combined shares amount to 40 percent of LTE's total stock.

Answer!

Phil thinks a merger would be expensive, doesn't he?	Yes, he thinks a merger would be expensive.
Do LTE's prospects look good or bad?	They look good.
They look so good that LTE might not want to sell, right?	That's right, they look so good that LTE might not want to sell.
Is there another way to get control of LTE?	Yes, there's another way to get control of LTE.
They could contact the largest stockholders individually, couldn't they?	Yes, they could contact the largest stockholders individually.
They could contact the largest stockholders individually and offer to buy their shares privately, right?	That's right, they could contact the largest stockholders individually and offer to buy their shares privately.
Do they need 100 percent of the shares to have control of the company?	No, they don't need 100 percent of the shares to have control of the company.
Do they need 50 percent or only 20 percent to have control of the company?	They only need 20 percent to have control of the company.

Very good!

Repeat!

The amount is 20 percent.
AP needs it.
The amount AP needs is 20 percent.
The company is LTE.
They're discussing it.
The company they're discussing is LTE.

The shares are expensive.
AP wants them.
Answer! The shares AP wants ...

The shares AP wants are expensive.

The stockholders are private.
Stan mentioned them.
The stockholders Stan ...

The stockholders Stan mentioned are private.

The stock is important.
They own it.
The stock ...

The stock they own is important.

The merger will be difficult.
They're considering it.
The merger ...

The merger they're considering will be difficult.

Very good! Now let's go back to the conversation.

Phil: Who's the largest of the stockholders?

Stan: A Mrs. Lamb. Almost all of her holdings are in LTE stock ... over 500,000 shares. Just that block alone would give us almost the entire 20 percent we need to acquire control of the company. But, I'm sorry to say, she recently passed away.

Phil: I see. Well, you never know in a situation like this, Stan. Her heirs might still be willing — even anxious — to sell off some of the shares.

Answer!

Does Mrs. Lamb own a large block of shares?

Yes, she owns a large block of shares.

Is she the largest or the smallest of the major stockholders?

She's the largest of the major stockholders.

Mrs. Lamb recently passed away, didn't she?

Yes, she recently passed away.

Does Phil think her heirs might be willing to sell off some of the shares?

Yes, he thinks her heirs might be willing to sell off some of the shares.

He thinks they might be willing and even anxious to sell off some of the shares, right?

That's right, he thinks they might be willing and even anxious to sell off some of the shares.

Very good! Listen again!

Stan: I think an offer of $6 over the present market price of $36 a share would be attractive. That would amount to over twenty million dollars!

Phil: That's a bargain, Stan. Why don't we get Peter Crawford's approval to draft a letter to the executors of Mrs. Lamb's estate? We should submit an offer to them in writing.

Stan: We can approach the other six major stockholders, too. Peter's called a meeting of our top people for next Tuesday. I'd like you to be there, Phil.

When he hears about the 20 million dollar offer, I may need to hire you as my legal counsel!

Answer!

Does Phil want to submit the offer over the phone?	No, he doesn't want to submit the offer over the phone.
He wants to draft a letter to the executors of Mrs. Lamb's estate, doesn't he?	Yes, he wants to draft a letter to the executors of Mrs. Lamb's estate.
They can approach the other major stockholders, too, can't they?	Yes, they can approach the other major stockholders, too.
They can approach the other major stockholders and make offers to them as well, right?	That's right, they can approach the other major stockholders and make offers to them as well.
Has Peter Crawford already approved the offer?	No, he hasn't approved the offer yet.
They're going to discuss it with him at the meeting next Tuesday, aren't they?	Yes, they're going to discuss it with him at the meeting next Tuesday.
He hasn't approved the offer yet, but they're going to discuss it with him at the meeting next Tuesday, right?	That's right, he hasn't approved the offer yet, but they're going to discuss it with him at the meeting next Tuesday.

Good! Very good! Well, it looks like a merger with LTE is getting closer. And we're getting closer, too — closer to the end of this tape, Tape 19. This is the end of Tape 19.

Tape 20   A MATTER FOR THE LAWYERS

Play World is a company that recently came up with a product almost identical to AP's Games Master. Peter Crawford had his legal department send a letter to Charles Campbell, president of Play World. Campbell has just phoned Peter Crawford.

Campbell: *Good morning, Mr. Crawford. This is Charles Campbell, president of Play World. I suppose you know why I'm calling.*

Crawford: *Yes, Mr. Campbell. I assume you received the letter from our legal department.*

Campbell: *It's right here in front of me. Let's see now ... Audio Performance is threatening legal action against Play World unless we stop the manufacture and sale of our Play Machine. You can't be serious, Crawford ...*

Crawford: I couldn't be more serious. Your product has been copied directly from AP's Games Master. Its technology was developed by AP and we hold patents on it.

Campbell: Now hold on a minute, Crawford! The machines may be similar, but they're not identical. If you sue us, we'll sue you for injury to the good name of our company. I'd think about that if I were you.

Crawford: I am. I'm also thinking that all this could be very expensive. Let me remind you, Mr. Campbell, Audio Performance is not a small company. We have a patent infringement on our hands, and we'll spend whatever it takes to protect our product.

Campbell: Look, Play World's a small firm. Why make all this trouble over a little game machine?

Crawford: I'll tell you why. AP has a lot riding on the Games Master. But more than that, we have to show our competitors that AP is willing to fight for its rights.

Campbell: Listen, I'm sure we can ...

Crawford: Now it's your turn to listen, Mr. Campbell! I'm not finished. As I was saying, we'll pay whatever it costs to set an example here and now. Maybe it'll discourage future attempts by others who think they can infringe on AP's patents.

Campbell: But, we haven't infringed on anything!

Crawford: Well, we think you have. And once this gets to court, we'll prove it.

Campbell: Listen, I'm sure we can reach a friendly settlement out of court.

Crawford: All I can say at this point is that you have our letter requesting you to stop all further manufacture and sale of your machine. The next move is up to you.

Now, let's listen to the first part of the conversation once more ... and then answer some questions.

Campbell: Good morning, Mr. Crawford. This is Charles Campbell, president of Play World. I suppose you know why I'm calling.

Crawford: Yes, Mr. Campbell. I assume you received the letter from our legal department.

Campbell: It's right here in front of me. Let's see now ... Audio Performance is threatening legal action against Play World unless we stop the manufacture and sale of our Play Machine. You can't be serious, Crawford ...

Answer!

Is Charles Campbell president of AP?

He's president of a company called Play World, isn't he?

No, he isn't president of AP.

Yes, he's president of a company called Play World.

425

Does his company manufacture the Games Master?

No, it doesn't manufacture the Games Master.

His company manufactures a product known as the Play Machine, doesn't it?

Yes, it manufactures a product known as the Play Machine.

Did Mr. Campbell recently receive a letter from AP?

Yes, he recently received a letter from AP.

Does AP's letter threaten legal action against Play World?

Yes, it threatens legal action against Play World.

Does AP want Play World to continue the manufacture and sale of the Play Machine?

No, they don't want Play World to continue the manufacture and sale of the Play Machine.

They want them to stop it, don't they?

Yes, they want them to stop it.

So, AP is threatening legal action against Play World unless it stops the manufacture and sale of the Play Machine, right?

That's right, AP is threatening legal action against Play World unless it stops the manufacture and sale of the Play Machine.

Very good! Listen again.

Campbell: *You can't be serious, Crawford ...*

Crawford: *I couldn't be more serious. Your product has been copied directly from AP's Games Master. Its technology was developed by AP and we hold patents on it.*

Campbell: *Now hold on a minute, Crawford! The machines may be similar, but they're not identical. If you sue us, we'll sue you for injury to the good name of our company. I'd think about that if I were you.*

Answer!

The Play Machine wasn't developed by AP, was it?

No, it wasn't developed by AP.

It wasn't developed by AP, but its technology was, right?

That's right, it wasn't developed by AP, but its technology was.

Who holds the patents on the technology, AP or Play World?

AP holds the patents on the technology.

Campbell didn't admit the machines were identical, did he?

No, he didn't admit they were identical.

He said the machines were similar, but not identical, right?

That's right, he said they were similar, but not identical.

AP hasn't filed suit against Play World yet, has it?

No, they haven't filed suit against Play World yet.

But if AP does file suit, Campbell said he'd sue AP, right?

That's right, if AP does file suit, Campbell said he'd sue AP.

He'd sue them for injury to the good name of his company, wouldn't he?

Yes, he'd sue them for injury to the good name of his company.

Good! Very good!

Repeat!

The Games Master was copied.
The Games Master seems to have been copied.

AP's technology was used.
AP's technology seems to have been used.

The patents were infringed.
Answer! The patents seem to have ...

The patents seem to have been infringed.

AP's business was damaged.
AP's business seems ...

AP's business seems to have been damaged.

Their ideas were stolen.
Their ideas ...

Their ideas seem to have been stolen.

Very good. Listen again.

Campbell: I'd think about that if I were you.

Crawford: I am. I'm also thinking that all this could be very expensive. Let me remind you, Mr. Campbell, Audio Performance is not a small company. We have a patent infringement on our hands, and we'll spend whatever it takes to protect our product.

Campbell: Look, Play World's a small firm. Why make all this trouble over a little game machine?

Crawford: I'll tell you why. AP has a lot riding on the Games Master. But more than that, we have to show our competitors that AP is willing to fight for its rights.

Answer!

Did Peter remind Mr. Campbell that AP was not a small company?

Yes, he reminded him that AP was not a small company.

He told him they would spend whatever it took to protect their product, right?

That's right, he told him they would spend whatever it took to protect their product.

Does AP have a lot riding on the Games Master?

Yes, they have a lot riding on the Games Master.

Peter said AP was willing to fight for its rights, didn't he?

Yes, he said they were willing to fight for their rights.

He said AP had a lot riding on the Games Master and that they were willing to fight for their rights, right?

That's right, he said AP had a lot riding on the Games Master and that they were willing to fight for their rights.

Good! Very good! Listen again.

Campbell:	Listen, I'm sure we can ...
Crawford:	Now it's your turn to listen, Mr. Campbell! I'm not finished. As I was saying, we'll pay whatever it costs to set an example here and now. Maybe it'll discourage future attempts by others who think they can infringe on AP's patents.
Campbell:	But, we haven't infringed on anything!
Crawford:	Well, we think you have. And once this gets to court, we'll prove it.
Campbell:	Listen, I'm sure we can reach a friendly settlement out of court.
Crawford:	All I can say at this point is that you have our letter requesting you to stop all further manufacture and sale of your machine. The next move is up to you.

Answer!

Peter wants to discourage future attempts to infringe on AP's patents, doesn't he?	Yes, he wants to discourage future attempts to infringe on AP's patents.
I beg your pardon? What does he want to do?	He wants to discourage future attempts to infringe on AP's patents.
Is Mr. Campbell starting to sound a little more friendly?	Yes, he's starting to sound a little more friendly.
He's now suggesting a friendly settlement out of court, isn't he?	Yes, he's now suggesting a friendly settlement out of court.

Very good! Well, it looks like AP and Play World may be able to settle this matter in a friendly way. Let's hope everything turns out all right in the end. And, speaking of the end, this tape, Tape 20, has now come to an end. This is the end of Tape 20.

Tape 21   THE TRU-TONE PICTURE BEGINS TO CHANGE

Sales director Ben Melnick has just returned from a trip to the New England area, where he had been testing a new ad campaign for the Tru-Tone line. He stopped by for a chat with Jane Collins, AP's executive assistant.

Jane:	I see you got some sun, Ben. The weather in New England must have been nice.
Ben:	Crystal clear skies the whole time, Jane. And the business part of the trip was just as bright.
Jane:	The new Tru-Tone ad campaign is going well, then.
Ben:	Sales are climbing in all ten cities where the new marketing is being tested. Six cities, including Boston, have almost doubled sales in the past month.

Jane: Now that is impressive. I wonder if Tru-Tone's problems are over after all ... if we've finally reached a turning point.

Ben: Well, the new advertising strategy is definitely on the right track ... no doubt about it. We seem to be hitting the market at just the right time.

Jane: Hmm ... but I do recall the marketing staff warning us how risky new ad campaigns can be. Sales could increase momentarily, but then level off — or even decline.

Ben: I don't think that's going to happen here, Jane. O.K., it's true the Christmas season is coming and sales should peak at that time anyway. But Steve's marketing studies point to a long, continued upward trend in sales.

Jane: And as we expand our T.V. and magazine promotions, more and more people will be exposed to the product. What about profits?

Ben: That's going to be troublesome for a while. We've increased adver-tising considerably and cut our prices, so profits will be off somewhat.

Jane: By how much, do you think?

Ben: I'd say about twelve to thirteen percent. But once the new marketing is introduced nationally, we'll be stepping up production and sales. And that should improve profits.

Jane: Sounds good. Who knows? All our ambitious plans may actually work out.

Ben: I don't doubt it for a minute. In fact, I'm going to my office right now and light up one of these cigars I picked up in Boston.

Jane: Well, it sure is nice to have you back, Ben — even with your cigars!

Now, let's listen to the start of the conversation again ... and then answer a few questions.

Jane: I see you got some sun, Ben. The weather in New England must have been nice.

Ben: Crystal clear skies the whole time, Jane. And the business part of the trip was just as bright.

Jane: The new Tru-Tone ad campaign is going well, then.

Ben: Sales are climbing in all ten cities where the new marketing is being tested. Six cities, including Boston, have almost doubled sales in the past month.

Answer!

Did it rain the whole time Ben was in New England?	No, it didn't rain the whole time he was in New England.
The skies were crystal clear the whole time he was there, weren't they?	Yes, the skies were crystal clear the whole time he was there.

Is the new ad campaign already under way?	Yes, it's already under way.
Is the new marketing being tested in 10 cities or 100 cities?	It's being tested in 10 cities.
The new marketing is already under way in 10 New England cities and going well, right?	That's right, the new marketing is already under way in 10 New England cities and going well.
Sales are climbing in all 10 cities where the new marketing is being tested, right?	That's right, sales are climbing in all 10 cities where the new marketing is being tested.
And in some cities, sales have almost doubled, haven't they?	Yes, in some cities, sales have almost doubled.

Very good! Now let's listen to some more of the conversation.

Ben: *Six cities, including Boston, have almost doubled sales in the past month.*

Jane: *Now that is impressive. I wonder if Tru-Tone's problems are over after all ... if we've finally reached a turning point.*

Ben: *Well, the new advertising strategy is definitely on the right track ... no doubt about it. We seem to be hitting the market at just the right time.*

Jane: *Hmm ... but I do recall the marketing staff warning us how risky new ad campaigns can be. Sales could increase momentarily, but then level off — or even decline.*

Answer!

Did Jane say the results of the new campaign were disappointing?	No, she didn't say the results of the new campaign were disappointing.
She thinks Tru-Tone's problems may be over after all, doesn't she?	Yes, she thinks Tru-Tone's problems may be over after all.
And what about Ben? Does he think the new advertising strategy is on the right track or the wrong track?	He thinks it's on the right track.
There's no doubt about it in his mind, is there?	No, there's no doubt about it in his mind.
Are new ad campaigns always safe or can they be risky?	They can be risky.
The marketing staff warned how risky new ad campaigns can be, didn't they?	Yes, the marketing staff warned how risky new ad campaigns can be.

Good! Very good!

Repeat!

How risky will the campaign be?
Jane wondered how risky the campaign would be.

How long will the campaign last? *Answer!* She wondered how long ...	She wondered how long the campaign would last.
Who will supervise the campaign? She wondered ...	She wondered who would supervise the campaign.
How much will the campaign cost? She wondered ...	She wondered how much the campaign would cost.
What will the results of the campaign be? She wondered ...	She wondered what the results of the campaign would be.

Very good! Let's return to the conversation.

Jane: *Sales could increase momentarily, but then level off — or even decline.*

Ben: *I don't think that's going to happen here, Jane. O.K., it's true the Christmas season is coming and sales should peak at that time anyway. But Steve's marketing studies point to a long, continued upward trend in sales.*

Jane: *And as we expand our T.V. and magazine promotions, more and more people will be exposed to the product. What about profits?*

Ben: *That's going to be troublesome for a while. We've increased adver-tising considerably and cut our prices, so profits will be off somewhat.*

Answer!

Tru-Tone sales should peak around Christmastime, shouldn't they?	Yes, they should peak around Christmastime.
Sales usually peak during the Christmas season anyway, right?	That's right, sales usually peak during the Christmas season anyway.
Recent studies don't point to a downward trend in sales, do they?	No, they don't point to a downward trend in sales.
Recent studies point to a continued upward trend, right?	That's right, recent studies point to a continued upward trend.
Will T.V. and magazine promotions be expanded or cut back?	They'll be expanded.
I beg your pardon? What will be expanded?	T.V. and magazine promotions will be expanded.
And that means more and more people will be exposed to the product, doesn't it?	Yes, that means more and more people will be exposed to the product.

As T.V. and magazine promotions are expanded, more and more people will be exposed to the product, right?

That's right, as T.V. and magazine promotions are expanded, more and more people will be exposed to the product.

What about profits? Will they increase right away or will they be off somewhat?

They'll be off somewhat.

Very good! Let's listen again!

Ben: ... so profits will be off somewhat.

Jane: By how much, do you think?

Ben: I'd say about twelve to thirteen percent. But once the new marketing is introduced nationally, we'll be stepping up production and sales. And that should improve profits.

Jane: Sounds good. Who knows? All our ambitious plans may actually work out.

Ben: I don't doubt it for a minute. In fact, I'm going to my office right now and light up one of these cigars I picked up in Boston.

Jane: Well, it sure is nice to have you back, Ben — even with your cigars!

Answer!

Is Tru-Tone's new marketing going to be introduced nationally?

Yes, it's going to be introduced nationally.

Does that mean AP will be reducing production?

No, that doesn't mean AP will be reducing production.

They'll be stepping up production, won't they?

Yes, they'll be stepping up production.

Once the new marketing is introduced nationally, AP will be stepping up production, right?

That's right, once the new marketing is introduced nationally, AP will be stepping up production.

Do Jane and Ben sound optimistic about the company's ambitious plans?

Yes, they sound optimistic about the company's ambitious plans.

Very good! Well, the Tru-Tone picture seems to be improving, and just in time. And speaking of time, that's all the time we have for this tape, Tape 21. This is the end of Tape 21.

Tape 22   FOCUSING ON EXPORT SALES

Alan Fischer has recently been appointed director of AP's export department. He's meeting with sales director, Ben Melnick.

Ben: We're pleased you've decided to join AP, Alan. You're just the person I need to head up our new export division. With your command of foreign languages and overseas contacts, we're going to take full advantage of you.

Alan: I hope so, Ben. I regard this as an excellent opportunity. I've enjoyed my stay in Los Angeles ... but the truth is, I've been anxious to get back to the European environment.

Ben: Well, after 15 years as a sales representative in Europe and Latin America, I suppose even L.A. might seem a bit ordinary. How do you feel about being stationed in London?

Alan: For one thing, it's definitely the right place for AP's sales office. And speaking for myself and my family, it's ideal. We spent several years there and loved it.

Ben: That should make it a lot easier for you to get settled. You won't have to familiarize yourselves with the place.

Alan: Quite right. The relocation should be no problem at all.

Ben: Which reminds me ... you'll soon meet Mr. Crawford's assistant, Jane Collins. She'll be getting estimates on airfare for you and your family and transportation of your personal belongings. She can also help arrange temporary housing until you find something permanent.

Alan: Thanks, Ben. Oh, I was told there was a gentleman ... a Mr. Water-man, I believe ... who'll be briefing me on AP's foreign operations.

Ben: Yes, Stan Waterman, our controller. He and I will bring you up-to-date on everything. It won't take you long to conclude that exports haven't been getting much attention around here.

Alan: While our competitors have been focusing on exports much more systematically ...

Ben: And more aggressively, too. No, Alan, I have to admit ... AP's overseas business has been developing more or less by itself. But, even so, exports have reached 16 percent of our total sales.

Alan: The market is there, Ben. We've just got to go after it. With a base in London, I can expand our sales network throughout Europe and streamline our procedures. In two years, I think we can double our export sales.

Ben: If you give me that kind of increase, I'll see to it that you stay overseas as long as you want. Alan, I have a feeling you're going to be a hit around here. Welcome aboard, old chap!

Now let's listen to the first part of the discussion again ... and then answer a few questions.

Ben: We're pleased you've decided to join AP, Alan. You're just the person I need to head up our new export division. With your command of foreign languages and overseas contacts, we're going to take full advantage of you.

Alan: I hope so, Ben. I regard this as an excellent opportunity. I've enjoyed my stay in Los Angeles ... but the truth is, I've been anxious to get back to the European environment.

Ben: Well, after 15 years as a sales representative in Europe and Latin America, I suppose even L.A. might seem a bit ordinary.

Answer!

How long was Fischer a sales representative in Europe and Latin America, for 15 years or 25 years?	He was a sales representative in Europe and Latin America for 15 years.
I beg your pardon? What did Fischer do for 15 years?	He was a sales representative in Europe and Latin America for 15 years.
He didn't say he was going to study a foreign language, did he?	No, he didn't say he was going to study a foreign language.
Does he already have a good command of foreign languages?	Yes, he already has a good command of foreign languages.
Has Fischer enjoyed his stay in Los Angeles?	Yes, he's enjoyed his stay in Los Angeles.
He's enjoyed his stay in Los Angeles, but he's anxious to get back to Europe, right?	That's right, he's enjoyed his stay in Los Angeles, but he's anxious to get back to Europe.

Very good! Let's go back to the conversation and find out more about Alan Fischer's overseas assignment.

Ben: How do you feel about being stationed in London?

Alan: For one thing, it's definitely the right place for AP's sales office. And speaking for myself and my family, it's ideal. We spent several years there and loved it.

Ben: That should make it a lot easier for you to get settled. You won't have to familiarize yourselves with the place.

Alan: Quite right. The relocation should be no problem at all.

Ben: Which reminds me ... you'll soon meet Mr. Crawford's assistant, Jane Collins. She'll be getting estimates on airfare for you and your family and transportation of your personal belongings. She can also help arrange temporary housing until you find something permanent.

Alan: Thanks, Ben.

Answer!

Will AP's European sales office be located in London or Paris?	It'll be located in London.
And that's where Alan's going to be stationed, isn't it?	Yes, that's where he's going to be stationed.

Will he and his family have to familiarize themselves with life in London?	No, they won't have to familiarize themselves with life in London.
They've lived there before, haven't they?	Yes, they've lived there before.
Who'll be getting estimates on airfare, Jane Collins?	Yes, Jane Collins will be getting estimates on airfare.
She'll be getting estimates on airfare and transportation of their personal belongings, right?	That's right, she'll be getting estimates on airfare and transportation of their personal belongings.
Will she also arrange temporary housing?	Yes, she'll also arrange temporary housing.
She'll arrange temporary housing until Alan finds something permanent, right?	That's right, she'll arrange temporary housing until Alan finds something permanent.

Very good!

Repeat!

Jane will arrange airfare for Alan.
He won't have to arrange it himself.

She'll get travel information for Alan's wife.
She won't have to get it herself.

She'll make hotel reservations for the whole family.

Answer! They won't have to ...

They won't have to make them themselves.

She'll find permanent housing for Alan.
He won't ...

He won't have to find it himself.

She'll handle the packing for Mrs. Fischer.
She ...

She won't have to handle it herself.

She'll take care of all the expenses for the Fischer family.
They ...

They won't have to take care of them themselves.

Good! Very good! Let's go back to the conversation.

Alan: *Oh, I was told there was a gentleman ... a Mr. Waterman, I believe ... who'll be briefing me on AP's foreign operations.*

Ben: *Yes, Stan Waterman, our controller. He and I will bring you up-to-date on everything. It won't take you long to conclude that exports haven't been getting much attention around here.*

Alan: *While our competitors have been focusing on exports much more systematically ...*

Ben: *And more aggressively, too.*

Answer!

Will Alan be briefed on AP's foreign operations?	Yes, he'll be briefed on AP's foreign operations.
He'll be briefed and brought up-to-date on everything, right?	That's right, he'll be briefed and brought up-to-date on everything.
Did Ben say exports had been getting a lot of attention up to now?	No, he didn't say they'd been getting a lot of attention up to now.
He said exports hadn't been getting much attention, right?	That's right, he said they hadn't been getting much attention.
Have their competitors been focusing on exports more systematically than AP?	Yes, they've been focusing on exports more systematically than AP.

Very good! Listen again.

Ben: *No, Alan, I have to admit ... AP's overseas business has been developing more or less by itself. But, even so, exports have reached 16 percent of our total sales.*

Alan: *The market is there, Ben. We've just got to go after it. With a base in London, I can expand our sales network throughout Europe and streamline our procedures. In two years, I think we can double our export sales.*

Ben: *If you give me that kind of increase, I'll see to it that you stay overseas as long as you want. Alan, I have a feeling you're going to be a hit around here. Welcome aboard, old chap!*

Answer!

Has AP's overseas business been well managed?	No, it hasn't been well managed.
It's been developing more or less by itself, hasn't it?	Yes, it's been developing more or less by itself.
I beg your pardon? What's been developing more or less by itself?	AP's overseas business has been developing more or less by itself.
Does Alan think there's a market for their products in Europe?	Yes, he thinks there's a market for their products in Europe.
He said the market was there and AP just had to go after it, right?	That's right, he said the market was there and AP just had to go after it.
Is Alan planning to streamline procedures or leave things as they are?	He's planning to streamline procedures.
He thinks he can double AP's export sales, doesn't he?	Yes, he thinks he can double them.

That would make Ben very happy, wouldn't it?	Yes, that would make Ben very happy.
If Alan can double sales, he'll be a real hit at AP, right?	That's right, if he can double sales, he'll be a real hit at AP.

Good! Very good! Well, it looks like Alan's foreign assignment will be interesting. He thinks he can produce good results, but he doesn't have much time. And, we don't have much time, either ... on this tape, Tape 22. This is the end of Tape 22.

Tape 23   A PREVIEW OF THE NEW PLANT

Vice president of planning, Jeff Martinelli, just received some architectural sketches of the new plant that AP is planning to build in Greenville, South Carolina. He took them over to show to Ed Pearson, AP's production manager.

Jeff: *Good morning, Ed. Have you got a minute to look at a preview of the new plant in Greenville? I have some more architectural sketches.*

Ed: *Sure, Jeff. Let me make some room here on the desk. ... There, that should do it.*

Jeff: *I wanted you to see this floor plan. It's slightly different from the one we looked at before.*

Ed: *Hmm, let's see. Executive offices, employee lounge, cafeteria ... all about the same as before.*

Jeff: *That's right. And we still have the 40,000 feet of manufacturing space. No change there, either.*

Ed: *Let's see ... the railroad siding and loading docks are still over here in back. Wait a minute, what's this over here? It looks like the ware-house area has been extended.*

Jeff: *That's the major difference from the previous plan, Ed. I'm proposing to add 34,000 feet of space here ... along the railroad siding.*

Ed: *Well, we won't have any shortage of space — that's for sure.*

Jeff: *If you need it, at least it'll be there. In the meantime, we can use the extra space to store raw materials, or even rent it out until we actually need it.*

Ed: *Sounds like a good idea. With all the new business that's in the works, we'll probably need the extra space sooner than we think. What about employee parking?*

Jeff: *We're providing more than 500 spaces — about 100 more than we'll need when the plant opens.*

Ed: *Hey, that reminds me. They've been having a lot of labor problems in the Greenville area, haven't they? Quite a few strikes?*

> **Jeff:** Yeah, it's been pretty rough down there. There's even talk of a truckers' strike. But the last I heard, negotiations were going well. I'm hopeful we can still break ground early next spring.
>
> **Ed:** And we can begin installing the new equipment by late summer or early fall. It is a beautiful building, Jeff. Congratulations on a terrific job.
>
> **Jeff:** You've been a big part of the planning, Ed. Now the question is ... how do we tell Peter that this plant's going to cost $14 million?
>
> **Ed:** Uh-oh. I just remembered, I'm due at a meeting of our production staff. Give my regards to Peter, won't you, Jeff?

Now let's listen to the start of the conversation again ... and then answer a few questions.

> **Jeff:** Good morning, Ed. Have you got a minute to look at a preview of the new plant in Greenville? I have some more architectural sketches.
>
> **Ed:** Sure, Jeff. Let me make some room here on the desk. ... There, that should do it.
>
> **Jeff:** I wanted you to see this floor plan. It's slightly different from the one we looked at before.
>
> **Ed:** Hmm, let's see. Executive offices, employee lounge, cafeteria ... all about the same as before.
>
> **Jeff:** That's right. And we still have the 40,000 feet of manufacturing space. No change there, either.

Answer!

Are Jeff and Ed discussing the new plant in Greenville?	Yes, they're discussing the new plant in Greenville.
Jeff wants Ed to look at some architectural sketches, doesn't he?	Yes, he wants him to look at some architectural sketches.
Did Ed say he was too busy to look at the sketches?	No, he didn't say he was too busy to look at them.
Where did he put the sketches, on his desk?	Yes, he put them on his desk.
Is the floor plan the same as the one they looked at before?	No, it's not the same as the one they looked at before.
It's slightly different from the one they looked at before, isn't it?	Yes, it's slightly different from the one they looked at before.
Will there be an employee lounge and a cafeteria?	Yes, there'll be an employee lounge and a cafeteria.
And there'll still be 40,000 feet of manufacturing space, won't there?	Yes, there'll still be 40,000 feet of manufacturing space.

Very good! Jeff and Ed are still discussing the floor plan of the new plant. Listen!

Ed: Let's see ... the railroad siding and loading docks are still over here in back. Wait a minute, what's this over here? It looks like the ware-house area has been extended.

Jeff: That's the major difference from the previous plan, Ed. I'm proposing to add 34,000 feet of space here ... along the railroad siding.

Ed: Well, we won't have any shortage of space — that's for sure.

Jeff: If you need it, at least it'll be there. In the meantime, we can use the extra space to store raw materials, or even rent it out until we actually need it.

Ed: Sounds like a good idea. With all the new business that's in the works, we'll probably need the extra space sooner than we think.

Answer!

Will the new plant have a railroad siding and loading docks?

Yes, it'll have a railroad siding and loading docks.

But that's not what's different from the previous floor plan, is it?

No, that's not what's different from the previous floor plan.

Will the loading docks be in front or in back?

They'll be in back.

What's different? Has the warehouse area been changed?

Yes, the warehouse area's been changed.

It's been extended, hasn't it?

Yes, it's been extended.

The major difference from the previous plan is that the warehouse area has been extended, right?

That's right, the major difference from the previous plan is that the warehouse area has been extended.

How much is Jeff proposing to add, 3,400 or 34,000 feet of space?

He's proposing to add 34,000 feet of space.

There won't be a shortage of warehouse space at the new plant, will there?

No, there won't be a shortage of warehouse space at the new plant.

How could they use the extra space? Could they use it to store raw materials?

Yes, they could use it to store raw materials.

They could even rent it out until they need it, couldn't they?

Yes, they could even rent it out until they need it.

Very good!

Repeat!

They won't have a lot less space.
They'll have a lot more space.

The plant won't be substantially smaller.
It'll be substantially larger.

439

It won't cost much less than they
expected.

It'll cost much more than they
expected.

Answer! It'll cost much more ...

It won't be far less efficient than the
other plants.
It'll be ...

It'll be far more efficient than the
other plants.

The production won't be considerably
lower than it is now.
It'll be ...

It'll be considerably higher than it is
now.

They won't have slightly less parking
than now.
They'll have ...

They'll have slightly more parking
than now.

Good! Very good! Let's return to the conversation now.

> Ed: *What about employee parking?*
>
> Jeff: *We're providing more than 500 spaces — about 100 more than we'll need when the plant opens.*
>
> Ed: *Hey, that reminds me. They've been having a lot of labor problems in the Greenville area, haven't they? Quite a few strikes?*
>
> Jeff: *Yeah, it's been pretty rough down there. There's even talk of a truckers' strike. But the last I heard, negotiations were going well. I'm hopeful we can still break ground early next spring.*

Answer!

Will the new plant have an employee
parking area?

Yes, it'll have an employee
parking area.

Will the parking area be larger or
smaller than they need?

It'll be larger than they need.

Will they have more or fewer spaces
than they need?

They'll have more spaces than
they need.

What about labor problems? Have
there been any labor problems in the
area?

Yes, there have been labor
problems in the area.

They've even had a few strikes, haven't
they?

Yes, they've even had a few
strikes.

Has there been talk of a truckers' strike?

Yes, there has been talk of a
truckers' strike.

Very good! Let's listen again.

> Jeff: *I'm hopeful we can still break ground early next spring.*
>
> Ed: *And we can begin installing the new equipment by late summer or early fall. It is a beautiful building, Jeff. Congratulations on a terrific job.*

Jeff: You've been a big part of the planning, Ed. Now the question is ... how do we tell Peter that this plant's going to cost $14 million?

Ed: Uh-oh. I just remembered, I'm due at a meeting of our production staff. Give my regards to Peter, won't you, Jeff?

Answer!

Does Jeff think they can begin construction next spring?	Yes, he thinks they can begin construction next spring.
He's hopeful they can break ground by then, isn't he?	Yes, he's hopeful they can break ground by then.
Can they begin installing new equipment in the spring?	No, they can't begin installing new equipment in the spring.
They can begin installing new equipment by late summer or early fall, right?	That's right, they can begin installing new equipment by late summer or early fall.
Is the new plant going to cost $4 million or $14 million?	It's going to cost $14 million.
Have they already told Peter how much the plant's going to cost?	No, they haven't told Peter how much the plant's going to cost yet.
They still have to tell him the plant's going to cost $14 million, don't they?	Yes, they still have to tell him the plant's going to cost $14 million.

Very good! Well, it looks like AP is going to have a new plant. Jeff and Ed's conversation is over now, and this tape, Tape 23, is over also. This is the end of Tape 23.

Tape 24   TO THE FUTURE!

It was a year ago that Peter Crawford was named president of Audio Performance. Today, he presented his year-end report to the Board of Directors at United Electronics, AP's parent company. He's at home now, with his wife, Helen.

Helen: Peter, you look exhausted. I guess the Board meeting was pretty rough, huh?

Peter: A little. I just hope the Board members didn't notice how nervous I was.

Helen: But you've met most of them on one occasion or another. I mean, it's not like you were walking into a roomful of strangers.

Peter: There's just something about a formal appearance before the Board. You never know what they're thinking or what the next question will be. The whole thing just makes me nervous every time.

Helen: Oh, come on. They must realize how successful you've been at AP.

Peter: Yes, but from the Board's point of view, it's all very risky. Who knows what's going to happen a year or two from now?

Helen:	I can't believe it! You make it sound as if you're barely managing to hold on to your job.
Peter:	That's not what I mean. But ... it's a very risky business ...
Helen:	O.K., Peter, that's enough! I saw that smile. Now tell me — how did the meeting really go?
Peter:	Hmm ... now that you mention it, there was one highlight. The Board said they wanted me to stay at AP long enough to put the finishing touches on all the projects that are in the works.
Helen:	So, they do like what you've been doing. I knew it! When you look back at all the long hours, the work you put in ... Wait a minute, what do you mean "stay at AP long enough"?
Peter:	Well, it seems United Electronics will soon be needing vice presidents at the divisional level. And that would mean managing several com-panies. The Board's already looking for some qualified people ... and who do you suppose they've had their eyes on?
Helen:	You?! I knew the news would be good, but this ... this calls for a toast. Well now, I propose a toast, Mr. Crawford — to the future!
Peter:	To the future, Mrs. Crawford ...

Now, let's listen to the start of the conversation again ... and then answer some questions.

Helen:	Peter, you look exhausted. I guess the Board meeting was pretty rough, huh?
Peter:	A little. I just hope the Board members didn't notice how nervous I was.
Helen:	But you've met most of them on one occasion or another. I mean, it's not like you were walking into a roomful of strangers.
Peter:	There's just something about a formal appearance before the Board. You never know what they're thinking or what the next question will be. The whole thing just makes me nervous every time.

Answer!

Where had Peter been, to a press conference or a Board meeting?

He had been to a Board meeting.

His wife, Helen, said he looked exhausted, didn't she?

Yes, she said he looked exhausted.

How did he feel during the meeting? Did he feel relaxed?

No, he didn't feel relaxed.

The whole thing made him very nervous, didn't it?

Yes, the whole thing made him very nervous.

Were the Board members all strangers to him?

No, they weren't all strangers to him.

| He had already met most of them, hadn't he? | Yes, he had already met most of them. |

Very good! Now let's go back to the conversation.

> Peter: *The whole thing just makes me nervous every time.*
>
> Helen: *Oh, come on. They must realize how successful you've been at AP.*
>
> Peter: *Yes, but from the Board's point of view, it's all very risky. Who knows what's going to happen a year or two from now?*
>
> Helen: *I can't believe it! You make it sound as if you're barely managing to hold on to your job.*
>
> Peter: *That's not what I mean. But ... it's a very risky business ...*

Answer!

Has Peter been successful at AP?	Yes, he's been successful at AP.
He's not sure what's going to happen a year or two from now, is he?	No, he's not sure what's going to happen a year or two from now.
Does Peter think he's about to lose his job?	No, he doesn't think he's about to lose his job.
That's not what he meant to say, is it?	No, that's not what he meant to say.

Good! Very good!

Repeat!

Peter's done a good job.
The job Peter's done has been good.

He's introduced important changes.
The changes he's introduced have been important.

He's taken risky steps. *Answer!* The steps he's taken ...	The steps he's taken have been risky.
He's put in long hours. The hours he's ...	The hours he's put in have been long.
He's hired qualified managers. The managers ...	The managers he's hired have been qualified.
He's made wise decisions. The ...	The decisions he's made have been wise.

Very good! Now let's go back to the conversation.

> Helen: *You make it sound as if you're barely managing to hold on to your job.*
>
> Peter: *That's not what I mean. But ... it's a very risky business ...*
>
> Helen: *O.K., Peter, that's enough! I saw that smile. Now tell me — how did the meeting really go?*
>
> Peter: *Hmm ... now that you mention it, there was one highlight. The Board said they wanted me to stay at AP long enough to put the finishing touches on all the projects that are in the works.*

Helen: So, they do like what you've been doing. I knew it! When you look back at all the long hours, the work you put in ...

Answer!

Helen asked Peter how the meeting had really gone, didn't she?	Yes, she asked him how the meeting had really gone.
The meeting didn't go so badly after all, did it?	No, it didn't go so badly after all.
Did Peter say the meeting had one highlight?	Yes, he said it had one highlight.
He said the Board wanted him to stay on at AP, didn't he?	Yes, he said the Board wanted him to stay on at AP.
Did they want him to put the finishing touches on all his projects?	Yes, they wanted him to put the finishing touches on all his projects.
They wanted him to put the finishing touches on all the projects that are in the works, didn't they?	Yes, they wanted him to put the finishing touches on all the projects that are in the works.

Very good! Let's listen again.

Peter: The Board said they wanted me to stay at AP long enough to put the finishing touches on all the projects that are in the works.

Helen: Wait a minute, what do you mean "stay at AP long enough"?

Peter: Well, it seems United Electronics will soon be needing vice presidents at the divisional level. And that would mean managing several com-panies. The Board's already looking for some qualified people ... and who do you suppose they've had their eyes on?

Helen: You?! I knew the news would be good, but this ... this calls for a toast. Well now, I propose a toast, Mr. Crawford — to the future!

Peter: To the future, Mrs. Crawford ...

Answer!

Will they be needing more vice presidents?	Yes, they'll be needing more vice presidents.
They'll be needing more vice presidents at the divisional level, won't they?	Yes, they'll be needing more vice presidents at the divisional level.
What does that mean? Does it mean managing several companies?	Yes, it means managing several companies.
The Board's already looking for qualified people, aren't they?	Yes, they're already looking for qualified people.
Did Helen propose a toast?	Yes, she proposed a toast.
Did she propose a toast to the past or the future?	She proposed a toast to the future.

Very good! Well, it looks like Peter may get another promotion. The Board is very satisfied with the progress he's made. We hope you're satisfied, too, with the progress you've made in this program — *Doing Business in English*. This, now, is the end of Tape 24, the last tape in the program. Congratulations! This is the end of Tape 24.

INDEX